State						
New Mexico	21	★	12 mo.	90 da.	30 da.	
New York	21	★(f)	1 yr.	4 mo.	30 da.	Annual
North Carolina	21	★	1 yr.	—	4 mo.	
North Dakota	21	★	1 yr.	90 da.	30 da.	
Ohio	21	★	1 yr.	40 da.	40 da.	
Oklahoma	21	★	1 yr.	6 mo.	30 da.	
Oregon	21	★	6 mo.	—	—	
Pennsylvania	21	★	1 yr.(u)	—	2 mo.	
Rhode Island	21	★	1 yr.	—	6 mo.	
South Carolina	21	★	2 yrs.(p)	—	4 mo.	
South Dakota	21	★	1 yr.	—	30 da.	Decennial
Tennessee	21	★	12 mo.	90 da.	—	
Texas	21	★	1 yr.	6 mo.	6 mo.	Annual
Utah	21	●(c)	1 yr.	4 mo.	60 da.	
Vermont	21	★	1 yr.	—	3 mo.(l)	
Virginia	21	★	1 yr.	6 mo.	30 da.	
Washington	21	★	1 yr.	90 da.	30 da.	
West Virginia	21	★	1 yr.	60 da.	—	
Wisconsin	21	★	1 yr.	—	10 da.	
Wyoming	21	★	1 yr.	60 da.	10 da.	
Alaska	21	★	12 mo.	—	30 da.(aa)	Every gen. elec.
Guam	21	★	2 yrs.	—	—	
Hawaii	21	★	1 yr.	—	3 mo.	
Puerto Rico	21	★	1 yr.	—	1 yr.	
Virgin Islands	21	★	1 yr.	—	60 da.	

* Reproduced by the courtesy of the Council of State Governments from *The Book of the States, 1954–55*, pp. 80–81.

(a) Poll or head taxes are levied in many other states. Those listed here, however, provide that payment of the poll tax is a prerequisite for voting.

(b) Must pay all poll taxes owed since 1901. Members of the armed forces are exempt from payment of poll taxes.

(c) Registration is permanent unless removed for cause.

(d) Conditioned upon voting and continued residence.

(e) Except for irrigation district elections.

(f) Must have been citizen ninety days.

(g) City or town, thirty days.

(h) All except certain minor elections.

(i) Must have been citizen five years.

(j) Under 1949 act, all voters must re-register and pass literacy test. Those failing test may qualify by answering 10 of 30 oral questions prescribed by law.

(k) For all state and federal elections.

(l) Township.

(m) Municipality, four months.

(n) In city or town.

(o) For vote on bond issues or special assessments only.

(p) Ministers of the Gospel and teachers in public schools may vote after six months' residence.

(q) Assessed upon citizens 21 to 60 years of age except those specifically exempted.

(r) Registration is for all elections of state and county, but voter must be registered in municipality also to vote in municipal elections.

(s) A person who became entitled to vote after January 1, 1922, must be able except for physical disability, to read and write English.

(t) Re-register in two years if not voting within that time.

(u) Six months if previously an elector or native of U.S.

(v) Ownership of property is an alternative to literacy.

(w) Constitution provides for registration in cities over 10,000, but no system exists. Poll tax receipts determine eligibility of voters aged 21 to 60 years; exemption certificates for those over 60 in cities over 10,000, and certain others.

(x) Must owe no past due taxes.

(y) Except in some cities.

(z) All elections except special elections.

(aa) Precinct.

(ab) Municipal election.

(ac) English or Hawaiian language.

(ad) Name subject to removal from registration list after failure to vote in a general election

AMERICAN
STATE AND LOCAL
GOVERNMENT

By the Same Author

AMERICAN GOVERNMENT: National, State, and Local, Second Edition

AMERICAN NATIONAL GOVERNMENT, Fourth Edition

GOVERNMENT IN THE UNITED STATES, Fifth Edition

AMERICAN STATE AND LOCAL GOVERNMENT

SECOND EDITION

CLAUDIUS O. JOHNSON

PROFESSOR OF POLITICAL SCIENCE
The State College of Washington

NEW YORK

Thomas Y. Crowell Company

1956

Library of Congress Catalog Card Number 55-12247

FIRST EDITION

First Printing, December, 1949
Second Printing, February, 1952

SECOND EDITION

First Printing, October, 1955
Second Printing, January, 1957

MANUFACTURED IN THE UNITED STATES OF AMERICA
BY THE VAIL-BALLOU PRESS, INC., BINGHAMTON, N.Y.

TO MARY

PREFACE TO THE SECOND EDITION

The principal purpose underlying the preparation of the First Edition of *State and Local Government* was to supply a text for a relatively short course in that subject. As that work appears to have met a certain demand, this new edition is now offered. It follows the same general plan of organization as the first, but it contains a new chapter—"The States in the American Federal System"—which seems essential for a broader grasp of the topic of intergovernmental relations. New material has been added in the other chapters and rewriting has not been shunned where I could improve my earlier presentation. Some excellent studies of the government of individual states are now appearing. Perhaps the volume on any particular state and this text, which tries to include them all, may find association as mutually supplementary companions.

In the Preface to the edition of 1950 I wrote: "I am indebted to other writers of textbooks on American government; to those who write articles for research and professional journals; to busy men, public officials and others, who so kindly answer my letters and often enclose with their answers supporting materials; and to a few talented and industrious citizens who fit into all these classes. Their names are not mentioned here, but this general thanksgiving is, I believe, made specific by suitable acknowledgment at appropriate places in the text." That expression of indebtedness and appreciation is sincerely renewed here.

C. O. J.

January 3, 1956

CONTENTS

CHARTS AND TABLES

AMERICAN
STATE AND LOCAL
GOVERNMENT

TO THE STUDENT

The Preface on the preceding pages is for your professor. The book is for you. In the thirty-odd years that I have taught government, it has been my constant endeavor to make the subject clear, direct, interesting, and personal. These ends I have held in view as I was writing this book. The "we" and "our" that so frequently appear on its pages were used designedly, to "personalize" the subject, to bring it home to us, to make us feel that we have a stake in our government, to convey the idea that each of us is a unit, however small, in the process of government. Please accept these minor intimacies of the printed page as an indication of my desire to eliminate a measure of formality from the study of state and local government and to make it a joint, pleasant, and profitable excursion for professors and students.

C. O. J.

CHAPTER 1

THE STATES
IN THE AMERICAN FEDERAL SYSTEM

The American states antedate the nation. Before winning independence the original states existed as separate British colonies, and as such they were subject in legal theory to the complete control of Crown and Parliament. In practice, however, they enjoyed a rather liberal allowance of local autonomy. In the later stages of their development the colonies conceded to the central authorities at London control only over their external affairs and asserted, in effect, that they were their own masters in internal affairs. American colonial experience was therefore with a governmental system in which the powers of government were informally divided (a principle always denied by the British) between a central authority and various regional authorities. It was but natural that, following the successful Revolution, the people of the independent states should establish a system of government in which national and state authorities were given separate and, to a degree, independent powers. This is, of course, the American federal [1] system. As our concern in this volume is with the states, it is the purpose of this chapter to indicate the place of the states in that system.

I. STATE POWERS [2]

The national government has all powers delegated to it under the Constitution [3] and such other powers as may be fairly implied from those delegated.

---

[1] The term "federal" in American usage has two meanings. One is to designate the dual system of government, the national-state system; the other is simply a term used interchangeably with "national." Thus we commonly hear "federal government" used for the more appropriate term "national government." In this volume the terms are used interchangeably—for variety.

[2] R. G. Gettell, *Political Science* (1949 ed.), Ch. 14; W. B. Graves, *American State Government* (1953 ed.), pp. 1–31; A. F. Macdonald, *American State Government and Administration* (1955 ed.), Ch. 2; A. T. Mason, "Our Federal Union Reconsidered," 65 *Political Science Quarterly* 502 (Dec. 1950); C. B. Swisher, *The Growth of Constitutional Power in the United States* (1946), Ch. 2.

[3] "Constitution," as capitalized throughout this volume, refers to the Constitution of the United States.

The states have all other powers except a few prohibited to them by the Constitution. The powers of the states are largely inherent and undefined. Because the Constitution deals almost entirely with national or federal powers and because the national authority over foreign relations and defense furnish so much of the drama of government, we are likely to overlook the great number of fundamental powers remaining to the states. The states have the power to tax; to borrow money; to make and administer the great bodies of civil and criminal law; to exercise the widest possible powers in connection with the health, safety, and well-being of their inhabitants; to establish schools and supervise education; to charter and control corporations; to regulate intrastate trade; to engage in business enterprises; to make practically all the suffrage and election laws; to administer welfare and correction; and to make all rules and regulations respecting local government. As for the individual, the state government is literally with him from the cradle to the grave. It issues his birth certificate and his burial permit; and between the Alpha and Omega of his mortal existence it protects his rights, penalizes his delinquencies, and regulates his conduct in scores of ways. If he goes hunting, it is under state permission. If he gets married, he must have a state license. If he is divorced, it is by a decree of a state court. Before he enters a profession, he must satisfy the state that he is competent.

Some readers may still be unconvinced, may yet maintain that most of the last hundred years have witnessed a steady increase of national power at the expense of the states. It is conceded at once that national power has been extended to subject matter that the framers of the Constitution probably did no dream of—to the regulation of business, labor-management relations, agricultural production, and communications, to mention only a few items. Federal exercise of such power does not mean, however, that the central government has usurped the functions of the states, but only that such government has found it desirable to employ powers it has always possessed in order to meet new demands and conditions. For example, it has exercised its original interstate commerce power, a power it was given in the days of the ox-cart and sail-boat, to deal with the particularly sensitive and tremendously significant problem of labor-management relations. And it has used another original power, that of appropriating money for the general welfare, to establish a national social security system. Even if, as a result of the entrance of the national government into certain fields, the states have lost some power that they once possessed, it does not follow that they "are on their way out." The states, like the national government, are constantly increasing their sphere of activity. If federal authority has increased its control over industrial relations affecting interstate commerce, the states have redoubled their efforts to regulate the same activities in intrastate commerce. The states have tapped and are continuing to tap their great reserve of governmental power. If the national government has expended billions for highway construction, the states have spent more billions and much of it on roads they ignored a hundred years ago. The states have always had full authority in relation to education, but it is only in the last hundred years (the last fifty in some states) that they have adopted comprehensive public education programs. Public health is a matter the states formerly did little about, but now with improved knowledge of that science they are moving forward rapidly in that area. It is of great interest (and some concern) that the states are now spending about thirty times as much per year as they spent in 1915. This increase is explained in part by the rise in the price level, in part by the increase in population, but principally by improvements in the standards of performance of old functions and the adoption of new functions.[4] It would seem unnecessary, then, that we should any longer seriously trouble ourselves about federal encroachment upon state powers, or over any lack of power remaining to the states. There are, however, certain limitations upon state power, or limitations upon the exercise of power, which we will now notice. We shall observe also that while the Constitution places limitations upon the states it extends to them advantages in equal or greater proportions.

II. CONSTITUTIONAL LIMITATIONS UPON THE STATES [5]

The limitations imposed by the Constitution upon the states may be divided into two classes—those that protect the civil rights of persons and the political rights of citizens and those that are designed to prevent the states from interfering with the functions of the national government, primarily those of commerce and finance.

A. To Protect Civil and Political Rights

General Provisions Protecting Civil Liberties

As we shall see in the next chapter, the states have provisions in their own constitutions designed to secure civil liberties, but our interest here is with similar provisions of the federal Constitution which are applicable to the states. "No state," reads the Constitution, "shall . . . pass any bill of attainder, ex post facto law or law impairing the obligation of contracts." [6] A bill of attainder is a legislative act by which an accused person is declared guilty and punishment is prescribed without judicial trial. It appears that not since Reconstruction times has a state legislature, even by inadvertence, passed a bill of attainder.[7] The words ex post facto mean "after the fact." The constitutional prohibition is against the enactment of any law which makes a deed done before its passage, and innocent at the time, a crime.

[4] Macdonald, *op. cit.,* p. 377.

[5] R. E. Cushman, *Leading Constitutional Decisions* (1955 ed.), Ch. 4; Claudius O. Johnson, *American National Government* (1955 ed.), Ch. 5; A. T. Mason and W. M. Beaney, *American Constitutional Law* (1954), Chs. 4, 5, 10–12, especially the Introductory Essays.

[6] Art. I. sec. x, cl. 1.

[7] But Congress passed such an act in 1943. See United States v. Lovett, 328 U.S. 303 (1946).

Furthermore, an act increasing a penalty, or changing the method of trial in such a way as to make conviction more certain, would be ex post facto for any person accused of having committed a crime covered by the act on a day prior to its passage. The prohibition against impairing the obligation of contracts is one that protects property rights, rights not easily distinguishable from personal rights. A simple example of the sort of thing prohibited occurs in the case of John Doe who holds a note from Richard Roe for $1,000, with interest payable at 6 per cent. Suppose the state legislature, during the life of the note, passes an act limiting the interest rate to 5 per cent. This law would impair the rights of John Doe under the contract, and it would be declared inapplicable to his case. It would, of course, properly apply to similar contracts made after its passage.

Due Process of Law

Far and away the most significant provision of the federal Constitution respecting the maintenance of individual liberty in the states is the Fourteenth Amendment. The essential clauses of it read: "No state shall . . . deprive any person of life, liberty, or property, without due process of law; nor deny to any person within its jurisdiction the equal protection of the laws." First we consider the meaning of that ancient term (it is at least 800 years old) due process of law. In broad non-technical language, it means that state and local governments in their actions respecting persons (corporations are also persons, artificial persons) shall not deal arbitrarily, unfairly, or in a discriminatory manner. Concretely, in criminal cases, it means among other things, that a formal and definite accusation must be furnished the person who is being put on trial, he must be given adequate opportunity to make his defense, and he must be allowed, and even furnished, counsel. Due process is violated when evidence is obtained from an accused by a coercive method —for example, by thirty-six hours of continuous questioning under powerful electric lights.[8] Furthermore, the penal laws themselves are held to violate due process if they are so vague in meaning that men of ordinary intelligence can only guess at their application to specific acts. In a civil case (suit between individuals) due process requires a regular proceeding before a court duly authorized to hear the case, and full hearing for the parties.

Due process and the police power. The states, in exercising their "police powers," that is, in legislating for the safety, health, morals, and general welfare of the public, must be careful that they do not deprive individuals and organizations of liberty or property without due process of law. Now almost any law restricting the operations of saloons or gambling places, requiring safety appliances on machinery or on vehicles of transportation, and fixing the maximum hours of labor or minimum wages will deprive someone of liberty and property (interfere with his operations and cost him some money). What due process prohibits is *unreasonable* and *arbitrary* inter-

---

[8] Ashcraft v. Tennessee, 322 U.S. 143 (1944).

ference with liberty and property.   For some years the Supreme Court of the United States was strongly inclined to hold that legislation which constituted an exercise of police powers was unreasonable, and therefore in denial of due process of law.   Since about 1915, however, the Court has shown a strong disposition to find the police regulations to be reasonable.   From time to time various statutes prescribing minimum wages for women and children were held to be in violation of due process of law, but in 1937 the Court decided that such laws represented a proper exercise of the states' duty to protect women and children in industry and therefore did not unreasonably deprive employers and employees of the liberty to make contracts of labor.[9]

DUE PROCESS AND THE FREEDOM OF EXPRESSION.   There are four freedoms of expression—of speech, of the press, of religion, and of assembly—that are protected by due process of law.   The courts will hold to be a deprivation of liberty an unwarranted or unreasonable state or local interference with any one of these rights.   Beginning to receive emphasis in the 1920's, this application of due process of law is a profoundly significant development, for among civilized people no liberty is so dear as that of expression.   To be sure, no liberty is absolute, and state laws against libel, slander, sedition, and similar abuses and offenses are not in violation of freedom of speech and of the press.   On the other hand, laws that prohibit full and free (or even absurd, ridiculous, and erroneous) expression on matters of popular interest are held to be in violation of freedom of expression and contrary to due process.   Religious freedom is not violated by state laws against blasphemy and laws establishing penalties for bigamy are valid even though the joint husband may have religious sanction for plurality in wives.   But laws are invalid that require religious workers to procure a license from a city official before distributing their literature.   Likewise, state laws or school board regulations are invalid that demand the "flag salute" in the public schools of children who regard the flag as a "graven image."   In America religious liberty means, among other things, the separation of church and state, a principle that is construed so strictly that a school board may not set up a program of religious instruction in the public schools.   The fourth of the freedoms under discussion, that of assembly, is indispensable to freedom of speech and religion.   Due process of law does not prevent the states from banning violent assemblies, or assemblies at utterly inappropriate times and places, but it secures to the people the right "peaceably to assemble," a right the courts protect by striking down state laws or local ordinances that would prevent such assemblies.[10]

The Equal Protection of the Laws

The most interesting and significant cases arising under the "equal protection of the laws" clause are those involving racial segregation.   Before

[9] See Johnson, *op. cit.*, pp. 107–109, or other texts on American government.
[10] Johnson, *op. cit.*, pp. 90–98.

1900 the Southern states enacted legislation requiring segregation of Negroes and whites in public transportation, schools, and other services and facilities. The Supreme Court sustained such acts on the theory that the "separate" accommodations imposed no racial discrimination, no denial of equal protection, considering that each race was furnished "equal" accommodations.[11] But one of the principal objections to the "separate but equal" doctrine was that the facilities offered Negroes were almost invariably inferior to those provided for others.   On occasion, Negroes were without any facilities, as when they desired to travel on a Pullman or attend a professional school.   A landmark was established in 1938, when the Supreme Court held that the State of Missouri, which provided no separate institution in which Negroes could be trained as lawyers, was denying them equal protection of the laws in not admitting them to the University of Missouri.[12]   In later cases it was held that Negroes, when admitted to such institutions, must not in any way be segregated from the other students.   In 1954 segregation in the public schools, quite aside from unequal facilities, was attacked as being of itself a denial of the equal protection of the laws.   The Supreme Court, speaking unanimously through Chief Justice Warren, ruled that "in the field of public education the doctrine of 'separate but equal' has no place."[13]   The Court very wisely left the states a reasonable time in which to adjust their public school systems to the requirements of the far-reaching desegregation decision.

Constitutional Safeguards Respecting the Suffrage

The original Constitution left entirely to the states the decision as to who should be granted the right to vote.   The right is still so determined, subject to the requirements of the Fifteenth Amendment (1870) that no citizen shall be denied the right to vote on account of race or color and to the Nineteenth (1920) that sex shall not be a disqualifying factor.   First by fraud and intimidation and later by cleverly designed statutes administered by "evil eyes and unequal hands" the Southern states, in effect, circumvented the Fifteenth Amendment and thus prevented from voting all except a very small percentage of Negroes.   In recent years, the repeal of the poll tax in about half the states below the Mason-Dixon Line, Supreme Court decisions favorable to the Negro's claim to the suffrage,[14] and some changes in the political climate of the South have contributed to increase the number of Negroes admitted to the franchise.   Fairly reliable estimates of Negro registration in the South place the figure for 1940 at 149,908 and for 1950 at 827,820,[15] a significant advance.

[11] Plessy v. Ferguson, 163 U.S. 537 (1896).
[12] Missouri ex. rel. Gaines v. Canada, 305 U.S. 337 (1938).
[13] Brown v. Topeka, 347 U.S. 483 (1954).
[14] See, for example, Smith v. Allwright, 321 U.S. 649 (1944), holding that preventing a Negro from voting in a primary election is contrary to the Fifteenth Amendment just as is excluding him from participation in a general election.
[15] T. I. Emerson and D. Haber, *Political and Civil Rights in the United States* (1952), p. 326.

B. To Strengthen National Powers

Certain constitutional restrictions upon the states are designed primarily to prevent the states from obstructing the functions of the national government. The following paragraphs are devoted to an examination of some of these restrictions and limitations.

Limitations upon Compacts between the States

The Constitution provides that "no State shall enter into any treaty, alliance, or confederation," and that "no State shall, without the consent of Congress . . . enter into any agreement or compact with another State or with a foreign power." [16]   The courts of the United States have been very liberal in interpreting the powers of the states under the second clause just quoted.   They have held that on a number of matters the states may make agreements without even asking the assent of Congress.   In the case of Virginia v. Tennessee,[17] the Court said: "If, for instance, Virginia should come into possession and ownership of a small parcel of land in New York which the latter state might desire to acquire as a site for a public building, it would hardly be deemed essential for the latter state to obtain the consent of Congress before it could make a valid agreement with Virginia for the purchase of the land."   But the consent of Congress must be obtained, continued the Court, for any compact "tending to the increase of political power in the states, which may encroach upon or interfere with the just supremacy of the United States."   One of the best known of interstate compacts is that under which New York and New Jersey established the Port of New York Authority (1921).   Recent difficulties involving racketeering and violence along the waterfront led the two states to enter upon the Waterfront Commission Compact, an agreement that received the prompt approval of Congress (June, 1953).[18]   In 1949 a significant division of waters agreement, the Upper Colorado River Basin Compact, was entered into by Arizona, Colorado, New Mexico, Utah, and Wyoming.[19]

Limitations in Respect to Foreign Commerce

Very material limitations are placed upon the states with regard to commerce.   Not only is the power given to Congress to regulate commerce "with foreign nations, and among the several States, and with the Indian tribes" (Art. I, sec. VIII, cl. 8); but "no State shall, without the consent of the Congress, lay any imposts or duties on imports or exports, except what may be absolutely necessary for executing its inspection laws"; nor may a state lay a duty of tonnage without the consent of Congress (Art. I, sec. x, cl. 10).

[16] Constitution, Art. I, sec. x.
[17] 148 U.S. 503 (1893).
[18] *Book of the States, 1954–55,* p. 16.
[19] See Jean S. Breitenstein, "The Upper Colorado River Basin Compact," *State Government,* Sept., 1949, pp. 214–216, 225.

An inspection fee, for example, a fee to cover fully the cost of inspecting the quality of tobacco intended for export, may be levied or imposed by a state without the consent of Congress, but it seems that it is for Congress to determine whether or not the charge made is more than is "absolutely necessary" to cover the cost of the inspection.[20]   If a state wishes to levy a duty or tonnage (the latter is a tax on the carrying capacity of a vessel entering or leaving a port), it may do so only after the assent of Congress has been given. Frequently, during the early years of the Republic, Congress permitted the states to make such levies for the purpose of improving local port facilities.

The prohibition of the Constitution regarding the imposition of import duties by the states is given a broad judicial interpretation.   It is construed to mean not only that the states shall not impose duties on articles at the time of their importation, but also that the states may not tax imported articles as long as they have not become a part of the general property in the state.   Thus, articles that remain the property of an importer in his warehouse are not subject to state taxation, for such a tax "is too plainly a duty on imports to escape the prohibition in the Constitution." [21]   States may, of course, tax imported articles along with other property after such articles have become commingled (placed on store shelves for sale, for example) with the general property in the state.

Limitations in Respect to Interstate Commerce

The Constitution gives Congress the power to regulate interstate commerce. The grant of this power to Congress does not exclude the states from passing considerable legislation on the subject, but it does limit the authority of the states in two significant ways.   First, when Congress acts to regulate a particular type of transaction in interstate commerce or an interstate carrier, the railroads, for example, all state law inconsistent with the national regulations must give way.   Second, even in the absence of any congressional legislation, state laws are regularly declared void if they relate to interstate transportation or trade that admits of only one uniform (and therefore national) system of regulation.

Permissible State Laws Affecting Interstate Commerce

Despite the restrictions mentioned in the preceding paragraph, the states still have some power over interstate commerce.   Long ago the courts held that the states, exercising their police powers, could make regulations in the interest of local health and safety, even though such regulations might incidentally interfere with interstate commerce.   Thus, when an epidemic of anthrax was raging among Louisiana livestock, the State of Texas prohibited the transportation of such stock from Louisiana into Texas, and the Supreme Court

[20] Patapsco Guano Co. v. N.C. Bd. of Agri., 171 U.S. 345 (1898).   The Chief Justice cites Justice Bradley, on circuit, in Neilson v. Garza.
[21] Brown v. Maryland, 12 Wheat. 419 (1827).

of the United States sustained this act.[22] Similarly, the Court has upheld the right of a state to require locomotive engineers to be examined and licensed; to regulate the heating of passenger cars; to require guard posts on bridges; and to limit the speed of trains at grade-crossings.[23] The proudest of the many interstate "cannon balls," "flyers," "rockets," and "zephyrs" may be validly required by city ordinance to slow down within the corporate limits and to refrain from making unnecessary noises. Many other state and local regulations promulgated in the interest of the health, safety, and convenience of the public have been sustained. Indeed, the delegation of the interstate commerce power to Congress, as that power has been interpreted by the courts, has not prevented the states from impeding and obstructing the flow of trade between the states.

Limitations on State Monetary and Taxing Powers

1. STATE BANKS AND BANK NOTES. "No state shall . . . coin money; emit bills of credit; [or] make anything but gold and silver coin a [legal] tender in payment of debts" (Art. 7, sec. x, cl. 1). This provision of the Constitution owes its origin to the unfortunate paper money experiments of the states during and immediately following the Revolution. The commercial classes were fully persuaded that the national government alone should have monetary powers.

We must note that the restrictive clause does not prohibit the states from chartering banks that compete with the national banks; nor does it prevent states from authorizing their banks to issue bills that may circulate as currency, although not as legal tender. State bank notes are kept out of circulation, however, by a statute of Congress that imposes a heavy tax upon their issue.

2. BILLS OF CREDIT. The courts have been liberal with the states in interpreting the prohibition with regard to bills issued on the credit of the state and designed to circulate as money. In only one case have state obligations been held void as bills of credit. This invalidation occurred when Missouri, more than a hundred years ago, made loans to her citizens in the form of certificates that were to be accepted as money for taxes and for salaries and fees of state officers. The more liberal view is illustrated by the following: Texas issued state warrants to pay its debts. They were made receivable for all taxes and public dues, and the law authorized state officers to pay public creditors with them if such creditors would receive them. When this paper was received back by the state, it was not to be reissued. Since it was not to circulate as money in ordinary business transactions, the Court held that the issue did not constitute bills of credit.[24]

3. INTERGOVERNMENTAL TAXATION. In his discussion of national suprem-

---

[22] Smith v. St. L. & S.W.R.R. Co., 181 U.S., 248 (1901).
[23] Southern Ry. Co. v. King, 217 U.S. 524 (1910).
[24] Huston, etc., Ry. Co. v. Texas, 177 U.S. 66 (1900).

acy Chief Justice Marshall laid down the rule that the states could not tax the operations of the national banks.[25]   Following the principle enunciated by Marshall, the Supreme Court has held that the states may not tax the property of the national government, its bonds, its franchises, the salaries of its officers, or otherwise by taxation obstruct the operations of the national government. However, Congress may authorize the states to levy certain taxes that might otherwise fall within the list of prohibitions.   For example, the states are permitted to tax the real property of national banks as they tax other real property, and they may tax the stockholders.   When the national government attempted to tax the salaries of state officers, the Supreme Court originally imposed the same rule of implied prohibition, holding that the central authority had no more right to interfere with the functioning of the state governments than those governments had to interfere with the processes of the central government.

Taxation of public salaries.   Formerly the Supreme Court made much of Marshall's extreme statement in McCulloch v. Maryland—"the power to tax involves the power to destroy"—and was quick to declare invalid any act of a state legislature that imposed a tax upon national agencies or officers on the theory that such a tax was the entering wedge that would "destroy" the national government.   Recently the Court has been less under the influence of Marshall's absolutes and it has been more under the guidance of the legal wisdom of the late Justice Holmes, who recognized few absolutes.   Holmes maintained that "distinctions of the law are distinctions of degree" and that "the power to tax is not the power to destroy as long as this Court sits." [26]

Approaching the problem of intergovernmental taxation with the distinctions of degree in mind, the Court now takes the view that a state tax, nondiscriminatory in character, that falls upon an agency or officer of the national government is valid if it is not an economic burden passed on to that government.   It no longer holds that taxing the salary of a government official has the same result as a tax on the government itself.   In Graves v. New York [27] the Court held that the New York State income tax law was valid when applied to the salary of an examining attorney for the Federal Home Owners' Loan Corporation.   This tax, said the Court, "is laid upon income which becomes the property of the taxpayer when received as compensation for his services; and the tax laid upon the privilege of receiving it is paid from his private funds and not from the funds of the government, either directly or indirectly."   By the same reasoning the national government was given the green light to tax the salaries of state officers.   In the Public Salary Act of 1939 Congress brought the salaries of state officers and employees within the federal taxing area, and authorized the states to impose nondiscriminatory taxes upon the salaries of officers and employees of the United States.   The demise of the old practice of intergovernmental salary tax exemption finds

[25] McCulloch v. Maryland, 4 Wheat. 316 (1819).
[26] Dissenting in Panhandle Oil Co. v. Mississippi, 277 U.S. at 223 (1928).
[27] 306 U.S. 466 (1939).

few mourners.   It was of no clear benefit to any government and it gave those receiving salaries for government services a privileged position.

Taxation of public enterprises.   The national government taxes state activities that are of a nongovernmental, or, to use the term generally employed, "proprietary" character.   The terms "governmental" functions and "proprietary" functions were invented by the courts; and, in the course of time, the tribunals listed as governmental the states' courts, the police systems, the public schools, the public hospitals, and waterworks under state ownership. These things, said the courts, the national government may not tax.   The courts also, in cases appropriately before them, ruled as proprietary the states' liquor business, state or municipally owned street railways, state banks, publicly owned wharfs, and state university football contests (but not the university—that was governmental).   These things the national government may tax.   The distinctions were not always convincing, but the general rule seemed to be that an activity of a state or one of its subdivisions that historically had been in the domain of private business could be taxed by act of Congress. But in 1946 the Supreme Court held that the State of New York must pay a federal gallonage tax on the sale of mineral water taken from Saratoga Springs.[28]   This decision was, of course, not in accord with the classification that put waterworks down as governmental and nontaxable functions.   As a matter of fact, the decision pretty well discards the classifications so painfully built up and seems to rely more upon whether the subject of the tax is traditionally within the national taxing power and whether the tax bears alike upon states and citizens.[29]   This sort of confusion has never arisen in respect to national functions or the state's power to tax them and for the simple reason that a state may not tax any national function, even a purely commercial activity.

III. OBLIGATIONS OF THE NATIONAL GOVERNMENT TO THE STATES [30]

The national government is under some specific obligations to the states. Article IV, section IV, of the Constitution reads: "The United States shall guarantee to every state . . . a republican form of government, and shall protect each of them against invasion, and on application of the legislature or of the executive (when the legislature cannot be convened), against domestic violence."

The Guaranty of the Republican Form of Government

The Constitution nowhere defines what is meant by the republican form of government.   Undoubtedly the framers were sure that the state governments as they were constituted in 1787 were republican.   Certainly also Congress,

[28] New York v. United States, 326 U.S. 572.
[29] David Fellman, "Federalism," in "Ten Years of the Supreme Court, 1937–1947" (R. E. Cushman, ed.), *Am. Pol. Sci. Rev.*, Dec., 1947, pp. 1157–1159.
[30] J. M. Mathews, *The American Constitutional System* (1940 ed.), pp. 57–63; W. W. Willoughby, *Principles of the Constitutional Law of the United States* (1930 ed.), Ch. XI.

by her acceptance of the constitutions of the new states, recognized them as having the essential features of republicanism. Republican government is thus understood to be a government in which a substantial body of the people have the right to choose their representatives and, in American practice, the right directly or indirectly to choose their executive.[31]

WHO APPLIES THE TEST FOR REPUBLICANISM? As the Constitution fails to define republican government, so it fails to specify what branch of the national government shall apply the republican test to a state's political institutions. Applying the test is rather obviously a political matter and, therefore, a power that naturally belongs to the political arms of the government—Congress and the President. Congress, through its power to admit new states and by its authority to exclude representatives from its membership, is in the best position to determine whether a state is republican and to enforce its ideas as to what constitutes that type of government. The courts have taken this view, at least; and they accept as republican any and all state governments that are expressly or tacitly recognized as such by Congress,[32] or by the President acting under the authority of Congress and the Constitution.[33]

Protection of the States Against Invasion and Domestic Violence

Closely connected with the guaranty of the republican form of government in the states is the guaranty that the national government shall protect the states against invasion and domestic violence. There is no difficulty in interpreting the meaning of this obligation with regard to invasion, for an invasion of a state by a foreign army would be at the same time an invasion of the United States, and no question exists as to the right and duty of the national government to resist such an attack. But when the internal order of a state is disturbed by rebellion or riot, the obligation of the national government is not so clear. The Constitution says that aid shall be extended to the states when the state authorities request it. If, however, the President feels that the state is capable of maintaining order and that it makes a request for national intervention because of timidity or for political reasons, he may refuse to send aid. On the other hand, when domestic disturbances in a state reach such proportions that the national property is in danger or the national services are interrupted, the President may send federal troops to the scene of the disorder, even against the protest of state authorities, as President Cleveland did in 1894 on the occasion of the serious railway strike in the Chicago vicinity.

IV. INTERSTATE RELATIONS [34]

The states, when acting within their spheres of government, are, in a legal sense, foreign to one another except where the Constitution of the United

---

[31] Willoughby, op. cit., pp. 139–140.
[32] Pacific States Tel. & Tel. Co. v. Oregon, 223 U.S. 118 (1912).
[33] Luther v. Borden, 7 Howard 1 (1849).
[34] W. F. Dodd, Cases on Constitutional Law (1954 ed.), pp. 379–400; Mathews, op. cit., Ch. VI; Willoughby, op. cit., Chs. XIII–XV.

States specifies to the contrary.   To be sure, foreign countries co-operate to a considerable extent under the rules of international law, but, in four important particulars, the Constitution establishes a much closer relationship among the states than is to be found between foreign states.   These relate to public acts, privileges of citizens, extradition, and the settlement of controversies.

Full Faith and Credit

In the first place, "full faith and credit shall be given in each State to the public acts, records, and judicial proceedings of every other State." [35]   In colonial times one colony treated the judgments of the courts of another as foreign judgments, allowing them to be re-examined on their merits and to be impeached for fraud or prejudice.   Such procedure operated as a considerable handicap upon intercolonial relations; and the men who drew up the Articles of Confederation, as well as those who drafted the Constitution, inserted the provision quoted above in order to establish more satisfactory legal relationships among the new states.

GENERAL ILLUSTRATIONS.   The "full faith and credit" clause does not require the courts of one state to enforce the penal laws of another.   The requirement covers only civil matters, and there are definite limitations even here.   For example, a state is not expected or required to enforce in its courts a contract made under a law of another state when to do so would be repugnant to good morals or lead to disturbance and disorganization of the local law.   But in an appropriate case the courts of one state must enforce the law of another.   Here are two concrete cases: A New York law imposed "double liability" upon owners of stock in New York banks.   When, in the great depression period (1929–1933), the superintendent of banks of the State of New York sought to collect the double liability from New Jersey residents who owned stock in a New York bank, the courts of New Jersey declined to entertain the action, holding that a New Jersey law protected the residents of the state from this sort of proceeding.   The Supreme Court of the United States decided otherwise, however, declaring that the subject matter was peculiarly within the regulatory power of the State of New York, and that New Jersey could not enable its residents "to escape the performance of a voluntarily assumed statutory obligation, consistent with morality, to contribute to the payment of depositors of a bank of another state of which they were stockholders." [36]   An electric light company and an individual made a contract of employment in Vermont, accepting the employment compensation act of that state.   The company had lines running into New Hampshire, and there the employee in the performance of his duties was killed.   It was held that the Vermont compensation act, not the compensation act of New Hampshire, should apply.[37]

These illustrations relate to the application, in appropriate cases, of the

35 Constitution, Art. IV, sec. I.
36 Broderick v. Rosner, 294 U.S. 629 (1935).
37 Bradford Electric Company v. Clapper, 286 U.S. 145 (1932).

laws of one state in the courts of another.   More significant and more commonly observed in operation is the requirement that the judgment of a court in one state shall receive "full faith and credit" in the courts of every other state.   If the duly attested record of the court giving the judgment in state A is presented, and if the court had jurisdiction (authority to hear and determine the case), the court in state B, in which the enforcement of the judgment is sought, is obligated to carry out the judgment of the court in state A.   To be sure, there are various complicating factors, but the basic rule is simple enough.   An individual wins a suit in one state, but before the judgment of the court is satisfied the defendant leaves the state, taking his property with him.   The successful litigant may then take the judgment to the state in which the elusive defendant is found and there institute suit upon the judgment.   It is not necessary for him to begin all over again—he simply brings a suit for the enforcement of the judgment.   It may happen that a litigant may win a judgment in state A and later have it enforced by a court in state B, even though under the laws of state B he could not have won the original judgment.[38]

APPLICATION OF FULL FAITH AND CREDIT TO DIVORCE.   A divorce granted to a spouse by a court of a state in which husband and wife are domiciled is a valid divorce anywhere, because there is no question of the jurisdiction of such a court.   Suppose that a spouse, a wife, let us say, leaves the state in which she was domiciled with her husband, takes up residence in another state, works as a secretary, and, after some years, gets a divorce in this state.   Does she have a decree that must be accepted as valid in the first state?   It would seem that the answer is "yes," for she had established bona fide (in good faith) domicile in the second state (not just a fake domicile for the purpose of a divorce).   Suppose, on the other hand, she did not establish bona fide domicile in the second state, but simply resided there the necessary 42 days, or whatever its law requires, in order to get the divorce.   Must the state in which she lived as a wife recognize her divorce?   The answer appears to be "no."   Here is such a case and the decision of the Supreme Court thereon: In 1940 the Nevada divorce mill granted decrees to husband A and wife B, who had motored from North Carolina and stopped for six weeks in a Nevada auto camp to establish domicile.   They married the same day they were divorced, and they returned immediately to North Carolina, where the former spouse of each resided.   Here they were convicted of bigamous cohabitation and sentenced to jail.   The Supreme Court of the United States set aside their conviction, holding that North Carolina, not having questioned the good faith of the Nevada domicile, must respect the divorce decrees.[39]   The Tar Heel State lost no time in setting the matter right.   It proceeded against the parties and clearly established the fact that they had gone to Nevada solely for the purpose of getting a divorce, that they had not taken up residence in Nevada

---

[38] Fauntleroy v. Lum, 210 U.S. 230 (1908), and Roche v. McDonald, 275 U.S. 449 (1928).
[39] Williams v. North Carolina, 317 U.S. 287 (1942).

in good faith. From these facts it contended that the accommodating state therefore had no jurisdiction to grant the divorces. This argument satisfied the Supreme Court.[40] The situation seems, then, to be this: a state may refuse to recognize a decree of divorce granted by another state, provided the first state can convince the Supreme Court of the United States that the second state assumed jurisdiction over a party who was not in fact a bona fide resident of the state, but had only remained in it long enough to get a "migratory" divorce.

This scant page on full faith and credit and divorce is an over-simplification of the subject. The problem has many angles, and Supreme Court decisions have not clarified all of them. In actual practice, however, only a few states, including New York and Pennsylvania, raise the question of the validity of a decree of divorce even when a state other than that of the marriage domicile grants it. In short, for most individuals, a divorce, "migratory" or otherwise, is effective everywhere.[41]

Privileges and Immunities

The second particular in which the Constitution brings about a much closer relationship among the several states than is found among foreign states is expressed in the provision that "the citizens of each State shall be entitled to all privileges and immunities of citizens in the several States." [42] The importance of preventing unjust and arbitrary discriminations by the states to the advantage of their own citizens and against citizens of other states was recognized from the first, for the Articles of Confederation contained a provision similar to that just quoted.

The object of the clause is to place the "citizens of each state upon the same footing with citizens of other states, so far as the advantages resulting from citizenship in those states are concerned. It relieves them from the disabilities of alienage in other states; it inhibits discriminatory legislation against them by other states; it gives them the right of free ingress into other states, and egress from them; it insures to them in other states the same freedom possessed by the citizens of those states in the acquisition and enjoyment of property and in the pursuit of happiness; and it secures to them in other states the equal protection of their laws. It has been justly said that no provision in the Constitution has tended so strongly to constitute the citizens of the United States one people as this." [43] The provision does not mean, of course, that a citizen of Texas who goes to California carries the laws of Texas along with him; but that when he is in California he must be treated by that state as it treats its own citizens.[44]

[40] Williams v. North Carolina, 325 U.S. 226 (1945).
[41] Estin v. Estin, 334 U.S. 541 (1948). For a learned article on certain aspects of full faith and credit and divorce, see E. N. Griswold, "Divorce Jurisdiction and Recognition of Divorce Decrees," *Harvard Law Review,* Dec. 1951, pp. 193–233.
[42] Constitution, Art. IV, sec. II.
[43] Paul v. Virginia, 8 Wall. 168 (1869).
[44] Neither aliens nor corporations reap any advantage from the clause under discussion, for neither are citizens.

In final analysis the privileges and immunities guaranties of the Constitution "forbid only such legislation affecting citizens of the respective states as will substantially or practically put a citizen of one state in a condition of alienage when he is within or when he removes to another state, or when asserting in another state the rights that commonly appertain to those who are part of the political community known as the people of the United States." [45]

Interstate Rendition

A third particular in which the states are brought a little closer together than are foreign states is in the matter of handling fugitives from justice. The nations commonly regulate the extradition of fugitives by treaty agreement. Our Constitution provides that, "a person charged in any State with treason, felony, or other crime, who shall flee from justice, and be found in another State, shall, on demand of the executive authority of the State from which he fled, be delivered up to be removed to the State having jurisdiction of the crime." [46]   Thus the international practice of extradition is made constitutional law in the American states.   As between our states, it is commonly referred to as "interstate rendition."

THE RENDITION PROCESS.   The process of rendition is regulated by an act of Congress that is supplemented by local statutes in most states.   It operates about as follows: A crime of robbery is committed in Maryland, and the person alleged to have committed the crime flees to New York.   His whereabouts having become known to Maryland authorities, the Governor of Maryland notifies the Governor of New York, who causes the arrest of the alleged fugitive.   The Governor of Maryland must present to the chief executive of New York a certified copy of the indictment or affidavit charging the person demanded with having committed the crime of robbery in Maryland.   If the Governor of New York (assisted, of course, by his legal advisers) is satisfied with the regularity of these papers, and if it appears that the individual demanded is probably a fugitive from Maryland justice, he will have him surrendered to an officer of the State of Maryland, to be carried back to that state for trial.[47]

RENDITION NOT COMPULSORY.   Ordinarily the requisitions of one governor to another are honored and the process of rendition works smoothly, but in no case may a governor be compelled to comply with a demand for an alleged fugitive.   Speaking of the rendition clause of the Constitution and of the act of Congress relating to it, Chief Justice Taney said: "Looking to the subject-matter of this law, and the relations which the United States and the several states bear to each other, the Court is of opinion the words 'it shall be the

---

[45] Blake v. McClung, 172 U.S. 239 (1898).

[46] Constitution, Art. IV, sec. II, cl. 2.

[47] Roberts v. Reilly, 116 U.S. 80 (1885).   Once back in Maryland, the accused may be tried for crime other than that specified in the request for his rendition.   Furthermore, he has no redress, even if he has been kidnapped and returned without lawful authority. Willoughby, *op. cit.,* p. 173.

duty' were not used as mandatory and compulsory, but as declaratory of the moral duty which this command created, when Congress had provided the mode of carrying it into execution.   The act does not provide any means to compel the execution of this duty, nor inflict any punishment for neglect or refusal on the part of the executive of the state; nor is there any clause or provision in the Constitution which arms the government of the United States with this power.   Indeed, such a power would place every state under the control and dominion of the General Government, even in the administration of its internal concerns and reserved rights." [48]

Controversies between States

The fourth constitutional provision that brings the states into a closer degree of relationship than is enjoyed by foreign powers is that clause which calls for judicial settlement of interstate controversies.   Sovereign states, such as the United States and Great Britain, may not sue each other unless both parties consent.   Where they are unwilling to submit their differences to an international court, they may exhaust the arts of diplomacy and risk the force of arms in reaching a settlement.   The states of the United States are forbidden to make war.   They must settle all of their disputes by agreement or judicial means.   Although many interstate disputes are settled by agreements between the states, the great majority of the more serious differences are brought to a solution through the operation of that incalculably valuable provision of the Constitution that extends the judicial power of the United States to controversies between the states.

ILLUSTRATIONS.   In a number of cases the Supreme Court of the United States has been called upon to settle boundary disputes between the states. Many cases of other types have been similarly adjudicated.   Missouri sued Illinois when the Sanitary District of Chicago, acting under state authority, constructed a drainage canal that carried sewage to the Mississippi, thus polluting the water supply for inhabitants of Missouri.[49]   Some years ago, Colorado took so much water from the Arkansas River for irrigation purposes that Kansas felt deprived of her share, and the Supreme Court upheld the right of Kansas to sue Colorado.[50]   When West Virginia came into the Union, she agreed to pay a fair part of the debt of Virginia as it stood January 1, 1861. It was necessary for Virginia to institute a number of suits in the courts of the United States before West Virginia would make a settlement.   This long-standing controversy over some $12,000,000 illustrates not only the importance of cases settled by judicial means, but also the rare tact and good judgment exercised by the Court in deciding such cases.[51]   Another case that aroused considerable interest was Arizona's unsuccessful attempt to secure a

[48] Kentucky v. Dennison, 24 How. 66 (1860).
[49] 180 U.S. 208 (1901) and 200 U.S. 496 (1906).
[50] 185 U.S. 125 (1902) and 206 U.S. 46 (1907).
[51] 246 U.S. 565 (1918).

Court injunction to prevent California, certain other states, and the Secretary of the Interior from carrying out the Boulder Dam project.[52]

V. FEDERAL AID TO THE STATES [53]

The topic to be discussed at this point differs materially from the preceding ones. The subjects discussed in the preceding sections are primarily legal and political in character. The present one, federal aid, has its legal and political aspects, to be sure; but its economic and social bearings are of much greater significance. Here we find the nation and the states co-operating in various governmental functions, and we find the lines that divide national and state activities a trifle dim in some cases. Federal aid to the states is not a new adventure in our system of government; but in recent decades it has increased both in amount and kind.

The authority to make such appropriations has been found long since. Indeed, Alexander Hamilton and John Marshall, although they might have objected to federal grants-in-aid on the grounds of policy, would have had no scruples on the question of the authority of Congress to make such grants. The authority comes from several provisions of the Constitution, the particular provision covering a specific grant depending upon the purpose of the appropriation. Congress has the power to regulate interstate commerce, and it follows from this power, for example, that Congress may make grants of money to protect the forests that hold the waters that feed the interstate rivers. Another example: Congress has the authority to "lay and collect taxes, duties, imposts, and excises" for "the general welfare of the United States." Congress has decided that appropriations for land-grant colleges, old-age assistance, and a host of other things are for the "general welfare of the United States." The Supreme Court has upheld the constitutionality of such acts of Congress.[54]

Aid without Strings Attached

Earlier federal aid to the states was usually in the form of land grants, which were received subject only to the understanding that they were to be used for specified purposes. This system had its origin in 1785, when the old Congress of the Confederation decreed that certain lands of the Northwest Territory should be set aside for public schools. When Ohio was admitted to the Union in 1802, Congress granted one section of land in each township for schools, a practice that was continued for states admitted thereafter. In 1848 the grant was increased to two sections, and even this was doubled for

---

[52] 283 U.S. 423 (1931).

[53] The Council of State Governments, *Federal Grants-in-Aid* (1949); The Commission on Intergovernmental Relations, *A Report to the President for Transmittal to the Congress* (1955); V. O. Key, Jr., *The Administration of Federal Grants to the States* (1937); Senate Committee on Expenditures in the Executive Departments, *Intergovernmental Relationships Between the United States and the States and Municipalities* (82nd Cong., 1st sess., Senate Report No. 94, 1951).

[54] Council of State Governments, *op. cit.,* pp. 15 ff.

Arizona, New Mexico, and Utah.   Higher education also received assistance, the common practice until 1889 being to grant to each newly admitted state at least two townships for a university.   States were also given lands for their seats of government, for building canals, for the stimulation of railroad construction, and for other purposes.

But these early grants contained no stipulations as to the minimum price the states should receive for the lands, nor were directions given for the administration of the funds thus acquired.   The result was that the state authorities did as they pleased; and what most of them pleased to do causes us to deplore the lack of foresight, to put it mildly, of the rugged individuals who sat in high places a few generations ago.   Often the land was sold at rates so low that the suspicion of corruption was persistent.   The best that can be said is that it was parted with light-heartedly and with the unjustified optimism that there would always be more.   In 1875, when much of the loss had already occurred, Congress began the practice of fixing a minimum price per acre at which the states might sell the lands, and from time to time has added more restrictions respecting sale and the administration of funds received.

Aid with Supervision

As just noted, supervision of the type of grant mentioned above came too late to conserve the grant in most states.   A new policy of "locking the stable before the horse was stolen" had its inception with the far-reaching Morrill Act of 1862, by which each state received 30,000 acres of land for each of its senators and representatives in Congress—such lands to be used for the establishment of colleges in which agriculture, mechanic arts, and other subjects should be taught.   Safeguards in the use of the lands were few and ineffective as measured by present standards of federal regulation of subsidies to the states, but a beginning was made.   Although failing to fix a minimum price at which land might be sold, Congress did establish requirements respecting the investing of the money obtained from sales and stipulated that the principal should not be expended.   Another important provision prohibited the use of any of the money for college buildings, building construction being fixed as the obligation of the states.   Here we see the beginning of the principle that a state, in order to receive federal aid, must itself assume a financial obligation.

The second Morrill Act (1890) provided cash appropriations for the land-grant colleges.   Appropriations under this act, the Nelson amendment (1907), and the Bankhead-Jones Act (1935) now average about $100,000 annually for each state.   Expenditure of any of this money for buildings is prohibited, as in the original act.   But the most important feature of the act of 1890 is that the Secretary of the Interior may withhold the allotment from any state that does not fulfill its obligations under the act.   At this point we see the introduction of the now very familiar and very powerful means of federal supervision.   When the kindly central government approached them "with its hand in its pocket," states found it expedient to forget their right of freedom from federal interference in their local affairs and accept the supervision.   Three years prior to the passage of the Second Morrill Act, Congress provided in the Hatch Act for cash contributions to the states and territories, the funds to be used for agricultural experiment stations.   Under this act and later supplementary acts, particularly the Bankhead-Jones Act (1935) and Public Law 733 (1946), each state and territory now receives an annual appropriation averaging approximately $200,000 for experiment stations established in connection with the agricultural colleges.   Although no adequate means of federal supervision of the expenditure of funds was provided for in the Hatch Act, federal authority in this direction was considerably strengthened by the Adams Act (1906).

Aid on the Fifty-fifty Basis Plus Federal Supervision

Some authorities have considered the Weeks Act (1911), which provided small federal payments to the states for protection from fire of the forested watersheds of navigable streams, as marking the beginning of modern federal-aid policy.   But a measure that appears to have the better claim to the honor is the Smith-Lever Act (1914), which provided for agricultural extension work through the co-operation of the federal government and the land-grant colleges.   Under this law each state was to receive a uniform lump sum grant of $10,000 each year, but a much larger amount (about $4,000,000) was to be apportioned among the states on the basis of rural population. More significantly, no state could get "its share" of the money so apportioned unless it matched the federal appropriation.   Furthermore, in order to get the money, a state had to secure approval of its plans of expenditure from the federal government.

In 1924 the Weeks Act was superseded by the Clarke-McNary Act, enlarging the scope of forest protection and requiring a state to match the federal allotment, an allotment to be determined by the Secretary of Agriculture on the basis of need.   The act further provided that funds were to be expended under the direction of state officials, but that federal inspectors were to audit accounts and in certain other particulars strive to keep state standards up to a satisfactory minimum.   The Federal Aid Road Act of 1916 authorized annual appropriations up to $25,000,000 for roads over which the mails were transported.   Dollar-for-dollar matching was required, and funds were allocated to each state as follows: one third according to population, one third according to area, and one third according to rural delivery mileage.   In addition, the act made provisions for advance federal approval of highway projects and for continuing federal supervision, and required each state to set up a department of highways.

The preceding paragraphs give examples of the standard type of federal aid.   The federal-grant policy has a certain flexibility, but it will be noticed that each grant mentioned above contained three basic features: apportionment of funds among the states on some reasonable and fair basis (for example, agricultural extension funds on the basis of each state's rural population), state matching of the federal appropriation, and federal approval and inspection of state projects supported by the grant. There are exceptions to these general requirements, particularly to the matching requirement, as instanced by the Bankhead-Jones Act of 1935, which very liberally supplemented the earlier grants for agricultural extension and omitted any state-matching-of-funds requirement.

FEDERAL AID TO STATE AND LOCAL GOVERNMENTS, BUDGET EXPENDITURES IN 1956

In Millions of Dollars

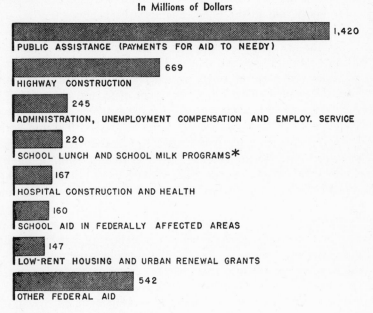

1,420
PUBLIC ASSISTANCE (PAYMENTS FOR AID TO NEEDY)

669
HIGHWAY CONSTRUCTION

245
ADMINISTRATION, UNEMPLOYMENT COMPENSATION AND EMPLOY. SERVICE

220
SCHOOL LUNCH AND SCHOOL MILK PROGRAMS*

167
HOSPITAL CONSTRUCTION AND HEALTH

160
SCHOOL AID IN FEDERALLY AFFECTED AREAS

147
LOW-RENT HOUSING AND URBAN RENEWAL GRANTS

542
OTHER FEDERAL AID

*Expenditures for school lunch include donation of commodities

From *The Federal Budget in Brief, Fiscal Year 1956,* p. 49.

Emergency Grants

During the depression years of the 'thirties the matching requirement was greatly relaxed and in a number of instances abandoned. In 1930 the federal government advanced $80,000,000 to the states to *enable them to match* the federal highway grants; two years later the Reconstruction Finance Corporation was authorized to advance $120,000,000 for similar purposes; and between 1933 and 1936 the National Industrial Recovery Administration and other relief agencies expended one billion dollars for highway purposes without any matching requirement. Between 1933 and 1935 the Federal Emergency Relief Administration distributed some three billion dollars (no matching requirement) among the states for relief. Thus the emergency grants made the regular grants puny by comparison.

Social Security through Federal Aid

Space cannot be provided for a discussion of each of the programs supported in part by federal aid, but the most significant federal-aid development must have attention.   The Social Security Act of 1935 carried provisions that revived grants for venereal disease control and for maternal and child health services and established other and new grant programs in public health.   But these provisions were hardly more than incidental when the main sections of the act are considered.   The act calls for grants for old-age assistance, aid to dependent children, aid to the blind, unemployment compensation, employment offices, child welfare, and crippled children services.   Every program authorized by the act, with the exception of the old-age annuity plan, is carried by the grants-in-aid system, that is, by federal and state appropriations and state administration in accordance with federal standards.

An examination of the trends in the amount of federal aid appropriations reveals that relatively large sums have been made available for highways since 1916, when the highway aid program got under way, and that appropriations for this function far exceeded those made for any other function until 1936, when the national government entered the social security field.   In 1952 federal aid expenditures for highways were slightly in excess of $400,000,000 and its expenditures for public welfare were nearly three times that amount.

Federal Recognition of Cities

Public officials and careful observers of the realities of government had for a long time been aware of city-federal associations in a number of functions, such as police protection, traffic control, and health administration, but it was the large federal loans and *direct* grants to cities during the tragic 'thirties that caused the rank and file of citizens to become thoroughly familiar with the fact that the cities and the federal government were on intimate terms; that the cities had a rich Uncle Sam who would hand money to them, if such direct subsidy seemed to be greatly needed.   Under the National Industrial Recovery Act loans were made available to cities for public works and publicly owned instrumentalities and facilities, and the NIRA came also bearing *gifts* up to 30 per cent of the cost of labor and materials for any such project. The Public Works Administration built city halls, hospitals, and schools, and constructed water and sewage disposal plants.   To be sure, PWA construction was chiefly through private contractors, but the cities profited to the extent that PWA carried a part of the cost of labor and materials.   These and other federal aids to cities no doubt had a permanent effect upon the relationships of the two governments concerned.   Some proof of a closer relationship is adduced by the fact that the Federal Aid Highway Acts of both 1944 and 1948 authorize specific and large sums for highway construction in urban areas, thus establishing a sort of urban federal-aid system.   But the Federal Airport Act of 1946, providing for an annual appropriation not to exceed $100,000,000 for airport construction on a federal-aid basis, went the whole way. This act authorizes the Civil Aeronautics Administration to deal directly with any city, county, village, or magisterial district, and it was the first continuing grant-in-aid act so to provide. The Federal Hospital Survey and Construction Act of 1949 provided $150,000,000 annually until 1955 to help communities build new hospitals. From these and other types of federal aid to cities it is apparent that a significant intergovernmental relationship has been established.

Federal Aid Attains Maturity

In 1953, in response to a recommendation of President Eisenhower, Congress created a Commission on Intergovernmental Relations and directed it to study the activities financed by the federal aid system, "including the ability of the federal government and the states to finance activities of this nature." At the time the Commission was set up it was generally believed that it would make sweeping recommendations for the reduction of federal aid and give great emphasis to the responsibilities of the states and local governments. But its report of June, 1955, although by no means ignoring state and local obligations, contained little that would disturb the proponents of the federal aid system. Rather the report characterized the federal grant as "a fully matured device of cooperative government" (page 120). It becomes rather obvious that federal aid is here to stay, but the permanence of the system does not imply that every program proposed for such "cooperative government" should be adopted, or that old programs should not be subject to periodic review and modification.

Reading List

The Council of State Governments, *The Book of the States, 1954–55,* Sec. I.
————, *Federal Grants-in-Aid* (1949).
R. E. Cushman, *Leading Constitutional Decisions* (1955 ed.), pp. 262–268, and Chs. IX and X.
W. F. Dodd, *Cases and Materials on Constitutional Law* (1954 ed.), 297–417.
F. Frankfurter, "The Compact Clause of the Constitution—A Study in Interstate Adjustments," *Yale Law Review,* XXXIV (1925), 685–758.
R. G. Gettell, *Political Science* (1949 ed.), Ch. 14.
Cullen B. Gosnell and Lynwood Holland, *State and Local Government in the United States* (1954), Chs. 20–24.
W. B. Graves, *Uniform State Action* (1934).
————, *American State Government* (1953 ed.), Chs. 24–25.
The Commission on Intergovernmental Relations, *A Report to the President for Transmittal to the Congress* (1955).
Claudius O. Johnson, *American National Government* (1955 ed.), Chs. 3–6.
V. O. Key, Jr., *The Administration of Federal Grants to the States* (1937).
A. F. Macdonald, *American State Government and Administration* (1955 ed.), Chs. 1–3.
J. M. Mathews, *The American Constitutional System* (1940 ed.), Chs. V–VI, XX.
R. V. Peel, *State Government Today* (1948).

J. A. Scott, *Law of Interstate Rendition* (1917).

State Government, "State Government at Mid-Century" (June, 1950).

C. B. Swisher, *The Growth of Constitutional Power in the United States* (1946), Ch. 2.

C. Warren, *The Supreme Court and Sovereign States* (1924).

W. W. Willoughby, *The Principles of the Constitutional Law of the United States* (1930 ed.), Chs. XI–XVI, XXI–XXVIII.

Questions and Problems *

1. Show that the states, despite "federal encroachment" upon their powers, are now exercising more powers of government than they did a hundred years ago.

2. Evaluate the advantages of constitutional restrictions upon the states in respect to civil liberties.

3. Does the Congress of the United States have the authority to abolish the poll tax as a qualification for voting?

4. Discuss the origin, the use, and abuse of the principle that the states may not tax the United States and that the United States may not tax the states.

5. Did Louisiana have a republican form of government when practically every officer of the state did Huey Long's bidding?

6. How do you square the refusal of a state to recognize certain out-of-state divorces with the "full faith and credit" requirement?

7. Show the extent to which the provision that "the citizens of each state shall be entitled to all privileges and immunities of citizens in the several states" means less than it appears to mean.

8. A fugitive from justice escaped from the penitentiary in state A eight years ago, and he has since resided as a good citizen in state B. His extradition is now sought by the governor of state A. What is the best course for the fugitive to follow?

9. Discuss the developments in federal aid to the states since the Second Morrill Act.

* These questions do not by any means cover the entire subject matter of this text. They are intended to be representative and suggestive, not exhaustive.

CHAPTER | 2

STATE CONSTITUTIONS

Although the Constitution of the United States lays some significant limitations upon the states and provides for some essential phases of interstate relations, it makes no specific requirement concerning the form of state government beyond the rather vague one that it shall be republican in character.[1] It is understood, of course, that a state constitution shall not violate the federal Constitution or the treaties or laws made under the authority of that instrument.[2] As our present-day state governments had their origin deep in English and colonial laws and practices, it is essential to begin the discussion of state constitutions with a brief sketch of colonial developments. Long ago a wise man said, "We cannot escape history." Certainly no student of government should make the attempt.

I. COLONIAL GOVERNMENT [3]

Different Types of Colonies

The thirteen colonies were founded at different times, Virginia being the first, in 1607, and Georgia the last, in 1732. Not only did the regions in which the colonists settled differ in climate, terrain, and in other respects, but the settlers themselves differed in background, purpose, and capacity. Moreover, the rights granted the colonies by the British crown also differed, although there was a strong tendency toward uniformity in the later colonial period. Eight of the colonies ultimately became royal colonies, that is, colonies governed by the "royal will and pleasure." Maryland, Pennsylvania, and Delaware continued under their proprietors and were called proprietary colonies. These proprietors held their grants in a semi-feudal fashion, administering them personally or through agents, but always under the general supervision of the British crown. The corporate colonies, Rhode Island and Connecticut, went their own way for a time under temporary provisions for

[1] On these points see Chapter 1.
[2] Art. VI, sec. II.
[3] M. W. Jernegan, *The American Colonies* (1929); A. H. Kelley and W. A. Harbison, *The American Constitution* (1948), Chs. 1–2; C. E. Merriam, *A History of American Political Theories* (1903), Ch. I; Gerald W. Johnson, *Our English Heritage* (1949).

government that was essentially democratic; the "Fundamental Orders of Connecticut" is one of the great documents of free institutions.   Later, both of these colonies received very liberal charters from the king, charters that gave legal sanction to the forward civil and political views of the founders of those colonies.[4]

Extent of Control by the British Crown

Each of the thirteen colonies was allowed a measure of self-government. The extent to which the colonies regulated their own affairs varied with the terms on which the crown authorized their establishment, with the interest of the British government in asserting its authority, and with the ability of the king's officers in restraining colonial legislatures, which were nearly always active in extending the sphere of their own authority.   In general, the London government retained the right to revoke or alter the charters (constitutions) of the colonies that possessed them; to veto, except for Maryland,[5] Rhode Island, and Connecticut, the laws enacted by their legislative bodies; to appoint or confirm the appointment of their governors, except in Rhode Island and Connecticut; and to hear appeals from the colonial courts.   It is hardly necessary to add that no colony was supposed to pass any act contrary to the laws of Great Britain.

Although there was no question concerning the complete legal authority of the British government over the American colonies, in the course of time these colonies came to regard themselves as practically independent of the mother country in their domestic affairs, and only grudgingly admitted the authority of the British to regulate their external affairs.   Facing this attitude, the officers of the crown frequently found it unwise and sometimes impossible to exercise their authority in the colonies.   It may be said, then, that although Britain had a rather strict control over the colonies on paper, in practice the colonies often had their own way, even to the extent of violating orders of the crown or of forcing governors to break the instructions of the crown.

Authority of the Colonial Governor

The governor was the most important official in the colonies, although his powers were much more limited in some colonies than in others.   He was the agent of the British crown, and as such it was his duty to issue all the orders of the crown and see that they were enforced, to supervise the work of other officers of the crown who were located in the colony, and to make reports and recommendations to the government at London.   His duties to the colony, as distinguished from those he owed the crown, were very similar to those of our present-day governors.   He enforced the laws enacted by the colonial assembly, was empowered to pardon all offenders except murderers and traitors, appointed various officers, was the head of the militia, and acted

---

[4] Jernegan, *op. cit.*, pp. 134 ff., 149–150, 273.

[5] Maryland was supposed to send her laws to England for approval, but this requirement was seldom observed. *Ibid.*, pp. 273–274.

as official spokesman for the colony. His authority in legislative matters was also similar to but greater than that exercised by state governors in our own day. He convoked assemblies, adjourned them, dissolved them, exercised an absolute veto on their bills, and even appointed the "upper house" in a number of the colonies. As a judicial officer he was the head of the colonial court. In Connecticut and Rhode Island, however, the governors were elected by the assembly, were very definitely responsible to that body, and, therefore, exercised no such wide powers as those named above.[6]

The Governor's Council

Councils of about a dozen men advised and in some cases, particularly in Rhode Island and Connecticut, directed the governors. In these two colonies the council was elected by the assembly, in Massachusetts by the assembly and the old council; but in the other colonies, council membership was determined by the crown and the governor or proprietors. In addition to giving the governor advice and direction, the council, or individual members of it, assisted the governor in various phases of his administrative work in some such manner as the secretary of state, the treasurer, the auditor, and other executive officers function in state administration at the present time. The council served with the governor as the highest court in nearly all the colonies; and in all except Pennsylvania, Delaware, and Georgia it sat as the upper house of the legislative body, thus performing the duties now discharged by our state senates. The council, with executive, legislative, and judicial functions to perform, thus defied the "separation of powers" that later came to be one of the principal features of American government.

Establishment of Representative Government

Representative government started early in the colonies. The same year (1619) that twenty slaves were sold by the Dutch to English planters at Jamestown, twenty burgesses met with the governor and his council in the church of that capital city and drew up laws designed to prevent idleness, drunkenness, and gaming; sought to curb the extravagance in dress of those days by taxing wearing apparel; and passed laws for the encouragement of agriculture.[7] In the course of time every colony had an assembly. Only those who possessed considerable property were eligible to the assemblies in the greater number of the colonies, and, in addition, a religious test was usually imposed. The men who voted for assemblymen had to show that they possessed a small amount of real property, and in some colonies they had to demonstrate further that they were correct in religion and morals.

In New England the basis of representation was the town, and in other colonies the county was generally used as the unit. At first each area had representation roughly proportional to its population; but, with the growth of settlements in the interior, the inhabitants of these "back-country" dis-

[6] Jernegan, *op. cit.*, pp. 273–276.
[7] L. G. Tyler, *England in America* (1904), pp. 79–81.

tricts made frequent, and usually unavailing, complaints against the original apportionments, which left them without their fair share of representation. By denying to these districts the number of representatives to which their population entitled them, the more conservative elements on the seaboard kept the liberals in the back country from getting control of the legislative bodies.[8]

THE ASSEMBLIES GAIN POWER.   In spite of the several undemocratic features of the colonial assemblies as judged by present-day standards, these bodies led in the movement for colonial rights—a movement the ultimate result of which was separation from Great Britain.   Through their control of finance, which they early secured, they forced governors, who had the legal authority to nullify their acts, to do their bidding or find no money appropriated to carry on the government.   A governor of New York wrote in 1741: "If a governor will not blindly consent to their bills, however unreasonable or contrary to [the governor's] instructions, they will starve him into compliance."   A member of the New Jersey assembly expressed the view of a number of his fellow legislators in these words: "Let us keep the dogs poore, and we'll make them do what we please." [9]   The assemblies claimed the right to legislate on all the internal affairs of the colonies and regarded themselves as parliaments.   An English officer in Virginia complained in 1703 that "the Assembly conclude themselves entitled to all the rights and privileges of an English Parliament, and begin to search into the records of the honorable house for precedents to govern themselves by." [10]

Significance of the rise of the assembly.   Although there is no doubt that some of the assemblymen were crude, self-seeking demagogues who secured their election by means not dissimilar to those employed by their kind in our own day, such qualities did not detract from the fact that they were paving the way for ultimate independence and to some extent fighting the battle for the people.   When the governor's council of New York, in 1711, sharply reproved the assembly for not allowing it to amend money bills, a power it claimed as a grant from the crown, the assembly made reply in a spirit that breathed of the free air of '76: " 'Tis true, the share the Council have (if any) in Legislation, (comes) only from the meer Pleasure of the Prince . . . On the contrary, the *inherent Right* the Assembly have to dispose of the money of the Freemen of this Colony, does not proceed from any commission, Letters Patent or other Grant from the Crown; but from the free Choice and Election of the People: who ought not to be divested of their Property (nor justly can) without their consent." [11]   When the British Parliament, in 1764 and following years, challenged the rights claimed by the colonial assemblies, asserting that it had the power to make all laws for the colonies if it cared

[8] See Jernegan, *op. cit.*, pp. 288–291, for these inequalities.
[9] Quoted, *ibid.*, p. 285.
[10] Quoted, *ibid.*, p. 287.
[11] Quoted, *ibid.*, pp. 286–287.

to exercise it, the break between the colonies and the mother country was made almost inevitable.

The Colonial Judiciary

Law and justice in the colonies followed the English models very closely. Indeed, the law enforced was for the most part the common law of England. It was supplemented by those statutes of Parliament that were made applicable to the colonies, and by an increasing number of laws enacted by the local assemblies. As in England, the justice of the peace was chosen from capable men of property who had the respect of the community. Sitting alone, one of these justices could hear and determine petty cases; sitting in a body, the justices of a county formed an intermediate or county court and heard the greater number of civil cases and criminal cases not involving loss of life or limb. The sheriff helped them in such matters as summoning juries; and constables made arrests, collected the fines imposed, and administered floggings.

The highest court in a colony was composed of the governor and his council or of a body of judges appointed by the governor. This court was primarily a court of appeals. It was not a court of final appeal, however, for cases might be carried from the supreme court of a colony to the Judicial Committee of the Privy Council in London. Decisions by this body three thousand miles away were frequently not well received in the colonies and in some cases they were successfully evaded.[12]

Local Government in the Colonies

THE COUNTY. As the people in a colony extended their settlements beyond the original location, the establishment of local government became necessary. The Virginia Assembly created counties as early as 1634. The county was the important unit of local government in the Southern Colonies and to a considerable extent in the Middle Colonies. County government in these colonies followed the English system very closely. It is an interesting fact that county government in some of the Southern states today is more like the English practice of the seventeenth century than is the present county system in England. In the counties the justices of the peace were the "statesmen of all work." Their part in the administration of justice has already been mentioned. In addition to their judicial duties, the justices of the peace administered practically all the other affairs of the county. Among their general duties may be mentioned the appointment of a number of officers of the county, the issuing of licenses, the letting of contracts for the construction of roads and bridges, the paying of bounties for the destruction of wild beasts, and the making of the county levies. The counties were divided into parishes governed by a vestry of twelve Anglican gentlemen. The vestry

---

[12] *Ibid.,* 77, 277 ff.; J. M. Mathews, *American State Government* (1934 ed.), pp. 387–388.

performed various local duties, including the supervision of the churches and the administration of poor relief. There was nothing of democracy in this local government. The justices of the peace and the vestrymen were appointed by the governor, and frequently an individual held several offices. This sort of government was, however, suited to the people and the times, and was reasonably good government.[13]

THE TOWN. The town was the basic unit of local government in New England. It was an area of land, usually about forty square miles, granted to a small group of proprietors, who held it in common. The proprietors were entitled to send representatives to the colonial legislative body, and they were allowed very extensive privileges in governing their own town. They levied taxes, elected officers, imposed fines and penalties, made rules for the good order and well-being of the town, and admitted new arrivals to citizenship. The government of these towns in time came to be essentially democratic, in sharp contrast to the system in the Southern counties, where all the important officers were named by the governor.[14] The town meetings, at which practically all matters of political or economic interest were attended to by the citizens in a body, won the praise of the great Virginia democrat, Thomas Jefferson, who saw them as splendid training schools for popular government, as indeed they were.[15]

Democratic Tendencies in the Colonies

The statement that there was little democracy in the colonies has been made frequently, and it is true in the main. Certainly the Cavaliers, who dominated the Southern Colonies and kept the offices and as many other good things as possible for themselves, were not democratic. Governor Spotswood of Virginia, one of the good colonial governors, was no more democratic than the others, and expressed the strongest disapproval of the growing tendency of the people to choose, as their representatives, persons of small means and low intelligence and those who inflamed the people with talk about the ruin of their liberties. Even William Penn recorded his disapprobation of the rank and file of Americans who were trying to obtain political power and who, having secured some recognition, thought nothing taller than themselves but the trees. The Puritans were very little, if any, more democratic than those who controlled the other colonies. They believed in spiritual equality but not in political equality. They were ready to oppose with vigor the attempts of the British crown to impose its authority over them, but they were not much concerned about the liberties of the individuals in their midst.[16]

There were, however, very definite signs of democracy in the colonies. We have just indicated that New England town government contained democratic

---

[13] Jernegan, *op. cit.*, pp. 76–78.
[14] *Ibid.*, pp. 166–168.
[15] Merriam, *op. cit.*, pp. 159, 160.
[16] *Ibid.*, pp. 15–16, 23–26, 32–34.

features. Rhode Island and Connecticut had liberal governments. The complaints of Spotswood and Penn noted above bear witness to the fact that there was a general movement toward a more popular control of government. The frontier has ever been fertile soil for the growth of democratic ideas, and the back country in the colonies proved no exception to that rule. The people who lived beyond the tidewater were to a considerable degree economically and socially equal, and they very naturally wanted to apply the principle of political equality as well.

The Great Awakening, which began in 1734, was essentially religious in character, but it reached into the whole life of the people. Its appeal was primarily to the inarticulate masses, to whom it gave hope, emotional stimulation, and ideas on political subjects as well as on those of religious and moral import. Opposition to this movement by the conservative and privileged classes had the very natural result of making its followers, the Methodists, Baptists, and Presbyterians, hostile to the aristocratic order, thus furthering the cause of democracy. The individualistic spirit of many of the colonists, their self-reliance, their remoteness from England, and the migration to the colonies of Scotch-Irish, Irish, and Germans were other factors that contributed to the growth of the democratic spirit. In the growing spirit of resistance to what they considered arbitrary government, the colonists found very encouraging examples in such English documents as the Petition of Right, the Grand Remonstrance, and the Bill of Rights.[17]

II. THE ORIGINAL STATE CONSTITUTIONS [18]

Although it was not until 1789, eight years after Yorktown, that the American Revolution led to the establishment of our federal system of government, it led almost immediately to the independence of the colonies and, of course, imposed upon the new states the necessity of setting up their own government. The purpose of this section is to note briefly the manner in which the public men set about that undertaking and to examine at a little more length the nature of the government they established.

Drafting and Adoption of the First State Constitutions

When the Revolutionary War began in 1775, the colonial governments crumbled one after the other. At first their places were taken by irregular authorities. Later, acting upon the rather vague advice of the Continental Congress of May 15, 1776, that they "adopt such government as shall in the opinion of the representatives of the people, best conduce to the happiness and safety of their constituents in particular, and America in general," [19] the states began to adopt constitutions. Eleven states had new constitutions

[17] Jernegan, op. cit., pp. 134–135, 271–272, 280–281, 407–412.
[18] Dumas Malone, Jefferson the Virginian (1948), Chs. XVII–XXVI; Merriam, op. cit., pp. 74–95; Allan Nevins, The American States during and after the Revolution (1924), Chs. IV, V, X.
[19] Journals of the Continental Congress, IV, 342.

in operation by 1780.   Rhode Island and Connecticut considered their liberal
colonial charters good enough for use in statehood.

In drafting their constitutions the statesmen of 1776, except in Massachusetts and New Hampshire, did not follow the method of having them
prepared by conventions chosen by the people for that one purpose, as is
the practice today.   Ordinarily, this work was done by the legislatures.   Nor
was the later method of submitting constitutions to the will of the voters
commonly employed.   Only in Massachusetts and New Hampshire was approval by the people regarded as essential, although in four other states the
constitutions were submitted to popular referendum.

Principles Embodied in the Original Constitutions

PROVISIONS FOR AMENDMENT.   What were the characteristics of these,
our first, state constitutions?   Present-day state constitutions contain very
detailed provisions for their amendment, but the framers of the early constitutions did not give this matter a great deal of attention.   Five states made
no provision for amendments, acting presumably on the theory that the legislatures or conventions would take care of amendments when the need for
them arose—in a sense a recognition of the sovereignty of the people.   Other
states provided for amendment by legislatures, by conventions, or by modifications of these methods.

GUARANTY OF CIVIL RIGHTS.   In these early constitutions civil liberties,
such as the right of trial by jury, the prohibition of excessive bail, the guaranty
against irregular search and seizure, the right of assembly and petition, religious toleration, and various guaranties for the protection of private property,
were secured.   As a measure of the importance attached to these guaranties,
they were given first place in the new political systems.

LIMITATION OF POLITICAL PRIVILEGES TO PROPERTY HOLDERS.   Political
privileges, however, were not conferred so freely as civil rights were guar-
anteed.   Although the authors of the constitutions denounced through the
paragraphs of these instruments the hereditary and aristocratic principle in
government, they, nevertheless, kept public affairs in the hands of the upper
classes.   In a number of the states the governor was required to show that
he possessed landed property to the value of $5,000, or $25,000, and in South
Carolina the value was fixed at $50,000.   For the lesser offices a smaller
estate was indicated, and for some offices there was no property qualification.
By constitution or by statute enacted in pursuance to the constitution, the
fathers of our state systems of government limited the right to vote to those
who held property, although the amount fixed as the qualification for voting
was usually not over two or three hundred dollars.   Even such men as Frank-
lin held the idea that a man with no property was a very irresponsible citizen
and should be denied the ballot.[20]

APPLICATION OF RELIGIOUS TESTS.   Although freedom of worship was
recognized by the new states, there was no considerable opposition to the

[20] Merriam, *op. cit.,* pp. 84–86.

governments' imposition of a religious test upon those who held office or upon the voters. Officers were commonly required to be Christians, frequently Protestants. No one could vote in Pennsylvania and South Carolina who did not believe in a future state of rewards and punishments. Only Protestants could vote in North Carolina and Georgia, and Delaware required its voters to believe in the Trinity and in the inspiration of the Scriptures. Rhode Island, Connecticut, New York, and Virginia made the nearest approaches to absolute religious freedom.[21]

Inconsistency of the "Fathers." Although those who established our first governments are supposed to have subscribed to the doctrine that all men were created equal, they obviously felt that certain modifications of the doctrine should be made in practice. The property qualifications and religious tests they imposed so commonly for officeholding and voting would seem to indicate that they believed in the equality of man as an aspiration for the future, not as a reality for immediate application. As for the Negro in bondage, only a few like Jefferson thought of his condition as otherwise than natural; to the great majority he was not in the picture.[22]

Yet we should not say that the "Fathers" were not democratic. The institutions they were establishing were democratic for their day. We have since gone beyond them and abolished the property qualifications and the greater number of the religious tests, but it is worth while for us to note that Pennsylvania and Tennessee still close their public offices to those who do not believe in a future state of rewards and punishments; that in a half-dozen other states officeholders must believe in God. In 1929, a judge in North Carolina, acting under a statute of 1777, stated that a witness's disbelief in a punishing God should lessen the force of her testimony, and added: "If I believed that life ends with death and that there was no *punishment* after death, I would be less apt to tell the truth." [23]

SAFEGUARDS AGAINST STRONG GOVERNMENT. The framers of the first state constitutions regarded government as an unreliable and untrustworthy servant of the people. Government was a necessary evil that must be watched at all times to prevent it from becoming oppressive and destructive of individual liberty. In order to hold government in check it was given minimum powers. Everywhere there was fear of strongly organized central governments.[24] The statesmen of '76 emphasized local government as the unit that would best secure their liberties; they were suspicious of state governments and fearful of a national government.

The new state constitutions further protected the people from arbitrary government by providing for frequent election of officers. John Adams once said that tyranny begins where annual elections end. Nearly all the state constitutions declared that long continuance in office was dangerous to liberty, and

---

[21] *Ibid.*, pp. 86–87.
[22] *Ibid.*, pp. 87–88.
[23] *Time,* Oct. 28, 1929.
[24] Merriam, *op. cit.*, pp. 76–78.

stated the principle of frequent elections and rotation in office as the best means of preventing those in authority from becoming oppressors of the people. In some of the states the annual changes in office were assured by constitutional provisions against officers' succeeding themselves. Despite the likelihood that such provisions will impair the efficiency of the government, a fact of which the patriots were doubtless aware, their first concern was to prevent governments from getting out of bounds.[25]

THE THEORY OF THE SEPARATION OF POWERS. At the time the state constitutions were being drafted there was much discussion of the separation of executive, legislative, and judicial powers as a means of guarding against arbitrary or tyrannical government, and this principle was stated in some of the constitutions. For example, the Massachusetts Constitution of 1780 carried the provision that no one of the three departments should exercise any of the functions of either of the other two, to the end that the government be one of laws and not of men.

The practice of legislative supremacy. In the actual construction of the framework of government, however, the powers were not effectively distributed among the three branches except in New York, Massachusetts, and New Hampshire.[26] In colonial times the governor was the officer against whom complaints of arbitrary conduct were frequently made, while the popular assemblies usually resisted the governor and the English crown and won the distinction of being the champions of liberty. It was but natural, then, that the legislatures of the new states should have the confidence of the people and that the governors should inherit, in the form of grave suspicion, the enmity formerly shown toward the chief executives in the colonies. As we have seen, the legislatures usually made the state constitutions, and they were thus able to take full advantage of the good esteem in which the people held them. They placed practically no limits upon their own power. Where the limitations embodied in the bills of rights were not so vague and general as to be inapplicable to any arm of the government, they applied primarily to the courts and executive officers, seldom to the legislatures.

Severe limitations of the governor's powers. The governor was limited to a very short term of office—only one year in seven states. In all states except Massachusetts and New York, where he was elected by the people, the governor was chosen by the legislature. Only in Massachusetts was the governor given the qualified veto power, but in New York he could exercise that power acting with his council. He had very little of the influence in connection with legislation that he enjoys today. His appointing power was severely limited, as were any other powers granted him.

Few changes in the judiciary. Few changes were made in the judiciary as the colonies passed into statehood. The law to be applied was still the common law and equity, and the statutes as enacted by the legislative bodies. The only changes necessary were those that had to do with the selection and

25 Merriam, *op. cit.*, pp. 82–83.
26 A. N. Holcombe, *State Government in the United States* (1931 ed.), pp. 54 ff.

tenure of judges. Judges had been appointed by the crown. The states provided for their appointment by the chief executives acting alone or with their councils, or for their selection by legislative bodies. Georgia alone adopted the method of popular election that has since come to be one of the generally approved methods of choosing state judges. Appointment was commonly for short terms, and judges were usually subject to removal by the legislatures— another manifestation of legislative supremacy.

Observations on the First State Governments

As a conclusion to this discussion of our early state constitutions, a few observations on the type of governments established should be made. (1) The elective officers were not numerous. Legislators were, of course, elected in all states, and in a few states important executive officers were elected; but other officers were chosen by the legislatures or appointed by executive authorities. The idea that practically all officers should be chosen by the people is a later democratic development. (2) The governments established were representative in character. Direct government through the use of such instruments of democracy as the referendum and the initiative was not seriously considered. (3) The constitutions were very short, probably averaging less than ten pages, and dealt, for the most part, with fundamentals State constitutions of our own day, with their many detailed provisions and regulations, frequently cover as many as fifty pages. (4) After making due allowance for English examples and colonial experience, we should still give our early statesmen credit for originality and good common sense for drafting in wartime practical schemes of government that served most of the states adequately until the next century was well advanced.

III. MODERN CONSTITUTION-MAKING [27]

The discussion in the preceding section makes clear that our first state constitutions were commonly made by legislative assemblies, or by conventions of more or less irregular character. In some states, constitutions may still be completely revised by the legislatures, subject of course, to popular approval; but the common practice is to assign this task to conventions chosen by the people for the sole and express purpose of drafting a constitution. The constitutions of about a fourth of the states do not provide for the calling of constitutional conventions; but it is held that, even where the provision is not made, the legislature may take the necessary steps for calling the convention. Since the states, unlike the nation, have not been slow to revise

[27] R. N. Baisden, *Charter for New Jersey: The New Jersey Constitutional Convention of 1947* (1952); W. B. Graves, *American State Government* (1953 ed.), Chs. 2 and 3, and "Constitutions" in *The Book of the States, 1954–55*, pp. 65–74; J. P. Keith, *Methods of Constitutional Revision* (1949); A. F. Macdonald, *American State Government and Administration* (1955 ed.), Ch. 4; V. A. O'Rourke and D. W. Campbell, *Constitution-Making in a Democracy* (1943); A. L. Sturm, *Methods of State Constitutional Reform* (Michigan Governmental Studies No 28, 1954); R. Uhl and Others, *Constitutional Conventions* (1951).

completely their fundamental laws, the number of such conventions has passed beyond the two hundred mark.   Among recent constitutional conventions, we may mention those in New York (1938), Missouri (1943), Rhode Island (1944), New Jersey (1947), New Hampshire (1948), and Tennessee (1953).

Calling the Convention

In most states the constitution provides that a convention may be called by the legislature, subject to majority approval in a popular referendum.   The same procedure is followed in those states whose constitutions make no provision for conventions.   The constitutions of New York, Ohio, and six other states require that the question of calling a constitutional convention be submitted to the people at regular intervals, a twenty-year interval being the most popular.   Under this plan the people of New York in 1936 voted for a convention, and the voters of Ohio in 1912, 1932, and 1952 decided against calling one.

Selection of Delegates

Usually, delegates are chosen from state legislative or senatorial districts. Sometimes a few delegates are chosen at large, that is, by the voters of the entire state.   By the latter method it is possible to secure the talent of several outstanding individuals who might live in the same district.   In any case, the personnel of a convention is usually somewhat higher than that of the ordinary legislature, for the reason that men who can ill afford to sit regularly in legislative bodies are willing to serve in this important capacity.

Organization and Procedure of Conventions

A convention's organization is not unlike that of the typical lower house of a state legislature.   The delegates elect a presiding officer and arrange for the various clerks and assistants needed by such bodies.   Rules of procedure are adopted, and a number of committees are appointed.   Each committee is made responsible for certain parts of the constitution.[28]   Committees receive proposals from members of the convention or from individuals outside the convention.   They listen to the exhortations and warnings of interested citizens whom they allow to appear before them.   From the mass of proposals and suggestions made and from the ideas of its own members, a committee prepares an article or sections of an article, which it presents to the whole body of delegates.   Here the proposal is discussed and possibly accepted.   It is more likely, however, to be adopted with amendments or re-

---

[28] Problems before the delegates are now so intricate and complicated that it is common practice for the states to designate special committees or commissions to prepare bulletins on the leading questions for the use of the delegates.   The legislative reference bureaus may also perform this service.   See Graves, *American State Government,* pp. 73–76; William Miller, "The Report of New Jersey's Constitutional Commission," *Am. Pol. Sci. Rev.,* XXXVI (1942), 900; Bill Logan, "Constitutional Revision for Oklahoma," *State Government,* June, 1949, p. 155; Kimbrough Owen, "Blazing the Constitutional Trail," *Nat. Mun. Rev.,* Mar., 1948, p. 140; Sturm, *op. cit.*

turned to the committee for further consideration. This process goes on until at length a constitution is drafted.

Popular Ratification of Constitutions

Although there are exceptions to the rule, the common practice is to refer the work of a convention to the people for their approval. The simplest method of doing this is to submit the whole constitution as a unit and let the voters accept or reject it as such. This method of submission is not altogether satisfactory, for the reason that an instrument containing a few features that do not commend themselves to the voters may result in the defeat of a constitution they would otherwise be pleased to accept. This method proved disastrous to the constitutions submitted by the New York Convention of 1915 and by the Illinois Convention of 1919, and it has not been commonly followed since the 1920's. It should be noted, however, that constitutions submitted as single units were approved by the voters of Missouri in 1944 and of New Jersey in 1947. A plan highly favored by a number of authorities and now in rather general use is that of submitting to the voters the proposed constitutions in a number of parts. Thus, in 1938, New York submitted the work of its constitutional convention to the people in nine proposals. One was an omnibus proposal including forty-nine miscellaneous and relatively noncontroversial provisions. The eight other proposals were specific and highly controversial. The omnibus proposal and five of the specific proposals were approved by the voters. Three of the specific proposals were rejected.

IV. AMENDING STATE CONSTITUTIONS [29]

Legislative Proposals

Amendments may be proposed by constitutional conventions, as in Tennessee in 1953, but simpler processes are commonly employed—proposals by the legislatures or by the voters. The method of amendment by legislative proposal dates from the time of the adoption of the first state constitutions. At the present time its use is authorized in all states except New Hampshire, in which state amendments may be originated only by a constitutional convention. The New Hampshire restriction does not, however, unduly impede the amending process, for the question of calling a constitutional convention must be submitted to the voters every seven years, and the old (1784) constitution has been amended more than a hundred times.

The process of legislative proposal varies somewhat, some constitutions requiring that proposals shall receive majority votes in the legislature, others three fifths of the votes, and still others two thirds. But whatever may be the legislative vote required, nearly all the constitutions stipulate that the vote shall be based on the number of members *elected to* the legislature, not simply on the number which happens to be present when the vote is taken. Further-

[29] See references in note 27.

GENERAL DATA ON STATE CONSTITUTIONS *
(as of January 1, 1953)

State or Territory	Total Constitutions	Dates of Adoption	Effective Date of Present Constitution	Age of Present Constitution(a)	Estimated Length of Present Constitution (words)	Total Amendments(b)	Constitutions Effective without Submission to Voters
Alabama	6	1819, 1861, 1865, 1868, 1875, 1901	1901	52	57,000	95	1819, 1861, 1865
Arizona	1	1911	1912	41	20,490	35	None
Arkansas	5	1836, 1861, 1864, 1868, 1874	1874	79	38,000	42	1836, 1861
California	2	1849, 1879	1879	74	85,000	272	None
Colorado	1	1876	1876	77	29,000	56	None
Connecticut	3(c)	1638–39, 1662, 1818	1818	135	9,100	47	1662
Delaware	4	1776, 1792, 1831, 1897	1897	56	20,000	21	1776, 1792, 1831, 1897
Florida	5	1838, 1861, 1865, 1868, 1886	1887	66	28,500	89	1861, 1865
Georgia	8	1777, 1789, 1798, 1861, 1865, 1868, 1877, 1945	1945	8	30,000	83	1777, 1789, 1798
Idaho	1	1889	1890	63	20,000	58	None
Illinois	3	1818, 1848, 1870	1870	83	18,754	10	1818
Indiana	2	1816, 1851	1851	102	9,064	18	1816
Iowa	2	1846, 1857	1857	96	9,990	20	None
Kansas	1	1859	1861	92	11,593	40	None
Kentucky	4	1792, 1799, 1850, 1891	1891	62	21,500	15	1792, 1799
Louisiana	10	1812, 1845, 1852, 1861, 1864, 1868, 1879, 1898, 1913, 1921	1921	32	184,053	302	1861, 1898, 1913, 1921
Maine	1	1819	1820	133	12,708	75	None
Maryland	4	1776, 1850–51, 1864, 1867	1867	86	40,000	69(d)	1776
Massachusetts	1	1780	1780	173	28,760	81	None
Michigan	4	1835, 1850, 1867, 1908	1909	44	21,000	55	None
Minnesota	1	1857	1858	95	25,800	76	None
Mississippi	4	1817, 1832, 1869, 1890	1890	63	18,800	35	1817, 1832, 1890
Missouri	4	1820, 1865, 1875, 1945	1945	8	31,000	4	1820
Montana	1	1889	1889	64	22,668	26	None
Nebraska	2	1866, 1875	1875	78	17,160	65	None

State							
Nevada	1	1864	1864	89	16,657	56	None
New Hampshire	2	1776, 1783	1784	169	10,562	105	1776
New Jersey	3	1776, 1844, 1947	1948	5	12,500	None	1776
New Mexico	1	1912	1912	41	22,400	27	None
New York	4	1777, 1821, 1846, 1894	1894	59	25,000	110	1777
North Carolina	2	1776, 1868(e)	1868	85	12,350	80	1776
North Dakota	1	1889	1889	64	31,500	63	None
Ohio	2	1802, 1851	1851	102	23,512	66	1802
Oklahoma	1	1907	1907	46	38,000	36	None
Oregon	1	1857	1859	94	26,000	92	None
Pennsylvania	4	1776, 1790, 1838, 1873	1874	79	19,800	53	1776, 1790
Rhode Island	2	1663, 1842	1843	110	17,000	32	None
South Carolina	7	1776, 1778, 1790, 1861, 1865, 1868, 1895	1895	58	35,000	215	1776, 1778, 1790, 1861, 1865, 1895
South Dakota	1	1889	1889	64	24,500	57	None
Tennessee	3	1796, 1834, 1870	1870	83	10,905	None	1796
Texas	5	1845, 1861, 1866, 1869, 1876	1876	77	39,000	110	None
Utah	1	1895	1896	57	18,000	52	None
Vermont	3	1777, 1786, 1793	1793	160	8,419	40	1777, 1786, 1793
Virginia	5	1776, 1830, 1851, 1867, 1902	1902	51	30,570	23	1776, 1902
Washington	1	1889	1889	64	19,360	28	None
West Virginia	2	1863, 1872	1872	81	17,500	27	None
Wisconsin	1	1848	1848	105	12,544	56(f)	None
Wyoming	1	1890	1890	63	17,260	18	None
Hawaii	1(g)	1950(h)	—	—	11,142	None	None
Puerto Rico	1	1952	1952	1	8,560	None	None

* From Albert L. Sturm, *Methods of State Constitutional Reform*, pp. 10–11, Michigan Governmental Studies No. 28, University of Michigan Press, 1954. By courtesy of the author and publishers.

(a) Computed from the effective date.

(b) Figures on amendments in the various states do not have the same basis. In some states, single amendments amend more than one section of the constitution; in others, changes in each section are counted as separate amendments.

(c) Including "The Fundamental Orders" of 1639 and the Royal Charter of 1662.

(d) An inaccurate figure since the charter of Baltimore is part of the constitution and there is no accurate accounting of charter amendments.

(e) The constitution of 1776 was revised in 1835, and the constitution of 1868 was extensively revised in 1876, leading some to claim 4 constitutions for North Carolina.

(f) Including 2 declared invalid by the Wisconsin Supreme Court.

(g) As a kingdom and a republic, Hawaii had 5 constitutions.

(h) Not yet accepted by Congress.

more, a few states require the affirmative action of two successive legislatures. In some states there are even more severe restrictions as to the manner of making proposals. For example, until 1953, the Tennessee constitution of 1870 prohibited the submission of amendments by the legislature more frequently than once in six years and it still provides that no amendment shall be submitted by the legislature to the people except by the affirmative action of a majority of the members of each house in one session and a two-thirds majority of such membership in the next succeeding session. Doubtless these restrictions largely explain why only about a dozen proposals for amendment were made over a period of more than eighty years.

Popular Approval of Legislative Proposals

When a constitutional amendment has been proposed by the legislature, it is then necessary, except in Delaware, to submit it to the people for their approval or rejection. The prevailing requirement is that approval by a majority of those voting on the amendment secures its adoption. But several states require for adoption of an amendment the approval of a majority of all those voting in a general election. The latter type of majority is much more difficult to win than a majority on the amendment, for many people who mark their ballot for candidates for various offices will, through failure to understand the proposed amendment or disinterest, neglect to vote on it. Formerly, in Illinois, amendments were often defeated although they were supported by substantial majorities voting on them. This could happen whenever the majority approving the amendment was less than a majority of all voters participating in the general election. The Illinois constitution stood unamended from 1908 to 1950, when the Gateway Amendment was approved. Under its provisions constitutional amendments may now be adopted with the approval of two thirds of those voting on the amendment. Until 1953 the Tennessee constitution required for ratification of an amendment the approval of a majority of those voting for candidates for the legislature, a majority never obtained. For eighty-three years the constitution stood without amendment; but in 1953 amendments proposed by a convention were adopted, and one of them changes the vote required for approval of an amendment from a majority of the votes cast for candidates for the legislature to a majority of the votes cast for candidates for governor. Such a majority may well be as difficult to obtain as the one formerly required. Special elections in which constitutional amendments alone are submitted would, of course, secure the ratification of amendments, if a majority of those voting approved them. A less expensive solution of the problem would be for the states that require a majority of those voting in the *election* to join the ranks of the greater number of the states that require only a majority of those voting on the *amendment*. Although the will of a majority of those interested enough to vote on the question may represent a minority of those voting in a general election, it is not likely to be unintelligent or capricious.

Amendment by Popular Initiative

Oregon having blazed the trail in 1902, thirteen states [30] now have constitutional provisions that authorize the amendment of their fundamental laws by popular initiative. An individual or a group may draft a proposal. The next step is to have the proposed amendment endorsed by the requisite number of petitioners. In Massachusetts and North Dakota the number required to make the petition effective is definitely fixed. Other states require a number of petitioners equal to a certain percentage of the vote cast in the last state election. This percentage is eight in California and Oregon, but the average requirement is about ten per cent. In order to insure against proposals having a purely local basis, several states require that signatures shall be secured in a number of counties or districts. For example, Nebraska requires ten per cent of the voters of the state and five per cent in each of two fifths of the counties for an effective petition. [31]

When a proposal has received the required number of signatures, it is then submitted to the voters of the state for their approval or rejection, [32] usually on a regular election date. In ten states, a proposed amendment is adopted if it is approved by a majority of those voting on it. But in Oklahoma and Nevada a majority of all those voting in the election is required, and the constitution of Massachusetts provides that the majority voting affirmatively on an amendment shall secure its adoption only when such majority is at least thirty per cent of the total votes cast in an election. [33]

Number and Character of Amendments

Most of the states use the amending process frequently. This practice prevails largely because state constitutions, particularly the newer ones, contain so many specific provisions that amendments are necessary to accomplish even the simplest changes in governmental organization or policy. It is a "poor" election year (the even year) if less than a hundred amendments are proposed to the people of the several states. If less than half that number is adopted, amending state constitutions still remains an active political industry; a state that has not during the last forty years amended its constitution twenty times is lagging behind the procession. Some amendments deal with affairs of significance, but the greater number relate to trivial matters or to minor phases of important matters. Amendments of consequence are those that relate to basic questions of state and local finance, the popular control of government, corporations, labor, education, industrial undertakings of the state, social security, and similar matters. Trivial amendments deal

---

[30] They are: Arizona, Arkansas, California, Colorado, Massachusetts, Michigan, Missouri, Nebraska, Nevada, North Dakota, Ohio, Oklahoma, and Oregon.

[31] *Book of the States,* pp. 68–73.

[32] In Massachusetts the petition must first be referred to the legislature, and it must be approved by one fourth of the members in two successive sessions before it may be referred to the people.

[33] *Book of the States,* pp. 68–73.

AMENDMENTS TO STATE CONSTITUTIONS *
(as of January 1, 1953)

State or Territory	Total Amendments		Legislative Proposals						Constitutional Initiative					
	Proposed	Adopted	Total Proposed	Total Adopted	Proposed 1938–52	Adopted 1938–52	Proposed 1952	Adopted 1952	Total Proposed	Total Adopted	Proposed 1938–52	Adopted 1938–52	Proposed 1952	Adopted 1952
Alabama	181	95	181	95	86	61	5	4	—	—	—	—	—	—
Arizona	87	35	49	23	19	11	1	1	38	12	10	3	0	0
Arkansas	(a)	42	(a)	26	15	8	3	2	(a)	16	21	11	0	0
California	482	272	408	251	90	59	17	14	74	21	19	5	2	1
Colorado	140	56	88	44	10	6	3	1	52	12	13	1	2	0
Connecticut	63	47	63	47	7	6	0	0	—	—	—	—	—	—
Delaware	41	21	41	21	16	9	1	0	—	—	—	—	—	—
Florida	140	89	140	89	61	37	11	1	—	—	—	—	—	—
Georgia	101	83	101	83	101	83	46	40	—	—	—	—	—	—
Idaho	96	58	96	58	21	17	1	1	—	—	—	—	—	—
Illinois	24	10	24	10	9	3	4	2	—	—	—	—	—	—
Indiana	37	18	37	18	6	6	2	2	—	—	—	—	—	—
Iowa	23	20	23	20	3	3	2	2	—	—	—	—	—	—
Kansas	66	40	66	40	7	7	1	1	—	—	—	—	—	—
Kentucky	37	15	37	15	11	6	0	0	—	—	—	—	—	—
Louisiana	347	302	347	302	222	184	34	34	—	—	—	—	—	—
Maine	93	75	93	75	19	15	0	0	—	—	—	—	—	—
Maryland	87	69	87	69	41	32	2	2	—	—	—	—	—	—
Massachusetts	98	81	54	49	9	9	0	0	1	1	1	1	0	0
Michigan	110	55	77	42	26	17	1	1	33	9	11	6	2	1
Minnesota	158	76	158	76	18	6	5	0	—	—	—	—	—	—
Mississippi	(a)	35	(a)	35	12	8	1	0	—	—	—	—	—	—
Missouri	7	4	7	4	7	4	2	2	46	10	11	1	0	0
Montana	41	26	41	26	11	5	1	0	—	—	—	—	—	—

State														
Nebraska	110	65	59	20	16	7	6	5	10	4	4	1	0	0
Nevada	92	56	92	56	9	9	0	0	0	0	0	0	0	0
New Hampshire	194(b)	105	—	—	—	—	—	—	—	—	—	—	—	—
New Jersey	0	0	0	0	0	0	0	0	—	—	—	—	—	—
New Mexico	76	27	76	27	36	13	0	0	—	—	—	—	—	—
New York	144	110	144	110	48	42	0	0	—	—	—	—	—	—
North Carolina	104	80	104	80	24	20	3	3	—	—	—	—	—	—
North Dakota	109	63	87	49	30	8	4	3	22	14	6	6	0	0
Ohio	132	66	52	24	9	7	0	0	32	9	5	3	0	0
Oklahoma	110	36	68	25	24	15	4	2	42	11	12	5	1	0
Oregon	206	92	128	65	31	21	7	6	78	27	12	4	4	2
Pennsylvania	77	53	77	53	12	9	1	0	—	—	—	—	—	—
Rhode Island	56	32	47	25	6	4	0	0	—	—	—	—	—	—
South Carolina	342	215	342	215	108	77	14	6	—	—	—	—	—	—
South Dakota	119	57	119	57	23	10	3	1	—	—	—	—	—	—
Tennessee	24	0	2	0	2	0	0	0	—	—	—	—	—	—
Texas	197	110	197	110	47	29	2	2	—	—	—	—	—	—
Utah	81	52	81	52	26	25	0	0	—	—	—	—	—	—
Vermont	120	40	14	14	0	0	0	0	—	—	—	—	—	—
Virginia	30	23	30	23	8	7	1	1	—	—	—	—	—	—
Washington	56	28	56	28	18	13	4	4	—	—	—	—	—	—
West Virginia	47	27	47	27	11	6	0	0	—	—	—	—	—	—
Wisconsin	87	56	87	56	11	7	0	0	—	—	—	—	—	—
Wyoming	36	18	36	18	10	7	0	0	—	—	—	—	—	—
Hawaii	—	—	—	—	—	—	—	—	—	—	—	—	—	—
Puerto Rico	—	—	—	—	—	—	—	—	—	—	—	—	—	—

43

* From Albert L. Sturm, *Methods of State Constitutional Reform*, pp. 54–55, Michigan Governmental Studies No. 28, University of Michigan Press, 1954. By courtesy of the author and publishers.

(a) Data not available.

(b) All proposed by conventions in New Hampshire.

with such propositions as increasing the salaries of state officials, authorizing counties to combine functions of certain offices, and changing the debt limit of some municipality, questions, that along with many others, the constitution should have left to the discretion of the legislature.

V. CONTENT OF STATE CONSTITUTIONS [34]

Having learned how state constitutions are made and amended, we are ready to examine their content.   In making this analysis, we shall at the same time note certain important changes that have taken place in the structure and character of state governments during the hundred and fifty years of their existence.   These changes, in the main, indicate the progress of democracy.   They show also that fewer important differences exist between the governments of the states at present than existed at the time they won their independence.   The primary cause for this growth in similarity is that the newer states, in framing their constitutions, consciously, sometimes almost slavishly imitated the older states, and that all the states, in revising or amending their fundamental laws, naturally adopted principles that were deemed to have worked well in other states.

1. The Bill of Rights

Every state constitution contains a bill of rights.   These rights include such cherished guaranties as indictment by grand jury, trial by a jury of twelve individuals, freedom of speech and of the press, and the right of petition. Several of these rights have been modified in a number of the states, especially in the newer states.   A few examples of these changes are submitted. As long ago as 1879, the California constitution provided that an accused might be held for trial upon information furnished by a magistrate, as well as by the time-honored method of indictment by a grand jury.   Other states have adopted this simplified process.   The jury trial itself has been modified. Utah authorizes the trial of cases by a jury of eight persons, whereas the old common law requires twelve.   Oklahoma authorizes a verdict in some cases by three fourths of the jurors, in place of the unanimous verdict required by the common law.   The old constitutions commonly provided that the privilege of the writ of *habeas corpus* should not be suspended except in case of rebellion or invasion, whereas some of the newer constitutions stipulate that it shall never be suspended by the state authorities.   Several recent constitutions, including those of New Jersey and New York, contain specific provisions designed to prevent various types of racial and religious discrimination.   If civil rights are to be kept up to date, there may be reason to revise them occasionally, discarding the outworn and adding those made necessary or desirable by modern developments.

[34] C. A. Beard, *American Government and Politics* (1949 ed.), pp. 539–545; Graves, *American State Government*, pp. 49–54; A. N. Holcombe, *State Government in the United States* (1931 ed.), Chs. IV–V.   All state constitutions may be found in Vol. III, New York State Constitutional Convention Committee, *Reports* (1938).

2. The Three Branches of Government

The second general division of a state constitution deals with the legislative, executive, and judicial departments.   The state legislature is the lawmaking body for a state as Congress is the lawmaking body for the nation.   Three states [35] started their careers with legislatures composed of a single chamber, but they later joined the ranks of their sister states who employed two legislative chambers from the beginning.   The fact that Congress was organized on the bicameral plan had a great deal of influence in bringing all the states to accept this system of representation.   The original idea was that property should have representation in the "upper chambers" of the state legislatures; but, one after another, the states adopted manhood suffrage for choosing the members of both branches of the legislature, so that property was no longer represented in one body more than in the other.   Yet the dogma that one house should and would check any hasty action of the other was generally accepted.   Furthermore, there was some reason for retaining the upper house because it had not only legislative powers but also certain executive and judicial powers.

THE LEGISLATURE.   The constitutions drafted during the Revolutionary period were most generous in granting power to state legislatures.   But it was not many years until the fear arose that the legislatures had too much power, and this fear was quickened by their unwise use of power.   Even before our federal Constitution was adopted, some of the states were beginning to withdraw powers from the legislatures.   Governors very early came to be elected by popular vote in nearly all the states.   Before 1850 the privilege of choosing judges and a number of other officers was very generally extended to the people.   Following the panic of 1837 it was found highly desirable to place a constitutional limit upon the amount of money a legislature might borrow on the credit of the state.   In like manner, legislative errors in bank regulation led to limitations upon their authority in this field.   When legislatures showed a tendency to abuse their powers to issue charters to cities and private corporations, the abuse was met by another constitutional limitation.   Indeed, a great deal of state constitutional history has to do with the curtailment of legislative powers.   Practically every state now has a long list of prohibitions addressed especially to the legislature.   Although the legislature still has substantial lawmaking power, it falls far short of the power with which the Fathers originally endowed it.

THE GOVERNOR.   The position of governor has steadily risen in the states. An officer very much dependent upon the legislature in the typical state a century and a half ago, he is now a chief executive of importance and he is expected to be a leader in the affairs of the state.   His emancipation began when the legislature lost the privilege of electing him.   From time to time, constitutions have added to the importance of his office by increasing his

[35] Pennsylvania (1776–1790), Georgia (1777–1789), and Vermont (1777–1836).   Nebraska's present-day experiment with the one-house legislature is discussed in Chapter 5.

appointing power; and the legislatures have frequently named the governor as the logical appointing officer, even where they might constitutionally vest that authority elsewhere. It must be said, however, that in the majority of the states the senate still has the authority to accept or reject the persons he names for office. Another significant power that two or three states gave their governors about 1780, and that is now withheld only in North Carolina, is the veto. In respect to an ordinary bill the governor must veto the whole of it or accept it (except in Washington); but more than two thirds of the states now authorize him to veto separate items of an appropriation bill. Washington even goes to the extent of authorizing the veto of a part of any bill. The general powers of the governor have been further augmented in those states that have reorganized their administrative system on the principle of concentration of authority in the hands of the chief executive.[36]

THE COURTS. The judiciary did not occupy the important place in our early state governments that it occupies today. Its authority and independence increased as state after state, during the first half of the nineteenth century, substituted popular election of judges for the earlier method of choice by legislatures. Furthermore, the states have come more and more to the practice of providing in their constitutions for the organization of the courts, thus increasing their independence of the legislatures in this respect, although the representatives still have considerable authority in relation to the details of judicial organization and procedure. Perhaps the most important aspect of the present independence of the judiciary is seen in its power to review acts of the legislative bodies. This authority to pass upon the constitutionality of statutes was exercised somewhat hesitantly at first; but its use by the Supreme Court of the United States, together with the general strengthening of the state judiciary during the fifty years following the establishment of our first state governments, definitely fixed the practice in the state governmental systems.[37]

From this brief survey of the three main divisions of power in the states, the conclusion is obvious that the executive and the judiciary have steadily grown in importance and that this growth has usually been accompanied by a diminution of legislative authority. In other words, a redistribution of functions has taken place that brings our state political systems much closer to the principle of the separation of powers than were the original systems, whose designers professed so much admiration for the principle.

3. Taxation and Public Debts

In addition to the bill of rights and the articles dealing with the three historic departments, present-day state constitutions usually contain other important articles dealing with finance, public and private corporations, education, the suffrage, and so on. Typical restrictions concerning taxation and state

[36] Examples: Illinois, New York, Washington.
[37] Holcombe, *op. cit.*, pp. 119 ff.

debts run as follows: Revenue shall not "exceed in any one year four mills on the dollar of the assessed valuation of all taxable property in the state. . . . Taxes shall be uniform upon the same class of property."   State "debts shall never in the aggregate exceed the sum of $200,000 exclusive of what may be the debt at the time of the adoption of this constitution. . . . The debt of any county, township, city . . . or any other political subdivision, shall never exceed five per centum upon the assessed value of the taxable property therein; provided, that any incorporated city may by a two-thirds vote, increase such indebtedness three per centum." [38]

4. Corporations

A number of states expressly restrict the method of chartering corporations and subject them to various conditions not required of individuals.   Thus the constitution of Ohio stipulates that corporations shall not be formed except by general laws, and that all such laws may from time to time be altered or repealed; that corporations may be classified and be made subject to supervision and regulation by officers of the state; that no right of way shall be appropriated to the use of any corporation unless full compensation be paid. Other restrictions of a similar nature are imposed, covering about a page in the constitution.   Some of the newer constitutions, especially those of the Southern and Western states, regulate corporations in much more detail. They impose restrictions with regard to rates and charges for service, make specifications concerning the quality of the service to be performed, forbid the granting of passes to public officers, prohibit monopolies, attempt to prohibit "stock watering," and establish corporation commissions to administer these and many other provisions which relate to incorporated enterprises.   In addition to these regulations vitally concerning corporate business, state constitutions commonly contain restrictions with regard to municipal corporations.   These have to do with the manner in which city charters may be issued, and with such matters as the limits on the power of the city authorities to tax, borrow money, and engage in business usually reserved for private individuals or corporations.

5. Education

State constitutions almost invariably contain sections with reference to education.   Such sections are found even in some of the older constitutions. For instance, Vermont's fundamental law, proclaimed in 1793, declared that "laws for the encouragement of virtue and prevention of vice and immorality, ought to be constantly kept in force, and duly executed; and a competent number of schools ought to be maintained in each town."   The newer constitutions almost invariably provide in some detail for public education.   Thus the constitution of North Dakota requires the legislature to establish and maintain "a uniform system for free public schools throughout the state, be-

[38] Constitution of North Dakota, Articles XI and XII.

ginning with the primary and extending through all grades up to and including the normal and collegiate course." Other provisions concerning the administration of schools and school lands cover four or five pages.

6. Labor

The states in our day not infrequently give labor some special consideration in their constitutions. For instance, in Oklahoma child labor is prohibited in hazardous employment; the eight-hour day is established for work underground; the right to contract for convict labor is denied; and other protection is extended to laborers.

Various other matters are touched upon in the typical state constitution. These include banking and insurance, charities and corrections, agriculture, public highways, county and township government, suffrage and elections, and provisions for amendment.

Length of State Constitutions

The older constitutions are relatively brief, as instanced by the fundamental law of Vermont, which occupies fourteen pages in Kettleborough's collection of state constitutions. The newer instruments of government are ordinarily much longer, those of California and Louisiana, the longest, covering about 150 and 300 pages, respectively. The difference in the length of constitutions does not necessarily indicate any great difference in the structure of state governments, for states with short constitutions frequently deal by statute with matters that are cared for in other states by constitutional provisions. If, for instance, the state's fundamental law does not contain elaborate provisions concerning the regulation of corporations, it does not follow that the state allows such organizations to follow their own sweet will in all things. It may quite adequately regulate corporations by statutes alone.

Constitutions and Statutes

This brings us to a brief consideration of the wisdom of detailed provisions in constitutions. Originally, constitutions laid down the fundamental principles of government and left to the state legislatures the authority to fill in the detail by the enactment of statutes. For a number of years, the tendency has been more and more to place this detail in the constitutions. Back in 1907, when Oklahoma presented the constitution with which she hoped to be admitted to the Union, President Roosevelt is reported to have remarked to a senator-elect from the territory, "I have only one criticism to make of the new constitution you have adopted. It fails to prescribe the kind of tooth powder a true Oklahomian must use. Why this omission when it regulated everything under the sun?" "It was an oversight, Mr. President," replied the senator-elect, "but we reckon on fixing that by statute." [39]

State constitution-makers might improve their product by more "oversights." Detailed provisions respecting the duties of officers, their salaries,

[39] E. E. Morison (ed.), *The Letters of Theodore Roosevelt* (1952), V, 809 n.

the organization of local government, taxation, and a number of other matters had much better be left for statutory elaboration. A constitution should not be a code of law but rather a framework upon which and about which a code can be fashioned.

Reading List

R. N. Baisden, *Charter for New Jersey: The New Jersey Constitutional Convention of 1947* (State Department of Education, Trenton, 1952).

J. E. Bebout, *The Making of the New Jersey Constitution* (1945).

Book of the States, 1954–55, pp. 65–74.

J. Bryce, *American Commonwealth* (1913 ed.), I, Chs. XXXVII–XXXVIII.

Commonwealth of Massachusetts, *Bulletins for the Constitutional Convention* (1918).

J. Q. Dealey, *Growth of American State Constitutions* (1915).

W. F. Dodd, *The Revision and Amendment of State Constitutions* (1922).

C. R. Erdman, *The New Jersey Constitution* (1934).

M. L. Faust, *Organization Manual* (Missouri Constitutional Convention of 1943, Columbia).

W. B. Graves, *American State Government* (1953 ed.), Chs. II–III.

C. G. Haines and B. M. Haines, *Principles and Problems of Government* (1934 ed.), Ch. XIV.

R. S. Hoar, *Constitutional Conventions: their Nature, Powers, and Limitations* (1917).

A. N. Holcombe, *State Government in the United States* (1931 ed.), Chs. II–V.

Illinois Legislative Reference Library, *Constitutional Convention Bulletins* (1920).

M. W. Jernegan, *The American Colonies* (1929).

Gerald W. Johnson, *Our English Heritage* (1949).

J. P. Keith, *Methods of Constitutional Revision* (Bureau on Municipal Research, University of Texas, 1949).

C. Kettleborough, *Constitution-Making in Indiana* (2 vols., 1916).

———, *State Constitutions* (1918).

I. Loeb, *Constitution and Constitutional Conventions in Missouri* (1922).

A. F. Macdonald, *American State Government and Administration* (1955 ed.), Ch. 4.

J. M. Mathews, *American State Government* (1934 ed.), Ch. VI.

——— and C. A. Berdahl, *Documents and Readings in American Government* (1940 ed.), Ch. XIX.

M. B. McCarthy, *The Widening Scope of American Constitutions* (1928).

C. E. Merriam, *A History of American Political Theories* (1903), Chs. I–II.

National Municipal League, *A Model State Constitution* (1948 ed.).

National Municipal Review, issue for March, 1948, "Modernizing State Constitutions."

Allan Nevins, *The American States during and after the Revolution* (1924).

New York State Constitutional Convention Committee, *Report* (12 vols., 1938).

V. A. O'Rourke and D. W. Campbell, *Constitution-Making in a Democracy: Theory and Practice in New York State* (1943).

B. M. Rich, "A New Constitution for New Jersey," *Am. Pol. Sci. Rev.,* Dec., 1947, pp. 1126–1129.

B. F. Shambaugh (ed.), *The Constitution of Iowa* (1935).

P. S. Sikes and J. E. Stoner, *Bates and Field's State Government* (1954 ed.), Ch. 4.

A. L. Sturm, *Methods of State Constitutional Reform* (Michigan Governmental Studies No. 28, 1954).

Raymond Uhl and Others, *Constitutional Conventions* (Bureau of Public Administration, University of South Carolina, 1951).

Harvey Walker, *The Legislative Process: Lawmaking in the United States* (1948), Chs. 3–4.

Questions and Problems

1. Show that the study of American state government appropriately begins in Great Britain.

2. Make a list of present-day organs of state government that had their origin in colonial times.

3. Discuss this statement: *American democracy had its beginnings in the colonies.*

4. How did the framers of the first state constitutions seek to guard against governmental "tyranny"?

5. Indicate the appropriate functions of constitutional commissions; conventions.

6. What are the provisions for constitution-making in your state? Suggest any needed changes in the process.

7. Prepare and defend what you consider a desirable method of amending state constitutions. Wherein does it differ from the system in your state?

8. What would be the nature of a state constitution that would need relatively infrequent amendment?

9. What inconsistencies do you find in the constitution of your state?

10. What provisions of the constitution of your state would be more appropriate in statutes?

CHAPTER | 3

NOMINATIONS AND ELECTIONS

No less significant than constitutions in the democratic process and somewhat more stimulating as a subject of discussion among both students and the public is the politics of nominating and electing officials. To be sure, the national political classic, the presidential race, commands the citizen's first interest. Nevertheless, state and local issues are not infrequently of more immediate concern to the voter than national questions, and the diversion of the voter's attention from state and local contests created by the national quadrennial sweepstakes is most unfortunate. Yet the former sometimes command wide and eager attention.

I. NOMINATIONS [1]

The people of the United States elect 435 members of the House of Representatives, 96 senators, about 10,000 state officers—governors, legislators, and others—and some 850,000 local officers.[2] Making nominations for these offices is an essential part of the election process.

A. The Era of the Caucus

Until the Jackson Era there were not many elective officers and the number of voters constituted only a small percentage of the population. In colonial times and in the early years of our independence a candidate announced himself, perhaps with the coy statement that he reluctantly consented to run because so many gentlemen had urged him to do so, or a group of politically minded persons at a rather informal meeting might name a candidate. This latter method was known as nomination by caucus.[3] Concerning the caucus, John Adams made an oft-quoted entry in his diary, February, 1763: "This

[1] Hugh A. Bone, *American Politics and the Party System* (1949), Ch. 19; R. C. Brooks, *Political Parties and Electoral Problems* (1933 ed.), Ch. X; V. O. Key, Jr., *Politics, Parties, and Pressure Groups* (1952 ed.), Ch. 14; C. E. Merriam and H. F. Gosnell, *The American Party System* (1949 ed.), Ch. XIV; Peter Odegard and E. A. Helms, *American Politics* (1947 ed.), Ch. XVI; H. R. Penniman, *Sait's American Parties and Elections* (1952 ed.), Chs. XIV–XIX, XXII–XXVII.

[2] Merriam and Gosnell, *op. cit.,* pp. 301–302.

[3] The word "caucus" is commonly held to have been derived from the Algonquian *kaw-kaw-wus,* meaning "to consult."

day learned that the Caucus club meets at certain times in the garret of Tom Dawes. . . . There they smoke tobacco till you cannot see from one end of the garret to the other. There they drink flip, I suppose, and they choose a moderator who puts questions to the vote regularly; and selectmen, assessors, collectors, fire-wards, and representatives are regularly chosen before they are chosen in the town." [4] In state and local political affairs the caucus became an established institution long before 1800. Local officers were nominated in some such manner as mentioned in Adams's diary; state officers by the members of a given party in the state legislature—the legislative caucus; and, beginning about 1796, candidates for the presidency by the party groups in Congress.

In 1824 the caucus was discredited as a method of choosing candidates for the presidency. Before this date the caucus had been greatly weakened in the states, and its life was probably not greatly prolonged by the introduction of the "mixed" or "mongrel" caucus—a caucus in which delegates from districts that had no party representatives in the state legislature would sit with their fellow partisans who held seats in that body and with them nominate candidates for office. Jacksonian Democrats opposed the caucus, whether pure or "mongrel," as undemocratic, corrupt, and as subversive of the cherished principle of the separation of powers. The triumph of Jackson meant the overthrow of "King Caucus," who had been sitting on a shaky throne for at least a decade.

B. The Delegate Convention

During the decade following 1820 the caucus ceased to be used except in the smallest political units—wards, towns, and townships. It was continued in these small districts for the purpose of nominating the party candidates for offices in these areas and for the additional purpose of naming delegates to city, county, and, in some cases, congressional district conventions. The delegates in any one of these conventions named the candidates for offices of the area that the convention represented, and selected delegates to a state convention and sometimes to a congressional district convention. These higher conventions, repeating the process of the county or city conventions, named the party candidates for elective offices within the state or district and selected the delegates for the great national convention. Thus the convention system was essentially democratic in theory, resting upon the small unit cells composed of the Toms, Dicks, and Harrys who might care to attend the local caucus. Democracy seemed to be satisfied—all candidates for elective office, from the smallest to the greatest, were nominated by the people or by their delegates, and, as the practice of adopting party platforms developed, the people's delegates drafted them. It appeared that about the last demand of popular government had been met and that the convention system would continue unchallenged.

4 Quoted in Brooks, op. cit., p. 254.

Unfair and Corrupt Methods of Choosing Delegates

But the convention hierarchy soon showed decided defects from the ground up. Frequently, the local caucus that selected the first set of delegates was composed only of very small-sized politicians and the "toughs" and "bums" of the community. It often met in saloons, or over livery stables, or in other places likely to discourage the attendance of the best citizens. It might meet in a room too small to hold all the voters who might try to attend; but the "gang," having been previously notified, would be there early and occupy all available space. Or the local machine might hold a "snap caucus"; that is, meet in advance of the time set, perhaps display enough conscience to turn up the clock, and complete the work at hand before the arrival of the independent members of the party.

If the delegates to the conventions were chosen by the indirect [5] primary ballot, which became a rather common practice, the results were hardly any better. The party would keep its polls open for a few hours, and frequently ballots would be cast only by "straight organization men" and their followers. The ballot box might be stuffed; non-organization voters might be forcibly prevented from casting a ballot, or they might not be able to find the polling place; or fraudulent returns might be made—to mention only a few of the methods by which the professionals controlled the old indirect primaries. Of course, not all the local caucuses and indirect primaries were run by professional politicians, tricksters, and "plug-uglies," but altogether too many of them were, especially in the cities.

Unfairness and Corruption in the Conventions

If the very foundation of the convention system—the caucus and the indirect primary—was grossly defective, it is not surprising that the convention itself failed to attain a high level. After the delegates were chosen, various politicians attempted to secure their support in the conventions by persuasion, entreaty, threats, promises of places on the public pay roll, and actual bribery. Frequently two different factions of the party sent rival delegations to a convention, where, with scant regard for the merits of the claims of the contesting delegations, the professional group that controlled the convention would seat the claimants who seemed most useful to that group. Sometimes individuals who had no notion of attending a convention would have themselves selected as delegates for the sole purpose of selling their credentials to the highest bidder. Conventions were usually run by masters of the art of politics—men who were wise to all the weaknesses of their fellow men and who were often unscrupulous enough to turn that wisdom to their own advantage.

There was money to be made in politics by men who possessed sharp wits and dull consciences. The ever-increasing number of public offices afforded positions for party men who paid a part of their salaries into the organization

---

[5] The indirect primary must be carefully distinguished from the later direct primary, a system by which voters actually nominate candidates for office.

treasury. More important sources of revenue for the party organizations and for the enrichment of party leaders and bosses were found in the unholy alliance between business and politics. Graft in the letting of public contracts, especially in cities, in the granting of franchises for public utilities, and in affording "protection" to vice and crime ran into millions. Said Big John Kennedy, "It's a pretty good game at that, is politics, and it can be brought to pay like a bank." [6] No wonder greedy professionals made every effort to control conventions. The loss of such control would mean a pass in dividends on the "good game."

True, there were honest conventions, and a larger number showed some evidence of responsibility to the general public. But the system taken as a whole was bad. Even the good conventions were beyond any effective popular control.

C. The Direct Primary

Following the Civil War the states made various attempts to limit abuses and corruption in the caucuses, primaries, and conventions; but gradually the idea spread that the solution of the problem lay in the direct primary, to be established by state constitutions and laws. The direct primary is a system by which the voters of a given party make their nominations directly in a party election, and it is to be distinguished from the old indirect primary in which the party voters elected delegates who then made the nominations at conventions. The direct primary is usually regulated in great detail by law; the indirect primary rested for the most part upon party rules.

Origin and Development of the Direct Primary

The direct primary seems to have originated in Crawford County, Pennsylvania, a few years after the Civil War.[7] From there it spread to counties of the West and came into even more general use in the Southern states. After 1900 the movement for it was nation-wide; and it was championed by such men as the senior Robert M. La Follette, William Jennings Bryan, Theodore Roosevelt, and Woodrow Wilson. Today the direct primary has supplanted the convention system or seriously threatened it in nearly every state in the Union. Rhode Island is the most recent "convert" (1948).[8] Only in Connecticut is the convention system still undisturbed. New York and a few other states employ the convention for state-wide offices, but not for local ones. Republicans, being decidedly in the minority in a number of the Southern states, often use conventions in that region. The states have widely different primary laws, but space permits no more than a general discussion of their provisions.

[6] Quoted in M. R. Werner, *Tammany Hall* (1928), p. xi.
[7] There is proof of some use of it in the same county as early as 1842. Brooks, *op. cit.*, p. 261.
[8] R. S. Childs, "Rhode Island Tries Primary," *Nat. Mun. Rev.*, Mar., 1949, p. 126.

"Designation"

The process by which aspirants get their names on the official primary ballot is called "designation." In a number of states, declaration of candidacy, usually accompanied by a small fee, is all that is required. The other common method of designation is by petition. The number of signatures required varies from state to state and in accordance with the importance of the office sought; but the number required is frequently excessive, running into hundreds or even thousands. If those who seek the nomination are backed by the party organization or machine, which is often the case, they are put to no inconvenience or expense in the circulation of the petition; but an independent candidate is at the disadvantage of having to circulate the petition himself, or having friends or paid workers do it for him. When a petition has received the requisite number of signatures, it is turned over to an officer authorized by law to receive it and pass upon its legality. If, upon examination, usually a very perfunctory one, the petition is found to meet the requirements of the law, the aspirant is entitled to a place upon the primary ballot.

Positions on the Ballot

In what order shall the names be placed on the ballots? One might think that an alphabetical list would take care of the matter very simply, but it does not. It has been found that those who stand at the top of the list have a much better chance of being nominated than the others. Consequently, a number of states have adopted a system of rotating the names. Assuming, for example, that Abel, Hanson, and Young are seeking the Republican nomination for governor, by this system the ballots will be so printed that each aspirant's name will appear first on one third of the ballots, second on another third, and last on the other third. In a few states the order of candidates on the ballot is determined by lot. That the position on the ballot should have anything to do with the prospects for nomination is, of course, an indication of the limitations of the direct primary.

Types of Primaries

"OPEN" AND "CLOSED" PRIMARIES. Primaries are classified as "open" and "closed." Under the "open" system, which is used in only eleven or twelve states, the voter is handed the ballots of all the parties. He retires to a booth, takes the ballot of his own party, and marks the name of the person he favors as the party candidate for governor, mayor, sheriff, and so on through the list. He then folds the ballot and deposits it. The ballots of the other parties he drops in a box for "blanks." The open primary has the commendable feature of preserving the secrecy of the ballot; but it is criticized on the ground that it is possible for persons to vote in either party without any regard to their political affiliation, thus destroying party responsibility.

The "closed" primary is used in the great majority of the states. By this plan the voter must declare his party allegiance. In a number of states a simple declaration is not sufficient—he may be required to take an oath that he has been affiliated or will be affiliated with the party. When the election officials are satisfied as to the voter's party affiliation, they give him the ballot of his party (but not the ballots of the other parties, as in the open system) and he retires to a booth and marks the names of persons he prefers as candidates for the various offices. One must not assume, however, that the closed primary is air-tight. On the contrary, we are informed that, even where the test of party affiliation is strict, it is usually possible for the determined or unscrupulous voter to step out of his own party and participate in the nominations of another.

THE "BLANKET" PRIMARY. A new form of ballot, the "blanket" primary ballot, is used in the state of Washington. All the candidates for nomination appear on the same ballot, the candidates being grouped under the title of the office to which they aspire, each candidate having his party affiliation opposite his name. Every primary voter is given this blanket ballot. He may confine his selections to one party, or he may vote for a Republican aspirant for the position of United States senator and for a Democratic aspirant for the post of governor and otherwise show his discrimination as a voter. The high man of each party for each office then appears on the ballot at the general election in November. Obviously, the blanket primary ballot makes for the greatest independence in voting in primary elections. For this reason it is very popular with the voters, and for the same reason it is very much disliked and feared by the old party "wheelhorses" and all good "organization" men.[9]

THE "RUN-OFF" PRIMARY. Nominations are commonly made by plurality (the greatest number) vote. If there are just two persons seeking nomination for an office, one will, of course, receive a majority. If there are three on the list, then we may find some such result as 35 per cent for A, 34 for B, and 31 for C. Under the plurality rule, applied in many states, the nomination would go to A, although it is clear that he is not the choice of a majority of the voters of his party. In order to prevent plurality nominations, several devices have been employed; but the only one used extensively is the double primary, employed by some six Southern states. By this system a first, or "free-for-all," primary is held. Aspirants who receive a majority of the votes are nominated in this first primary. But in respect to those offices for which no aspirants receive a majority, a second, or "run-off," primary is held to choose between the two who stood highest in the "free-for-all." This double system is troublesome and expensive; but, since the Democratic nomination is tantamount to election in these states, they naturally prefer conclusive primaries.[10]

[9] C. O. Johnson, "Washington Blanket Primary," *Pacific Northwest Quarterly*, XXXIII (Jan., 1942), 27. See also Daniel M. Ogden, Jr., "The Blanket Primary and Party Responsibility in Washington," *Pacific Northwest Quarterly*, XXXIX (Jan., 1948), 33.

[10] Georgia provides for nominations by a county unit vote system, a plan under which the candidate who gets the highest popular vote in a county is awarded from 2 to 6 nominating votes, the number depending roughly upon the population of the county.

THE NONPARTISAN PRIMARY.   Many judicial and local officers are elected, in theory at least, on a nonpartisan basis.   They are therefore nominated in the primaries on a nonpartisan ballot.   On this ballot all the aspirants for nonpartisan offices are listed in groups, according to the office sought. All the voters, without any regard to political affiliation, are given the same ballot.   For each nonpartisan office to be filled, the voter marks the name of his choice.   When the ballots are counted, the two leading aspirants for any particular office are declared nominated for that office, and they will then appear as candidates on the nonpartisan ballot at the regular election that follows.   It may be unnecessary to state that the nonpartisan primary does not prevent partisans from appearing on the ballot.   It is only the partisan designation that is abolished.

Comments upon the Direct Primary

CRITICISMS.   Many of the earlier advocates of the direct primary saw in it a method by which the people would in periodic expressions of civic righteousness nominate the most capable and honest men for office, while its opponents alleged that the candidates so nominated would be much inferior to those named by the conventions.   After more than fifty years authorities still disagree concerning the relative merits of candidates chosen by conventions and direct primaries.   This writer suggests that the product is about the same, except that the convention system was more likely to produce a representative of special interests and the primary system a demagogue.

In the second place the direct primary is criticized because of the added expense it entails.   The government must pay the cost of the primary election, and the candidates and their backers must pay the cost of the primary campaign.   Those who advance this criticism not infrequently assert that the high cost of campaigns gives rich candidates an advantage over the poor candidates, but many poor men have been nominated in the primaries and it is common knowledge that large expenditures either by an aspirant or by others on his behalf have often failed in their purpose.   We can derive considerable encouragement from the fact that a candidate with only money to offer may lose to an opponent who has ideas and plans.

Third, other critics of the direct primary assert that it breaks down party responsibility.   Such critics say that under the convention system the party leaders are responsible for the nominations made, and that under the direct primary system everybody, and hence nobody, is responsible.   It is true that leaders and bosses were responsible in a sense under the convention system, but the voters found no satisfactory means of enforcing this responsibility. With our direct primaries, the leaders and bosses are still functioning; but

---

The plan is weighted heavily in favor of the rural county, for no matter how small the population, it has two votes, and the largest urban county gets only six votes.   Thus it happened that Eugene Talmadge, whose strength was primarily in rural communities, won the nomination for governor in 1946, although one of his opponents, James V. Carmichael, was well ahead of Talmadge in the popular vote column.

they are subject to a much closer check by the voters than they were in the heyday of conventions.

A fourth charge against the direct primary is that, unlike the convention, it furnishes no means by which very desirable compromises may be reached between factions in the party. But the party leaders frequently hold consultations before the primary and propose candidates for the various offices, and this "organization slate" is often ratified by the voters in the primary.[11]

When all the arguments against the direct primary have been heard, it is apparent that the principal one is that there is no official way in which party responsibility for the candidates may be maintained. The central problem of the direct primary then becomes that of devising a scheme whereby the party organization and the voters will each have an appropriate and effective part in making nominations. Any plan that achieves these ends must give the party organization a right to pass on the candidates and must at the same time leave the final decision respecting nominations to the voters. Such a plan has been suggested.

A Proposed Primary System

The National Municipal League's Committee on the Direct Primary (Professor Joseph P. Harris, chairman) has devised a new primary system that a number of students of government look upon with favor. The essential features of the proposed plan [12] are as follows:

1. Pre-primary conferences, under direction of the party organization, should recommend candidates to the voters, such candidates to be designated on the ballot as having the endorsement of the party leaders. The plan would also permit nominations by petition, thus avoiding the restoration of an irresponsible party oligarchy. Pre-primary recommendations by the party organizations were long ago proposed by Charles Evans Hughes, when he was Governor of New York. Such a plan has been in use in Colorado since 1912, and it was recently adopted by Nebraska (but repealed in 1953), Rhode Island, and Utah.

2. Individual candidates should be permitted to file for nomination in only one political party. This would prevent "dual" or "cross filing," as extensively practiced in California. The committee would not, however, prohibit a party organization from endorsing the candidate of another party.

3. The direct primary system should be required of all parties that polled as much as 10 per cent of the vote at the preceding general election.

4. The states could use the "closed," "open," or "blanket ballot," as they might see fit. (The writer joins Professor Harris in favoring the wide-open "blanket" system.)

5. The Committee listed as number 1 in its recommendations the principle of the short ballot, declaring that all offices except those responsible for the major policies of government should be filled by appointment.

---

[11] Merriam and Gosnell, *op. cit.*, pp. 307–308.
[12] *Model Direct Primary* . . . , National Municipal League (1951).

As there is no doubt that the direct primary is with us to stay, it is most appropriate that our efforts should be directed at its improvement. The plan briefly outlined above contains well-considered suggestions and might be studied with profit by both friends and foes of the direct primary.

Party Platforms Under the Direct Primary

How are party platforms made under the direct primary system? Clearly, the whole body of voters cannot make them. Consequently, the work must be done by conventions or by party councils. If the convention meets before the primary is held, there is no assurance that the platform drafted will conform to the views of the candidates nominated; but if the convention meets after the primary, the platform will very properly reflect the views of the nominees who have just been named by the voters. In a number of states the platform is framed by a party council after the primary has been held. This council is ordinarily composed of the candidates for important offices and a few others, such as members of the party who hold high public office or high party office. This method of framing a platform has decided merit, in that the framers are those who are directly responsible for carrying it into execution. In the State of Washington, where the conventions meet before the primaries are held, the Republican platform of 1952 "was adopted without a dissenting vote and without even being read. It was getting late by the time it came up." [13] This kind of action is to be expected where there is practically no association between platform and candidates.

II. POLITICAL CAMPAIGNS [14]

In the states the sovereign electors choose governors, other executive officers, legislators, and judges; in the counties, sheriffs, commissioners, surveyors, assessors, school superintendents, and coroners are among those to be elected; and in the cities, mayors, councilmen, and a number of other officers are to be chosen by the people. Not all of these officers are elected on the Tuesday after the first Monday in November in the even years, the date of the national elections; but many of them are elected at that time, and the candidates must necessarily compete for the voter's attention with candidates for national office in the unequal contest, a very unequal contest in presidential years.

Controlling Factors in State and Local Campaigns

National issues are often controlling factors in state campaigns, and not infrequently in local campaigns. This unfortunate situation prevails because many state and local elections, with the exception of city elections, occur on the national election days, and national issues are usually the center of interest. The typical voter, obeying his own partisan impulses, or too much a victim of inertia to vote for candidates in different party columns, or hearken-

[13] *Spokesman-Review*, May 25, 1952.
[14] Bone, *op. cit.*, Chs. 21–22; Key, *op. cit.*, Ch. 16; Merriam and Gosnell, *op. cit.*, pp. 390–392; Odegard and Helms, *op. cit.*, Chs. 17–18.

ing unto the voice of party leaders to vote the ticket "straight," marks his cross
in the big circle at the top of the party list, thus supporting his party for all
offices from President to constable.

But at times the states and local communities have great concerns of their
own; they will not subordinate their problems to the national issues.   Personal or factional feuds, struggles of the public against the interests of railroads, power magnates, local public utilities, insurance companies, mining
and manufacturing interests, labor unions, social security organizations, and
various other groups, may temporarily or for a considerable period of time
bring parties, factions, and voters to consider issues or problems in their states
or counties or cities independently from those of the nation.   As a result
states sometimes, and cities frequently, elect the candidates of one party to
national office and the candidates of another to their own offices.   This division of the honors of office comes about not only for the reasons just given,
but also because the ties of party do not bind the voter in state and local campaigns, particularly in the latter, as they do in national campaigns.   Even in
national elections a lapse of party regularity is now condoned or easily for-
given, a tolerance quite unknown thirty or forty years ago, when "scratching
the ticket" in such elections was little short of treason.

Campaign Methods

The methods of reaching the voter in state and local campaigns are, in
general, about the same as those employed in the national contests.[15]   There
are important shades of difference, however.   Merriam and Gosnell tell us
that personal squabbles, factional strife, class consciousness, sectional jeal-
ousies, race prejudice, and religious antipathies are found in more intense
form in individual states than in the country as a whole, thus giving state campaigners more delicate problems of strategy than the national campaigners
may meet.   The local communities may be said to hold the same difficulties
for the campaigner as the state.

Two general courses are open to the candidates: they may walk the tight
rope, sidestep, wiggle, wobble, and "weasel" in the attempt to win votes from
all groups or factions; or, they may pick out the classes that have the greatest
number of votes, pose as the champions of their interests, and make capital
of their declared hostility to, let us say, Wall Street, "bloated bondholders,"
"soulless corporations," and "haters of the old folks."   The latter method is
more likely to prove effective if the candidate is a practical psychologist.
Candidates are, of course, backed by various party organizations, which help
them with speakers, "literature," and money.   In the local areas the candidates can do a great deal for themselves through personal contact with a large
number of voters, sometimes all the voters in their district.

PETTINESS AND PERSONALITIES IN CAMPAIGNS.   Sometimes state and local
political contests are conducted on the somewhat dignified plane that usually
characterizes the national campaigns.   At other times militant gubernatorial

[15] See Johnson's *American National Government* (1955 ed.), Ch. 9.

or mayoralty candidates with burning issues and eager backers conduct "hammer-and-tongs" campaigns. Not infrequently our campaigns, other than national, degenerate to trivialities and personalities.

Here is a rather extreme example of the latter type. The fact that it comes from a Texas "run-off" primary does not impair its value as an illustration; for, there, success in the Democratic primary is equivalent to election. In 1930 Mrs. Miriam A. ("Ma") Ferguson, the state's chief executive during 1925–1927, and wealthy Ross A. Sterling were candidates for governor. Retiring Governor Dan Moody fired the heaviest projectiles against "Fergusonism" for Sterling, while Mrs. Ferguson's husband, removed (1917) from the executive mansion of the state by impeachment, championing the cause of the "common people," mixed the poison for the "millionaires." "Husband Ferguson drew enormous crowds, set them wild with denunciations of Messrs. Moody and Sterling. Newspapers were given libel law waivers by Candidate Sterling to print anything Stumpster Ferguson said against him, but Mrs. Ferguson would not grant the press the reciprocal privilege. Her husband, appealing to the 'common folks at the fork of the creek,' mocked and jibed at Candidate Sterling's handsome Bay Shore house, declared it had no less than 27 bathrooms." [16] Sterling, who was no public speaker and left the stumping to others, did feel called upon to explain just why he needed *eight* bathrooms in his home, and he expressed the hope that every citizen of Texas might have at least one bathroom. Sterling won this particular campaign, but two years later he lost to Mrs. Ferguson in a similar "run-off" contest.

III. THE VOTING PROCESS [17]

The health and strength of democracy depends in considerable measure upon the integrity of the ballot. With a large majority of the population eligible to vote in nearly every section of the Union,[18] the conduct of an election is an undertaking that calls for planning and organization, for officers and party watchers, for ballots and machines, for polling places (more than a hundred thousand of them), and above all for careful attention to details.

The Polling Place

The country or city is divided into precincts or districts, each of which contains several hundred voters. Each precinct has its polling place. Formerly, the prevailing practice was to rent private property for this purpose; but as this gave too much opportunity for graft and favoritism, the tendency now is decidedly in the direction of requiring the use of school buildings, police stations, or other public structures. Sometimes churches are used. A few states blessed with good climates make considerable use of tents.

[16] *Time*, Sept. 1, 1930, p. 19. For a more recent example of the same sort of thing (Theodore Bilbo in Mississippi), see V. O. Key, Jr., *Southern Politics* (1949), pp. 241–243.
[17] Spencer D. Albright, "Elections," *Book of the States, 1954–55*, pp. 75–91; Bone, *op. cit.*, pp. 658–679; Brooks, *op. cit.*, Ch. XV; Key, *Politics, Parties, and Pressure Groups*, Ch. 22; Merriam and Gosnell, *op. cit.*, Chs. XVII–XVIII; Penniman, *op. cit.*, Ch. XXVII.
[18] For number of voters, potential and actual, see Johnson, *op. cit.*, pp. 210–211.

Election Officers

When the voter enters the polling place, he finds that several individuals, almost invariably one or two from each of the great parties, are serving as inspectors or judges of elections. These persons are responsible for the proper conduct of the election in the precinct. If they are corrupt, elections become frauds in spite of volumes of laws intended to keep them pure; for, as a learned judge once said, no statute has yet been drafted that will serve as a substitute for an honest man. The theory that dishonest inspectors of the two major parties will check each other and thus keep an election pure has some fatal defects in practice, and the soundness of the theory may well be questioned. Two dishonest men who happen to belong to different political parties are no more likely to give us an honest election than two wrongs are to make a right. These men may put personal gain above party advantage and sell out; or it may be to both their personal gain and party advantage to trade in election frauds.

A number of cases have been exposed in which party machines have reached agreements to "count out" third-party candidates. Some years ago in Chicago an election official, in imminent danger of being detected at this particular crime against the voters, actually ate twenty-eight ballots that had been cast for the "wrong" candidates. Sometimes the machines agree to trade votes, for example, presidential votes for gubernatorial votes. In such cases it may become the "duty" of the inspectors to make the exchange. It is encouraging to note that authorities are practically unanimous in the conclusion that such frauds are much less common now than they were a generation ago.

Watchers

In addition to the election officers the voter will find watchers at the polls. These individuals represent the different parties and candidates, and they have the right to see everything that is done by the election officials, in regard to both casting and counting the ballots. If they are honest, alert, familiar with the election laws, and know many of the voters, they can do a great deal to preserve the integrity of an election in their precinct.

Methods of Voting

ORAL VOTING. A century and a quarter ago a number of states used the oral (*viva voce*) system of voting. The voter simply approached the county polling place, where the candidates for county and sometimes higher offices and frequently a considerable crowd had collected. Upon being recognized by the judges and being told by them to vote, he pronounced the names of his candidates, whose words of thanks were often drowned out by the applause and jeers of opposing partisans. This oral pronouncement was considered by many leading citizens to be the only manly way to vote, and it was still preserved in a few states until after the middle of the nineteenth century.

PARTY BALLOTS. The party ballot, which was very generally substituted for oral voting a century or more ago, was no great improvement over the latter. The ballots were printed by the party, contained only the names of the candidates of the party, were distributed by the party's "ticket peddlers," and were cast in the open. The fact that a ballot contained only the names of the candidates of one party made it impossible for a voter to divide honors between parties, unless he "scratched" some names on his ticket and wrote in the names of other candidates. If he had the energy or independence or courage to do this, he was almost sure to be detected and rebuked or even slugged by party workers. The old type of ballot made machine control of elections very easy, because watchers could see how everybody voted and could therefore see that "the goods paid for were actually delivered."

THE AUSTRALIAN BALLOT. In 1888 a ballot long used in Australia, and therefore known as the "Australian ballot," was introduced in the United States. It is now used in some form by all the states except South Carolina. This ballot is printed and distributed at public expense; it bears the names of all candidates; it is given to each voter only at the polling place; it is marked by the voter in secret. The original Australian ballot did not designate the parties of the candidates. It simply listed each group of candidates under the office they sought.

Because of the multiplicity of offices, and in the interest of parties, we have modified the Australian plan. In Massachusetts and in some twenty other states all the candidates for each office are listed in separate groups; but the party of each candidate is printed after his name. According to the Massachusetts plan the voter marks the name of the candidate of his choice for each office, although some states employing that plan provide for "straight" ticket voting by a single mark.

In the greater number of states the Australian ballot has been still further modified. Each party is given its own column on the ballot; and the voter, by simply putting his mark in the big circle at the top of his party column, votes for the candidates of his party for all the offices to be filled. If the voter wishes to "scratch" or "split" his ticket, that is, vote for candidates of another party for some of the offices, then he puts the cross in the circle of his favorite party and makes a cross opposite the name of each candidate he prefers who is in the column of another party. It is clear that the party column type of ballot makes it easier for one to vote the "straight" party ticket; that it tends somewhat to discourage independent voting; and that for these reasons it is favored by the politicians.

A majority of the states place the candidates for all offices on the same ballot. Several states, however, have separate ballots for different types of offices—national, state, county, and city. Separate ballots may have some influence in the direction of independent voting, since they do in a physical sense separate candidates for the different types of offices. A number of states present initiated and referred measures on separate sheets, and thereby emphasize those questions as distinct from the election of officers.

Nonpartisan offices. It is generally recognized that partisanship is to be deplored in relation to judicial and local offices. Consequently, in a number of states, candidates for such offices are now placed on the ballots in true Australian style; that is, without party designation. One would be foolish to say that this prevents all partisanship, but there is no doubt that it lessens the intensity of it and stimulates independent voting. In a few states candidates for public school superintendents are listed on a nonpartisan ballot, and in Minnesota and Nebraska candidates for the legislature—surely a political and partisan organ of government—are so listed.

Casting the ballot. We return now to our voter, whom we left at the polls while we were discussing ballots. When he has satisfied the election officials that he is duly qualified to vote, he is given the ballot or ballots and retires to the privacy of a booth to do the marking. An illiterate or physically incapacitated voter may have the assistance of election officials, and, in some states, the assistance of other voters, in marking his ballot. The marking being completed, the voter folds the ballot according to directions previously given and returns it to an inspector who, if he is satisfied that it is the same ballot that was given the voter, deposits it in the box.

VOTING MACHINES. A majority of the states now make varying degrees of use of the voting machine. It is a complicated mechanism, but like many other such mechanisms it is very easy to operate. The name of each candidate appears under a lever, and the voter indicates his choice by pulling the lever over the candidate's name. A number of states have the machines so constructed that an elector may vote the straight ticket by simply pulling down the lever of his party. As the machine is enclosed by curtains, the voter has absolute secrecy in indicating his choices. If he votes in secret, what prevents him from operating the machine several times? The answer is that the machine records only the last movement of the levers, and it will not record that until the voter opens the curtain to leave the booth. The machine adds the votes as the levers are pulled for the various candidates, parties, or measures. When the polls are closed, all that the officers have to do to learn the results of the election is to unlock the machine and read the totals. The chief advantages of the machines are: they can be operated more quickly than a paper ballot can be marked; they are accurate; they are so constructed that a voter cannot spoil his ballot; the absolute secrecy of the ballot is preserved; and they afford no opportunity for election officials to invalidate any votes as they can by mutilating or destroying paper ballots. The cost of installing machines is very high and, except in the larger precincts, this initial cost is not offset by savings on ballots and other reductions in election costs that the machine makes possible.

In spite of the obvious advantage of the voting machine over the paper ballot, it has been slow coming into general use. It is not available for any large percentage of voters, except in New York and eight or nine other states. The chief obstacles to its adoption are: its initial cost; the distrust of a mechanical device that does not show how each vote is cast; and the determined opposition of corruptionists, who find the voting machine much more rigid in resisting election trickery and fraud than the paper ballot.

Counting the Votes

With the closing of the polls, the counting of votes begins.   We have just observed that where a voting machine is used, the counting officers have nothing to do but unlock the machine and read the totals.   But counting paper ballots is a tedious job, and it may occupy election officials, who have already been busy at the polls all day, through the better part of the night.   Even honest election officials will grow weary and make mistakes.   Party watchers who were annoyingly alert in the morning measurably relax their vigilance as the night advances.   To lessen the strain on tired election officials, some twelve states have provided for special counting boards.   These may begin their work a few hours after the polls open, and they will have the results totaled by midnight, or perhaps even earlier.   The count as announced from the many precincts gives, unofficially, the results of an election.   Several days later an official canvass is made by authorities, usually county officers, designated for that purpose.   These canvassing boards send all the election figures that relate to the state or districts larger than the county to the state canvassing board.

Absentee Voting

It always happens that many qualified voters are absent from their counties or states on election day.   Nearly all of the states extend to certain classes of absentees the privilege of voting.   A few states accord the privilege only to those absent in the military or naval service; a few other states allow any absentee the privilege; but the typical provision is that all those whose business or profession renders their absence necessary shall be entitled to the absentee voter's ballot.   Most of the states allow those who are ill or physically disabled (although actually present in the precinct) the privilege of absentee voting.   A large majority of the states permit an individual to have an absentee ballot either when he is outside his county or his country and state.

A few states require the absentee to exercise his privilege on election day. The voter may go to any polling place in his state, make an affidavit, receive a ballot, and vote in the usual manner.   The affidavit and the ballot are then forwarded to the election officers of the county in which the voter resides.   The more common provision concerning the time and method of absentee voting is that the absentee shall by affidavit apply to designated officers of the county in which he is a registered voter for the absentee voter's ballot.   Upon receipt of the ballot, the absentee signs an affidavit and returns the marked ballot to the place of his registration, where it is counted with the other ballots on election day.   The voters show scant appreciation of the privilege, as very few of the tens of thousands who might avail themselves of it take the trouble to do so.[19]

[19] Albright, in *Book of the States,* pp. 88–91; Brooks, *op. cit.,* 452 ff.; Penniman, *op. cit.,* pp. 512 ff.

THE ARMED SERVICE VOTE. Arrangements, usually inadequate, have been made for members of the armed forces to vote during all our major wars. In 1942 Congress authorized members of the armed forces who were qualified (registration and poll-tax payments were expressly excepted as qualifications) to vote in their states, to vote in national elections. Servicemen had to request their state secretaries of state to send them a "war ballot." Only 28,051 members of the armed forces actually received and returned the ballots in accordance with the federal law and the laws of their states. It was obvious that a more satisfactory arrangement should be made for 1944. But politics and constitutional questions (politics under the cover of the Constitution, one is tempted to say in this case) prevented the enactment of a comprehensive statute. The act that finally passed Congress gave state ballots the right of way over the ballot authorized by federal law, the latter ballot to be used only where the state ballots were not available. A number of states hastened to enact laws that would give the servicemen a reasonable opportunity to vote, and the result was a rather agreeable surprise. Approximately 2,800,000 members of the armed services voted.[20] Under the laws of most of the states armed forces personnel on active duty, whether in peace or war, now have the privilege of an absentee ballot.

The Voter's Burden

In our country we have placed ever-increasing burdens upon the voter. He is expected to choose presidential electors, members of both Houses of Congress, several executive officers of his state, state legislators, judges in many states, and scores of county, city, and other local officers. Furthermore, we call upon the voter to nominate nearly all of these officers in the primary elections. But these electoral activities do not end his task. He must vote upon state constitutions and their amendments in practically every state. In about twenty states he must vote upon ordinary bills that have been "initiated" or "referred." He is sometimes asked to pass upon city charters and ordinances. Finally, in some states and local areas he may be summoned to the polls to vote in "recall" elections.

Formerly, a voter who did his best to exercise the privilege of the franchise in Chicago had to register twice, go to the polls five times, and weigh the merits of candidates for fifty offices within a year. The same type of voter in Colorado at a typical general election marked his ballot for candidates for thirty offices and voted on sixteen measures; and the faithful elector in Los Angeles performed the same operations for forty-five offices and fifty-eight measures.[21] The voter of San Francisco who did his full duty marked his ballot for some two score offices and thirty-nine measures, one of which was a proposed amendment to the city charter that would give a detective sergeant

[20] Boyd A. Martin, "The Service Vote in the Elections of 1944," *Am. Pol. Sci. Rev.,* XXXIX (Aug., 1945), 720.

[21] Spencer Albright, "How Does Your Ballot Grow?" (Bulletin, Am. Legislators' Association, May 10, 1933); Penniman, *op. cit.,* pp. 495–496.

a right to a hearing before being transferred.[22]   Of course these are rather extreme cases and there has been some shortening of the ballot in recent years, particularly in cities; but the average ballot is far too long, listing from twenty to thirty offices, the greater number of which would be much better filled by appointment than by election.   In states that employ the initiative and the referendum, the ballots usually contain some measures on which none but the most exceptional voters can express an intelligent opinion, and not infrequently they carry measures of such small consequence that they should be determined by minor public officials in the routine discharge of their duties.

Obviously, in view of the burden placed upon the voter, he cannot discharge his duties intelligently.   He may be able to inform himself concerning the qualifications of the candidates for important offices, but even the most conscientious and intelligent voter is practically helpless in an attempt to make a wise choice of candidates for the dozens of minor offices.   All the voter can do is to vote the straight party ticket and hope that the party organization which vouches for the candidates has played no trick upon him.

THE SOLUTION.   The conditions can be improved, and they have been improved to some extent.   The short ballot is the remedy.[23]   The ballot can be shortened by lengthening the terms of offices.   Where four-year terms are substituted for two-year terms, the voter's job is cut in half.   But the principal means of shortening the ballot is in the reduction of elective officers. Why should the people be asked to elect an inspector of elections, a public weigher, a clerk of a municipal court, a hide and animal inspector, and a host of others whose duties are technical and administrative?   Our practical statesmen and students of government agree that there is no reason whatever for burdening the voter with such tasks.   They propose that the people elect such important political officers as governors, legislators, mayors, and councilmen; and that all other officers be appointed by the elected executive officers or by them in co-operation with the legislative bodies.

As everyone knows, the only national officers elected by the people are the President and congressmen—all other national officers are appointed.   It is proposed that the states and the local governments follow the national plan. Some of the states have taken measurable strides in that direction; many of the cities have done so.   The short ballot is the only democratic ballot, if democracy has any relation to intelligent voting.   The short ballot brings us responsible government, if, as is true in all business concerns, responsibility can be established by giving the chief officers the authority to name their assistants.   The movement for the shorter ballot would perhaps make more progress but for the fact that it is as undramatic as civil service reform and shares with the latter movement something of the spoilsman's opposition and the public's apathy.

22 *The New York Times,* Oct. 26, 1930.
23 R. S. Childs, *Short Ballot Principles* (1911).   Childs continues in the faith.   See, for example, his "We Must Keep Ballot Short," *Nat. Mun. Rev.,* July, 1949, p. 328. Leading public men and editors generally favor the short ballot.   *The New York Times,* editorial, Sept. 24, 1954, states concretely the case for it.

Reading List

Hugh A. Bone, *American Politics and the Party System* (1949), Chs. 19, 21–24.
The Book of the States, 1954–55, pp. 75–91.
R. C. Brooks, *Political Parties and Electoral Problems* (1933 ed.), Chs. X–XIII, XV–XVI.
H. R. Bruce, *American Parties and Politics* (1936 ed.), Chs. XI–XV, XVII.
G. M. Connelly and H. H. Field, *The Non-Voter, Who He Is, What He Thinks* (1945).
T. W. Cousens, *Politics and Political Organization in America* (1942).
J. Daniels, *Tar Heel Editor* (1939).
E. C. Evans, *A History of the Australian Ballot System in the United States* (1917).
H. F. Gosnell, *Getting Out the Vote; an Experiment in the Stimulation of Voting* (1927).
P. Herring, *The Politics of Democracy* (1940).
A. N. Holcombe, *State Government in the United States* (1931 ed.), Chs. VIII–IX.
V. O. Key, Jr., *Politics, Parties, and Pressure Groups* (1942 ed.), Chs. 14, 16, 22.
———, *Southern Politics in State and Nation* (1949).
F. R. Kent, *The Great Game of Politics* (1923).
C. E. Merriam and H. F. Gosnell, *Non-Voting: Causes and Methods of Control* (1924).
———, *The American Party System* (1949 ed.), Chs. XIV–XX.
C. E. Merriam and L. Overacker, *Primary Elections* (1928).
Warren Moscow, *Politics in the Empire State* (1948).
National Municipal League, *Model Direct Primary* . . . (1951).
P. H. Odegard and E. A. Helms, *American Politics* (1947 ed.), Chs. XVI–XXI.
Howard R. Penniman, *Sait's American Parties and Election* (1952 ed.), Chs. XVII–XIX, XXII–XXVII.
J. T. Salter (ed.), *The American Politician* (1938).
———, *Public Men In and Out of Office* (1946).
E. R. Sikes, *State and Federal Corrupt Practices Legislation* (1928).
J. A. Woodburn, *Political Parties and Party Problems in the United States* (1924 ed.), Chs. XVI, XVIII, XXI.

Questions and Problems

1. Assess the gains and losses resulting from the overthrow of the legislative caucus as a nominating agency.

2. Is any type of nominating caucus now in use in your state?

3. Discuss the theory and practice of the delegate convention as a nominating body. To what extent is it still used?

4. Consider these propositions respecting the direct primary: It (a) destroys party responsibility; (b) enables anybody to become a candidate for office; (c) makes it easier for the rich man to buy a nomination; (d) results in the nomination of mediocre men; (e) stops boss control of politics; (f) makes the people politically intelligent and alert; (g) prevents the drafting of satisfactory party platforms.

5. To what extent do the partisan divisions in an election campaign remain firm after the newly elected officers take over? Consider the divisions in the legislature, the alignment of legislators with the governor, etc. in your state.

6. Trace the efforts made and the progress achieved in ballot reform in the United States.

7. Should people who seldom vote be deprived of the right to vote? Should we have compulsory voting laws? Pick out six persons of different types, each of whom you consider an intelligent voter; then try to decide just what qualities make him such a voter.

8. Show how constitutions and laws might be changed to aid the voter in casting his ballot intelligently.

CHAPTER 4

THE STATE EXECUTIVE SYSTEM

The American state executive system has experienced fundamental changes in the course of the years. Beginning our independence with a profound distrust and suspicion of governors (a heritage from the colonial era), we fashioned our state constitutions in such a manner as to give the governors short terms and few independent powers. Fondling the doctrine of the separation of powers, the first state constitution-makers gave practically all of them to the legislature. State constitutional history is very largely the story of correcting the balance, restoring the governor to his rightful place as the head of the state.[1] Unlike the President of the United States, he must still share executive power with other elective officials, but, during the past fifty or sixty years, developments in a number of states have placed the governor in an executive position comparable to that of the President and in practically all the states his legislative powers are relatively no less significant than those of the President.

I. THE OFFICE OF GOVERNOR: GENERAL FEATURES

Qualifications

State constitutions commonly stipulate that the governor shall be a citizen of the United States; that he shall have resided in the state for a specified number of years—usually five; and that he shall have attained an age—thirty is the usual requirement—which is supposed to indicate maturity. None of these qualifications need be expressed in constitutions or law, for they would be enforced by the voters in any case. One can easily imagine the opposition's attacks upon the candidate who lacked them or any of them. "Are we going to let this 'foreigner' rule over us?" "Can this drawling Southerner tell us Westerners how to run our state?" "The little child shall lead them!" On rare occasions a man may move from private life to the governor's chair; but usually he has served as Congressman, or in some executive position in the state, or in the state legislature, or in some other public office.

[1] This history is skillfully sketched by Leslie Lipson in *The American Governor: From Figurehead to Leader* (1939), Ch. II.

Nomination and Election

In nearly all the states the candidates for governor are nominated by the direct primary. The peculiar "county unit" primary system employed in Georgia has been noted (page 56). The convention system is used in New York and a few other states. Except for slight variation in Mississippi and Vermont, governors are elected by direct vote of the people.[2]

Term and Tenure

The framers of the original state constitutions feared "tyranny," and one of their means of guarding against it was the short term of office. Consequently, governors were commonly given one-year terms. It developed, however, that such short terms were not only unnecessary but decidedly disadvantageous, calling for frequent elections and all too frequent turnovers in state administration. During the past century the tendency has been in the direction of lengthening the terms. The term is now fixed at two years in twenty states, and at four years in the others. A few states, fearing the construction of a political machine by the governor and its use in continuing him in power, have made the chief executive ineligible for the term next succeeding. In other states it is not uncommon for the governor to serve two or even three consecutive terms. Alfred E. Smith and Herbert H. Lehman each served four terms as governor of New York, but Thomas E. Dewey, who was elected for three four-year terms, has the record for length of service as governor of that state. Albert C. Ritchie set the national record—sixteen years as governor of Maryland.

Removal from Office

IMPEACHMENT. In every state except Oregon the governor and other civil officers may be removed from office by impeachment. The charges are commonly voted in the lower house of the state legislature, and the question of guilt is decided by the state senate. Governors so removed include Sulzer of New York (1913); James E. Ferguson of Texas (1917); J. C. Walton of Oklahoma (1923), and Henry S. Johnston of the same state (1929). Impeachment proceedings are frequently criticized because on occasion they are used for political reasons rather than for any high crimes or misdemeanors a governor may have committed. The impeachment method is further criticized on the ground that it is difficult to bring it into use when it is needed. Regular sessions of the legislature are ordinarily held only once in two years; and, since they are short, there is little time for an impeachment. Usually special sessions may be called only by the governor, and he is not likely to

[2] The Mississippi plan, somewhat on the order of the presidential electoral system, calls for election by a popular and electoral vote. If no candidate receives a majority of the electoral vote, the lower house of the legislature chooses a governor from one of the two highest on the list. In Vermont, if no candidate receives a majority of the popular vote, the two houses of the legislature in joint session choose a governor from one of the three highest on the list.

call a session to consider his own impeachment. Impeachment is a gun practically without stock or barrel as far as the governor who holds office only two years is concerned, for the legislature meets about the time he takes the oath of office and adjourns almost before he has had time to become guilty of serious misconduct in office.[3]

THE RECALL. In realization of the limits of impeachment and in accordance with democratic tendencies in government, about a fourth of the states have adopted the recall. It may be used against public officials generally, although in some states judges are excepted from its operation. In practice, executive officers, state and local, have been most likely to feel its force. After a petition for recall has been signed by the number of voters required by the constitution or law, the day is fixed for the recall election, and on that day the electors go to the polls and vote for or against an officer's removal. In respect to state executive officers the advantages of the recall over impeachment (local officers are not subject to impeachment) are that it may be invoked at any convenient time and on any charge, political or legal, whereas impeachment may fairly be used only when the executive has violated the laws respecting his duties. In 1921 Governor Lynn J. Frazier and several other officers of North Dakota were recalled. It is an interesting commentary on democracy that Frazier was elected to the United States Senate a year later.

Although Governor Frazier was guilty of no crime or misdemeanor, there is no grave charge to be lodged against the people of North Dakota for his recall. That procedure is political in its design. On the other hand, impeachment is supposed to be judicial in character, and the legislatures, which have not infrequently employed it as a political weapon, are subject to severe censure. It should be a matter of national gratification that the political impeachment of President Johnson failed to result in conviction, and a point of deep regret that political impeachments in the states have not similarly failed.

As might be expected, if, for political reasons, governors guilty of no crime have been removed by impeachment proceedings, a few crooked and jailbird governors have, for the same reason, been left undisturbed by the impeachment process. On occasion, the courts are called upon to take action before impeachment proceedings are instituted, or when such proceedings seem not to be contemplated. Federal courts have sent several governors to the penitentiary. It is a pleasure to report, however, that the great majority of American governors have not merited retirement to private life by extraordinary means and that still fewer of them have been guilty of crime. Some charlatans and demagogues there may have been among them, but as a class they have shown devotion to public duty.

[3] On impeachment see N. F. Baker, "Some Legal Aspects of Impeachment in Louisiana," *The Southwestern Pol. and Soc. Sci. Quart.*, X (March, 1930) 359; F. M. Stewart, "Impeachment in Texas," *Am. Pol. Sci. Rev.*, XXIV (Aug., 1930), 652; C. A. M. Ewing, "The Impeachment of Oklahoma Governors," *Am. Pol. Sci. Rev.*, XXIV (Aug., 1930), 648; R. L. Miller, "The Gubernatorial Controversy in North Dakota," *Am. Pol. Sci. Rev.*, XXIX (June, 1935), 418.

Gubernatorial Succession

The recall operates very much the same as a regular election, the governor (or any other official) against whom the recall is invoked and other candidates for that office being listed on the ballot. If the recall is successful, a new governor is elected at the same time. But in case of the impeachment, death, or resignation of a governor, the officer designated by the constitution as his successor is elevated to the place, just as the Vice President succeeds to the presidency. In some thirty-five states the lieutenant governor takes the governor's chair. In other states, the president of the senate or the speaker of the lower house takes the office.

Compensation

The governor's salary is fixed by the constitution in some states; but fortunately there is a growing tendency to leave the amount of compensation to legislative determination, which makes possible the much-needed increase without the hazard of a popular vote on the question. The salary is usually low, averaging about $15,000 per annum. Eight or nine states pay salaries ranging from $20,000 to $50,000, and these may be regarded as the only states in which any liberality is shown in the matter of compensation. The states commonly furnish an executive mansion and often allow modest sums of money for expenses that are not entirely of a public nature. In spite of the relatively small compensation governors receive, the office does not go begging.

POSSIBILITY OF FUTURE HONORS. Many able and distinguished men are glad to accept the office. In addition to being the place of highest honor in the state, it is by no means a blind alley politically. Literally scores of governors have become United States senators; a number of others have received important federal appointments; some have been made Vice President; and everyone knows that Cleveland, McKinley, the two Roosevelts, Wilson, Coolidge, and several other Presidents touched the governor's round in their climb to fame.

II. THE GOVERNOR'S EXECUTIVE POWERS [4]

The governor is not the only executive officer of the state. The executive power is divided among the governor, secretary of state, and other officers. The governor is usually designated by the constitution as the "supreme executive" and charged with the duty to see "that the laws are faithfully executed"; but the courts have almost invariably held that these seemingly broad grants of power give the governor no definite authority—that his powers

---

[4] W. F. Dodd, *State Government* (1928 ed.), Ch. VIII; J. A. Fairlie, "The Executive Power in the State Constitution," *Annals of the Am. Acad. of Pol. and Soc. Sci.* (Sept., 1935), pp. 59–73; A. N. Holcombe, *State Government in the United States* (1931 ed.), pp. 333–352; Lipson, *op. cit.*, Chs. III, VII–VIII; J. M. Mathews, *American State Government* (1934 ed.), pp. 302–320.

must come from other and specific provisions of the constitution or statutes. In other words, in construing the clauses of the constitution relating to the governor's powers, the courts have followed the principle of strict construction, with the result that the executive powers of the governor have not been developed through the years as have those of the President. We should add, however, that a number of states have been strengthening the position of the governor as an executive during the past half century. Acting primarily in the executive capacity, the governor exercises some supervision over administration, a limited appointing power, a still more limited power of removal, grants pardons and reprieves (a restricted power in some states), and performs miscellaneous duties incident to the executive power.

1. Supervision of Administration

The governor's power to supervise the state administration is often grossly inadequate. The other executive officers elected along with the governor very naturally feel their responsibility to the people rather than to him. The governor's power to appoint subordinate administrative officials is subject to considerable limitation, and his removal power is severely restricted. The duties of state executives and administrative officers are rather minutely regulated by statutes. The control over them is legislative and judicial rather than executive. In a number of states the governor may force his "subordinates" to act only by the cumbersome method of instituting court proceedings against them. Furthermore, in taking care that the laws are faithfully executed, the governor must depend not only upon state officers but upon local officers such as sheriffs and district attorneys—officers over whom he has even less control than over the state officers, except in five or six states. In short, in many states the governor as a director of administration is far from being in the independent position occupied by the President. The national administration is largely centralized. Lower officers are responsible to higher officers, and these to still higher officers, until the responsibility rests finally with the President. In most of the states there is no hierarchy of administration, each office or board or commission being regulated rather minutely by law, the administrative "superiors" usually having only a shadowy directing power.

Still, the people expect the governor to see that the laws are faithfully executed, and these executives usually do the best they can with the means at their disposal. They use the powers of appointment and removal as far as they have them; they require reports from the various administrative officers concerning the work of their departments; they investigate the conduct of officers; they make use of whatever political influence they have in securing effective co-operation of officeholders; and the more skillful of them may use publicity as a means of forcing desired action on the part of officers over whom they have no definite control.

INCREASING THE POWERS OF DIRECTION. In a number of states that have reorganized their administrative system, the governor is placed in a position from which he can exercise a much more effective control.   Thus, in 1917, Illinois gathered together a tangled wilderness of some sixty state agencies and placed them in nine departments (later increased to thirteen), each headed by a director appointed by the governor and senate for a term of four years.   Assistant directors and bureau chiefs are appointed in like manner, but they work under the immediate supervision of the department heads. The governor directs administration through the thirteen heads of departments, and he may form a cabinet with them if he cares to do so.   About half the states—including New York, Pennsylvania, Virginia, and Washington—have followed in the main the Illinois plan.

2. Appointments

The excesses of democracy before the middle of the nineteenth century deprived the governor of practically all the power of appointment.   But the choice of administrative officers by popular election (or sometimes by legislative election) proved unsatisfactory in most cases, and in many instances notoriously corrupt.   Consequently, since about 1850, the governor has been recovering his appointing power, until in most states he now names the great majority of the principal administrative officers.

LIMITATIONS ON POWER OF APPOINTMENT.   It cannot be said, however, that the governor's appointing power is as large as it should be, or, relatively, as extensive as that of the President; for even in those states in which the governor's power has been recently increased, the secretary of state, the treasurer, the auditor, the attorney general, and perhaps others are commonly either elected by the people or chosen by the legislature.   Furthermore, many states have administrative officers whose terms overlap the term of the governor, and, in consequence, he has subordinates who are not of his appointment.   Again, in making appointments, the governor is often limited by statutes that prescribe the qualifications the appointees shall possess.

In the case of the appointment of important officials, the most common requirement is that the nomination shall be made by the governor and that confirmation shall be by the senate.   The governor must name the "right" men, or the senate will not confirm his appointments.   He must consult party leaders to learn who the right men are, and sometimes this consultation amounts to dictation by a leader or boss.   Even Theodore Roosevelt frankly confessed that as Governor of New York he had to consult Boss Platt with regard to his appointments or find them failing of confirmation in the senate. In other words, the appointing power is not infrequently in the hands of the man who stands behind the governor's chair rather than in those of the man who sits in it.   Sometimes, of course, the governor is himself the party leader in the state, in which case his appointments may be of an independent character, although that does not necessarily mean that they are any better than those an invisible leader might prompt him to make.

It seems that the more sordid type of politics is much more likely to enter into appointments by a governor than into those made by the President, for the state party organization is smaller and more unified than the national organization and therefore easier for small groups and bosses to control. In addition, the citizen is often more interested in what is taking place at Washington than he is in what his local rulers are doing, a deplorable fact which the powers that be in a state know how to use to their advantage. Conditions in respect to the choice of administrative officers in the state might be improved by vesting their appointment solely with the governor, for it is in connection with securing the confirmation of the senate that the governor often finds that he must bow to the sinister power of the boss and the machine.

3. Removals

It will be recalled that the President may remove from office any executive officer or employee of the United States. This power, like all others, is subject to abuse, but it is essential for good administration. Few governors have as complete freedom in the matter of removals as the President, who may make a removal for any cause; but in many states the governor may now remove not only those officers whom he appoints on his sole authority, but also, for proper cause, those whose appointment he shares with the senate.[5] This is one phase of the story of the modern tendency to make the governor chief executive in fact as well as in name. Rather extensive powers of removal are granted in Michigan, where the governor may remove elective state officials when the legislature is not in session, and any elective county official. In giving the governor the power to remove local officials, Michigan is joined by New York and a few other states, the power usually being limited, however, to law enforcement officers.

4. Pardons and Reprieves

The power to grant pardons and reprieves is held by the governor alone in some states; in others, a pardon may not be granted by the governor except upon the recommendation of a board of pardons; and in a third group of states, pardons are granted by a board of which the governor is simply a member. This power to grant pardons, reprieves, and paroles often places a heavy burden upon the governor, one that takes much of his time and (in those cases in which the death penalty has been imposed) subjects him to serious emotional strain.[6]

No doubt executive clemency has been exercised too freely or for the wrong motives in some cases, as when a governor of Arkansas liberated about three hundred prisoners to call to the attention of the public the evils of contracting prison labor. Perhaps clemency should be exercised with a leaning toward generosity, and few would argue that the ill health of a prisoner, youth, doubt of guilt, the recommendations of a trial judge (or jury), family need, good prison record, and similar factors should not constitute strong inducements for the extension of clemency. But the job is too much for a governor,

[5] W. B. Graves, *American State Government* (1953 ed.), p. 334.
[6] See Alfred E. Smith, *Up to Now, an Autobiography* (1929), pp. 306–308.

with his many other duties, to carry alone. He needs the help of a board, at least some members of which should have more than a passing knowledge of the problem.

5. Other Executive Powers and Duties

As the ceremonial head of the state, the governor is present at many important public gatherings, receives distinguished visitors, attends (a number of them do) the inauguration of the President, meets his fellow governors at conferences, and lends his name to numerous affairs and enterprises, public or private.   Acting more definitely in an official capacity, he formally accepts the service of legal papers issued against the state, sends to and receives from governors of other states requisitions for persons alleged to be fugitives from justice, takes care of communications between the state and the national government, and performs other duties of a similar character. He is invariably the commander-in-chief of the state militia, except when it is in the service of the United States, when it is under the command of the President. The governor is empowered to call out the militia to suppress riots or prevent serious disorders.   Formerly, the state's chief executive was usually an *ex officio* member of a large number of boards and commissions, and in many states he still has the duty of serving on a dozen or even a score of such agencies. His significant executive duties are such that even if he could devote his time exclusively to them he would have plenty to do. But he is called upon to discharge many purely routine and time-consuming functions hardly more than clerical in nature. Furthermore, he must travel, speak, shake hands, give interviews, and do many similar things to please the public and keep his political fences in repair. A good governor must be versatile, quick, healthy, and able to stand an eighty-hour week.

III. THE GOVERNOR'S LEGISLATIVE POWERS [7]

However far behind the President the governor may lag in executive and administrative powers, in most states he has authority in legislative matters that compares very favorably with that of the President, and in some states he has a distinct advantage over the President. Even before the executive hand was strengthened, as indicated in the last paragraph of subsection 1 above, the governor's lack of executive power failed to serve him as a defense against the people who had elected him and who wanted promises performed. Consequently, governors turned their efforts to legislation as the most promising field for achievement, and in this field a number of them won notable success. As the advantages of legislative leadership and power in the hands of the governor became apparent, more authority was vested in him, until now, even in those states that have bolstered up his administrative powers,

[7] Dodd, *op. cit.*, pp. 190–196 Holcombe, *op. cit.*, pp. 115–119, 352–370; Lipson, *op. cit.*, Chs. IV, IX; Mathews, *op. cit.*, pp. 289–302; Mathews and Berdahl, *Documents and Readings in American Government* (1940 ed.), Ch. XXII; F. W. Prescott, "The Executive Veto in American States," *Western Pol. Qt.*, III (1950), 97–111.

his opportunities in legislation are probably superior to those in administration.

1. General Legislative Powers

In every state the governor may call the legislature into special session, and in a few states he must do so when petitioned by a specified number of the legislators. In about half the states he has an advantage over the law-makers when they are in special session, in that they may not legislate upon matters other than those for which the session is called. A second legislative power of the governor is the authority to adjourn the two houses when they cannot agree upon a date for terminating their labors. This power is seldom used, because many states fix the length of legislative sessions by constitutional provision, and because in other states the houses are usually able to reach an agreement.

More important than the power either to call special sessions of the legislature or to fix the date for its adjournment, is the governor's authority and duty to send messages to it. Like the President's messages to Congress, the messages of the state's chief executive are sent regularly at the beginning of a session of the legislature and at such other times as may seem desirable. The governor follows the federal model, reporting on the condition of the state and recommending needed legislation.[8] On the average, his messages are as effective in securing desired legislative action as are the messages of the President—perhaps more so—for the state assembly is usually of short duration, its deliberations must be somewhat hurried, and the majority of its members are more likely to welcome than to resent the governor's efforts to help them.

2. The Veto

Without any question, one of the most material powers of the governor in relation to legislation is the veto power. North Carolina is the only state that has not authorized its use. When the legislature passes a bill, it is sent to the governor, who is allowed a few days, varying among the states from three to ten, in which to consider it. If he signs it, it becomes a law. If he allows the allotted days to pass without acting upon it, it still becomes a law. But if he vetoes the bill, it is returned to the legislature for further consideration. In some twenty states (see accompanying table on the Executive Veto) the veto may be overcome only by a two-thirds vote of the *total* membership of each house of the legislature, and in about a dozen states the veto may be overcome by a two-thirds vote of the members *present*. All other states, except Connecticut, require a vote larger than a simple majority of the members present to "override" the governor's veto.

Originally, the governors who had the veto power used it sparingly and chiefly as a means of preventing unconstitutional legislation, as did our early

---

[8] See "Governors' Messages—1953," *State Government*, March, 1953, and "Trends in State Government—1954: the Governors' Messages," *State Government*, March, 1954.

Presidents. Nowadays, it is used practically without let or hindrance for any reason a governor may have in mind. At times the veto amounts to a slaughter, but it is usually a slaughter of defectives. Professor F. W. Prescott gives us some interesting figures.[9] In 1947 the Governor of New York vetoed 329 of 1,245 measures (near the executive average in that state); California's Governor, 175 of 1,752; and governors of some other states also made high scores. Professor M. N. McGeary finds that between 1939 and 1945 the Governor of Pennsylvania vetoed 229 of 2,174 bills.[10] More important than the number of vetoes is the question of their effectiveness. Does the veto axe deal a death blow to a bill? Ordinarily it does. In 1947 the legislatures were able to override only about 2 per cent of the vetoes, and about one half of such overriding occurred in two states in which the executive and legislative branches were decidedly out of harmony.[11] In New York, Pennsylvania, and some other states the veto is almost never overridden. This relatively absolute veto is made possible by the high majorities required to override it and by the fact that most bills go to the governor when the legislature is about to adjourn.[12]

THE VETO FOLLOWING THE ADJOURNMENT OF THE LEGISLATURE. Most Americans have heard of the President's pocket veto and a few of them understand that it operates only on those measures left with the President at the time Congress adjourns; that nonaction by the President on such measures within ten days of their passage pocket vetoes them, kills them. In about a fourth of the states bills left with the governor at the time the legislature adjourns are killed by his failure to approve them, although in most of those states, the time given the governor to consider bills after adjournment is longer than the time allowed him during the period the legislature is in session. Thus, in New York, while the legislature is in session, the governor has ten days in which to exercise his veto power, and if he does not veto a bill during that time it becomes a law; but after the legislature has adjourned, the governor has thirty days in which to consider measures left for his decision. Bills not approved within the thirty-day period could be pocket vetoed, but New York governors usually accept the responsibility of registering vetoes on measures of which they disapprove. During the past twenty-five years more than 90 per cent of the New York vetoes have been exercised during the after-adjournment period.

A majority of the states do not permit the pocket veto. Their constitutions provide that, despite the adjournment of the legislature, a bill becomes a law unless vetoed by the governor. The greater number of these states give the

---

[9] *Op. cit.,* p. 102 (Prescott's table is reproduced on pages 106–107).

[10] M. N. McGeary, "The Governor's Veto in Pennsylvania," *Am. Pol. Sci. Rev.,* Oct., 1947, p. 941. The veto record of the governor of California for the legislative session of 1949 is as follows: Bills passed, 1603; bills vetoed during the session, 24 (none were overridden by the legislature); bills pocket vetoed, 86. In 1955 the Governor of New York vetoed 327 of 1,199 bills submitted by the legislature.

[11] Holcombe, *op. cit.,* p. 354; Prescott, *op. cit.,* p. 103.

[12] McGeary, *op. cit.,* pp. 944–945.

The Governors' Veto *

State	Days after Which Bill Becomes Law (before Adjournment) unless Vetoed (Sundays excepted)	Fate of Bill after Adjournment		Item Veto on Appropriation Bills	Votes Required in House and Senate to Pass Bills or Items over Veto(a)	Constitution Prohibits Governor from Vetoing	
		Days after Which Bill Passes unless Vetoed (Sundays excepted)	Days after Which Bill Dies unless Signed (Sundays excepted)			Initiated Measures	Referred Measures
Alabama	6	—	10	★	Majority elected	(b)	(b)
Arizona	5	10	—	★	Two-thirds elected(c)	★	★
Arkansas	5	20(d)	—	★	Majority elected	★	★
California	10	30(d)	30	★	Two-thirds elected	★	★
Colorado	10(d)	15(d)	—	★	Two-thirds elected	★	★
Connecticut	5(e)	—	30(d)	★	Majority present	(b)	(b)
Delaware	10	10(d)	—	★	Three-fifths elected	(b)	(b)
Florida	5	—	—	★	Two-thirds present	(b)	(b)
Georgia (f)	30	—	(g)	★	Two-thirds elected	(h)	—
Idaho	5	10	—	★	Two-thirds present	(b)	—
Illinois	10	10	—	★	Two-thirds elected	(b)	(b)
Indiana	3	5(d,i)	—	—	Majority elected	(b)	(b)
Iowa	3	(j)	30	—	Two-thirds elected	—	—
Kansas	3	(k)	—	★	Two-thirds elected	(b)	(b)
Kentucky	10	10(d)	—	★	Majority elected	—	—
Louisiana	10(d,l)	20(d)	—	★	Two-thirds elected	(b)	(b)
Maine	5	(m)	6(p)	—	Three-fifths elected	(b)	(b)
Maryland (o)	6	—	—	★	Two-thirds present	(n)	★
Massachusetts	5(e)	—	(q)	★	Two-thirds present	(b)	(b)
Michigan	10	—	5	★	Two-thirds elected	★	★
Minnesota	3	—	3	★	Two-thirds elected	★	★
Mississippi	5	(m)	—	★	Two-thirds elected	(b)	(b)
Missouri	(r)	—	15(d,s)	★	Two-thirds elected	(b)	(b)
Montana	5	—	—	★(t)	Two-thirds present	★	★
Nebraska	5	5	—	★	Three-fifths elected	★	★
Nevada	5	10	—	—	Two-thirds elected	★	★
New Hampshire	5	—	(g)	—	Two-thirds elected	(b)	(b)
New Jersey	10(u)	45	—	★	Two-thirds elected	(b)	(b)
New Mexico	3	—	6(s)	★	Two-thirds present	(h)	—
New York	10	—	30(d)	★	Two-thirds elected	(h)	—
North Carolina	(v)	(v)	(v)	(v)	....	(b)	(b)
North Dakota	3	15(d)	—	★	Two-thirds elected	★	★

State			★		Vote required to pass over veto		
Ohio	10	10		—	Three-fifths elected		
Oklahoma	5	—	★★	15	Two-thirds elected	★★	★★
Oregon	10(d)	20	★★(w)	—	Two-thirds present	(b)	(b)
Pennsylvania	10(d)	30(d)	★★	—	Two-thirds present	(b)	(b)
Rhode Island	6	10(d)		—	Three-fifths present	(b)	(b)
South Carolina	3	(m)	★★	—	Two-thirds elected	★	★
South Dakota	3	10(d)	†	(g)	Two-thirds elected		
Tennessee	5	20(j)	★★	—	Majority elected	(b)	(h)
Texas	10	10	★★	(g)	Two-thirds present	(b)	(b)
Utah	5	—		10	Two-thirds elected	(b)	(b)
Vermont	5	—	★★(y)	—	Two-thirds present	(b)	(b)
Virginia	5	5(d)		6(l)	Two-thirds present(x)	★	★
Washington	5	—	★★	—	Two-thirds elected	(b)	(b)
West Virginia	5(z)	15(d)		3	Majority elected	(b)	(b)
Wisconsin	6(l)	—	★★★★★★	30(g)	Two-thirds present	(b)	(b)
Wyoming	3	—	★★★★	10(p)	Two-thirds elected	(b)	(b)
Alaska	3	3		30	Two-thirds elected	(b)	(b)
Guam	10	30(g)		—	Two-thirds elected	(b)	(b)
Hawaii	10	10(p)			Two-thirds elected	(b)	(b)
Puerto Rico	10	30			Two-thirds elected		
Virgin Islands	—	—			Two-thirds elected		

* Reproduced by the courtesy of the Council of State Governments from *The Book of the States, 1954-55*, p. 103.

† Author's note: By a constitutional amendment of 1953 a bill becomes a law if not vetoed within 10 days. The governor is also authorized to veto or reduce items in appropriations bills. Note (g) is no longer valid.

(a) Bill returned to house of origin with objections, except in Georgia, where Governor need not state objections, and in Kansas, where all bills are returned to House.

(b) No provision for initiative or referendum in state.

(c) Three-fourths in case of an emergency measure.

(d) Sundays not excepted unless last day is Sunday.

(e) Sundays and legal holidays excepted.

(f) New constitution, passed by General Assembly, withholds right to veto constitutional amendments.

(g) Unsigned bills do not become laws after adjournment.

(h) No provision for initiative in state.

(i) Bill becomes law if not filed with objections with Secretary of State within five days after adjournment.

(j) Sundays not excepted.

(k) In practice, the legislature closes consideration of bills three days before adjournment *sine die*, where all bills are considered.

(l) Governor has 10 days (in Wisconsin 6 days) from time bill was presented to him in which to approve or disapprove.

(m) Bill passed in one session becomes law if not returned within 2 days (Maine and Mississippi 3) after reconvening.

(n) Constitution provides that Governor may veto initiated measures and if legislature sustains veto, measure is referred to vote of people at next general election.

(o) 1950 Constitutional amendment requires any bill vetoed after adjournment, or dying because of pocket veto after adjournment, to be returned to the legislature when it next convenes, for a vote on overriding the veto.

(p) Within 6 days (in Hawaii 10 days) after presentation to the Governor, regardless of how long after adjournment.

(q) Within 5 days of receipt by Governor. In practice General Court not prorogued until Governor has acted on all bills.

(r) If Governor does not return bill in 15 days, a joint resolution is necessary for bill to become law.

(s) Governor must file his objections with Secretary of State.

(t) Governor may not veto items in budget submitted by himself after it has passed legislature with three-fifths vote.

(u) If house of origin is in temporary adjournment on 10th day, becomes law on day house of origin reconvenes unless returned by Governor on that day. Governor has power of veto after repassage of bills in amended form with condition bill must be approved in 10 days or pocket veto.

(v) No veto; bill becomes law 30 days after adjournment of session unless otherwise expressly directed.

(w) Also may veto items in new bills declaring an emergency.

(x) Including majority elected.

(y) May veto items in any bill containing items or sections.

(z) Budget (appropriation) bill not submitted to Governor after passage.

governor more time to consider bills after the legislature has adjourned than while it is in session.   For example, in Pennsylvania, when the legislature is in session, the governor has ten days in which he may exercise his veto power, and, when the legislature has adjourned, he has thirty days.   The significant point is that, even after the legislature has adjourned, he must actually veto a measure or it becomes a law.   The governor is thus given a responsibility and a reasonable time in which to exercise it.

THE ITEM VETO.   Thirty-nine states now give the governor the authority to veto separate items of an appropriation bill, and in a number of states he may also reduce such items.   These powers, like the power to veto whole bills, are freely exercised.   The item veto, especially when the right to reduce items is combined with it, gives the governor a broad and very useful negative in regard to appropriations—a negative that legislators who for political reasons vote for extravagant appropriations often secretly hope he will exercise.[13] This particular type of veto serves also as a most effective instrument against the mounting of "riders" on appropriation bills.   Although nearly all the states feel that they have gone far enough with the item veto when the governor is empowered to strike out or reduce parts of an appropriation bill, Washington authorizes him to veto a part of any bill and Oregon to veto items in new bills declaring an emergency.

EXECUTIVE RECOMMENDATION OF AMENDMENTS.   Alabama, Virginia, Massachusetts, and New Jersey (since 1947) give the governor a choice of vetoing a bill or returning it to the legislature with proposed amendments. In the latter event the legislature accepts or rejects the governor's proposal by a simple majority.   In case of acceptance the amended bill goes back to the governor, who very naturally signs it.   If, on the other hand, the governor's amendments are rejected, then the original bill goes back to him for his approval or veto.   This plan of allowing the governor to suggest changes in a bill seems to make the occasions for the use of the veto much less frequent, and, to that extent at least, brings about a more harmonious relation between the executive and legislative branches of the state government.   The same sort of plan may be used and is being used unofficially in other states. Legislators in touch with the governor will let his views be known on projected bills; or the governor may publicly speak his mind; or the legislature may, upon the governor's request or upon its own motion, recall a bill it has sent to him.   Any one of these steps may lead to the incorporation of amendments that will make a bill acceptable to the chief executive.

THE VETO AS AN EFFECTIVE INSTRUMENT.   Few authorities will deny that the extension of the veto power has improved our state lawmaking systems. The power has been extensively, effectively, and, on the whole, wisely used. Governors have often prevented the enactment of defective or otherwise ob-

---

[13] R. H. Wells, "The Item Veto and State Budget Reform," *Am. Pol. Sci. Rev.,* XVIII (1924) 782–791.   But some authorities hold that the widespread adoption of budget procedures by the states has lessened the need for the item veto.   See Graves, *op. cit.,* pp. 338–339.

jectionable legislation, and perhaps even more frequently they have blocked excesses in appropriations.   Legislators themselves, unable to resist the pressure of powerful interests in their constituencies, not infrequently vote for an indefensible bill or item of appropriation and wait in confidence for the governor's veto.   Thus, the legislator may save his head with his constituency, while the governor, who serves the whole state, incurs the wrath of some of its citizens by beheading the legislator's measures.   Although it is unfair to the governor, of course, to pass such tasks to him, he can better afford to risk the hostility of voters in a particular locality than their delegate in the legislature can, for the governor's loss in one community may be made up by gains in another.

Formerly, long orations were made on the advantages of the bicameral legislative system, laying great stress upon the dogma that one house would kill the "bad" bills that emanated from the other.   All too often the other chamber has failed to serve as executioner.   It is the opinion of students of state government that in a number of states, including New York, the chief executive now "exerts a more powerful and beneficial check upon legislation adopted by both houses than either house does upon that adopted by the other." [14]   In those states in which he is given a few weeks' time to consider bills after the legislature has adjourned, he sits as a sort of third chamber. "He grants hearings to advocates and opponents of measures which have received legislative approval, refers legal and financial questions to his attorney general or other advisers, and in general does what he can to determine for himself whether the measures adopted by the legislature should be enacted." [15] It would be absurd to make the governor out a hero, defending, in every instance, the interests of the people against ignorant, careless, or corrupt legislators.   Governors, as well as members of the legislative branches, have sometimes failed in their trust.   Nevertheless, the governor and his advisers are ordinarily better qualified to pass upon bills than is the average legislator; and when we combine the governor's advantage with the fact that the eyes of the whole state are upon him, we have reason to expect that the affairs of the whole people will be better served by the governor than by individual legislators.

3. The Governor and the Budget

We consider the subject of state finance in a later chapter; but we must record here that the governor's part in relation to state revenues and appropriations has greatly increased in many states during the past thirty or forty years.   We noted above the governor's negative and older power over appropriations through the item veto.   A number of states now authorize or require him to initiate the budget, that is, the state's financial program for the ensuing

[14] From Holcombe, *op. cit.,* p. 356.   By permission of the Macmillan Company, publishers.   Professor Holcombe's statement is equally applicable twenty years later.   See Prescott, *op. cit.,* and S. R. Solomon, "The Governor as Legislator," *Nat. Mun. Rev.,* Nov., 1951, pp. 515–520.

[15] From Holcombe, *op. cit.,* p. 355.

fiscal period.   The essence of the plan is that the governor, or officers responsible to him, collect information concerning the financial needs of the various government agencies and institutions of the state, decide how much should be appropriated for each, make an estimate of revenues to balance these appropriations, and submit the whole program to the legislature.   The governor, who is actively working for the state all the time, who is in constant contact with its problems, and who bears the brunt of the responsibility for efficiency and economy, is the logical official to prepare the budget.   The legislature may disregard his recommendations, but it at least has a financial program upon which to work; and if the program has public approval, the legislature will not lightly pass it by.

4. The Governor's Leadership in Legislation

In considering the powers of the governor we must look beyond the constitutions and statutes.   As the highest officeholder in the state, the governor is quite likely to be a man of considerable influence in his party, and there are many examples of governors who have dominated the party organization. Sometimes the members of his party who are in the legislature are glad to follow him; at other times they may follow him reluctantly under the dictates of political wisdom.

More than forty years ago Governor Woodrow Wilson went before the Democrats in the New Jersey legislature and said: "I have been elected Governor of New Jersey by the people of New Jersey, selected by the convention of the Democratic party, and I thereby have become the responsible leader of the Democratic party in the State.   I will be held responsible by the people at the polls. . . .   Each of you gentlemen will be held responsible in the districts where you were elected.   I am held responsible as well as you by the same people.   I am the only person in the whole State, however, to express approval or disapproval on behalf of all the people, and I will express that approval or disapproval by determining what we should do." [16]   There was no denying this logic, and when Wilson immediately followed it by presenting a program (a thing that seldom emanates from a legislative group), the Democratic lawmakers adopted it unanimously.

The governor is probably more of a chief legislator now than he was in Wilson's time.   Nor can it be said that improvements in administrative organization in a number of states have caused him to give more thought to executive and administrative functions and less to legislative matters.   On the contrary, it might be demonstrated that strengthened executive leadership contributes to stronger legislative leadership.   Administrative reorganization has enabled the governor to get a better over-all view of the needs of the state, has provided him with agencies to help prepare his program, and in other ways improved his position for legislative leadership. [17]   But whether a state

[16] Quoted in F. A. Ogg and P. O. Ray, *Introduction to American Government* (1945 ed.), p. 794 n, from David Lawrence in the Springfield *Republican,* Feb. 29, 1924.
[17] See Lipson, *op. cit.,* pp. 206 ff.

has strong or weak administrative organization, the governor has come to be the authority to whom the people look for action, whether administrative or legislative, and nothing so clearly indicates the significance of his rôle in legislation than the fact that in any passable gubernatorial campaign the candidates give practically all their attention to issues, to questions of policy, to a program to be presented to the legislature. There is every evidence that the voters want it that way. Writing of developments in New York, but in language that is applicable to many states, Professor Samuel R. Solomon submits the following:

. . . The governor has emerged as chief legislator because of the acclimatization of the electorate to the belief that the democratic tradition of representative government is best upheld when chief reliance is placed in the governor rather than in the legislature.[18]

IV. OTHER STATE EXECUTIVE AND ADMINISTRATIVE OFFICERS [19]

Every state has a score or more of executive officers to whom, excepting the lieutenant governor, we give the general designation of department heads. Some of these offices have a long history, dating from colonial times, but most of them are relatively new, having been established since the Civil War or even since 1930. Nearly all of the old historic offices are constitutional and elective, and they include the few traditional functions deemed appropriate (and still important) for state government a century or more ago.

Lieutenant Governor

About three fourths of the states have a lieutenant governor, who, as we said earlier, succeeds to the governorship in case of the resignation, death, or impeachment of the governor, and in a number of states exercises the functions of governor during the temporary absence of that official from the state. Except in Massachusetts he presides over the senate. Many students of government consider the office of lieutenant governor unnecessary. Obviously, the senate would not object to choosing its own presiding officer; and it is more desirable to have as the governor's successor the secretary of state, or some other officer who is more closely associated with the government of the state.[20]

The Historic Department Heads

SECRETARY OF STATE. Each of the states has a secretary of state. A few of his duties are prescribed by the constitution, but most of them are imposed by legislative acts. He may keep the records of the state, supervise

[18] "The Governor as Legislator," *Nat. Mun. Rev.*, Nov., 1951, p. 520.

[19] Dodd, *op. cit.*, pp. 225–231; Graves, *op. cit.*, pp. 363–369; A. F. Macdonald, *American State Government and Administration* (1955 ed.), pp. 227–234.

[20] See W. R. Isom, "The Office of Lieutenant Governor in the States," *Am. Pol. Sci. Rev.*, XXXII, (Oct., 1938), 921, and Robert B. Crosby (Lieutenant Governor of Nebraska), "Why I Want to Get Rid of My Job," *State Government*, July, 1947, p. 193.

elections, issue certificates of incorporation and motor vehicle licenses, and perform other administrative work of a similar character. His duties are numerous and often unrelated.

ATTORNEY GENERAL. Another essential officer is the attorney general, no state being without one. Like the secretary of state, his duties are mainly prescribed by statute. It is his duty to give legal advice to the governor and other administrative officers and agencies when requested to do so, to appear in court in all cases in which the state has an interest, and to institute proceedings against violators of state law where the general public is adversely affected. In a few states he has some authority to direct the work of the prosecuting attorneys in the counties.

SUPERINTENDENT OF PUBLIC INSTRUCTION. Either the constitution or a statute provides for a superintendent of public instruction in each state. In most states his legal powers are not very comprehensive. In general, he has some authority to supervise the administration of schools in counties and other local districts, to apportion school funds among such districts, and to make various investigations. Regardless of his legal powers a high-class superintendent will have a major influence in shaping the state's educational policy.

TREASURER. A treasurer in every state receives the revenues and makes disbursements. He has little discretion beyond the authority to choose the banks in which the state funds shall be deposited, and often even this discretionary power is limited.

AUDITOR. The acts of the treasurer are checked by an auditor or comptroller, who is a more important financial officer than the treasurer. The auditor's chief duty is to see that the funds are being lawfully expended. A number of states have given the auditor the authority to require uniform methods of accounting in the administrative departments, and in some states he may exercise supervision over the accounts of local government agencies.

The Modern Departments

As the functions of state government increased over the years it was found necessary to add new administrative agencies. At first the tendency was to establish boards or commissions rather than single-headed executive departments; but eventually the advantages of the latter type of organization came to be recognized and the practice of setting up a department headed by one individual became wide-spread. More will be said about this subject in the chapter on state administration, but we may say here that in such reorganized states as Missouri, New Jersey, and New York nearly all of the essential functions of modern government are conducted by departments, headed by single executives who are appointed by and responsible to the governor. Among such departments are those of revenue, agriculture, highways, labor, health, public welfare, and conservation, departments that have been made necessary by both the expansion of old functions and the addition of new functions.

The Executive Cabinet: Its Retarded Development

In a few states the governor has a council, a survivor from colonial times. It is elective in New Hampshire and Massachusetts, appointive in Maine, and it is composed of *ex officio* members in North Carolina. In the three New England states the council has varied duties in connection with state finances and state institutions and its concurrence is required for certain of the governor's appointments. In North Carolina its duties are purely advisory.

A cabinet in the states in any sense analogous to that of the President was, of course, impossible in the days of elective department heads, boards, and commissions. On the other hand, it might be expected to come into successful operation in those states that have reorganized administration and have constituted departments with appointive heads responsible to the governor. Under the newer administrative set-up some governors did indeed hold cabinet meetings, but, in general, the idea did not take root. There is now, in all probability, less use made of state cabinets than there was twenty years ago. Professor Leslie Lipson suggests that there may have been less actual need for cabinet discussion after the new administrative system became a going concern; and he also notes that temperamental difficulties prevented some governors from making the best use of a cabinet, and he calls attention to the fact that a number of department heads are specialists, experts, whose contribution to the discussion of general policy would be of little value.[21]

V. THE GOVERNOR'S POWER IN THE MODEL CONSTITUTION

For more than a score of years, the National Municipal League has had a Committee on State Government, which from time to time has published a *Model State Constitution*.[22] It is worth our while to notice briefly what the latest edition (1948) of this "Constitution" proposes on the executive department. It would make the governor the chief executive in fact as well as in name, and would establish closer and more formal relations between him and the legislature in such ways as to strengthen his leadership as a law-maker. The Model draft states that "the executive power of the state shall be vested in a governor," and it then proceeds to relegate to the scrap heap of "Model T" political institutions the independent executive departments with which we have too long been familiar. The Model authorizes the governor to appoint an administrative manager, to serve at the governor's pleasure, and to perform such duties as the chief executive might delegate to him. Administrative departments, not exceeding twenty, may be created by act of the legislature. Heads of departments are to be appointed and removed by the governor.

The governor, the administrative manager, and the heads of departments may sit in the legislature, introduce bills, and participate in the discussion of measures, but they are given no vote. The governor is authorized to order

[21] *Op. cit.,* pp. 166 ff.
[22] The Fifth Edition, published in 1948, is printed in the Appendix of this volume.

a referendum on any bill that fails to pass the legislature; and that body may, by majority vote, order a referendum on any measure vetoed by the governor and failing to receive the two-thirds majority in the legislature necessary to override such veto. The experts' plan gives the governor wide powers over state finance. He is required to prepare and submit to the legislature the budget, together with revenue and appropriation bills. And he is authorized to veto separate items of appropriation bills or to reduce such items. These provisions are included in the Model plan after years of careful consideration, and they have probably had considerable influence in a number of the states, particularly in respect to administrative organization.

Reading List

H. A. Barth, *Financial Control in the States, with Emphasis on Control by the Governor* (1923).

G. C. S. Benson and E. H. Litchfield, *The State Administration Record in Michigan* (1938).

F. L. Bird and F. M. Ryan, *The Recall of Public Officials in California* (1930).

Book of the States, 1954–55.

A. W. Bromage, *State Government and Administration in the United States* (1936), Ch. VIII.

F. G. Crawford, *State Government* (1931), Chs. IX–X.

W. F. Dodd, *State Government* (1928 ed.), pp. 190–196, and Ch. VIII.

J. A. Fairlie, "The State Governor," *Mich. Law Rev.,* X (1912), 370–383, 458–475.

J. H. Finley and J. F. Sanderson, *The American Executive and Executive Methods* (1907), Chs. V–XIV.

J. A. Friedman, *The Impeachment of Governor William Sulzer* (1939).

H. F. Gosnell, *Boss Platt and His New York Machine* (1924), Chs. VI–VIII.

Governors' Conferences, *Proceedings* (Annual since 1909).

W. B. Graves, *American State Government* (1953 ed.), Ch. 9.

A. N. Holcombe, *State Government in the United States* (1931), Ch. XI.

C. Jensen, *The Pardoning Power in the American States* (1922).

R. M. LaFollette, *A Personal Narrative of Political Experience* (1913).

Leslie Lipson, *The American Governor: From Figurehead to Leader* (1939).

A. F. Macdonald, *American State Government and Administration* (1955 ed.), Ch. X.

J. M. Mathews, *American State Government* (1934 ed.), Ch. XII.

——— and C. A. Berdahl, *Documents and Readings in American Government* (1940 ed.), Ch. XXII.

George H. Mayer, *The Political Career of Floyd B. Olson* (1951).

National Municipal League, *Model State Constitution* (1948 ed.).

Theodore Roosevelt, *An Autobiography* (1913), Ch. VIII.

Homer E. Scace, *The Organization of the Executive Office of the Governor* (Institute of Public Administration, New York, 1950).

P. S. Sikes and J. E. Stoner, *Bates and Field's State Government* (1954 ed.), Ch. 11.

Alfred E. Smith, *Up to Now, an Autobiography* (1929).

———, *The Citizen and His Government* (1935).

W. C. Williams, *Sweet of Colorado* (1943).

Questions and Problems

1. What are the provisions in the constitution of your state concerning the qualifications, term, and tenure of the governor? Which of these provisions do you regard as unnecessary?

2. Show the difference in purpose and in operation between impeachment and the recall.

3. What powers as a supervisor of administration has the governor of your state?

4. What additional powers, if any, does the governor of your state need to enable him to be the chief executive in fact as well as in name?

5. How are pardons granted in your state? Is there any abuse of the power?

6. Does your governor have the item veto? The pocket veto? Look up his veto record for a recent session of the legislature.

7. What responsibilities has your governor in relation to the preparation of the budget?

8. To what extent is your governor a leader in legislation? Give specific examples of this leadership.

9. What executive officers in addition to the governor are elected in your state? Outline their duties.

10. How nearly does the distribution of executive power in your state conform to that recommended in the Model State Constitution?

CHAPTER | 5

STATE LEGISLATURES
AND THE LEGISLATIVE PROCESS

The preceding chapter on the State Executive System contains incidental reference to the legislature in the discussion of the governor's relations with it. Here the purpose is to proceed from this oblique approach to a direct consideration of the legislature. In a number of states the Initiative and Referendum are firmly established as supplements to the legislature, a fact which requires that these twin instruments of democracy also be given more than passing mention in this chapter.

The legislature is the organ of government that, within constitutional limits, must make the decisions on what the state shall do and on where the money is to come from. The governor recommends and advises, and he may use the veto as a brake; pressure groups of every shade and description may play upon the legislature in a thousand ways; but the responsibility, the decision, is with the legislature. Its position is basic and fundamental in democratic government. And in consequence its structure, organization, procedure, powers, and limitations demand careful study.

I. LEGISLATIVE STRUCTURE, SESSIONS, AND PERSONNEL [1]

The Bicameral System

POPULAR ACCEPTANCE. Nebraska is the only state without a bicameral legislature. If an individual who is not a student of politics thinks of bicameralism at all, he thinks of it about as he does of a law of nature. It simply must be so. If one asks why there must be two chambers, the typical citizen probably regards him with mingled contempt and suspicion, and then speaks

[1] *The Book of the States, 1954–55,* pp. 95–154; W. B. Graves, *American State Government* (1953 ed.), pp. 187–223; Graves (ed.), "Our State Legislators," *Annals of the Am. Acad. of Pol. and Soc. Sci.,* Vol. 195 (Jan., 1938); A. N. Holcombe, *State Government in the United States* (1931 ed.), pp. 282–291; A. F. Macdonald, *American State Government and Administration* (1955 ed.), Ch. 8; P. S. Sikes and J. E. Stoner, *Bates* (1948), Ch. VIII; Belle Zeller (ed.), *American State Legislatures:* Report of the Committee on American Legislatures, Am. Pol. Sci. Assn. (1954), Chs. 2–6. The last-named work is most useful.

with that strong emphasis which comes from assurance: "Why, one house serves as a check upon the other. Either house might hastily pass some villainous bill; the other house will probably give the measure more consideration, defeat it, and that will be one more bad law that we won't have to bother with." If the inquirer is not made ashamed of his "ignorance" by this reply he might ask: "Why, then, should we not have three houses, or four? Certainly we have plenty of bad laws passed by the two houses. Maybe four houses, with all the checks they would provide, would succeed in checking out practically all the unwise bills." At this point the "informer" might become a bit irritated and say that every fool knows that there should be two houses, and just two; that they probably check each other as much as is desirable; that, in any case, the men who wrote the state constitution knew what they were doing when they gave the legislature an "upper" and a "lower" house, following the plan adopted by the Philadelphia Convention for Congress. At the mention of the fact that the states have the legislative system which the enlightened patriots in 1787 deemed sufficient for the needs of the national government, the inquirer is probably silenced. We, however, have the duty of pushing the inquiry a little farther.

REASONS FOR ITS ADOPTION. The student knows, of course, that most of the colonies employed the bicameral legislative system, patterned after the two Houses, Lords and Commons, of the British Parliament. Following the British and colonial models, nearly all the state governments organized during the Revolution adopted the dual plan. In some of the states the rank and file of citizens elected the members of the lower house, and the propertied classes elected the upper house. This distinction was never made in other states, and the states that adopted the plan soon gave it up and allowed the same electors to choose members of both branches of the legislature. Not only that, but, with a few exceptions, population came to be accepted as the basis of representation in the upper as well as in the lower house. There was, then, no essential difference between the two houses; and the main excuse for the two was that one would check the other, or, to put it affirmatively, that bills would be more carefully considered by two houses than by one.

The framers of the federal Constitution prescribed the bicameral system for the national government not only because past practice in Great Britain and America stamped it with approval, but also because it made possible the great compromise on representation—representation in the House of Representatives according to population, and in the Senate an equal representation of the states. The states were strongly influenced by the federal system, and those that started with the unicameral type of legislature abandoned it for the bicameral plan.[2] With only one dissenter, the states continue with the dual type of legislature. Yet it has been discovered in recent years that ideas can be changed rather quickly, and other states may try the Nebraska experiment.

---

[2] Georgia (1789), Pennsylvania (1790), and Vermont (1836). See D. B. Carroll, *The Unicameral Legislature of Vermont* (1933), and I. A. Watts, "Why Pennsylvania Abandoned Unicameralism," *State Government,* March, 1936, pp. 54–55.

Do the houses check each other?   Some studies [3] have been made of the of bills passed by one house are killed in the other; but the killing is usually working of the bicameral principle, and these do not show that the two houses effectively check each other, except perhaps in a few states.   True, a number indiscriminate.   True, also, one house amends many bills originating in the other; but, here again, the amending may be good, bad, or indifferent.   Consideration by two houses often means only two hasty considerations, or simply a hasty consideration in the house in which a bill originates and the acceptance of its conclusions by the second house without any consideration.

It is further charged that the bicameral plan enables party leaders or the "organizations" to control legislatures in an irresponsible manner.   Here is an example.   The public seems to want enacted a law that the leaders secretly oppose.   The leaders have a different bill introduced and passed in each house.   Then a conference committee, under the control of the leaders, of course, goes through the form of attempting to agree upon a measure acceptable to both houses.   By previous arrangement the conference committee fails to agree, and no law is enacted.   Nevertheless, by this subterfuge, both houses go on record as approving a measure that the leaders deftly beheaded.[4] It would seem, then, that the bicameral system not only frequently fails to insure adequate consideration of bills and to accomplish the defeat of unwise ones, but also that it may be used as a means of dodging responsibility.[5]

More effective checks.   After all, whether or not the houses check each other is not a very material point, for legislation is checked by a number of other means that we deem quite sufficient.   The committees of each house, although far from perfect, do a great deal to improve the quality of legislation by their preliminary studies of the bills introduced.   The governor's veto, discussed in the preceding chapter, often proves to be an effective guaranty against faulty legislation.   Then, we must not forget the courts with their power to nullify unconstitutional acts.   In particular, we must remember that the federal courts will void state laws that violate such important provisions of the federal Constitution as the clause that prohibits the states from passing laws depriving any person of life, liberty, or property without due process of law, and the clause that prohibits the states from impairing the obligation of contracts.   Considering that legislatures are held in check by these agencies, it hardly seems desirable that the bicameral check, usually fictional, seldom a positive good, and on occasion mischievous, should be retained.

[3] D. L. Colvin, *Bicameral Principle in the New York Legislature* (1913); Mona Fletcher, *A Decade of Bicameralism in Ohio with Special Reference to the 1930's* (Abstract of Doctoral Dissertations, No. 59, Ohio State University Press, 1950); Thelma I. Griswold, *Bicameralism in Ohio* (1937); Dorothy Schaffter, *The Bicameral System in Practice* (1929).

[4] Holcombe, *op. cit.,* p. 307.

[5] The typical member of the legislature usually stresses the value of the "checks" under the bicameral system, but several members have frankly told the writer that they need "that protection"—the privilege of dodging responsibility.

The Case for a Unicameral Legislature

With the foregoing considerations in mind it is not surprising that many students of government advocate a unicameral system for the states.[6] They argue that this system will expedite the business of the legislature; prevent the leaders from dodging responsibility; and, by reducing the number of legislators, enable states to pay adequate salaries to those remaining. They point out, further, that the single chamber has given satisfactory results in several Canadian provinces, in Swiss cantons, and in other countries. Advocates of the single chamber make a strong argument for it when they show that the cities have long since abandoned the bicameral council in favor of the single-chamber council.

THE NEBRASKA EXPERIMENT. A generation ago attempts were made in several states to secure the adoption of the unicameral plan. Constitutional amendments were submitted in Oregon (1912 and 1914), Oklahoma (1914), and Arizona (1916); but they were defeated in each case. In 1913 Governor Hodges of Kansas proposed a single chamber, to be composed of less than a score of members, who should be experts in legislation and give their full time to affairs of state. His novel and interesting proposal was not submitted to the voters.[7]

Despite the fact that ten states gave thought to the unicameral idea between 1910 and 1934, Nebraska is the only state that adopted it. The proposal was brought forward in that commonwealth from time to time for twenty years and there is little doubt that it would have remained in the proposal state for another twenty years had not Nebraska's elder statesman, the late Senator George W. Norris, in 1933 and 1934, actively sponsored the unicameral plan. Opposed by practically every newspaper of the state as "radical," "revolutionary," and "dangerous," the constitutional amendment was adopted by the voters in November, 1934.[8] The amendment provides for a chamber of not less than thirty, nor more than fifty members, and the legislature fixed the number at forty-three, to be chosen on a nonpartisan ballot. The plan went into operation with the legislative session of 1937. Competent observers are well pleased with the results, and the citizens of Nebraska now appear to take their unicameral legislature for granted. In its representative character, in its procedures, and in its output, it is deemed to be superior to a majority of the legislatures of other states. The Committee on American Legislatures of the American Political Science Association commends it, and sees no valid reasons against other states following the Nebraska example.[9]

---

[6] See, *Model State Constitution,* Art. III, in Appendix; Zeller, *op. cit.,* Ch. 4.

[7] Carrol, *op. cit.,* pp. 4 ff.

[8] J. P. Senning, in his *The Unicameral Legislature* (1937) gives an account of the movement for it.

[9] Zeller, *op. cit.,* pp. 52–59 and Appendix A. See also R. C. Spencer, "Nebraska Idea 15 Years Old," *Nat. Mun. Rev.,* XXX (1950), 511, and R. V. Shumate, "The Nebraska Unicameral Legislature," *Western Pol. Qt.,* 5 (1952), 504.

But the bicameral tradition is strong, as already indicated, and party men outside Nebraska generally regard unicameralism with disfavor.

The Size of the Chambers

The number of state senators and representatives is rather rigidly fixed by the constitutions in some states, but in the greater number of states the constitutions simply impose general limitations and leave the legislatures to determine the exact number. Senates vary in size from 17 in Delaware and Nevada to 67 in Minnesota, with less than half the states having as many as 40. The lower houses are considerably larger than the senates, varying in size from 35 in Delaware to 400 in New Hampshire, but the number is usually somewhere between 100 and 150. Nearly all the large lower houses are in the New England states, because the system of town representation, still in use there, necessitates a large number of representatives. It is generally agreed among authorities that the size of both the senate and the house is, in most states, larger than necessary.

The Basis of Apportionment

For purposes of representation the typical state is divided into two sets of districts—one set for members of the lower house, and the other for the upper house. The counties serve as convenient units for representation in the lower house in most of the states, except in New England, where the town is the unit. Counties usually have representatives in proportion to their population,[10] but the general rule is that a county shall have at least one representative. Except in Maine and Massachusetts, the New England system of town representation pays scant attention to population, particularly in Vermont and Connecticut, the former state giving every town, regardless of size, one, and only one, representative, the latter allowing large towns a maximum of two representatives. Apportionment in the senate is usually on the basis of the population of the counties, although some of the New England states use the town as the unit, practically disregarding the difference in population. Small or sparsely settled counties may be combined to form a senate district, and densely populated counties may be divided into several districts. A few states make use of the same districts for senators and representatives.

DISCRIMINATION AGAINST URBAN AREAS. Inequalities in representation, sometimes amounting to gross discriminations, occur in those states that have large urban populations. In more than a majority of the states the constitutions favor the rural areas in the apportionment of seats for one house or the other. Furthermore, legislatures, dominated by representatives from rural areas, often fail to carry out the clear constitutional mandate to reapportion seats. The Illinois legislature, which at this writing has made no reapportionment since 1901, is only one of the worst examples of such neglect

---

[10] In some states representation is determined by citizen population and in Massachusetts and Tennessee apportionment is based upon the number of legal voters. Zeller, *op. cit.*, pp. 32–33.

of duty.[11]   About half the state legislatures have similarly failed to discharge this particular obligation.

Although the courts may grant relief in cases in which a legislative apportionment violates such a constitutional requirement as that "districts shall be equal," they hold that the decision to make an apportionment is political and that the courts cannot control a legislature in such matters.   In a few states reapportionment is more or less automatic, is handled by an authority outside the legislature, and in Arizona and perhaps two or three other states it seems to have achieved satisfactory results.   Automatic reapportionment is recommended by the Committee on American Legislatures of the American Political Science Association.[12]

In the meantime the inequalities continue, either as a result of constitutional provisions or of the failure of legislatures to act in compliance with them. As of 1948, the United States Conference of Mayors listed such inequalities in twenty states, a few of which are here submitted.   In Colorado, Denver County had 21,500 population per representative and Basa County 6,207. Hartford and Colebrook, Connecticut, each had two representatives, the former with a population of 166,000 and the latter with a population of 547; the population of St. Louis County was 816,000 and that of eighteen other counties 158,000, but the city and county-group each had the same number of representatives.   In Wisconsin, urban assembly districts averaged 67,446 population and rural districts 15,827.   New Jersey presents a very special case.   Although urban counties containing about 80 per cent of the state's population had only eight senators and rural counties with the other 20 per cent of the population had thirteen senators, the delegates to the constitutional convention of 1947 had to take a pledge not to propose legislative reapportionment.[13]

Reasons for discrimination.   Originally, the states were predominantly rural and equal numbers of representatives from counties or towns, resulted in few gross disproportions.   With the growth of cities, however, "equal" representation produced the inequalities noted above.   In most states concessions were made to the urban areas by increasing their number of lawmakers, but the increase was seldom in proportion to population.   Delegates in legislatures and constitutional conventions, regarding cities as full of irresponsible nonproperty owners, foreigners, and radicals, or even as cesspools of iniquity, and likely to disturb the political and social order if given the power to do so, used their original advantage of numbers and voted against making fair concessions to the urban dwellers.   A statesman so broad of

---

[11] In 1954 the people adopted a constitutional amendment directing the legislature to make a reapportionment giving Cook County 24 senatorial districts and downstate 34, and Cook County 30 representative districts and downstate 29, area being the prime consideration in forming the senate districts and equal population the house districts.

[12] Zeller, *op. cit.*, p. 46.

[13] See table in Graves, *American State Government*, p. 203.   See also David O. Walter, "Reapportionment and Urban Representation," *Annals of the Am. Acad. of Pol. and Soc. Sci.*, 195 (Jan., 1938), 11.

mind as Jefferson had the gravest misgivings when he contemplated the untoward political and social damages that might be wrought by urban electorates. Discrimination continues not only because many "good" people see it as a means of curbing excesses for which large representations from cities might be responsible, but also because it is to the economic and political advantage of those who have control under the present system to continue it.

Some results of discrimination. Rural populations and their representatives, despite certain populistic tendencies, are essentially conservative on the great problems of the day; certainly more so than city people. Legislative apportionment favoring rural areas thus means that conservatism has more than its share of representation in the legislature. Whether or not this is a "good thing" depends upon one's point of view; but it is suggested that we assume a great deal when we say that a farmer and his hired man (two voters) are entitled to a voice in government equal to that of a banker, a clerk, and a factory laborer (three voters).

Another consequence of this discrimination is that a number of states may find themselves with Republican legislatures and Democratic governors, the reason being that over-represented rural districts (outside of the South) are predominantly Republican, whereas the under-represented cities are more often Democratic. It is true that legislatures and governors of opposite political parties have, on occasion, established working relationships, but if they are of the same political persuasion "the going" is usually smoother. Still another point of significance should be mentioned. It is unfortunate that rural members of a legislature who understand nothing of the problems of municipal transportation, police, and similar complicated subjects have such a large voice in determining what shall be done about them. And it is as ridiculous as unfortunate that rural legislators should decree that there shall be no sports on Sunday, no Sunday movies, or lay down similar prohibitions designed to regulate the habits and morals of urban dwellers.[14]

Do Legislatures Represent?

It is often said that, broadly speaking, legislatures are fairly representative of the larger economic and social groups. Although few of the lawmakers carry union cards or have other direct affiliations with labor, it is stated that other voices are frequently raised on behalf of labor. There is no doubt that business and agriculture are directly and well represented in the legislature; it is certain that labor, both industrial and agricultural, and some other economic and professional groups are not directly represented in proportion to their numbers in the population, and it is debatable whether they are adequately represented by legislators who have their life among other interests and organizations. In any event, it may be argued that legislatures as now constituted are not truly representative of the many interests of the whole

[14] On the shortcomings of rural legislators in respect to city problems, see Richard L. Neuberger, "The Country Slicker vs. the City Yokel," *The New York Times Magazine*, July 31, 1949, p. 17.

population of a state.   This deficiency in representation is explained in part by the fact that legislators are commonly chosen by single-member districts. It is, of course, impossible for more than one to be chosen from such a district, and this means that those of the minority party, even though they may number just a few less than the majority, go unrepresented as far as that particular district is concerned.   Where there are three parties in a district, it is possible for a candidate to win who has only thirty-four per cent of the votes, thus leaving sixty-six per cent of the voters unrepresented.

PROPORTIONAL REPRESENTATION.   In order to give the parties fair quotas of the representatives, plans of proportional representation have been proposed.   In one form or another, "P.R." is now employed in a number of European countries and in a few American cities.   Without going into technicalities,[15] we will simply say here that, if applied to the election of members of the lower house of a state legislature, it would mean that our single-member districts would give way to large districts, each sending some half a dozen members to the lower house.   The votes would be cast and counted in such a way that parties or groups which cast one third of the votes in the district would elect one third of the representatives, and other parties or groups would in like manner receive their fair proportion of the representatives.   Of course, it would never give the parties representation in strict mathematical proportion to their voting strength, but proportions would be approximately fair— much fairer than under our present system.

Objection to P.R.   Nevertheless, the principle of proportional representation does not meet with any particular enthusiasm in this country.   It is argued that, by giving smaller third parties an opportunity to elect their candidates to office, our two-party system, in which we take so much pride and in which we place so much reliance, will be disrupted.   With this development, it is feared that frequently no party would have a majority in the lawmaking body, and that we would have to resort to a "bloc" system of government, the working of which in Continental European countries has not favorably impressed us.   It is said further that, as between the two major parties, the present system works out with reasonable fairness in the long run; that disproportions favoring a party in one district are equalized by disproportions favoring the other party in another district.   This comforting conclusion, however, is not warranted.   A party with a majority will almost invariably win more than its fair quota of seats under the present arrangement.   Although admitting this to be true, the advocate of party government will nevertheless say that the majority party needs this extra "unearned" majority in order to carry out its program.   Even though we concede that there are certain very clear, if somewhat theoretical, advantages on the side of proportional representation, the exigencies of practical politics relegate it to the background.

[15] There are a number of books and articles that fully set forth the details.   C. G. Hoag and G. H. Hallett, Jr., *Proportional Representation* (1926), covers the field thoroughly. Articles and items on P.R. appear regularly in the *National Municipal Review* (monthly).

Terms, Qualifications, Compensation, and Immunities of Legislators

Thirty-two states fix the terms of senators at four years; other states at two years. In the lower house the term is two years in forty-three states, and four years in four states. Nebraska elects her single chamber biennially. The terms may be too short, but the voters generally turn down any proposal that they be lengthened.[16]

Senators and representatives must meet the state constitutional requirements of citizenship in the United States, residence in the districts they represent, and age. These requirements are of no particular importance, for, regardless of whether or not they are fixed by a constitution, few candidates could hope to be elected who lacked such qualifications.

Compensation of state lawmakers is low. The amount is fixed in many state constitutions, and until recently, it was found difficult to secure the approval of amendments granting increases or granting the legislature the authority to make highly desirable adjustments. It is probably much better to leave the matter of compensation to the legislature itself, but in some states where an increase has been authorized, the rate is still rigidly fixed by constitutional amendment.[17] Formerly, the prevailing practice was to pay legislators a per diem for attendance at sessions. More than a majority of the states now pay salaries, but only New York, Illinois, and four or five other states make them reasonably adequate. It is doubtful if the average compensation amounts to more than $25 per day for the legislative session. Some fourteen states, following the example set by Congress in 1946, now provide retirement benefits for legislators, usually by including them in a general retirement plan for elected officials.

Just as congressmen do, state senators and representatives enjoy immunity from arrest while in attendance at sessions and in going to or coming from the same, except in case of treason, felony, or breach of the peace. Again, as with their national prototypes, they are accorded freedom of speech and debate in their respective houses.

Personnel of Legislatures

The composition of the typical state legislature (see table) bears a strong similarity to the personnel of Congress. Many lawyers are present, often relatively young lawyers who experience no particular difficulty in getting away from their few clients for the session and who lose no large volume of income in so doing. In fact, experience in the legislature may improve the professional status of the young attorneys and bring them more clients and larger fees. Next to the lawyers, the farmers, many of them well along in life, have the largest delegations. Then there are merchants, insurance men, bankers, and other businessmen—enough in these combined callings to outnumber the lawyers. They are all there—the able, the mediocre, the selfless,

[16] Zeller, *op. cit.*, p. 64 n.
[17] As in Tennessee in 1953.

the selfish, the incorruptible, and the men who have a price.   In their qualifications for their duties they rise well above the general run of voters who
sent them to the capitol, and their devotion to the public interest may in like
manner exceed that of the electorate.   The number of women serving in legislatures now ranges around 250, a number not sufficient to produce any marked
changes in legislation, even if women's interests were markedly different from
those of the men.

OCCUPATIONS OF STATE LEGISLATORS, 1949 *

Occupation	House	Senate	Total
Lawyers	1078	596	1674
Farmers	1110	358 ·	1468
Merchants	795	268	1063
Insurance	236	75	311
Banks and trusts	101	41	142
Real estate	174	38	212
Doctors	46	34	80
Teachers	155	33	188
Laborers	129	16	145
Craftsmen	191	31	222
Undertakers	31	9	40
Retired	286	41	327
Other	1318	285	1603
GRAND TOTALS	5650	1825	7475

* Reproduced from Belle Zeller (ed.), *American State Legislatures,* Report of the Committee on American Legislatures,
American Political Science Association, Thomas Y. Crowell
Company, New York (1954), p. 71.   By courtesy of the Committee and the publisher.

HIGH TURNOVER.   The turnover in legislative personnel is high, too high.
Professor Charles S. Hyneman has said that a member must serve in three
sessions before he can hope to become effective.   In 1938 Hyneman reported
on his findings respecting tenure in ten states over a period of ten years.   In
only four of the twenty chambers studied were there as many as 50 per cent
of the members who had completed three sessions.   And in seven chambers
less than 25 per cent could show experience in three previous sessions.[18]

The American Political Science Association's Committee on State Legislatures found a very similar condition in 1950.   These experts noted further
that a number of committee chairmen were first-termers.   We are cautioned,
however, against drawing any firm conclusions from the large turnover; re-
minded that it might be only an indication of the political instability of our
time.[19]   Yet whatever the cause may be, it is unfortunate that our legislatures
do not contain a higher percentage of members who have had longer experience in the legislative process.

[18] "Tenure and Turnover of Legislative Personnel," *Annals of the Am. Acad. of Pol.
and Soc. Sci.,* 195 (1938), 24.
[19] Zeller, *op. cit.,* pp. 65–70.

Legislative Sessions

In the early days of the Republic, the annual session of the legislature was the accepted standard. But fifty years ago nearly all of the states had gone over to the biennial plan. Just now ten states hold annual sessions,[20] and the tendency seems to be in that direction. In about three fourths of the states the legislatures convene in regular session in January of the odd year. The time the legislature may remain in session is stipulated in the constitutions of approximately two thirds of the states, sixty days being the most common limit. To put it shortly and bluntly, the time limit was placed upon legislatures in order to lessen their opportunities to do evil, a strange reaction of the people to their chosen representatives. The Committee on State Legislatures of the APSA reports as follows:

Limiting sessions intensifies all evils associated with legislative halls. Taking advantage of the short time for deliberation, a strong minority may thwart the interest of the majority through delaying tactics. Bills piled up at the end of the session are rushed through without adequate consideration. . . . The restriction on length of sessions are the real reasons for bad laws—not extended periods of discussion. Certainly it would be impossible to say that legislation or the quality of legislators has been improved by limiting the session.[21]

California and several other states have tried the experiment of the split session, but it appears to be in current operation only in the state named. Under the California plan the legislature meets for a period of not more than thirty days for the purpose of introducing bills and disposing of certain preliminary matters. Then, it must take a recess for a period that may run as long as six weeks, the assumption being that during this period the members will think about legislative problems and mingle with their constituents to learn their will on pending legislation. When the legislature reassembles, no new bills may be introduced in either house except by the consent of three fourths of the members thereof. The split session has not convincingly demonstrated its utility beyond the fact that it gives legislative counsel time to prepare digests of the bills introduced.

SPECIAL SESSIONS. The legislature may be called into special session by the governor. It would seem appropriate for the members of the legislature to call a special session, but in only a few states is this procedure authorized. Not only does the authority to call special sessions rest solely with the governor in most states, but in about half of them the legislature may consider only such subjects as are recommended by him. Another limitation upon the special session is that of time, nineteen states' constitutions imposing a limit from 15 to 60 days. Special sessions are rather common, particularly in those states in which a time limit is placed upon the regular biennial session.[22]

---

[20] But in three of these states, California, Colorado, and Maryland, the even-year session deals only with revenue and appropriations.

[21] Zeller, *op. cit.*, p. 93.

[22] *Ibid.*, pp. 90–91.

II. LEGISLATIVE ORGANIZATION AND PROCEDURE [23]

The Speaker

The lower house in every state is presided over by a speaker. Theoretically he is chosen by the members, but actually by the caucus of the majority party—the caucus, in turn, being controlled by a few leading members of the party or even by a party boss who may not have a seat in the legislature. Occasionally the leaders of the two parties reach an understanding concerning the speakership, and in such cases the presiding officer is somewhat limited as to the extent to which he may use his office for the advantage of his own party.

In the typical state the speaker is more powerful than his counterpart in the national House of Representatives. Professor Holcombe summarizes his powers as follows: [24] the power to recognize (and, of course, to refuse to recognize) members who wish to be heard on the floor; to make rulings on points of order, subject to an appeal to the whole body of members—which appeal is usually ineffective, owing to the fact that the majority ordinarily sustains the speaker; to appoint committees—through which power he rewards and disciplines members, and largely determines the character of party leadership in the house; to refer measures to committees—a power that often enables him to determine the fate of important bills; to control the committee on rules—a power that does not exist in all legislatures, and that is important only in those in which the rules committee is a highly privileged one. In controlling the house, the speaker relies very heavily upon the majority floor leader, particularly for making the necessary motions and explanations at the proper moments to enable the party to manage the house.

The Presiding Officer of the Senate

In about three fourths of the states there is a lieutenant governor whose duty it is to preside over the senate. He is elected by the people, and he may therefore belong to the minority party in the house over which he presides. Not being a member of the senate, he ordinarily has no vote except in case of a tie. As presiding officer, his powers are similar to those of the speaker of the lower house, with the exception that in nearly half the states he has no power to appoint committees or to control the committee on rules. The majority party in the senate elects a president pro tempore, who presides in the absence of the lieutenant governor, and who, with other party leaders, generally exercises the political powers that fall to the speaker in the lower house. Under ordinary circumstances, therefore, the leading figure in the

[23] *Annals of the Am. Acad. of Pol. and Soc. Sci.*, 195 (Jan., 1938); Graves, *op. cit.*, Chs. 7–8; Holcombe, *op. cit.*, pp. 256–271; The Council of State Governments, *Our State Legislatures* (1948); Macdonald, *op. cit.*, Ch. 9; Sikes and Stoner, *op. cit.*, Ch. 10; Walker, *op. cit.*, Chs. XI–XVII; C. I. Winslow, *State Legislative Committees* (1931); Zeller, *op. cit.*, Chs. 6–13.

[24] *Op. cit.*, pp. 294–296.

senate is not the lieutenant governor, but the president pro tempore, or some other majority party leader or leaders.   In those states that have no lieutenant governor, it is, of course, the senate's privilege to elect its presiding officer, and in such states his powers are likely to be very similar to those of the speaker of the house of representatives.

Other Legislative Officers and Employees

Each house elects a clerk, a sergeant-at-arms, a doorkeeper, a chaplain, and a postmaster.   Numerous secretaries, stenographers, policemen, and pages are elected, or designated by leaders, and a few may even be selected by the rank and file of members as their part of the legislative "spoils."   Frequently, legislatures have many more employees than they need, and at times their salaries and wages may run to exciting figures.

In 1944 a grand jury investigation in New York uncovered what was known about the State Capitol as the "wonderful lu-lu system."   For years the men at Albany had voted sums of money (never a large sum at any one time) "in lieu of detailed, itemized expenditures."   Some of this "lu-lu" went to certain members of the legislature, some to increase the compensation of regular employees of the legislature, and some went to individuals whose employment by the legislature was only fiction.   One "employee" who had received a $1,000 "lu-lu" squirmed that he "didn't do much of anything for the state."   Another whose "lu-lu" take ran to the same figure sweated but could not "recall doing a single thing for that money."   This "lu-lu" sounds less like peanuts when it is totaled.   In 1943 it cost the state $1,433,544.[25]

The Committees

The work that a legislature must now perform is not only almost staggering in quantity but it is also perplexing in its variety.   No chamber of a legislature could "turn a wheel" without committees.   How good is the committee system?   There are plenty of committees, the average being 32 for the house and 25 for the senate.   But they are not so constituted that the work can be properly distributed among them, the result being that a few are overworked, some have moderate loads, and a few have nothing at all to do.   Further shortcomings of the committee system of the typical legislature are sufficiently revealed by the recommendations of the Committee on American Legislatures of the APSA for their improvement.   They are as follows:

1. Reduce the number of committees to 12 or so, leaving one to deal with each major subject, such as revenue, appropriations, agriculture, labor, health and welfare, conservation, local government, and the judiciary.   This suggestion is in line with the improvements made in the committee system of Congress in 1946.

2. Make extensive use of joint committees as is the practice in Massachusetts, Maine, and Connecticut.   Joint committees remove the necessity for dual consid-

[25] John W. Lederle, "New York's Legislature under the Microscope," *Am. Pol. Sci. Rev.,* XL (June, 1946), 521; and *Time,* Dec. 18, 1944, p. 18.

eration of bills, make for co-ordination between the two houses, and otherwise promote legislative efficiency.

3. Reduce committee assignments.   The average member now serves on four or
five committees with the result that the work on some or all of them must be slighted.
The reduction in the number of committees would, of course, make feasible the
reduction in committee assignments.

4. Balance qualifications and interests of members with political requirements in
making committee assignments.   The 25-odd senates and houses that follow the
seniority rule in designating committee chairman should reconsider that rule.

5. Adopt rules that will assure prompt and orderly consideration of bills by committees; require scheduled hearings on appropriate bills and the keeping of adequate
committee records; and prevent a committee from killing a bill by failure to report.

6. Provide an adequate technical staff to aid each committee in assembling data,
preparing bills, and so on.[26]

A few legislatures are not so far from the goal thus fixed, but the great
majority of them are nearer the other end of the field.

Party Organization

Party leadership in the legislatures varies considerably from state to state.
A number of states, most of them in the South, are one-party states, and
there is no reason for the tight party organization and control that might be
desirable in the two-party legislatures.   In the latter type of legislature, as
in Colorado, Indiana, and New Jersey, the caucus of the majority party wields
significant power in determining the officers and committees, although it may
not exercise great force in respect to legislative policy or program.[27]   In the
legislatures of other states leadership may be found in a steering or policy
committee, in chairmen of committees, in some informal party oligarchy, or
in the executive mansion.   Legislation in the states is often nonpartisan
in character (more so than in Congress), and party lines are broken more
frequently and completely than in Congress.   After all, parties are built
primarily around national issues and such issues are not ordinarily present
in the problems facing a state legislature.   There is then a certain artificiality
in party lines in the legislature, and the divisions there are quite as likely to
be rural vs. urban, or right wing vs. left wing, as Republican vs. Democratic.
Sometimes the leaders of the two parties, or of factions in them, ostensibly
in opposition, reach an understanding concerning both legislative organization

[26] Zeller, *op. cit.,* pp. 95–104.

[27] A very estimable lady with little knowledge of the ways of caucuses was elected to a
house in which the majority party's caucuses played a leading role.   Her party caucus
endorsed by a very small majority a candidate for speaker who was not acceptable to her,
and she had no intention of voting for him in the house.   Before the vote was taken, however, she learned that the vote on the caucus nominee for speaker was an acid test of party
allegiance.   Quickly smothering her conscience and summoning her party loyalty, she
voted for the nominee, who was easily elected speaker, since his party had a majority.
While the lady was hoping that nothing like this would happen again soon, the clerk appointed her on the committee to conduct the speaker-elect to the chair!   Her lessons in
practical politics were coming fast.

and program.   Such bipartisan combinations are not likely to produce the best results for the state, for in such cases there is no effective minority to safeguard the people's interest.

The Introduction of Bills

Bills are introduced by individual members or by committees.   The great majority of them are presented by individual members, and the overwhelming majority of these relate to some matter of interest only to the individual who introduces it, or to his constituency, or to a few voters in his constituency. Many such bills are introduced "by request," which notation on the bill indicates to the committee to which it is referred that the measure may be allowed to die in committee for all its ostensible sponsor cares.   Important bills may emanate from the powerful committees, and some of these originate with the governor and are proposed by the committee as "administration measures."

In order to give the legislature opportunity to consider the measures before it, a time limit on the introduction of bills is fixed by the constitution or by legislative rules in some states.   This limitation usually takes the form of prohibiting introductions after the legislature has been in session a specified number of days.   It cannot be said that these provisions are particularly effective, for certain types of bills are ordinarily exempted from the prohibitions and others may usually be exempted with the consent of special majorities of the members.

Bills in Committee

Upon the introduction of a bill, it receives its first reading, in most states, by title only.   The bill is then referred to a committee, and the committee considers it or does not consider it, very much after the manner of a congressional committee.   In about one third of the states all bills must be reported by the committees.   But in the great majority of the states (including a few in which committees are required to report) the committees may kill measures by failing to consider them or by not reporting them after consideration.   True, it is ordinarily provided that the majority (one third in Missouri) of the house may recall a bill from a committee; but since the principal committees are invariably controlled by the majority leaders, whom the rank and file of the party membership cannot afford to offend, this power to "discharge a committee," and thus place a bill on the chamber's calendar, is seldom exercised.

The common practice, then, is for the chairman and the majority of a committee to select for consideration only such bills as meet with their approval, and to report to the house only the bills they want enacted into law.   In making these selections, the chairmen of the committees usually keep in close touch with the speaker of the house, or, in the case of senate committees, with the president pro tempore of the senate.   Occasionally, bills are reported unfavorably; but, as we have just noted, bills not favored by the committee are usually not reported at all. Measures that are reported favorably have a good chance of passage; those reported unfavorably and those not reported have practically no chance. Thus, the committees, "little legislatures," working with the party leaders, have the power of life and death over the great majority of the bills referred to them.

Bills Before the House

When a committee reports a bill favorably, it is ordinarily placed on the house calendar and is ready for its second reading. This reading may be in full or by title only. In any case the reading is of no importance except that it indicates a stage in the advancement of the bill. It is at this time that debate on a bill ordinarily takes place, amendments are offered, and strategy for defeating it brought into play. At this stage important bills are often considered in committee of the whole, which, technicalities aside, is simply the house sitting informally. In committee of the whole there is opportunity for general debate, but the time is limited. When the house is in formal session, there is comparatively little debate, because of the pressure of time or other reasons that the leaders often have for wanting the matter disposed of with little or no debate.

When a bill has passed its second reading, it is then engrossed. This process may amount to a redrafting of the bill if many changes have been agreed upon during the second-reading stage. Engrossed bills are placed on the calendar for third reading and are taken up for consideration in the order of their appearance, unless, as is often the case with important bills, they are made the subject of a special order. Debate on third reading is ordinarily confined to the bill as a whole, not to its parts, and amendments must have unanimous consent. With the conclusion of the debate on third reading, the bill is up for final passage.

TIME-SAVING DEVICES. State legislative bodies save time and rush bills to a vote in very much the same manner as our national House of Representatives. We take a few examples of these short-cut methods. The time a member may spend in debate is ordinarily limited by the rules. The presiding officer may refuse to recognize a member who wishes to speak. The "previous question" may be ordered, which means that debate must cease and the main question be voted upon. In many states the committee on rules brings in special rules from time to time, making a bill a special order on a given date, limiting the time that may be spent in debate, or setting the time when the final vote shall be taken. In no state is there that freedom of debate which is such a marked feature of procedure in the United States Senate. State lawmakers may object to these timesaving and often "steamroller" devices, but it is seldom that the majority will stage a protest, for the lowly member must follow the leaders, or he will have no share of the legislative patronage and no consideration will be given to the measures he proposes. A time-saving device that no one should object to is the electrical roll call, now used in one or both houses in nearly half the states.

Legislative and Executive Action on Bills in States and Territories, 1947 *

State	Bills Introduced	Bills Passed in Both Houses	Percentage of Bills Passed	Bills Vetoed and Pocket Vetoed	Percentage of Passed Bills Vetoed	Veto Overridden	Became Law	Number of Joint and Concurrent Resolutions Adopted and in Effect †	Percentage of Bills Introduced Which Became Laws	Percentage of Bills Passed Which Became Laws
Alabama	1,482	623	42.0	18	2.7		605	74	40.8	97.1
Alaska	235	101	42.9	5	5.0	1	97	5	41.3	96.0
Arizona	482	148	30.7	12	8.1	5	141	6	29.3	95.3
Arkansas	844	464	54.9	36	7.8	2	430	7	50.9	92.7
California	4,318	1,752	40.5	175	10.0		1,577	(203)	36.5	90.0
Colorado	1,629	349	21.4	6	1.7		343	(38)	20.8	98.3
Connecticut	2,348	1,076	45.8	12	1.1		1,064	—	45.3	98.9
Delaware	848	346	40.8	21	6.1		325	35	38.3	93.9
Florida	2,496	1,402	56.2	23	1.6		1,379	—	55.2	98.4
Georgia	680	404	59.4	12	3.0		392	36	57.6	97.0
Hawaii	1,504	268	17.8	24	7.5		248	(16)	16.5	92.5
Idaho	418	279	66.7	4	1.4		275	(44)	65.8	98.6
Illinois	1,675	738	44.0	37	5.0		701		41.8	95.0
Indiana	815	406	49.8	32	7.9		474	(19)	45.9	92.1
Iowa	1,049	358	34.1	12	3.1		347	9	33.1	96.9
Kansas	808	492	60.9	5	1.0		487	3	60.3	99.0
Kentucky (a)	794	275	34.6	32	11.6	5	248	66	31.2	90.2
Louisiana (a)	1,032	410	39.7	26	6.3		384	33	37.2	93.7
Maine	2,314	600	25.9	4	0.6		596	185	25.8	99.4
Maryland	1,418	1,011	71.3	84	8.3		927	22	65.4	91.7
Massachusetts	3,007	701	23.3	18	2.3	2	685	79	22.8	97.7
Michigan	945	381	40.3	10	2.6		371	4	39.2	97.4
Minnesota	2,960	650	22.0	8	1.2		642	(24)	21.7	98.8
Mississippi (a)	1,630	692	42.4	3	0.4		689	30	42.3	99.6

Missouri	724	221	30.5	25	11.3		196	1	27.1	88.7
Montana	603	354	58.7	13	3.6		341	26	56.5	96.4
Nebraska	568	362	63.7	6	1.7		358	—	63.0	98.9
Nevada	443	284	64.1	5	1.8	2	279	—	63.0	98.2
New Hampshire	616	404	65.6	2	0.5		402	(b)	60.6	99.5
New Jersey	846	487	57.5	70	14.2		418	10	49.4	85.8
New Mexico	566	238	42.0	16	6.7		222	32	39.2	93.3
New York	5,313	1,245	23.4	329	26.4		908	(4)	17.1	72.9
North Dakota	627	376	59.9	3	0.8		373	(39)(c)	59.5	99.2
Ohio	852	248	29.1	5	2.0	2	245	(16)	28.8	98.8
Oklahoma	795	389	48.1	9	2.3		380	9	47.8	97.7
Oregon	1,019	605	59.4	11	1.8	1	595	(58)	58.4	98.3
Pennsylvania	2,223	720	32.4	57	7.9		663	(5)	29.8	92.1
Rhode Island	893	326	36.4	6	1.8		320	(77)	35.8	98.2
South Carolina	855	606	70.8	3	0.5		603	— (b)	70.5	99.5
South Dakota	577	430	74.5	3	0.7		427	5	74.0	99.3
Tennessee	2,774	1,120	40.4	6	0.4		1,115	37	40.2	99.6
Texas	1,335	470	35.2	12	2.6		458	9	34.3	97.4
Utah	596	163	27.3	9	5.5		154	(25)(c)	25.8	94.5
Vermont	403	260	64.5	0	0.0		260	49	64.5	100.0
Virginia (a)	687	406	59.1	6	1.5		400	(3)	58.2	98.5
Washington	931	309	33.2	20	6.5		289	(12)	31.0	93.5
West Virginia	834	184	22.1	1	0.5		183	(15)	21.9	99.5
Wisconsin	1,220	624	51.1	10	1.8	1	615	(75)	50.4	98.6
Wyoming	273	171	62.6	7	4.1	1	165	11	60.4	96.5
TOTALS	62,304	24,928	40.0	1,253	5.0	22	23,796	1,481	38.2	95.0

* From F. W. Prescott, "The Executive Veto in American States," *Western Pol. Qt.*, III (1950), 102, by courtesy of the author and editors.

† One Joint Resolution each in Alabama, Iowa, New Jersey, Tennessee, Wyoming, and four in Hawaii were vetoed and included in the number of bills vetoed. Joint Resolutions in parentheses indicate adoption without action of governor.

(a) Figures for 1946 regular sessions.

(b) Joint Resolutions not reported separately are included in columns for "bills" and "laws" respectively.

(c) Indicates division between resolutions signed by the governor and those adopted without signature.

The Conference Committees

When a bill has passed one house, it must be sent to the other, where it runs the legislative gauntlet a second time.   If the second house amends the bill, it must be returned to the first house for action upon the amendments. In case the two houses cannot agree on the amendments, the conference committee comes into play.   This committee may disagree quite honestly, or it may fail to agree because the leaders find in it a convenient means of defeating the will of the members of both houses.   In any case, failure of a committee to agree means that no bill will be passed.   On the other hand, it may add some entirely new provisions to a measure and thus secure what the leaders were not otherwise able to get from the legislative bodies.   When a bill has finally passed both houses, it is sent to the governor, whose powers of approval and veto were discussed in the preceding chapter.

The Lobby

Those who follow the work of state legislatures often speak of the legislators' lack of information on the subjects upon which they legislate and of their lack of knowledge as to where information can be obtained.   The lobbyist is sometimes the sole authority on which legislators base their opinions, and not infrequently legislators publicly admit their appreciation of the help of lobbyists.[28]   Of course lobbyists have a right to be present and to state the case for this or that interest or group; but it is not in the public interest that lawmakers, so often lacking information from unbiased sources, should rely upon them so heavily.   The lobby is probably more powerful and sinister in the general run of state legislatures than it is in Congress, for the searchlight of publicity is not always glaring in state capitols and the legislators are less experienced and perhaps more likely to be influenced than congressmen. Newcomers in the legislature are easy marks for the lobbyists, often receiving from these experienced men their schooling in the intricacies of legislative organization and procedure and other "freshman days" helps and tips.   It is too much to expect that none of these freshmen will in turn do their teachers a favor that may not be in the interest of all the people.

A provision of long standing in the constitution of Georgia declares lobbying to be a crime and a similarly ancient and obsolete clause of the fundamental law of California defines lobbying as the attempt to influence the vote of a member by bribery or other dishonest means.   Lobbying is now accepted as standard procedure and the lobbyists are sometimes referred to as the "third house."   There is every reason why citizens should be permitted to approach the legislature either directly or through their agents, lobbyists. The problem is not how to abolish the lobby, but how to prevent abuses. Some thirty states now have laws of varying degrees of stringency and effectiveness relating to lobbying.   The common requirement is that paid legisla-

[28] See the articles on Lobbies and Pressure Groups in *Annals of the Am. Pol. and Soc. Sci.,* 195 (Jan., 1938), and Zeller, *op. cit.,* Ch. 13.

tive agents or legislative counsel shall register, giving name and address, name
~lover, and the nature of the legislation he is seeking to influence.
states prohibit the payment of contingent fees to lobbyists (so ιι. introduced, so much if passed, etc.). About an
equal number ot sι. require a statement of expenditures paid, incurred,
or promised. California, one of the states in which the lobby had made
a rather bad reputation, has one of the most elaborate and perhaps one of
the best laws regulating it. An amendment to the act in 1950 imposes upon
the lobbyist such conduct as the following:

To perform no act that places a member of the legislature under a personal obligation to him; to deceive no member on any material fact pertaining to legislation;
never to influence the introduction of a bill for the purpose of later being employed
to defeat it; not to represent that he can control the vote or action of any member
of the legislature; and not to appear as an advocate for an interest adverse to his
employer nor represent employers whose interests are known to him to be adverse.

But, however inclusive the regulatory statutes may be, the problem of controlling the lobby will remain with us. Enforcement is difficult, and new
types of lobbying activity are constantly being developed.

The Legislative Council

The quantity and complexity of the work that now comes to the legislature is far beyond what it can cope with without special aid. The kind
of help legislatures need is only incidentally and occasionally supplied by
lobbyists. Legislators must have their own special sources of information
upon which they can rely. One of the most promising agencies for relieving
the legislature of some of its burden and at the same time improving its product is the legislative council. Originating in Kansas in 1933, the plan has
spread to more than two thirds of the states. The council is composed of
a dozen or more members of the legislature, and is commonly appointed by
the presiding officers with due regard for the minority party. During the
long periods between legislative sessions, the council meets from time to time
(quarterly, monthly, or at irregular intervals), considers legislative problems,
and prepares reports and recommendations for the next session.

How can a few members of the legislature, meeting for a day or two, four,
or five times a year, plan a program? They cannot by themselves. But
the council, any effectively functioning council, has a permanent staff headed
by a director of research. This staff assembles the materials, makes the
studies, and reports to the council. To be sure, council members may and
should do some of this work, but for the most part they rely upon the staff.
In a number of states the reports and recommendations of the council find
ready acceptance in the legislature. It requires no imagination to understand that a legislature having a limited period for its session might be grate-
ful to a council and its expert staff for this preliminary work and that such
work is usually much better done than it would be if left to a standing com-

mittee during the crowded days of a session.   Authorities on state legislatures are unanimous in their endorsement of the council, their only fears being that it might not be properly supported or adequately staffed.[29]

Legislative Reference Service

A source of aid to legislators that is older than the council and now practically indispensable is the legislative reference service.   In 1901 Wisconsin established a legislative reference library and New York did likewise about the same time.   Forty-four states now have some such library or service.   In some states the service is decidedly limited because of insufficient appropriations and staff, but in a number of states it functions with a degree of adequacy in collecting available information on any subject on which the legislature might take action, assembling legislation from all the states as well as pertinent material on its operation, stocking such works of reference as may be of general use to legislators, and making research studies.   The service functions the year around, but during a legislative session, it often increases its staff and keeps workers on duty day and night.[30]   Other sources of information available, at long range, to legislators include the Legislative Reference Service of the Library of Congress and facilities of the Council of State Governments at 1313 East 60th Street, Chicago.

BILL DRAFTING.   Legislators have been deficient in the art of drafting bills.   It is one thing to decide that a law is needed to prevent or encourage a particular thing, and quite another to draft a statute that will accomplish the purpose intended.   Drafting is a technical matter.   The statute must be so constructed that neither more nor less than is intended is expressed, that its meaning not only may be understood but cannot be misunderstood. Some will seek to expand the terms of a statute; others will seek to make it meaningless.   A law that serves the original purpose of its makers, despite all the controversy and litigation over its meaning, is a rare product.   It is obvious that the average member of a state legislature is wholly incapable of drafting a bill in the proper form; for many of them not only lack the technical knowledge necessary, but they are also deficient in the rudiments of ordinary English composition.   The bill-drafting follies of legislatures are often illustrated by an extreme example: "When two trains approach each other at a crossing they shall both come to a full stop and neither shall start up until the other has gone." [31]

Lacking the qualifications of bill drafters, formerly many legislators relied upon lawyer constituents or upon lobbyists, the latter being only too glad to

---

[29] Graves, *American State Government*, pp. 256 ff.; F. H. Guild, "Legislative Councils," *State Government*, Sept., 1949, pp. 217 ff.; W. J. Siffin, "Footnote to the Legislative Council Movement," *State Government*, July, 1955, pp. 156 ff.; Zeller, *op. cit.*, Ch. 8.

[30] C. L. Larsen and M. F. Ryan, Jr., *Aids for State Legislators* (1947), pp. 29–30; E. E. Witte, "A Law-Making Laboratory," *State Government*, April, 1930, and his "Technical Services for State Legislators," *Annals of the Am. Acad. of Pol. and Soc. Sci.*, 195 (Jan., 1938), 137.

[31] Sikes and Stoner, *op. cit.*, p. 226.

frame statutes embodying the principles for which they were laboring. Nearly all the states now provide some type of bill drafting assistance. The office of the attorney general may serve as the sole agency, or it may be simply one such agency. Some states delegate this duty to the legislative reference service, others to the legislative council, and still others to a statutory and code revision authority.

III. LEGISLATIVE POWERS AND LIMITATIONS [32]

As explained in Chapter 1, section I, all the powers of the national government are delegated to it by the Constitution or are implied from those delegated by that instrument, and all other powers of government are reserved to the states, subject to a few important prohibitions laid upon them by the federal Constitution. The states thus have jurisdiction over a much wider range of subjects than has the government of the United States. Each state, through its constitution, determines in the main what its governing authorities shall be, what powers they shall have, and, to a considerable extent, how these powers shall be exercised. In this division of powers within a state the legislature always receives the lion's share. Its powers are, for the most part, legislative, but some are judicial and still others are executive and administrative in character.

Legislative Powers

The legislature elaborates the constitution of the state through the enactment of innumerable statutes. Where the constitution leaves off in providing for the machinery of government for the state, the legislature takes over and completes the task, a not inconsiderable one. The legislature is responsible, subject to constitutional limitations, for fixing the organization and functions of city, county, and other units of local government. It has the weighty responsibility of preparing the state's financial program, of enacting its revenue laws and voting appropriations. It must protect individuals and the general public through the enactment of the necessary criminal laws, and it must by law provide for the regulation of business and various other activities and relationships of individuals.

Then to the legislature goes the responsibility of determining what the states shall do regarding numerous matters which were seldom or not at all the subject of legislation a hundred years ago. What educational advantages shall the state offer its citizens in high schools, colleges, and universities? What highway construction program shall it adopt, and what measures shall it design to promote safety on the highways? What are its obligations to agriculture, and what measures shall it promulgate for the conservation of natural resources? How shall public utilities be regulated and by whom? And is the state to favor "public power" or "private power" or develop a

[32] Dodd, *op. cit.*, pp. 173–177, 190–222; Graves, *American State Government*, pp. 280–289; Holcombe, *op. cit.*, pp. 275–288; J. M. Mathews, *American State Government* (1934 ed.), pp. 242–249; Sikes and Stoner, *op. cit.*, Ch. 9; Zeller, *op. cit.*, Ch. 11; "Action by the Legislatures," *State Government*, July, 1955, pp. 147 ff.

well-rounded program that utilizes both? How can the state balance the claims of labor and management and at the same time adequately protect the public interest? What health measures are necessary or desirable, and how much social security should the state offer? The legislature must deal with these and many similar questions, the answers to which constitute the very essence of modern statecraft.[33]

Judicial Powers

In about half the states the legislature is authorized to decide contested elections, a power that is judicial (or should be) in its nature and from which there is no appeal from the legislative decision. In all states except Oregon [34] the governor and other civil officers may be removed by impeachment. The "articles of impeachment" are voted in the lower house and the trial is conducted by the senate, except in Nebraska, where the articles are voted by the one-house legislature and the trial is conducted by the state supreme court. It will be made clear in the chapter on the State Judicial System that the courts not only look to the legislature for the laws they are to enforce, but also find their organization and procedure, except as specified in the constitution, fixed by the legislature.

Executive and Administrative Powers

Quite commonly the governor's appointments must be validated by senatorial confirmation, and in several states certain judicial and executive officers are chosen by the whole legislature. Ordinary removals (to be distinguished from removal by impeachment) may be made in a number of states by joint action of the governor and senate or by joint action of the legislative bodies. State legislatures have sometimes fallen willing victims to a temptation to which Congress has often yielded, the temptation to regulate the details of administration. For example, legislatures have not only decided what departments shall be organized, but they have prescribed in great detail the internal organization of the departments—a function that administrative authorities could discharge much better and save the time of the legislatures while so doing. Legislatures have not only enacted laws for the protection of fish and game, but they have prescribed the most detailed and technical regulations as to how fish and game shall be protected; and laws enacted for the purpose of eradicating or controlling the hoof-and-mouth disease have contained the most minute directions as to just how this shall be done. Now, authorities will agree that the legislature should provide for the protection of fish and game and for the eradication of the hoof-and-mouth disease, but they will also agree that the legislature should stop with the statement of the objects to be accomplished and the creation of the agencies for accomplish-

---

[33] Some interesting reflections on the problems the legislators face in reaching their decisions on matters of policy are found in T. V. Smith's "Two Functions of the American State Legislator," *Annals of the Am. Acad. of Pol. and Soc. Sci.*, 195 (Jan., 1938), 183.

[34] In Oregon corrupt and otherwise delinquent officials are supposed to be dealt with by the courts as ordinary criminal offenders. Macdonald, *op. cit.*, p. 184 n.

ing them, leaving the details to be worked out by the administrative agencies. Legislatures have neither the time nor the technical information necessary for making administrative regulations.

It is indeed encouraging to see that the practice of leaving details to be worked out by administrative authorities is growing. Boards of health are being given the authority to draw up sanitary codes; industrial commissions are being empowered to make rules and regulations for guarding against fire hazards, personal injuries, disease, etc.; and public utility commissions, for some time, have been authorized not only to make ordinary rules and regulations respecting public utilities, but also to fix the rates that may be charged for services. Since about 1930 this desirable movement has proceeded at a rapid rate, leaving the legislatures more time to devote to what should be their chief function, the formulation of policies.[35]

LEGISLATIVE OVERSIGHT OF ADMINISTRATION. Let no one fail to note, however, that the legislature has a most significant and appropriate function in relation to the executive department and that is to exercise broad control over it to the end that the legislature has assurance that the policies it has adopted are being carried out and that the funds it has appropriated are being expended according to law. Obviously it becomes necessary for the legislature, through its committees or officers responsible to it, to have a look at the administration from time to time, and on occasion the legislature must take corrective action. This legislative oversight of administration must be balanced against the need for executive independence in matters of detail and in the discharge of functions, like appointment and removal, that are purely executive. The maintenance of this balance between executive responsibility and legislative oversight of administration can be achieved only where both branches of the government are well organized for the performance of their appropriate functions and are guided by leaders who, most of the time, rise above personal and petty politics.

Limits on Legislative Powers

In colonial times, especially during the period immediately preceding the Revolution, the people thought of their legislatures as strongholds of defense against the attacks made on their liberties by the governors who represented the British crown. When independent state governments were established after 1775, it was but natural that this confidence in the legislatures should continue, and that these bodies should retain all the powers they previously possessed and acquire a number of those formerly held by the governors. Prior to 1800 practically the only limitations on the powers of the legislatures were in the provisions for frequent elections and in the bills of rights.

FORFEITURE OF PUBLIC CONFIDENCE. The legislatures did not keep for long, however, the high place they held in public esteem. From the very first, land speculators intrigued with legislators for grants of large tracts

[35] Kansas Legislative Council, "Legislative Functions of Administrative Agencies" (1938); Macdonald, *op. cit.,* pp. 223–225.

of western lands at nominal prices—the land to be developed and advertised and sold at advanced prices, to the enrichment of the land companies and not infrequently to the profit of accommodating legislators. A little later there was great demand for roads, bridges, canals, and, after 1830, railroads. To secure their construction, legislatures granted to various concerns charters of incorporation, amounting in many cases to monopolies, and, along with the charters, most liberal, even prodigal, grants of land. In connection with these charters and grants the opportunities for corruption were too frequent and tempting to be resisted at all times by all legislators. In like manner, much unwisdom and some corruption were shown in the ease with which legislators granted bank charters to irresponsible promoters, with the result that the people suffered greatly, particularly in the West, from the operations of "wildcat" banks. Not only were the states too liberal in granting privileges to private corporations, but the states themselves went into banking and also undertook the construction of roads, canals, and railroads on a grand scale.

When the panic of 1837 struck, a number of the states were heavily in debt and some of them repudiated part of their obligations. Let us not suppose that the constituents had been prophesying that dire results would follow the prodigality of their representatives. Rather was it in response to the voice of the people that these programs were undertaken. Nevertheless, when the mistakes and blunders stood revealed, the legislatures were not saved by the plea that they had given the public what it wanted.[36] Consequently, a large part of the history of state legislatures, especially since the middle of the nineteenth century, is written in the limitations placed upon them.

PRESENT LIMITATIONS AND RESTRICTIONS. Legislatures are now commonly limited in respect to organization and procedure by constitutional stipulations on such matters as the number of members, length of sessions, rate of pay, the manner in which bills, especially money bills, may be introduced, the steps in the passage of a bill, and the method of voting. More important than these restrictions are the constitutional limitations on the scope of legislative action.

1. Matters of finance. The financial mistakes and excesses noted above led in many states to severe restrictions on taxation, appropriations, and debts. Constitutions generally stipulate that taxes shall be uniform and equal on all types of property, although this provision is frequently modified by such exceptions as the authorization of an income tax and the permission to classify property for purposes of taxation. Constitutions sometimes limit the rate of taxation, both state and local, and, in order that the rates shall be kept down and vicious favor seeking shall be avoided, frequently deny legislatures the right to exempt from taxation, persons, corporations, or localities. However, exemption is ordinarily authorized for private schools and religious and eleemosynary institutions.

---

[36] See discussion of abuse of legislative power in Sikes and Stoner, *op. cit.*, pp. 202 ff.

In making appropriations, legislatures must restrict themselves to those designed for a public purpose. Donations to individuals or private corporations are commonly forbidden. The form of appropriation bills is usually specified by some such provision as: "The general appropriation bill shall embrace nothing but appropriations for the different departments of the state, for state institutions, for public schools, and for interest on the public debt. All other appropriations shall be made by separate bill, each embracing but one subject." [37]

The authority of both legislatures and local governing bodies to borrow money is commonly restricted to specified amounts or to a small percentage of the assessed valuation of taxable property. However, it is usually provided that these amounts may be exceeded with the approval of the majority of the voters in the area for which the indebtedness is proposed, an approval that in practice has been relatively easy to obtain. In like manner, the constitutions usually prohibit the states and their various subdivisions from making loans to individuals, associations, or corporations.

2. *Special laws.* The majority of the states, in order to save the time of legislatures and to prevent abuses, now have constitutional prohibitions against the enactment of such local and special laws as those preventing the throwing of sawdust in Big Ivey Creek in Buncombe County and the shooting of firecrackers within one mile of the post office at Haw River,[38] granting a special privilege or franchise to a corporation, and voting a special charter to a city. A common prohibition is that no special law shall be enacted when a law of general application can be made to serve. This prohibition is ineffective in many states because the legislature itself passes upon the question of the necessity of a special law. But in the few states in which the courts determine the matter, the restriction is usually effective.

More important than this general prohibition against special legislation, is the specific enumeration of subjects on which the legislature shall pass no special law. This list, which may run as high as thirty or more, includes such subjects as the granting of divorces, the chartering of corporations (both private and municipal), changing the rules of evidence, changing the names of individuals, the punishment of crimes and misdemeanors, locating or changing county seats, and laws affecting the estates of deceased persons or of minors. The question as to whether an act violates any of these prohibitions is determined by the courts, not by the legislature.

Another method of limiting the activities of legislatures in passing special bills is found in procedural requirements. For example, in New York a two-thirds vote of the entire membership is required to pass a special or private bill appropriating money, and in several states, including New York, acts that apply to particular localities must be referred to such areas for their approval.

[37] Constitution of Arizona, Art. IV, sec. 20.
[38] See Mathews, *op. cit.,* p. 247 n., for a list of such local laws enacted by a North Carolina legislature.

It should be noted that prohibitions against special legislation do not prevent the legislatures from making reasonable classifications.   For instance, a prohibition against granting special charters to cities does not prevent legislatures from classifying cities according to population and giving the different classes different charters.   In like manner, the Fourteenth Amendment of the federal Constitution, which prohibits the states from denying to any person the equal protection of the laws, does not mean that the legislatures may not make reasonable classifications of persons and corporations for purposes of taxation and regulation.   Thus, doctors may be subject to one set of regulations, lawyers to another, and mechanics to none at all.   Railroads may be taxed by one method, and ordinary property by another.[39]

3. Indirect limitations.   Legislatures are limited not only by constitutional provisions that apply directly to them but also by provisions and extraconstitutional developments that transfer power from legislatures to other organs of government.[40]   We have already learned that the veto enables the governor to wield a tremendous power over the legislature in practically every state. The growth of his authority over the budget and appointments indicates some decrease in legislative power over these subjects.   With the general approval of the public, the governor frequently assumes the reins of legislative leadership in formulating and securing the adoption of policies, thereby decreasing the importance of the legislature in a field peculiarly its own.

In the early days the courts took a broad and liberal view of legislative powers.   Thus, in North Carolina, in 1794, the supreme court held that the people did not adopt a bill of rights "against a power they supposed their representatives might usurp, but against oppression and usurpation in general." [41]   Contrast this with the declaration of the Texas court, in 1918, to the effect that, since the constitution of that state directed the legislature to pass a local option law, it prevented the legislature from controlling the liquor traffic in any other way.   Other cases of this kind could be cited to show that, despite the theory that a legislature has all powers not denied it by the Constitution of the United States and the constitution of the state, the courts are now inclined to hold that authorization or direction to take certain action serves as a prohibition against taking other, although similar, action.[42]   Indeed, the marked tendency of the courts to apply the doctrine of "implied limitations" to legislative powers has led some authorities to say that it should be checked by constitutional means, and the constitution of Oklahoma follows this suggestion in a provision that reads: "Specific grant of authority in this constitution upon any subject whatsoever shall not work a restriction, limitation, or exclusion of such authority upon the same or any other subject or subjects whatsoever."

[39] Mathews, *op. cit.,* pp. 247–249.
[40] Sikes and Stoner, *op. cit.,* pp. 207–213.
[41] Quoted in *ibid.,* p. 212, from 1 Hay, N.C. 29.
[42] *Ex parte* Myer, 207 S.W. 100 (1918).

IV. THE INITIATIVE AND REFERENDUM [43]

In a number of states a lack of confidence in the legislatures is expressed in the initiative and refendum. Through the initiative the voters may themselves enact a measure their representatives will not pass; through the referendum, they may defeat a measure their representatives have passed. The initiative is positive in character; the referendum is negative. The former has been described as "a spur on the flanks," the latter as "a bit in the mouth," of the legislative steed.[44] Manifestly, those who fear these institutions of democracy because of their alleged radical character should concentrate their efforts against the initiative, since all the referendum can do is to hold the legislature in check. It was never intended by the most earnest advocates of the initiative and referendum that they should supplant representative (republican) government. This was simply the time-honored "scarecry" assertion of those who would frighten the electorate into voting against their adoption. The I and R were intended for emergency or special use, the presumption being that the legislature would ordinarily enact the measures that had popular support and fail to enact those that had it not.

Extent of Their Use

Although the referendum had been in pretty general use during the nineteenth century as a means of having the people pass upon proposed state constitutions and amendments thereto, and in the local communities of some states as a means of giving them their "local option" on the saloon question, neither the referendum nor the initiative was used for ordinary statutes in this country until 1898, when South Dakota introduced both.[45] Other states followed in rather rapid succession until about 1912, when the movement lagged. Twenty-one states (see page 119) now have constitutional provisions authorizing direct legislation, and it is a rare election year (even year) in which the total number of amendments and statutes voted upon by the people of these states does not exceed seventy-five. The number of submissions varies considerably in the states. California, with 48 (but about half these proposals were submitted by the legislature) in 1914, seems to hold the record; but Oregon, Colorado, and some other states have made relatively high scores. A number of cities have the I and R for their local charters

[43] R. C. Brooks, *Political Parties and Electoral Problems* (1933 ed.), Ch. XVII; Colorado Legislative Reference Office, *The Initiative and Referendum in Colorado* (1940); Dodd, *op. cit.*, Ch. XX; H. F. Gosnell and Margaret J. Schmidt, "Popular Law Making in the United States, 1924–1936," in New York State Constitutional Convention Committee's, *Problems Relating to Legislative Organization and Powers* (1938); Holcombe, *op. cit.*, Ch. XVI; Claudius O. Johnson, "The Initiative and Referendum in Washington," *Pacific Northwest Quarterly,* Jan., 1945, pp. 29–63; V. O. Key and W. W. Crouch, *The Initiative and Referendum in California* (1939); James K. Pollock, *The Initiative and Referendum in Michigan* (Bureau of Government, University of Michigan, 1940); Waldo Schumacher, "Thirty Years of the People's Rule in Oregon," *Pol. Sci. Qt.,* XLVII (June, 1932), 242.

[44] Brooks, *op. cit.,* p. 498.

[45] Switzerland authorized the use of the referendum and initiative for statutes some years before.

and ordinances, particularly those cities that have adopted the newer commission and manager forms of government; and as a rule the urban voters are not slow to avail themselves of their privileges.   The student knows, of course, that there is no provision for the use of these direct legislative methods in our national system, and we may add that there is little or no movement for their adoption.

Referendum Procedure

Although both the initiative and referendum differ in the details of their operation in the several states, the general principles are the same, and we shall describe them without greatly concerning ourselves with the variations.

1. COMPULSORY.   Every state except Delaware has the compulsory referendum on constitutional amendments, and many states require that form of referendum on banking laws and on incurring a debt beyond a certain minimum.   That is to say, constitutional amendments and statutes on the subjects mentioned, having passed the legislature, *must* be referred to the voters and be approved by them before they become effective.   In like manner, many cities have the compulsory referendum on charter amendments, incurring indebtedness, and other matters.   The compulsory referendum, as we observed above, is not new.   In fact, we have long accepted it as a matter of course, and hardly think of it as a referendum at all.

2. OPTIONAL.   What we commonly have in mind when we speak of the referendum is the optional referendum, which did not come into general use until after 1900.   It operates as follows.   The legislature passes a statute to which some of the voters object.   During the period, usually ninety days, before the statute becomes effective, the opposition circulates a petition for a referendum.   If the requisite number of voters, varying in the twenty states from five to ten per cent, sign the petition, the statute must then be held in abeyance until submitted to the whole body of voters for their decision.   In ten or eleven referendum states the legislature may on its own motion refer a bill to the people.   The submission is usually made on the regular election dates.

Manifestly, some measures are designed to meet crises and are needed immediately, and a referendum on them, with the delays it entails, would be intolerable.   Consequently, it is customary to give the legislatures the power to designate such bills as "emergency measures" and thus exempt them from the operation of the referendum.   Legislatures sometimes abuse this privilege by designating as emergency measures, bills that are not such measures in fact.   In order to correct this abuse, some states require an extraordinary majority of the legislature to attach the "emergency clause"; others allow the governor to veto the clause; still others enumerate the subjects that may not be legislated upon under the emergency classification.   No system, however, will eliminate all of the abuse either on the part of legislatures or of voters who originate petitions.

State	Initiative — Voters Signatures Necessary for Petitions	Initiative — Vote Required for Enactment	Referendum — Submission by — Petition	Referendum — Submission by — Legislative Action	Referendum — Voters Signatures Necessary for Petitions	Referendum — Vote Required for Enactment
Arizona	15%	Majority	★(a)	★(a)	5%	Majority
Arkansas	8%(b)	Majority	★	—	6%(b)	Majority
California	8%(c)	Majority	★	★(a)	5%(c)	Majority
Colorado	8%(e)	Majority	★	★	5%(e)	Majority
Idaho	10%(f)	Majority	★	★	10%(f)	Majority
Maine	10%(f)	Majority	★	★	10%(f)	Majority
Maryland	Does not use initiative system		★	—	10,000	Majority
Massachusetts	3%(f)	Majority & 30% of total votes cast at election	★	—	1½%–2%(f,g)	Majority(h)
Michigan	8%(f)	Majority	★	★	5%(f)	Majority
Missouri	5%	Majority	★	★	5%	Majority
Montana	8%(i)	Majority	★	★	5%(i)	Majority
Nebraska	7%(j)	Majority & 35% of total votes cast at election	★	—	5%(j)	Majority & 35% of total vote cast at election
Nevada	10%	Majority	★	—	10%	Majority
New Mexico	Does not use initiative system		★(k)	—	10%–25%(l)	Majority(m)
North Dakota	10,000	Majority	★	—	7,000	Majority
Ohio	3%	Majority	★	—	6%	Majority
Oklahoma	8%	Majority	★	★	5%	Majority
Oregon	8%(n)	Majority	★(o)	★	5%(n)	Majority
South Dakota	5%	Majority	★	—	5%	Majority
Utah	10%	Majority	★	—	10%	Majority
Washington	50,000	Majority & ⅙ of total votes cast at election	★	★	30,000	Majority & ⅙ of total votes cast at election

* Reproduced by courtesy of the Council of State Governments from *The Book of the States, 1954–55,* p. 143.

(a) Legislative acts not subject to referendum if they contain emergency clause or provide appropriations for state departments or institutions.

(b) Petition requirements refer to percentage of votes cast for Governor at last preceding election. Also, from each of 15 counties, there must be signatures equal to at least one-half of the designated per cent of the voters of such county.

(c) Petition requirements refer to percentage of votes cast for Governor at last preceding election. If initiative proposal is for submission to legislature, only 5% is required.

(d) Legislature may submit to referendum only proposals to amend previously adopted iniative acts.

(e) Petition requirements refer to percentage of votes cast for Secretary of State at last preceding election

(f) Petition requirements refer to percentage of votes cast for Governor at last preceding election.

(g) 2% if operation of law is to be suspended pending referendum; 1½% otherwise.

(h) Disapproval of legislation requires not only a majority of vote on the subject, but also at least 30% of votes cast in the election.

(i) Also must have signatures of 8% of voters on initiative petitions and 5% of voters on referendum petitions in each of two-fifths of the counties.

(j) Also must have signatures of 5% of voters on petitions in each of two-fifths of the counties.

(k) Laws cannot be subject to referendum if they are appropriation acts, provide for payment or refunding of debt, maintenance of schools or institutions, or provide for preservation of public health, peace or safety.

(l) 25% if operation of law is to be suspended; 10% otherwise. Also, petitions must have signatures of like percentages of voters in each of ¾ of the counties.

(m) Disapproval of legislation requires not only a majority of votes on the subject, but also at least 30% of votes cast in the election.

(n) Petition requirements refer to percentage of votes cast for Justice of the Supreme Court at last preceding election.

(o) Referendum not permitted on laws necessary for immediate preservation of public health, peace or safety.

Initiative Procedure

1. DIRECT.   If certain voters desire a constitutional amendment which the legislature will not propose or a measure which that body will not enact, they draft it, or have it drafted, and then circulate a petition on its behalf.   In the nineteen states which authorize the enactment of statutes by the initiative, the number of signers required is usually a little higher than for the referendum; and in the thirteen states (see page 42) in which the constitution may be amended by the initiative, seven require more petitioners for proposing amendments than for proposing statutes.   A petition in favor of a measure, signed by the requisite number of voters, places the measure on the ballot at the next regular election, when the entire electorate determines its fate as in the case of a referred measure.   This is called the direct initiative because the proposal goes directly to the voters.

2. INDIRECT.   In five or six states, the indirect initiative must be employed. The petition for a proposed measure is first submitted to the legislature; if the bill is passed by that body, the matter is settled and the necessity of a popular vote on the question avoided.   If not passed, some states require that the proposal be submitted to the people without further formalities; but in other states, additional signatures or other requirements must be met before it can be submitted.   In California and Washington either the direct or indirect initiative may be use.

The Initiative and Referendum in Operation

Direct legislation has now been in operation long enough and under sufficiently varying conditions to enable us to reach several fairly safe conclusions respecting its use.

1. EFFECT UPON THE LEGISLATURE.   The system of direct legislation has not encroached upon the regular legislative bodies to any considerable degree. Even in those states that resort most frequently to direct legislation, the legislatures continue to enact practically all the laws.   Nor does it appear that the initiative and referendum have brought about any important change in the personnel of legislatures.   The caliber of our lawmakers is pretty much the same as it was a generation ago.   As to whether or not the "bit in the mouth" and the "spur on the flanks" have improved the output of the duly elected legislative bodies, it is difficult to determine.   Perhaps it can be said that the existence of the I and R has at times caused legislators to consider their responsibilities more seriously.

2. EFFECT UPON THE BALLOT.   Direct legislation has unquestionably added to the tasks of the voter.   He must now vote on both men and measures.   Although certain measures will receive a relatively high vote in many instances, the fact remains that a large number of voters do not officially express their opinions upon the ordinary measures referred to them.   A business man, in telling his wife how to discharge her obligations as a citizen in a particular election, explained that she would be given two ballots; that one

contained the names of the candidates, and that the other "had some laws or something on it." He advised her to follow his example and not bother about voting on the laws.

3. POSSIBILITIES OF MINORITY GOVERNMENT. The fact that a considerable portion of the electorate is not interested in referred or initiated measures often makes it possible for a minority (although a majority of those voting on a measure) to carry its point. The situation is not so serious as it may appear to be, for government policies are often determined by minorities. Those who are in any degree familiar with our history know that the federal Constitution was adopted by convention delegates chosen by a minority of the adult males of the country. A policy determined by an intelligent minority is certainly not greatly to be feared. On the other hand, however, minorities of the "lunatic fringe" variety may plague the electorate by submitting to it foolish and absurd measures, and the indifference of the rank and file of the voters may occasionally result in the passage of a measure of this type. Some states have guarded against this by providing that no measure shall become a law unless a certain percentage of all those voting in the election (as distinguished from those voting on the particular measure) shall have voted on the measures.

4. TYPES OF LAWS SUBMITTED. Measures laid before the people cover a wide range; but the greater number of them have to do with minor changes in the organization of government, state and local. A fair number of them relate to finance—the authorization of an indebtedness, changing the system of taxation, and the like. Public utility measures have not been so numerous; but they have usually caused the most lively interest on the part of the electorate and, more particularly, the business group concerned. Some important measures have related to schools, roads, alcoholic beverages, and social security. These examples by no means exhaust the list, but they do cover practically all the subjects on which important measures have been referred to the electorate. It is of interest to note that the initiative has not deluged us with radical proposals; that conservatives have learned to use it quite as effectively as "radicals"; and that the groups that use it, be they the respectable or the disinherited, are those groups that are in a minority in the legislature.

5. THE QUESTION OF THEIR EDUCATIONAL VALUE. It is often said that the initiative and referendum educate the electorate; that they stimulate interest in government in general. This can hardly be questioned, but the extent to which they stimulate the voters to intelligent action is by no means certain. In a few states "publicity pamphlets" are mailed to each voter or household, but the evidence does not indicate that the voters read them or any part of them with particular care. This show of indifference does not mean, however, that the citizens do not receive some civic enlightenment from the discussions of the measures, but only that they may rely chiefly upon the spoken rather than the written word. Written appeals may move the educated classes, but the rank and file prefer the oral medium. Undoubtedly direct legislation creates a greater interest on the part of the electorate in

state policies, and it cannot be said that the interest does not run high when major questions are up for decision. Without having made any exhaustive study of the question, but having resided in states that have and in those that do not have direct systems of legislation, the writer is of the opinion that the voters in the former states are more intelligently concerned about public affairs than the voters in the latter.

Probable Future of Initiative and Referendum

A generation ago the lines on direct legislation were drawn, broadly speaking, between the liberals, who favored it, and the conservatives, who opposed it. Since neither the hopes of the former nor the fears of the latter have been realized, the lines have tended to break somewhat. It is an interesting fact that "tories" often used the I and R in the New Deal period when "radicals" and "reds" controlled the legislatures! It is a matter of who controls the legislature. If that body gives you what you want, you oppose the I and R; if it doesn't, then you are for direct legislation.

Students examine the record of the I and R, admit their shortcomings, point out their desirable features, and give them cautious endorsement. It is altogether probable that they will be retained by the states that now have them, and very unlikely that many other states will adopt them. It is also likely that changes will be made in their operation: through authorizing and requiring a greater use of the indirect initiative and the submission by the legislature of a substitute measure for the one originally proposed; through lengthening the list of subjects on which the people may not legislate directly; through providing more official help for the drafting and scrutinizing of initiated measures; and through other provisions of a similar character.

The 1948 edition of the *Model State Constitution* has some suggestions relative to the initiative and referendum that public men and students of government might well consider. One such suggestion, as explained in the chapter on the governor, is that the chief executive be authorized to call a referendum on any bill which fails to pass the legislature, and that the legislature be authorized, by majority vote, to submit to the people any measure vetoed by the governor, if, upon reconsideration by the legislature, it is not approved by a two-thirds vote but is approved by at least a majority vote. Another suggestion is that so-called "emergency measures" be made subject to the referendum, but that such measures be operative during the period between the filing of the referendum petition and the date of the election. This provision would eliminate some of the abuse to which legislature have put the "emergency clause."

A suggestion of particular significance is that "The initiative shall not be used as a means of making appropriations of public funds, nor for the enactment of local or special legislation. No measure submitted by the initiative shall contain therein the name of any person to be designated as administrator of any department, office, or agency to be established by the proposed law or constitutional amendment." The committee of experts probably had in mind certain types of pension proposals submitted in recent years to electors in various states, and the section by which such proposals would be rendered invalid might be characterized as the "anti-ham-and-egg" proviso.[46]

Reading List

Bower Aly (ed.), *Unicameral Legislatures* (1950).

A. E. Buck, *Modernizing Our State Legislatures,* Pamphlet series No. 4, the American Academy of Political and Social Science (1936).

D. B. Carroll, *The Unicameral Legislature of Vermont* (1933).

J. P. Chamberlain, *Legislative Processes: National and State* (1934).

D. L. Colvin, *The Bicameral Principle in the New York Legislature* (1913).

Council of State Governments, *The Book of the States* (biennially).

————, *Our State Legislatures* (1948).

H. W. Davey, "The Legislative Council Movement in the United States, 1933–1953," *Am. Pol. Sci. Rev.,* XLVII (1953), 785.

W. F. Dodd, *State Government* (1928 ed.), Chs. VI–VII, XX.

W. B. Graves, *American State Government* (1953 ed.), Chs. VI–VIII.

———— (ed.), "Our State Legislators," *Annals of the American Academy of Political and Social Science,* 195 (Jan. 1938).

Thelma I. Griswold, *Bicameralism in Ohio* (1937).

F. H. Guild, "Legislative Councils: Objectives and Accomplishments," *State Government,* Sept., 1949, pp. 217–219, 226.

F. H. Guild and C. F. Snider, *Legislative Procedure in Kansas* (Governmental Research Series, University of Kansas, 1946).

L. G. Harvey, "Reapportionment of State Legislatures—Legal Requirements," *Law and Contemporary Problems,* 17 (1952), 364.

A. N. Holcombe, *State Government in the United States* (1931 ed.), Chs. X, XVI.

"The Initiative and Referendum," *Bulletins for the Constitutional Convention, Mass.* (1917–18), Vol. I, No. 6.

"The Initiative, Referendum, and Recall," *Illinois Constitutional Convention Bulletin* (1919), No. 2.

R. Luce, *Legislative Assemblies* (1924).

————, *Legislative Procedure* (1922).

A. F. Macdonald, *American State Government and Administration* (1955 ed.), Chs. 7–9.

J. W. Manning, *Unicameral Legislation in the States* (1938).

Richard Neuberger, *Adventures in Politics: We Go to the Legislature* (1954).

New York State Constitutional Convention Committee, *Problems Relating to Legislative Organization and Powers* (1938).

James K. Pollock, *The Initiative and Referendum in Michigan* (1940).

T. H. Reed (ed.), *Legislatures and Legislative Problems* (1933).

Dorothy Schaffter, *The Bicameral System in Practice* (1929).

Waldo Schumacher, "Thirty Years of the People's Rule in Oregon," *Pol. Sci. Qt.,* XLVII (June, 1932), 242.

---

[46] For particular reference to California's difficulties see A. F. Smith, "Can We Afford the Initiative?" *Nat. Mun. Rev.,* Oct., 1949, p. 437.

K. C. Sears, *Methods of Reapportionment* (1952).

J. P. Senning, *The One-House Legislature* (1937).

C. W. Shull, "Political and Partisan Implications of State Legislative Apportionment," *Law and Contemporary Problems,* 17 (1952), 417.

P. S. Sikes and J. E. Stoner, *Bates and Field's State Government* (1954 ed.), Chs. 7–10.

T. V. Smith, *The Legislative Way of Life* (1940).

State Government (published monthly by the Council of State Governments).

Harvey Walker, *The Legislative Process: Lawmaking in the United States* (1948).

C. I. Winslow, *State Legislative Committees* (1931).

Belle Zeller, *Pressure Politics in New York* (1937).

—————— (ed.), *American State Legislatures,* Report of the Committee on American Legislatures, American Political Science Association (1954).

Questions and Problems

1. Summarize the arguments for and against the bicameral state legislature.

2. How nearly does your state approximate representation according to population in the lower house?   In the upper house?

3. What is the composition of your state legislature in respect to age, sex, profession, and education?

4. Comment upon the constitutional limitations as to the time a legislature may remain in session.

5. Estimate the value of joint committees in the work of the legislature.

6. What technical assistance is commonly available for a legislature?   In what particulars could this service be substantially improved?

7. How far does your state constitution's provisions for the legislature fall short of those recommended in the Model State Constitution?

8. Make a list of the provisions of your state constitution that indicate a lack of confidence in the legislature.

9. Write a 200-word essay on the relations of limitations on legislatures to the problem of improving legislatures.

10. Are the initiative and referendum in conflict with the republican form of government?

11. Can it be said that direct legislation is a tool of the "radicals" and "crack pots"?

CHAPTER | 6

THE STATE JUDICIAL SYSTEM

Students and citizens generally will read of the organization and activities of executives, administrators, and legislators, and they will discuss these with some assurance. But when it comes to the courts, they hesitate, finding them too technical; and they leave their consideration and discussion largely to the lawyers. True, the law and court procedures are often technical and only those with special training can hope to understand them. It is, however, an error to assume that intelligent laymen, including the common garden variety of college and university students, cannot learn enough about the courts and their operations to enable them to make penetrating judgments on the judicial system and to make some contribution to the administration of justice. Furthermore, a review of our state judicial system is not a dreary assignment. The courts deal with life—sometimes in the raw. The judges themselves are human, and we need not hesitate to discuss them and their work.

I. ORGANIZATION AND JURISDICTION OF STATE COURTS [1]

Types of Courts

In practically every state the courts are established by the state constitution and by legislative acts in pursuance thereof. Although the details of the judicial structure vary considerably from state to state, its fundamental aspects are essentially the same in all the states. Every state has a highest court of appeals, many have intermediate courts of appeals, all have various local courts of original jurisdiction, and all have minor courts.

1. THE SUPREME COURT. The highest court in the state is ordinarily styled the "supreme court"; but it also goes under such titles as the "supreme judicial court," "supreme court of errors," and "court of appeals." The number of justices varies from three to nine. Because of the pressure of business before the courts, there is a tendency to increase the number and permit them to sit in separate divisions, thus expediting the handling of cases.

[1] Council of State Governments, *State Court Systems* (1951 ed.); C. N. Callender, *American Courts* (1927), Ch. II; W. B. Graves, *American State Government* (1953 ed.), Ch. 17; P. S. Sikes and J. E. Stoner, *Bates and Field's State Government* (1954 ed.), Ch. 18.

125

Supreme courts have very little original jurisdiction, their work being confined almost entirely to the hearing of appeals. In some states, appeals lie to the supreme court from the intermediate courts of appeals only; whereas in others, appeals may be made from some of the lower courts. It is a rather common practice in the states to allow appeals to the supreme court only if the amount involved exceeds a certain sum, final decision in lesser cases being made by the intermediate courts. Supreme courts are always given ultimate jurisdiction in all cases requiring an interpretation of the state constitution; and, subject to review by the Supreme Court of the United States, they may interpret such parts of the federal Constitution, laws, and treaties as may come before them. Indeed, it is the duty of all state courts to apply the federal Constitution and laws to appropriate cases.

Judicial review. In interpreting either the state or federal Constitution, the state supreme court [2] may exercise the power of judicial review; that is, it may pass upon the validity of a statute of the state legislature under either of these instruments. A state court may even pass upon the validity of provisions of the state constitution if the question of their being in violation of the federal Constitution is raised. This authority to declare null and void state laws and provisions of state constitutions has been used rather freely by the state courts, perhaps more freely than by the federal courts. Because of the detailed provisions of state constitutions and particularly because of the many restrictions they impose upon legislatures, those bodies should move with great circumspection in order to avoid the enactment of unconstitutional measures. They do not always so move. Indeed, sometimes they quite frankly pass a measure of questionable constitutionality and leave the responsibility with the courts.

Advisory opinions. By constitutional provision in six or seven states and by statute or custom in several others, the supreme court is required to give advisory opinions when requested to do so by the governor or legislature. Such an opinion is not ordinarily requested except upon an important matter. When given, it is not considered as having the weight of a judicial precedent, inasmuch as the court hears no opposing arguments and decides no actual case.[3] These opinions are probably given a weight that falls between the opinions of an attorney general and court decisions in litigated cases. Eminent authorities differ on the wisdom of passing this function to the courts, and the legal profession very generally opposes it.

2. INTERMEDIATE COURTS OF APPEALS. The less populous states have no appellate courts except the supreme courts; but a number of the more densely

[2] The obligation of state courts to void state statutes that are in contravention to the federal Constitution is in its provision that "the judges in every state shall be bound thereby, anything in the constitution or laws of any state to the contrary notwithstanding" (Art. VI). See also People v. Western Union, 70 Colo. 90 (1921). All courts are bound to interpret the Constitution, but since the supreme courts have the final word, the practical result is that a law is not actually void until they so declare.

[3] In Colorado, however, such opinions have the same effect as opinions given in litigated cases. Graves, *op. cit.*, p. 638 n.

NEW JERSEY'S COURT SYSTEM
UNDER THE CONSTITUTION OF 1947

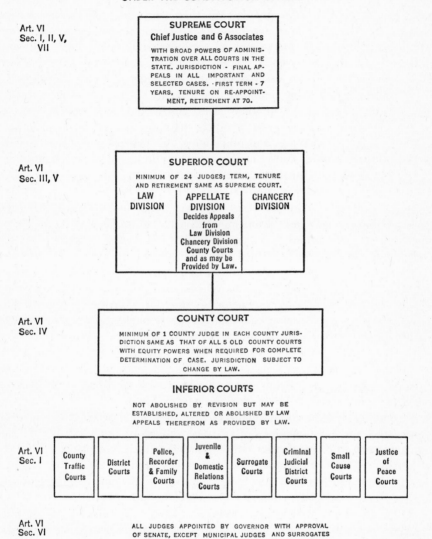

Art. VI Sec. I, II, V, VII

SUPREME COURT

Chief Justice and 6 Associates

WITH BROAD POWERS OF ADMINIS-
TRATION OVER ALL COURTS IN THE
STATE. JURISDICTION - FINAL AP-
PEALS IN ALL IMPORTANT AND
SELECTED CASES. · FIRST TERM - 7
YEARS, TENURE ON RE-APPOINT-
MENT, RETIREMENT AT 70.

Art. VI Sec. III, V

SUPERIOR COURT

MINIMUM OF 24 JUDGES; TERM, TENURE
AND RETIREMENT SAME AS SUPREME COURT.

LAW DIVISION	APPELLATE DIVISION	CHANCERY DIVISION
	Decides Appeals from Law Division Chancery Division County Courts and as may be Provided by Law.	

Art. VI Sec. IV

COUNTY COURT

MINIMUM OF 1 COUNTY JUDGE IN EACH COUNTY JURIS-
DICTION SAME AS THAT OF ALL 5 OLD COUNTY COURTS
WITH EQUITY POWERS WHEN REQUIRED FOR COMPLETE
DETERMINATION OF CASE. JURISDICTION SUBJECT TO
CHANGE BY LAW.

INFERIOR COURTS

NOT ABOLISHED BY REVISION BUT MAY BE
ESTABLISHED, ALTERED OR ABOLISHED BY LAW
APPEALS THEREFROM AS PROVIDED BY LAW.

Art. VI Sec. I

County Traffic Courts | District Courts | Police, Recorder & Family Courts | Juvenile & Domestic Relations Courts | Surrogate Courts | Criminal Judicial District Courts | Small Cause Courts | Justice of Peace Courts

Art. VI Sec. VI

ALL JUDGES APPOINTED BY GOVERNOR WITH APPROVAL
OF SENATE, EXCEPT MUNICIPAL JUDGES AND SURROGATES

Prepared for the New Jersey Committee for Constitutional Revision by Joseph Harrison;
Reproduced by Courtesy of Joseph Harrison and the Editors of the *Journal of the American Judicature Society*.

populated states have established intermediate courts of appeals, which correspond somewhat to the federal circuit courts of appeals. Some of the states have just one such court, and others have several. They are known by various titles, such as "courts of appeals," "district courts of appeals," and "superior courts." Like the supreme courts, each of these courts has several judges.

Their jurisdiction varies greatly, but their purpose is always the same, namely, to carry a part of the burden of appeals for the supreme court. Sometimes their jurisdiction extends to appealed cases in which the amounts in controversy fall between a certain stipulated maximum and minimum (say, $4,000 and $200), cases above the maximum going to the supreme court and cases below the minimum being finally decided in a lower court. The decision may be final in some cases, and in others an appeal may lie to the supreme court. Appeals involving the constitutionality of laws, titles to the state offices, felonies, and other important matters, in some states go directly from the lower courts to the supreme court, and in others must be carried first to the intermediate court of appeals.

3. COURTS OF ORIGINAL JURISDICTION. Local state courts have original jurisdiction in practically all cases of importance, and ordinarily an appellate jurisdiction in cases from minor courts. As a class they are often referred to as "trial courts" or "courts of first instance." The business before these courts may be divided into four types: civil cases at common law; equity suits; criminal prosecution; and probate matters, that is, matters relating to wills and the estates of deceased persons. These courts of original jurisdiction have various names—"superior," "district," and others—which do not always indicate the nature of their jurisdiction. In a number of states such courts handle all four types of litigation noted above; but a few states have special equity or chancery courts and some twenty states have probate courts.

4. MINOR COURTS. Below the ordinary courts of original jurisdiction there are courts that have original jurisdiction in petty cases. Although these may be designated as minor courts, they are not of minor importance, since the great majority of persons who go or are brought to court are concerned with trivial cases only. The office of justice of the peace had its origin in England centuries ago, and it has been an established institution in America from the beginning. In Britain the justice of the peace has jurisdiction in petty criminal cases only; but in America he may hear small civil cases as well, subject usually in both types of cases to appeal. In major criminal offenses, he may hold preliminary hearings and have accused persons held in custody. In addition to his judicial duties the justice of the peace may perform marriage ceremonies and attest formal documents.

Justices of the peace have fallen into disrepute. Professor W. Brooke Graves summarizes their defects as follows: they are "usually local politicians of the smallest caliber;" they know nothing of the law and little of anything else; they are paid on a fee basis and consequently have a strong tendency to decide for the plaintiff in order to collect a fee; many of them have entered into combinations with other local officials in establishing "speed traps" and otherwise harassing motorists, particularly those who are strangers.[4]

The justice of the peace functions in the rural districts. His city counterpart is the magistrate, and in many urban areas his reputation is hardly better than that of the justice of the peace. He is often subject to political influence to the extent that his decisions are made not on the basis of justice but on a tip from a wardheeler. A number of cities have improved the administration of justice through the establishment of municipal courts, giving them a wider jurisdiction than the magistrate's court enjoyed, and staffing them with competent judges. Such systems are commonly unified and under the administrative direction of a presiding judge. The results in Chicago, Detroit, and several other large cities are encouraging.

The Need for Judicial Organization

State courts were originally organized to meet the relatively simple needs of a rural society. As the country grew and an industrial civilization with all its complexities became established in most of the states, great changes in judicial organization were needed. There was a need for more courts, more judges, better systems of gathering and correlating judicial statistics, and, above all, for organization of the courts into a unified system. More courts were created and more judges were authorized from time to time, but that was as far as the legislatures usually went in meeting the new needs.

As a result of this halfway program the judicial system became more disorganized than ever. Some districts had more courts and judges than were needed; some had too few; and there was no higher court or administrative body with the authority to make proper adjustments. Furthermore, since there was no central judicial authority to make the rules of the courts, they were made by the legislatures, a task for which such bodies are not well fitted. In short, cumbersome and inflexible organization and rigid and ill-suited rules of procedure prevented, and in a number of states still prevent, the courts from performing their true function of administering justice speedily and free from unnecessary technicalities.

PROPOSED REMEDIES. A number of remedies have been designed for the improvement of judicial organization and procedure in the states. Here we shall give brief consideration to two of the most important of these—the unified court system and the judicial council.

The unified court system. Under this system all of the courts of the state would be organized as divisions or branches of a single, large judicial body. The chief justice or some other appropriate official would supervise the work of this consolidated court. Such a judicial system would make possible a division of judicial labor among various types of courts —civil, criminal, equity, and probate; the assignment of judges to tasks for which they are especially competent; dispatch in the settlement of cases; and the attainment of the goal that courts exist primarily for the benefit of

[4] *Op. cit.*, p. 596.

Classification of Courts and Terms of Judges *

State	Appellate Courts		Major Trial Courts					Courts of Limited Jurisdiction				
	Court of Last Resort	Intermediate Appellate Court	Chancery Court	Circuit Court	District Court	Superior Court	Other Trial Courts	Probate Court	County Court	Municipal Court	Justice, Magistrate or Police Court	Other Courts
Alabama	6	6	—	6	—	—	—	6	—	—	4	—
Arizona	6	—	—	—	—	4	—	—	2	4	4	2(a)
Arkansas	8	—	6	4	—	—	—	—	2	6	2	—
California	12	12	—	—	—	6	—	—	—	4	6	4(a),6(b)
Colorado	10	—	—	—	6	—	—	2	4	4	2	4-12(a)
Connecticut	8	—	—	—	—	8	—	4	—	4	2	—
Delaware	12	—	12	—	—	12	4-6(c)	4	4	2-4	4	4(b)
Florida	6	6	—	6	—	—	—	4	4	1-4	4	6(b)
Georgia	6	6	—	—	—	4	—	2	—	—	4	—
Idaho	6	—	—	—	6	—	6(d)	4	4	—	2	4(b)
Illinois	9	3	—	6	—	6	—	4	4	6	4	4(b)
Indiana	6	4	—	6	—	4	4(e)	4	—	4	4	—
Iowa	6	—	—	—	4	—	—	2	2	4	2	—
Kansas	6	—	—	—	4	—	—	2	4	2	4	—
Kentucky	8	—	—	6	—	—	—	—	—	4-6	4	6-8(b)
Louisiana	14	12	—	—	6(f)	—	—	4	—	—	4	—
Maine	7	—	—	—	—	7	—	4	—	4	2	—
Maryland	15	—	—	15	—	—	15(g)	4	—	8(h)	3	Life(i)
Massachusetts	Life	—	—	—	Life	Life	—	Life	—	—	4	6(a)
Michigan	8	—	—	6	—	6	6(j)	4	—	6	4	—
Minnesota	6	—	—	4	4	—	—	4	4	4	2	—
Mississippi	8	—	4	6	—	—	4(a)	4	—	—	4	4(k)
Missouri	12	12	—	—	4	—	—	4	4	2	4	—
Montana	6	—	—	—	4	—	—	—	—	4	2	—
Nebraska	6	—	—	—	4	—	—	—	4	4	2	6(r)

State	Term values (by court type)
Nevada	6 — — — — 4 — — — 6 2 —
New Hampshire	To age 70, 7 with reappointment for life — — — — — — — To age 70, 3 5 —
New Jersey	1 — — 5(l) — — 5 — 2(b) — 2(m), 5(b,n)
New Mexico	8 — — — 2 6 — — 6 2 —
New York	14 5 — 6(l),14(o) 6 2 2-6 — 4 4 —
North Carolina	8 — — 8 — — 2 2 — 2-6 2(b)
North Dakota	10 — 6 — 6 2-4 4 2 6 2 —
Ohio	6 6 — 6(a) 6 2 — 6 — 4 6(b)
Oklahoma	6 — 4 — — 4 — — 2 2 4(a),6(b)
Oregon	6 6 — — — — — — — 2 —
Pennsylvania	21 10 — 10(a) 10 10 — — 2 5 —
Rhode Island	Life — Life — 10 10 — — — — 3(s),10(b)
South Carolina	10 — 4 — 4 4 4 4 — 2 —
South Dakota	6 — 4 — — 2 2 2 — 2 —
Tennessee	8 8 8 8(e) — 4 4 — 4 6 —
Texas	6 6 6 — — 2 2 2 — 2 —
Utah	10 — — — — — — — 6 4 4(b)
Vermont	2 — — 2(l) 2 — 4 — 2 2 —
Virginia	12 — 8 8(p) — — — — — 2 —
Washington	6 — — 4 — — 4 — — 4 4-6(b)
West Virginia	12 — 8 — — — 4 — — 4 —
Wisconsin	10 — 6 — — 6 6 6 2-6 2 —
Wyoming	8 — 6 — 6 6 6 — — 2 4-6(b),6(q)
Hawaii	4 — 4 — — — — — — 2 2(s)
Puerto Rico	To age 70 — 12 — — — — — — 4 8(s)

* Reproduced by courtesy of the Council of State Governments from *The Book of the States, 1954-55*, p. 435.

(a) Courts of common pleas.
(b) Juvenile courts.
(c) Courts of record.
(d) City courts.
(e) Criminal courts.
(f) Judges in New Orleans serve 12 yrs.
(g) Supreme Bench of Baltimore.
(h) People's Court of Baltimore.
(i) Land Court of Massachusetts.
(j) Recorder's Court of Detroit.
(k) St. Louis Court of Criminal Corrections.
(l) County Courts.
(m) County traffic courts.
(n) Criminal judicial district courts.
(o) Supreme Court and Court of General Sessions.
(p) Corporation and hustings courts.
(q) Statutory courts; superior, district, civil, and small claims.
(r) Workmen's Compensation courts; Court of Industrial Relations.
(s) District courts.

litigants. A rather high degree of unity may be brought about without complete unification of the courts. This may be done through an administrative judge with power to assign judges to congested courts and to council with them on judicial problems. California, Maryland, Missouri, New Jersey, and several other states have made progress along this line.

The judicial council. Back in 1921 the Model State Constitution carried the significant proposal that the states set up judicial councils. What is more, the proposal has borne fruit, about thirty of the states having adopted it in some form. These councils are composed of representative judges of the various courts (the chief justice is commonly the head of the council), perhaps the attorney general, some practicing attorneys, probably a few members of the legislature, and often some laymen. The council is not a legislative or judicial body. It makes no laws, it decides no cases. Some of them have a few administrative powers, but the council must be considered primarily as an advisory and investigating body. Its administrative duties relate to the collection of statistics and other information essential to the efficient operation of the judicial system, and in some states the council may transfer judges from districts with light dockets to districts with crowded dockets.

Perhaps the chief duty of the council is to make rules of general practice. During the past century a number of states gave this power to the supreme court, but with the establishment of the judicial councils, it has been thought better to transfer the power to them. If a state should continue to vest this power in the supreme court, the authorities insist that the council should be assigned the task of taking the initiative, gathering data, drafting rules, and discussing their proposals with the bar, finally passing the rules up to the court for adoption. It seems to be very generally agreed that the legislature is not the body to make rules of general practice.

Attention to the problem of improving the organization and functioning of the judiciary is continuous. In 1949 the annual Conference of (State) Chief Justices was instituted. Some idea of the work of this conference may be gained by noting that in 1953 the chief justices concentrated their attention on judicial councils and conferences, and several other appropriate subjects. They recommended the judicial council for every state, and they recommended also a judicial conference (a larger body than the council but similar in personnel), suggesting that a state might desire to use either the council or the conference or both. Another recommendation was that an administrative officer be designated to discharge the many business and administrative duties now carried on by judges in most of the states. The federal courts have had such an office since 1939, and it has amply demonstrated its usefulness. The states are now following suit, beginning to provide for similar administrative assistance.[5]

[5] *Book of the States, 1954–55,* p. 431; "The Conference of Chief Justices," *State Government,* Oct., 1953, p. 241; E. W. Hudgins, "The Judicial Council and Judicial Conference in Virginia," *State Government,* Jan., 1954, p. 17; W. G. Woelper, "Administering the Courts in New Jersey," *Journal of the American Judicature Society,* XXXVI (Oct., 1952), 70.

II. STATE JUDGES [6]

Selection

Federal judges, as everyone knows, are appointed by the President subject to confirmation by the Senate. A similar method of appointment was used in the colonies; but during the Revolution and immediately following it, the legislature took a larger part in the selection of judges. As the nineteenth century advanced, the democratic and pioneer influence led to the establishment of popular choice as the chief method of selection. At present only eight states have their judges chosen by the governor—or by the governor subject to legislative approval, or by the governor and the judicial council; four leave this function to the legislature; and three fourths of the states leave the choice of judges to the sovereign people.

SHOULD JUDGES BE APPOINTED OR ELECTED? Judges are supposed to stay out of politics, to be independent. The question arises as to what method of selection is least likely to bring the judiciary into politics. It is commonly agreed that choice by the legislative body is the most political of all the methods of selection, and there is no strong movement in its favor at present. The issue is rather between executive appointment and popular election. The advocates of the appointive system speak of the high quality of the English and of our own federal judges, obtained under that system; of the fact that only in the American states are judges elected. They allege that an elective judiciary is, of necessity, a political judiciary; that candidates must descend from the bench and mount the rostrum or yield the judgeships to those who will do so. It is said that the people have no notion as to the competence of candidates for judicial office; and that in districts where so many judges are elected, popular choice is bound to be a farce.

But the advocates of the appointive system have perhaps overdrawn the picture. The facts are that the people have often made excellent choices, and that governors have not always made wise and nonpolitical appointments. Moreover, whether the elective or appointive method is used, the bar association, the best informed body on candidates for the judicial offices, exercises considerable influence with the voters or with the governor, as the case may be. Further, since the judges do decide political questions in passing upon the constitutionality of certain types of statutes, it is only proper that some political considerations should enter into their selection. Then, too, it may be observed that the election of judges is not ordinarily attended by partisan appeals. Sixteen states employ nonpartisan ballots for these elections, which, although they do not necessarily remove all partisan influences, nevertheless operate to reduce such influences. Not infrequently judges are re-elected solely on their records and without opposition. Yet we would

[6] A. A. Bruce, *The American Judge* (1924); M. Dawson, "Judging the Judges," *Harper's*, Sept., 1934, pp. 437–448; Dodd, *op. cit.*, pp. 312–319; Graves, *op. cit.*, pp. 609 ff.; *Book of the States, 1954–55*, pp. 435 ff.; Sikes and Stoner, *op. cit.*, pp. 529–537.

be less than candid not to admit that, if partisan considerations are usually absent in the process of selecting judges, the personal interests of the candidates are almost always present, and it cannot be doubted that some candidates have made popular appeals, the effect of which has been to lower the prestige of the courts and even threaten the independence of the judiciary. It is even a fact that some judicial nominations have been bought and paid for.   There are some methods of selecting judges that are decided improvements over those commonly employed.   One of the best of these shall have attention.

The Missouri plan of judicial selection.   In 1940 Missouri, following a plan approved by the American Bar Association, adopted a new system of selecting judges.   It provides that whenever a vacancy exists in the supreme court, in the courts of appeals, and in certain other courts in Kansas City and St. Louis, a nominating commission, composed of both lawyers and laymen, shall nominate three candidates, and the governor must appoint one of these nominees.   After serving twelve months this judge goes before the people upon his record and with no competing candidate.   The question for the voters to decide is: Shall he continue in office?   The people vote on the same question in reference to any judge whose term of office is about to expire.   In the event a majority of the voters are against his continuance in office, the nominating commission gives the governor a new list of nominees, the governor makes a new appointment, and after the judge has served for one year, the people vote on the question of his continuance in office.   It will be noticed that this plan is designed to provide a method of appointment which is relatively free from politics and, at the same time, to reserve to the people the right of ultimate control.

The political struggle through which the state of Missouri passed in securing this plan should not be passed by.   In 1940 the people adopted the amendment that provided for it by a majority of 95,000 votes.   Near the end of the next session of the legislature, the time when deals are most commonly made and the will of the people flouted, the legislature proposed an amendment to repeal the amendment adopted in the previous election.   In November, 1942, the people turned down this repeal amendment by a majority of 173,000.   The increased majority by which the people of Missouri expressed themselves in favor of removing judges from politics was a tribute to their intelligence and their interest in good government, and it was also a testimonial to the effectiveness of civic leadership on that question.[7]

[7] John Perry Wood, "Missouri Victory Speeds National Judicial Selection Reform," *Journal of the AJS*, XXVI (Feb., 1943), 142.   See also "Missouri and California Lawyers Appraise Judicial Selection Methods," *ibid.*, XXXI (April, 1948), 176; "Missouri Bar to Supplement Court Plan," *ibid.*, XXXII (June, 1948), 23; and L. M. Hyde, "Choosing Judges in Missouri," *Nat. Mun. Rev.*, Nov., 1949, p. 491; G. R. Winters, "A Better Way to Select Our Judges," *Journal of the AJS*, XXXIV (April, 1951), 166; Allen T. Klots, "The Selection of Judges and the Short Ballot," *Journal of the AJS*, XXXVIII (1955), 134, and "How Much Do Voters Know or Care About Judicial Candidates," *ibid.*, 141.

Terms and Tenure

The independence of judges is commonly considered as being determined not only by the method of selection but also by the length of their terms. The terms vary a great deal in the several states and within the individual states. The highest justices usually have the longest terms. Their term is for life in Massachusetts and Rhode Island; to the age of seventy in New Hampshire; twenty-one years in Pennsylvania; fifteen years in Maryland; fourteen years in Louisiana and New York; seven years with reappointment for life in New Jersey; and a lesser number of years in other states—six years being the most common. In more than half the states judges of the lower courts hold office for shorter terms than the judges of the supreme court. There is no doubt that the long term increases the independence and learning of a judge, and the practice of re-electing competent judges, which obtains in several states, serves as a fairly good substitute for the longer term.

Qualifications

State judges are almost invariably selected from the bar. The duties of the practitioner and the judge are really quite different, and in some countries there is a definite distinction between the two. In France, for example, young men are trained as lawyers or as judges, and the judicial profession is filled by those who have special training for it. No doubt our system has certain advantages over that of the French; but the fact remains that the duties of the advocate and the judge are different and that when a lawyer becomes a judge he must take himself in hand for some very important readjustments. As an attorney, he was a partisan, a talker, probably a specialist, and possibly unconcerned about the broader social problems of the state. As a judge, he must be an arbiter, a listener, learned in the whole field of the law and conversant with economics, history, and sociology. He must strive to gain a "full sense of the seamless web of life." He must become a "statesman as well as a jurist, thinker as well as lawyer." [8]

Manifestly it is exceedingly difficult, even under the most favorable circumstances, to find men who measure up to this standard; and it is not surprising that politics in selections, short terms, and inadequate salaries often produce state judges who are far below it. Indeed, in some states, judicial office, particularly that of trial judge, is not at all attractive to the best legal talent, and it not infrequently goes to second-class men or to young men who may hope to use it as a stepping-stone to a later lucrative practice. Although, broadly speaking, state judges are less likely than federal judges to be learned and independent, it should be said that a number of states have maintained very high judicial standards. And among the state judges who belong to a select company of statesmen-jurists we mention Cooley of Michigan, Doe of New Hampshire, Clark of North Carolina, Holmes (appointed to the Supreme Court of the United States in 1902) and Shaw of Massachusetts,

[8] H. J. Laski, "Mr. Justice Holmes," *Harper's,* March, 1930, p. 415.

Mitchell of Minnesota, Winslow of Wisconsin, and Kent and Cardozo (the latter appointed to succeed Justice Holmes in the Supreme Court of the United States in 1932) of New York.

Salaries and Retirement Annuities

In a few states the salary of judges is fixed by the constitution; but usually it is very sensibly left to the legislatures to decide, subject to a few constitutional limitations. Adequate salaries are paid in New York, New Jersey, Pennsylvania, and several other states, but the average is not high. A salary of $13,000 for supreme court justices and $11,000 for the judges in the courts of original jurisdiction may be taken as a rough average. It is fair to assume that more liberal salaries would elevate the standards of the state judiciary; for at present, in many states, competent men are loath to give up lucrative private practice for the relatively small compensation allowed judges. But progress is being made in the direction of increasing the salaries, and practically all the states have provided retirement pensions, a number of which are rather generous.

Removal of State Judges

Judges may be removed by impeachment in every state; but the political squabbles that commonly attend impeachment proceedings are so out of keeping with the nature of the judicial office that this method of removal is rarely used. Furthermore, impeachment requires a trial and a conviction for a specific offense. A more satisfactory method of removal, employed in a number of states, provides that the governor may at his option remove a judge upon address by both houses (usually a special majority) of the legislature. No trial or conviction is necessary, thus enabling the political authorities to remove a judge who for one reason or another may be incapacitated. One of the best examples of this type of procedure is provided for in the New Jersey Constitution of 1947. Under this provision the supreme court certifies to the governor that a particular judge is believed to be substantially incapacitated; the governor then appoints a commission of three persons to make inquiry; and on the recommendation of this commission the governor may retire the judge, "on pension as may be provided by law." In some states judges may be removed by a special majority of both houses of the legislature, the governor having no part in the matter.

In eight states [9] the people may remove a judge by recall; that is, by a special election ("diselection") held when 10–25 per cent of the voters officially request it. Back in the Progressive Era, when the recall was instituted, conservatives argued that the recall of judges would deal a terrible blow to the independence of the judiciary; that judges would be recalled every time they gave decisions which ran counter to the will of a bare majority of the voters; that the recall of judges meant, in effect, that the people would

[9] They are: Arizona, California, Colorado, Kansas, Nevada, North Dakota, Oregon, and Wisconsin.

set themselves up as judges. As a matter of fact, the people have shown great restraint in the use of this emergency weapon. No supreme court justice has ever been recalled. Only a few inferior judges have been so removed and these almost without exception for personal deliquencies rather than for unpopular decisions. Whatever arguments may be advanced against the popular dismissal of judges, experience has demonstrated thus far that the judiciary is in no particular danger from this source.

III. THE LAW IN THE STATES [10]

The student may possibly think of the law in the states, the law applied in state courts, as being that enacted by the legislatures. It is quite true that this statute law, as it is called, forms a large and growing part of the law the courts are called upon to enforce. But in order to have a grasp of the legal system of the states, it is necessary to look beyond the statutes, to take brief notice of our legal heritage.

The Common Law

The laws of the states consist very largely of the common law (often called simply "law") and equity, which the colonists brought over from England. To be sure, this legal heritage has been changed by statute, more in some states than in others; but the basic principles of the English common law system still apply in the American states, except in Louisiana. How did this English law develop and how did it come to be our law?

After the Norman Conquest and particularly during the reign of Henry II (1154–1189) the rather diverse systems of local law and judicial administration gave way to a centralized system. Justices were sent out from London "on circuits," and they held court in the various counties, acting under the authority of the king. In deciding the cases that came before them, they ascertained what the local customs were and ordinarily applied them in their decisions. Back in London, these justices no doubt related their experiences among themselves with mutual profit. On circuit again, a judge might have a case dissimilar to any he had decided before, and, furthermore, a controversy on which the customs of the community seemed conflicting, or, if uniform, contrary to justice. What did he do? He recalled that one of his brethren had a similar case a few months before; he followed the decision of his brother judge. And so it went on, the judges applying the customs of the communities where they seemed to do justice and using each other's decisions as precedents in other cases. In the course of time, a body of law *common* to the whole kingdom was developed. As the years passed, the judges came to rely much more upon earlier decisions than upon the customs of the communities. Finally, and long before the English colonies were planted in

[10] Z. Chafee, Jr., *Some Problems of Equity* (1950); Graves, *op. cit.,* Ch. 16; J. W. Hurst, *The Growth of American Law: the Law Makers* (1950); Richard O'Sullivan, *The Inheritance of the Common Law* (1950); Roscoe Pound, "Common Law," *Encyclopaedia of the Social Sciences.* IV, 50.

America, previous decisions rather rigidly established the principles to be followed in later cases. It must not be understood, however, that the law became absolutely fixed. One of the glories of the common law is that it has always submitted to gradual changes. But the trouble has been that the changes come just a little too gradually.

Equity

As already stated, the common law became too rigid. One could get redress only through the use of writs, which were limited in number and very technical in form. For many an injury there was no writ, and no writ meant no remedy. For example, there was no writ that would cover a breach of an ordinary oral contract, leaving such contracts to be broken with impunity. Again, if one lost title to his land by the fraud of another, the common law afforded him no remedy. In any case, the common law provided a remedy only after damage had been suffered. This was a major defect, since for many injuries the payment of damages, however large, is no adequate compensation. Something was needed to supplement the common law. This was found in *equity*. It developed in this way. Since the courts were the king's courts and acted under his authority, a person who failed to get justice in them turned to the king with his complaint. As an act of grace, the king might grant the relief prayed for. These petitions became so numerous that the king referred most of them to his chancellor and chaplain, "the keeper of the king's conscience." In the fourteenth century a special court, the court of chancery or equity, was permanently established for such cases. But let us not suppose that the chancellor and other equity judges had no other guide than conscience. Very soon equity came to have its own system of rules and remedies, and they are now hardly more elastic than those of the common law. It nevertheless continues to supplement, and at certain points to overlap, the common law. One other important fact should be noted. It is, that "law" and "equity" combined long since fell short of the needs of advancing civilization. They both remain, to be sure; but they have been modified and supplemented by acts of Parliament as often as that body has felt changes to be necessary.

Common Law and Equity in the States

As shown above, the English colonists carried the English system of law to America and to all other new lands in which they settled. The American Revolution did not change the law in the states. Indeed, it may be said that our courts applied the common law more whole-heartedly after the Revolution than before, although certain principles which seemed inapplicable in America were never enforced here. Even now, our courts occasionally consult the decisions of British courts in common law cases. A comparatively recent (1949) example comes from Arkansas, where the supreme court, finding no state law making the concealment of a dead body punishable, turned to the English common law of 1607 and found that "indecent treatment" of a body was a misdemeanor.   In like manner, the courts of Britain sometimes turn to American decisions.   In neither case, however, are the decisions of the courts of one country binding in the other; but they have great influence. The principles of equity, with certain modifications, also came into our legal system from Great Britain.   In England law and equity are still administered in separate courts; in America, except in a few states, they are administered by the same courts.

SOME EXAMPLES.   In order to make the distinction between law and equity clear, we shall take a few examples of how the two operate in civil controversies in the states.   Suppose A has been ousted from his land by B. A has a remedy at common law.   He may recover his land through an action of ejectment.   A may also claim damages from B because B temporarily deprived him of his rightful possession.   Suppose C breaks a contract with D.   For this breach of contract, C may be sued at common law. Taking one other example, suppose E has through his negligence caused F a personal injury.   F may sue E for damages at common law.   Now, suppose A conveys a piece of land to B, and in the deed the area of the land is incorrectly described.   The common law does not afford an adequate remedy; but equity will compel A to execute a new deed correcting the mistake.   Suppose C has secured a contract with D through fradulent devices; the common law damage suit is again no adequate remedy.   But in a court of equity D may prove the fraud and have the contract canceled. On the other hand, suppose E has entered into a perfectly valid contract with F to sell him a particular piece of property.   If E fails to make delivery, F may sue him for damages at common law.   Now, F may have a very special use for that particular piece of property—no other will serve his purpose. What he wants, therefore, is the property, not the insufficient damages he might get at law.   He goes to a court of equity, and that court will command E to deliver the property in accordance with the contract.   For the final illustration, take the case of a property owner who is about to extend his house beyond the building line and seems to be about to cut down one of his neighbor's fine trees.   The neighbor will hasten to an equity court and secure an injunction against the adjoining property owner.   He might wait until the damage is done and then sue at common law; but he wants his property preserved, not damages for its impairment or destruction.   From these examples it should be clear that equity fills in two very big gaps in the common law: it provides for relief against threatened wrongs; and it redresses certain injuries not covered by the common law.

Statutes and Codes

As the inadequacies of common law and equity led the British Parliament to supplement them by statutory law, so the American states have, in varying degrees, supplemented and changed them by statute.   A number of states have enacted complete codes dealing with particular fields of law.   It is sometimes said that the code abolishes the common law; but the code almost invariably draws very heavily from that law and is construed in the light of the common law. What the code actually does, in addition to making certain changes in the law, is to bring together all the laws on a given subject, as distinguished from the common law method of leaving them scattered about in thousands of judicial decisions. For example, many states have enacted criminal codes putting most of the old common law crimes on the statute books, dropping a few, and adding some entirely new crimes. Similarly, a number of states have established codes of criminal procedure and codes of civil procedure. Efforts are also made to secure uniform laws among the states on such subjects as negotiable instruments and sales. This movement is sponsored by the National Conference of Commissioners on Uniform State Laws, a body that has drafted about seventy statutes and has had the satisfaction of seeing at least a score of them quite generally adopted by state legislatures.[11] A few states have attempted to codify the whole body of law. Louisiana practically started her career as a state with a code modeled after the French civil law. In more recent years some other states of the South and some west of the Mississippi have adopted more or less complete codes.[12]

Is THE CODE DESIRABLE? Although some advantages are to be gained by codifying certain branches of the law, particularly by revising and simplifying the rules of common law pleadings and enacting comprehensive statutes on subjects that the common law covers inadequately, there is some question as to the wisdom of codifying the whole field of law. One of the reputed advantages of the code system over the regular common law system is that the former brings all the law together, whereas the latter is found in thousands of judicial decisions—precedents. To this contention, the reply is often made that it is impossible to get every fragment of the common law in a code; that cases will arise that are not provided for in that compilation. To the argument that the code makes the law certain and definite, it is replied that the code itself requires judicial interpretation, because cases constantly arise that fall within the twilight zone of its provisions. Further, it is said that the code is less flexible than the common law; that under the code necessary changes must depend upon the legislature, whereas under the common law new cases may be fitted in and old precedents occasionally overruled by the courts themselves. Finally, it may be said that the members of the legal profession, who should know more than the rest of us about the relative merits of the code and the old common law system, generally look with disfavor upon the attempts of a state to codify the whole domain of law.[13]

Particular attention should be directed to the work of the American Law Institute in restating the common law and in formulating codes of procedure. Many eminent scholar-lawyers have contributed to its research and publica-

---

[11] Graves, *op. cit.*, pp. 854 ff. See also his volume, *Uniform State Action: A Possible Substitute for Centralization* (1934); *Book of the States, 1954–55*, pp. 145–148; and A. J. Harno, "Uniform State Laws and the Federal System," *State Government*, Nov. 1948, pp. 225–227, 236.

[12] C. A. Beard, *American Government and Politics* (1949 ed.), p. 640.

[13] *Ibid.*, pp. 640–641.

tions and the results have received wide praise. In 1932 it published the *Restatement of the Law of Contracts,* its first project. This was followed by restatements on trusts, judgments, torts, and other subjects, running to twenty volumes. The "Restatement" is not an authorized code, not law in the sense that a state code is law, but is a scholarly work that simplifies and clarifies the law. It has had the widest influence with lawyers and judges, having been cited some 20,000 times by federal or state judges. As a modern interpretation of the common law it stands in a class all to itself.

Other Law

It seems hardly necessary to mention that state courts are bound by the state constitution, which is the highest law of a state, and by the still higher law of the nation—the Constitution, acts of Congress passed in pursuance thereof, and treaties. Furthermore, administrative rules and regulations issued by executive officers under the authority of the state constitution or of the legislature have the force of law.

IV. CIVIL LAW AND PROCEDURE [14]

Distinction Between Civil and Criminal Law

The law may be divided into two fields, civil and criminal. At the risk of stating the obvious, a brief distinction will be drawn between the two. A murder has been committed; a man has been robbed; a car has been stolen; a child has been kidnaped. These are a few examples of crime. The state assumes the duty of apprehending, prosecuting, and punishing those guilty of such offenses, although the victim of a crime or his relatives and friends may assist the state in some respects. The following are examples of civil wrongs: A passenger has been killed in an accident; a car has been damaged through the carelessness of the driver of another car; a citizen has distracting noises and noxious fumes coming from his premises to such an extent as to disturb his neighbor in the use and enjoyment of his property; an individual has refused to pay his landlord, his grocer, or others who have performed services for him. The law provides remedies for such wrongs, but the state will not take cognizance of them unless the person wronged brings them to court. The distinction between criminal and civil cases is now clear. In criminal cases, the state is the plaintiff and judge; in civil cases, the aggrieved individual is the plaintiff and the state is the judge. The alleged wrongdoer in both types of cases is the defendant. It may happen that a wrong may be at the same time both civil and criminal. For example, if a grossly negligent driver injures another, the state may prosecute him for crime and the injured party may sue him for damages.

---

[14] In the discussion of both civil and criminal law the writer has followed the excellent summaries in Beard, *op. cit.,* pp. 641 ff., and in Sikes and Stoner, *op. cit.* On procedure Callender, *op. cit.,* has been followed. For extended discussion of contracts and other aspects of business law, see various texts, such as Joseph L. Frascona, *Business Law* (1954) and Harold F. Lusk, *Business Law* (1951 ed.).

Law students take several courses on criminal law and procedure and course after course on civil law. Here we can only summarize, giving in this section some indication of the content of civil law and the manner in which its remedies are sought and applied. The section that follows defines the major crimes and gives an outline of procedure in criminal cases.

Civil Law

1. PROPERTY. Private property is one of the basic factors of our civilization. The laws relating to it form the most important subdivision of the field of civil law. In legal theory there is no such thing as absolute ownership. For example, the state may take a piece of land from a private owner for a public building site or a road. The owner has a right to compensation and the state will compensate him, but he cannot hold "his" land against the needs of the state. What one has, then, are certain *rights* to use and dispose of property, not absolute ownership. However, ownership is the term we use in common parlance, and it will suffice here. Property is divided into two main divisions, real and personal.

(*a*) *Real.* Real property, generally speaking, consists of land and whatever is erected or growing upon it or affixed to it. An individual who buys a piece of land is said to have an *estate in fee simple.* This is the nearest thing to absolute ownership. He may use his estate as he sees fit, subject to the condition that he respect his neighbor's rights. Another form of estate is known as a *life estate.* A widower in most states has this right in the real property of his deceased wife. Similarly, a widow has a life estate in a part of her deceased husband's real property. One who has a life estate may not, of course, will it to another, that being a right held only by the owner in fee simple. Real property in lands and buildings is called *corporeal* or *tangible.* Certain other kinds of real property are designated as *incorporeal* or *intangible.* For example, the rights that one landowner may have to use the land of an adjoining owner for access to a highway, for pasture, for hunting, and for many other purposes belong in this class.

(*b*) *Personal.* Personal property consists primarily, though not exclusively, of movable things. This property is commonly classified as follows: (1) *real chattels,* for example leases on land for terms of years; (2) *personal chattels*—ordinary movable property such as everyone owns—jewelry, clothing, books, and the like; (3) *choses in action,* which include bonds, stocks, claims one may have against debtors, and similar intangible rights; and (4) rights one may hold in patents and copyrights.

INHERITANCE. Property of deceased persons is inherited in accordance with the law, which differs somewhat in the several states. If the deceased has made a will that meets the requirements of the law, the executor, who is usually named in the will, after payment of the debts of the deceased, proceeds to distribute the property according to the stipulations of the will. If one dies intestate, that is, having made no will or one that is defective in form, the property is distributed to the heirs in accordance with the law and by an administrator appointed by a probate court. The law relating to wills and inheritance is exceedingly complex, and not infrequently there is prolonged litigation over the division of the decedent's estate. If one dies intestate without heirs, his property escheats, that is, reverts, to the state, the original and ultimate proprietor.

2. TORTS. Any violation by one individual of the rights of another, such as his right to personal security, liberty, property, and reputation, is called a *tort,* and the injured party may institute a suit for damages. No definition of the term is satisfactory; it can be understood only by examples and explanations.

(*a*) *Against the person.* Certain torts are committed against the person. Arrest without probable cause belongs to this class. An ancient and homely illustration of this particular tort is furnished by a landlord who was forced to pay damages to a lodger whose arrest he had caused on a suspicion that she had stolen about half the feathers from a bed in her room.[15] A similar tort is the institution of legal proceedings against one with malice and without probable cause. The fact that the law affords protection against the institution of malicious proceedings must not be construed to mean that any time a defendant wins a judgment he may then collect damages from the unsuccessful plaintiff. In order to collect damages the successful defendant must show that the suit was maliciously instituted. Another tort against the person is *assault,* which is an attempt, real or apparent, to do bodily harm. Thus, a threatening shake of a fist under another's nose or a rush toward another with intent to strike him constitutes assault. If bodily contact is made in such cases, another tort, *battery,* is committed. Of a number of other torts that are primarily against the person, we may mention enticing children away and alienating the affections of a wife or husband. *Slander* and *libel* constitute two well-known torts against the person. The former is a defamation of character published orally; the latter is the same published in writing, print, or figure.

(*b*) *Against property.* Certain torts are primarily connected with property. For example, A, without lawful excuse, interferes with B's attempts to secure contracts; or, A, having knowledge of a contract between B and C, influences C to break the contract. Again, A makes a fraudulent representation to B in a business deal, which B to his damage believes to be a truthful representation. *Trespass* covers a wide variety of torts, such as, the unlawful taking of personal property, forceful damage to such property, and nuisances to land. Indeed, the term is so broad that some of the torts mentioned under other headings, assault and battery, for example, are often classed as trespasses.

(*c*) *Against person and property.* Manifestly, a number of torts may affect both the person and property. Thus loud noises, noxious odors, or dense fumes, which discolor buildings and ruin the housewife's curtains,

---

[15] Allen v. Wright, Common Pleas of England, Nisi Prius, Trinity Term, 1838, 8 Car. & P. 522.

are nuisances that not only disturb persons in their use and enjoyment of property but also lower the value of such property. Similarly, the many torts grouped under the familiar term *negligence,* such as careless or reckless driving, may cause both personal injury and damage to property.

Although damages may be recovered for a tort, it does not follow that damages will be awarded every time one receives an injury. Suppose two negligent drivers have a collision, and one is injured. The injured party's "contributory negligence" bars him from collecting damages. By the same token, an employer is not liable at common law for the injuries of an employee who was negligent. Furthermore, the old common law doctrine of "fellow servant" prevented a workman from recovering damages if his injury was due to the negligence of another employee. In both these cases, however, the liability of the employer has been established by statute in most states.[16]

3. CONTRACTS. The making and enforcing of contracts is an indispensable practice in business. An agreement to sell a piece of property for a specified sum, to pay, at a specified time for value received, the principal and a certain rate of interest on a note, to carry goods from one point to another for a consideration, to pay a stipulated premium in return for insurance protection, and many similar agreements are contracts. The important contracts must ordinarily be written in order to be enforceable in court. Others may be oral. An individual who has been shown a hat to his liking and walks out of a store with it without saying a word is understood to have made a contract, an implied contract, to take the hat and pay the price for it. For breach of contract one may collect damages at common law, and in certain cases, as already indicated, get an order for "specific performance" in an equity proceeding.

4. BUSINESS ORGANIZATIONS. Another significant group of laws has to do with business organizations. Of particular interest are the partnership and the corporation.

(*a*) *Partnerships.* The partnership represents a relatively old form of business combination, but many small enterprises and some large ones are still carried on under this form. Its advantages are perhaps obvious enough, but it has certain disadvantages. For instance, it is dissolved when one of its members withdraws or dies. Also, the debts of the partnership are the debts of the individual members, which joint obligation means that a large debt may be saddled upon one solvent member, or that a too trusting individual may find himself ruined by the knavery of his partner.

(*b*) *Corporations.* The corporation is the institution through which most large businesses have come to be conducted in the last hundred years. It comes into being through a charter issued by the state to a group of natural persons. This legal person so created may sue and be sued, buy and sell property, and exercise certain other rights, just as natural persons do. The term of its life is fixed by the charter, not by the death or withdrawal of a

---

[16] See "Workmen's compensation," Chapter 9, section II.

member or members. The membership may change, but the corporation goes on. This power of "perpetual succession" is one of the features of the corporation that make it superior to the partnership for business purposes. Another advantage it has over the partnership is that the individuals who hold the stock are liable only to the extent of the par value of that stock. Thus, a man who has $1,000 in the stock of a particular corporation will lose only that amount if the corporation should fail. His other property cannot be seized to pay the debts of the corporation.[17]

5. DOMESTIC RELATIONS. A word must be said about one other large body of private law, the law of domestic relations.

(a) *Marriage and divorce.* Marriage licenses are issued and weddings solemnized in accordance with state law. Persons below a certain age and within a certain degree of kinship are not permitted to marry. Certain types of marriages, for instance, those entered into under fraud or duress, may be annulled. Divorces are granted by the courts under the authority of a legislative act, although it was not until 1949 that South Carolina abandoned the old practice of leaving the granting of divorces entirely to the legislature. The only ground for divorce in some states is adultery; other states add such grounds as desertion, conviction of crime, and incurable insanity; and some states are very liberal, allowing dissolution of the marriage on such grounds as "mental cruelty" and "incompatibility of temperament." It is notorious that persons who live in states having strict divorce laws often go to more liberal states to obtain their "freedom." On occasion some difficulty arises over the refusal of the state in which the parties actually live to recognize the validity of a divorce which one of them obtained while residing temporarily in another state.[18]

(b) *Status of married women.* Some twenty-five hundred years ago King Ahasuerus laid it down as one of the laws of the Medes and the Persians "that every man should bear rule in his own house." The old common law was somewhat in accord with that rule. At common law the husband was the guardian and protector of his wife, and it followed more or less logically that her property became his, even her clothing. The wife could make no binding contracts, and her husband could recover damages for any injury done her. On the other hand, the husband was obliged to support his wife and was held liable for any torts she might commit, for the necessities of life furnished her, and for the contracts she had entered into before marriage. Such, in substance, was the common law on the status of married women, a status that caused women struggling for emancipation to say they were "dead in the law."

During the last hundred years this status has been modified materially by liberal judges, and particularly by statutes. In some of the states, wives now enjoy practically the same rights as their husbands; but the forces that

---

[17] Only private corporations are discussed here. There are various other corporations, such as municipal corporations, which have governmental or quasi-governmental purposes.

[18] See Chapter 1, section IV, under "full faith and credit," for a brief discussion of this complicated problem.

contend for absolute equality the nation over still have a few strongholds
to take. In general, however, it can safely be said that such inequality of
the sexes as remains is due to physiological, psychological, and social causes,
rather than to legal discriminations.

(c) *Status of children.* In the old days a child was practically under
the absolute control of the male parent, but modern law protects the child
in various ways; for instance, in his right to support, and in guarding him
against abuse. Children may be taken away from grossly incompetent parents and placed under guardians. The custody of children of divorced parents is left to the courts, subject only to very general statutory provisions.
The courts consult the child's welfare, and as between the parents, allow the
innocent rather than the guilty to have custody of the child. Occasionally,
a child is placed in the custody of some third person. Children of divorced
persons are commonly supported from the father's income or estate.

Civil Procedure

The brief survey of the rules of substantive civil law must now be followed
by a discussion of the rules by which this substantive law is enforced, the
rules of civil procedure. A simple illustration will show the difference between substantive and procedural law. A is injured by the negligence of B.
His right to damages is covered by substantive law; the method by which
he legally recovers damages is a matter of procedure. Common law procedure was formerly used in all the states; but its technicalities were such that
justice was often defeated, and, as a result, the states were led to modify
the common law procedure by statutes, or by judges acting under the authority
of statutes. At present the system of procedure differs somewhat in the several states, but a general discussion of it will suffice.

1. PLEADINGS: In some of the minor courts the parties to a suit simply
go to court and tell their story, and the justice decides the case. This
method has not been found satisfactory in the regular trial courts; consequently, they continue to use a rather formal system of pleadings.

(a) *Preliminaries.* The plaintiff goes to an attorney and tells his story,
and the attorney directs the clerk of the court that has jurisdiction to issue
a writ of summons. This writ directs the defendant to appear in court at
a specified time to answer the plaintiff. It is given to the sheriff, whose
duty it is to find the defendant or his attorney and serve the writ. Ordinarily,
the action cannot proceed until actual service has been made; but in certain
cases, for example, divorce actions, where the defendant is outside the jurisdiction or residing in parts unknown, publication in newspapers is deemed
sufficient. If the defendant has not already engaged a lawyer, he should do
so at once, for failure to enter appearance in connection with the suit will
mean that judgment will be entered against him by default. The attorney
"files an appearance" for his client with the clerk of the court. He then notifies the attorney for the plaintiff that the appearance has been filed, and the

two attorneys thereafter notify each other of all the subsequent steps taken in the case.

(*b*) *The declaration and answer.* The next move is for the plaintiff to file a declaration (sometimes called a "complaint" or "petition"), setting forth his cause of action. It must be very carefully drawn, for it must show a cause of action sufficient in law to warrant a judgment for the plaintiff. This declaration is filed with the clerk of the court, and a copy of it is served on the defendant, together with a notice that he shall file an answer to the declaration within a certain date. The defendant, acting through his attorney, of course, may file a demurrer; that is, he may admit the facts as set forth by the plaintiff, but deny their legal sufficiency. In common parlance a demurrer is. "Yes; but what of it?" This demurrer passes the question of the sufficiency of the declaration to the judge. If he adjudges it legally sufficient, he "over-rules" the demurrer and the plaintiff wins his case, unless the court, as it generally does, allows the defendant to file an answer to the declaration. If the demurrer is sustained, the defendant wins this point and would have judgment in his favor but for the fact that the court then generally permits the plaintiff to remedy his declaration by amendment. Assume, now, that the defendant answers the declaration of the opposing party. This answer or plea may admit certain allegations of the plaintiff and deny others. The points on which the declaration and answer differ are the points which will be in issue at the trial. The nature of the defendant's answer may be such as to warrant a response by the plaintiff; and in a number of states this replication (or reply) is permitted, in order that all the points at issue may be brought out clearly. It often happens that the defendant's answer does not constitute a sufficient defense. It is now the plaintiff's privilege to demur, which he does by asking the court to enter judgment for him "for want of a sufficient answer" from the defendant.

Settlement out of court. After the parties have "agreed to disagree" on certain points, as shown in the declaration and answer, the case must be prepared for trial. The lawyers on both sides interview their clients and witnesses, and make every legitimate effort to forge chains of evidence that cannot be broken. As the day of the trial draws near, both sides may feel somewhat uncertain and they may reach a settlement out of court, much to the relief of all parties. Occasionally, just before a case is called, the judge may encourage the contending parties to reach a settlement, sometimes with good effect.

Pretrial conference. A pretrial conference is now common in the federal courts and in the courts of more than half the states. Under this plan the judge may direct the attorneys in a case to appear before him to discuss the possibilities of adjustments that will clarify the issue and simplify trial procedure. In three cases out of four, and quite incidental to its main purpose, pretrial results in complete settlement. Although the pretrial conference has experienced most of its development in the past twenty years, it appears to have demonstrated its utility and to have the general support of both the bench and the bar.[19]

2. THE JURY. If no settlement is made, the case comes up for trial in due time. The judge presides over the court and passes on points of law, and a jury is usually called to decide the questions of fact. If both sides agree, the jury may be dispensed with, and the case is tried before the judge alone. Let us follow the steps of a case that is tried by jury. A number of citizens have been previously summoned for jury service; and when a particular case is to be tried, twelve persons (a smaller number in some states) are selected for this case. Counsel for either party may challenge any juror for cause; that is, on the ground that he is mentally defective, has business connections with the other party, is prejudiced, or on some other grounds. The judge will excuse such jurors as are shown to be unfitted for the service. Each party is also allowed several peremptory challenges, challenges for which no causes are assigned but which are made on the basis of "intelligent hunches" as to what jurors probably would be unfavorable to the party's case. Citizens ordinarily have an aversion to jury service, and they are often excused for rather flimsy reasons. Yet the average person will learn a great deal on a jury that he would never learn otherwise, and certainly a good citizen should be willing to make a temporary sacrifice for the good of society.

3. THE TRIAL. The jury having been secured and sworn, the judge orders the attorneys to proceed with the case. Thereupon the counsel for the plaintiff rises and makes the opening statement. He informs the court and the jury of the facts in the plaintiff's case, of the nature of the evidence he will offer to prove these facts, and of the damages he asks for his client. He does his best to create a favorable impression for his client with the jury. His case may be won or lost by this initial effort. In some courts this statement is immediately followed by the opening statement of the defendant's attorney, but in others this may be delayed until the evidence for the plaintiff has been offered. In any case the opening statement for the defendant has the same general purpose as that delivered for the plaintiff.

Examination of witnesses. The attorney for the plaintiff now proceeds to examine his witnesses, probably beginning with the plaintiff himself. He must be careful not to ask a witness a "leading question"; that is, a question that suggests to the witness the answer the attorney desires. Also, he must guard against asking questions that are not relevant to the issue; for instance, questions relating to the number of the defendant's dependent children, if the matter in controversy is the amount of damages to be allowed for a personal injury. When the plaintiff's lawyer has examined the witnesses for his side, the attorney for the defendant may then cross-examine them. His purpose is, of course, to expose the weak spots in their testimony and discredit them with the jury. This cross-examination often makes a good

[19] There is considerable literature on the pre-trial conference. See in particular *Journal of the AJS*, XXV (1941), 24, 120; XXVI (1942), 36; XXVIII (1945), 156; and XXX (1947), 25. See also H. D. Nims, *Pre-Trial* (1950).

"show" in court; but if the attorney is not considerate in his treatment of witnesses, he is likely to turn the jury against his client's case. Witnesses for the defendant are examined and cross-examined in similar fashion. During the examination of witnesses one attorney may "object" to questions asked by the other, and the judge overrules or sustains the objection. In either case one of the lawyers is ruled against, and he may "take an exception" to the judge's ruling. These exceptions often constitute grounds for appealing the case.

4. THE VERDICT. If the evidence submitted indicates that one side or the other has failed to make out a case, the judge may, on motion of the attorney who considers his client entitled to the verdict, direct the jury to bring in a verdict for the defendant, or the plaintiff, as the case may be. The judge probably will decide, however, that sufficient evidence has been offered on each side to warrant the deliberation of the jury. If so, he directs the attorneys to "go to the jury." Each lawyer then makes an argument summarizing the points on which he rests his client's case. Following these, the judge delivers the "charge to the jury." In a number of the Western states the judge's charge precedes the arguments of the attorneys. This procedure has been criticized because it tends to leave the minds of the jurors on the eloquence of counsel rather than on the principles of law applicable to the case. The charge to the jury is often a rather long discourse. The judge explains the law applicable in the case, emphasizing that the jury must take his word for the law; that the jury is to decide the facts. He helps the jurors with this duty by reviewing the evidence offered and by giving them a great deal of good advice as to how evidence should be weighed, cautioning them at the same time that in reaching a verdict they must be governed by their own recollections of the evidence. It should be noted that in many jurisdictions the judge is rather severely limited by statute or rules as to the nature of the help he may give a jury, a limitation which most modern authorities consider unfortunate.

The jury then retires, somewhat bewildered, perhaps, by all the judge has told them, but having, in the ordinary case, pretty good idea as to which party is entitled to a favorable verdict. The jurors deliberate, and usually compromise before reaching an agreement. The compromise is frequently necessary because twelve persons seldom see things alike and the majority of the states require a unanimous verdict. The jury may decide for the plaintiff or for the defendant; occasionally it is unable to reach an agreement. If it decides for the plaintiff, it must also fix the damages (the amount being another matter for compromise). In the event the jury disagrees, the case must be tried again with a new jury.

5. APPEALS. Sometimes both parties are disappointed in the verdict; usually one of them is, and he and his attorney may attempt to get a new trial. The argument for a new trial rests upon various grounds, such as judicial error in a ruling concerning the admissibility of evidence or in instructions to the jury, or a verdict contrary to the evidence. This argument will

be heard by the judge who presided at the trial.   If the judge refuses to grant
a new trial, the losing party's next move in the fight is to take an appeal.   Frequently there is no right of appeal in certain types of cases, such as those
involving small amounts; but important cases, such as those in which the
amounts in controversy are considerable or in which constitutional questions
are involved, may be appealed as a matter of right.

Generally, in an appellate court, only points of law are at issue and there
is no jury.   Lawyers prepare their "briefs" and shape their arguments to
convince the judges, reserving their oratorical and emotional efforts for the
trial courts in which the jury is employed.   The appellate court may sustain
the judgment of the lower court, or it may point out certain errors in that
court's proceedings and direct the court to hold a new trial.   In a few cases,
those requiring a construction of the Constitution of the United States being
most common, appeal may be had from the highest state court to the Supreme
Court at Washington.   Trial, appeals, new trials, and perhaps more appeals,
require a great deal of time.   Sometimes a controversy may be in the courts
for several years.[20]

Executing a Judgment

Assume that in the course of time a plaintiff gets a judgment against a
defendant.   The defendant may be "judgment-proof," having no property
with which to satisfy the judgment.   In Dickens's day he was not "jail-
proof," however, his creditor being permitted to cause him to languish in
confinement until he paid or until the creditor was convinced that he could
not pay.   Imprisonment for debt is now abolished;[21] but, for obvious reasons, it was never a satisfactory method of collecting a debt from an insolvent
debtor.   Ordinarily the defendant has the means to satisfy the judgment,
since the plaintiff and his attorney usually do not take the trouble to start suit
against one who is insolvent.   If the defendant should refuse to pay the
damages allowed, the plaintiff's lawyer will get an order from the court directing the sheriff to sell certain properties of the defendant and to pay the plaintiff
the amount of the judgment out of the proceeds.

Equity Proceedings

The procedure as outlined above is that generally followed in suits at common law.   A brief discussion must now be devoted to proceedings in equity
cases.   The plaintiff files a "bill," stating his complaint and asking the court
for relief.   The defendant may demur, as in suits at common law, or he may
answer the bill.   The case goes to court on the points at issue shown by

[20] For the types of delays that occured under the system employed in New Jersey before
1947, see Joseph Harrison, "Judicial Reform in New Jersey," *State Government,* Oct., 1949,
p. 233.

[21] Individuals may still be imprisoned, however, for certain kinds of debts; for example,
those involving fraud or willful disobedience of a court order.   It seems that in Vermont
an individual may be held in jail if he is unable to pay damages assessed by a court in
certain tort cases.

the bill and answer. A noteworthy feature of equity procedure is that a jury is seldom used. Occasionally a judge will direct that certain questions of fact be referred to a jury, although the verdict is advisory only, serving somewhat as a guide to the judicial conscience. A few states have granted by statute the right of jury trial in equity cases, and in such states the judge is bound by the jury findings in equity cases as in cases at common law.

Equity courts move more quickly than common law courts. Often no oral testimony is introduced, the bill, the answer, perhaps a replication, and depositions of witnesses being held sufficient. Not infrequently the judge will refer a complicated case to an examiner or master in chancery, who will investigate the case and make a report to the court. The court then makes its decree on the basis of this report although it is not bound to accept the findings of the examiner or master. As just indicated, equity courts give their decision in the form of decrees. The defendant may be ordered to execute a contract, cancel a mortgage, or to do or not to do various things. Failure to comply with the decree constitutes contempt of court and is punishable by fine or imprisonment.

Declaratory Judgments [22]

It is understood that the common law provides remedies only after damage has been done, and that equity is often used to prevent an impending injury. But even equity stops short of the need in some cases. Parties often want to know, without the necessity of instituting ordinary suit, their rights under certain provisions of a will, a contract, or other instrument. Of course, one may consult a lawyer; but, valuable as his legal advice may be, it is often felt that something more in the nature of a judicial opinion is desirable. This is now provided for in a large majority of the states through the device known as the "declaratory judgment." A party having an interest in such an instrument as mentioned above institutes the proceeding; the court then calls in the other party or parties, hears them, and gives the declaratory judgment, thus settling the issue without giving a judgment for coercive relief. In 1933 declaratory judgment procedure received a decided impetus, when the Supreme Court of the United States held that it could review any such judgment of a state court if the facts of the case were such as to constitute a "case or controversy" between the parties, thus bringing the case within the range of federal judicial authority.[23]

Conciliation and Arbitration

Still less formal and less expensive than the declaratory judgment procedure, conciliation and arbitration have significant places in the administration of civil justice. Under concilation procedure a duly authorized person,

[22] C. S. Potts, "The Declaratory Judgment," *Journal of the AJS,* XXXVIII (Oct., 1944), 82.
[23] Nashville, C. & St. L. R. Co. v. Wallace, 288 U.S. 249 (1933). The next year Congress passed the Federal Declaratory Judgment Act.

usually a court official, attempts to find a solution for an issue between two parties. He talks the matter over with them, quietly explaining the law and giving his opinion on its application in this case. He may mention the great expense of going through regular court procedure, and the case may be such as to prompt him to suggest that such a proceeding would be folly. The conciliator has no authority to bind the parties to the dispute, but tactful men, full of mellow wisdom, often suggest solutions that are mutually satisfactory to the disputants. Since 1913 the city of Cleveland has made extensive use of conciliation procedure, and New York City and several other cities have developed the practice. In 1921 North Dakota adopted a state-wide conciliation plan.

Almost all the states have enacted some type of arbitration law, although only a few of the states measure up to the fairly adequate standards set by California, Massachusetts, New York, and one or two other states. The arbitration system works about as follows: Parties to a dispute, let us say over the fair value of services rendered, select an arbitrator, and, of equal importance, agree to abide by his decision. After appropriate hearings and deliberation, the arbitrator makes his decision, a decision that may be enforced as if it were a regular court judgment. An appeal lies to a court to determine whether the procedure was in accordance with law, but not as to the facts found by the arbitrator. This is the way the system operates in the states that have effective arbitration laws. In other states—in most of them, in fact—individuals may not be compelled to arbitrate, even though they agreed to do so in advance of any dispute, and appeals are permitted on both law and facts.

Arbitration has unquestionably demonstrated its feasibility. It only remains for legislatures in most of the states to rid themselves of the old idea that all cases should proceed, or should be allowed to proceed, to the stage of formal controversies, to be settled in the regular courts, where there are attorneys to argue, judges to rule and advise, and juries to deliberate. Perhaps we prefer to have our justice highly flavored with drama and cloaked in formality; or it may be that we are suspicious of an award that does not cost us a good round sum.[24]

V. CRIMINAL LAW AND PROCEDURE [25]

Crimes

An individual who commits a wrong does not necessarily commit a crime. For one thing, the wrong may simply be against an individual, a tort, as explained in the preceding section. For another thing, his act may be wrong in the sense that it is generally considered reprehensible, but it may not be

---

[24] *Annual Report of the American Arbitration Association,* 1955; A. F. Macdonald, *American State Government and Administration* (1955 ed.), pp. 257–258.

[25] Callender, *op. cit.,* Chs. XII–XIII; Livingston Hall and Sheldon Glueck, *Cases and Materials on Criminal Law* (1940); J. J. Kearney, *Clark and Marshall's Law of Crimes* (1940 ed.); L. B. Orfield, *Criminal Procedure from Arrest to Appeal* (1947).

punishable under the law. Only those acts that society (government) has defined and made punishable by the state are crimes. They are commonly divided into three classes: treason, felonies, and misdemeanors.

TREASON. At common law treason was the compassing of the king's death, aiding and comforting his enemies, counterfeiting coin, and performing certain other acts that interfered with the process of government. Under our Constitution, treason consists only in levying war against the United States or in adhering to its enemies, giving them aid and comfort. The other acts that were treason in England are felonies in the United States.

FELONIES. At the top of the list of felonies is, of course, murder. It consists of the unlawful killing of a human being with malice aforethought, express or implied. In many of the states the statutes define murder in the first degree as an actual deliberate, or premeditated intent to kill, or a homicide committed, even though unintentional, in the perpetration of such felonies as burglary or robbery. Other homicides that are included in the definition of murder are designated as murder in the second degree.

Manslaughter is defined as a homicide committed without justification or excuse, but without malice aforethought, expressed or implied. If the homicide is committed in sudden passion caused by a reasonable provocation, and not with malice aforethought, it is voluntary manslaughter; if committed unintentionally, but without excuse and not under circumstances suggesting malice, it is involuntary manslaughter. Killing an individual caught in adultery with one's spouse is an example of the first; homicide resulting from gross negligence in driving a car is an example of the second.

Kidnaping is the unlawful seizure and secreting of an individual and extorting something from him or another person. Having carnal knowledge of a woman by force and without her consent constitutes rape. In many states the definition of rape has been broadened by statute so that it includes carnal knowledge of minors, with or without their consent.

All of the felonies listed above are against persons. Burglary and arson are against the habitation as well as the person. Burglary at common law is the breaking and entering of a dwelling house of another at night and with the intent to commit a felony therein. Statutes have very generally extended the definition to include stores and shops, and in a number of states it includes daytime breaking and entering. Arson is the wilful and malicious burning of a dwelling house of another. Again, this common law definition has been expanded by statute to include the burning of buildings other than dwellings.

There are a number of felonies against the property of individuals. Robbery is the unlawful taking of the property of another from his person or his presence by violence or putting him in fear. The ordinary hold-up is a common example of robbery. Larceny is something different. It is the taking and carrying away of the personal goods of another with the intent to steal such goods. The goods that may be taken are numerous and include water and electricity as well as fur coats and money. The crime of embezzlement differs from larceny in that it consists of a servant or agent appropriating to his own use money or property lawfully in his possession that belongs to a principal or employer.

There are still other felonies; perjury and bigamy, for example. The list of felonies in one state might not be the same as those in another, but the major crimes are felonies everywhere. It appears that the actual test of whether or not a particular offense is a felony or misdemeanor in a state depends upon the punishment prescribed. The crime for which the conviction carries a penitentiary sentence is understood to be a felony.

MISDEMEANORS. The typical justice of the peace and police court cases, punishable by small fines and short jail sentences, are classed as misdemeanors. Defacing public property, illegal driving and parking, the use of profane or blasphemous language, the exhibiting of indecent pictures, the keeping of disorderly establishments, and the maintenance of various other nuisances go in this class. A man who makes a great noise at night with a speaking trumpet, to the disturbance of the neighborhood, may find himself in the police court for creating such a nuisance. A woman who had the habit of scolding on all occasions in such a manner as to constitute a common nuisance was convicted some years ago in New Jersey.[26] But a devout worshiper in North Carolina, whose voice was heard at the end of each verse of a hymn after the congregation had ceased and whose peculiarity in this manner excited mirth in one portion of the congregation and indignation in the other, although held to be a proper subject for discipline in his church, was discharged by the court as being innocent of any public offense.[27] A number of offenses that were mentioned under torts may also be misdemeanors. Thus, assault and battery may give rise to civil action on the part of an injured person and at the same time be of such a nature as to constitute offenses against the public. The same may be said of libel and slander and some other wrongful acts.

CRIMINAL INTENT. Intent as well as the act is a basic element in crime unless the law specifies otherwise. Breaking and entering a house with the *intention* of committing a felony therein constitutes burglary, whether the felony be actually committed or not. But one who takes property unlawfully under a *bona fide* claim of right is not guilty of larceny; the intent to steal is absent. Young children and insane persons cannot commit crimes, for they are irresponsible; intent cannot be shown. Drunkenness, however, is no excuse, though in some instances it may reduce the degree of the crime.

ACCESSORIES. A person who assists a felon is, of course, guilty of a crime also. He is designated as an "accessory before the fact," if, being absent at the time the crime was committed, he procures, counsels, or commands another to commit it; and he is an "accessory after the fact," if, knowing a felony to have been committed, he receives, relieves, or otherwise assists the felon. For treason and all offenses below the degree of felony there can be no accessories, all who would be classed as such in other crimes being

26 Baker v. State, 53 N.J. Law 45 (1890).
27 State v. Linkhaw, 69 N.C. 214 (1873).

treated as principals.   In some jurisdictions there is no important distinction in any crime between an accessory before the fact and a principal, both being subject to the same penalty.

Criminal Procedure

The public is perhaps more interested in the trial of criminal cases than in the law respecting various crimes.   This interest is not entirely misplaced, since the apprehension and prosecution of criminals constitutes a much greater problem.[28]

1. WARRANTS AND ARRESTS.   When a crime has been committed, the first thing, of course, is to arrest the guilty or suspected persons.   Arrests may be made with or without a warrant, according to circumstances.   In general it may be said that if one is seen in the act of committing a crime, or, if there is reasonable ground for belief that an individual has committed a felony, an arrest may be made without a warrant.   In other cases a warrant must be had.   It is usually issued when some person makes a sworn charge that a crime has been committed by another at a particular time and place.   It should be stated here that the person making the charge must have reasonable grounds for it; otherwise the individual against whom complaint is lodged may sue him for causing his false arrest.   When the complaint is duly made, a magistrate issues the warrant directing the apprehension of the individual named.   Naturally, arrests are commonly made by officers; but individuals may make them also, acting upon their own initiative when they have witnessed a crime, or assisting an officer whenever called upon to do so.

Summary trials.   If one is accused of a minor offense, of such a misdemeanor as exceeding the speed limit, parking in a prohibited area, or committing an ordinary nuisance, the trial is conducted by a magistrate or justice of the peace.   This officer hears the case and decides questions of both law and fact, trial without jury in such cases not being held to violate the constitutional guaranty of trial by jury.   The accused may have counsel if he desires it, and he may stand on his right to refuse to testify.   The magistrate is commonly empowered to impose a small fine or a short jail sentence upon minor offenders.   Appeals are allowed from the magistrate's court; but one convicted in such a court usually feels that there is more to be risked than gained by an appeal.

2. PRELIMINARY HEARINGS.   When an arrest is made for a major offense, the individual is brought before a magistrate for a preliminary hearing. The magistrate does not conduct the trial; but rather, decides whether, considering the evidence against the accused, there are sufficient grounds to hold him for trial.   The magistrate does not ordinarily hear evidence on both sides but hears only evidence against the accused.   However, the accused must be allowed to testify on his own behalf if he cares to do so.   If

[28] See National Commission on Law Observance and Enforcement, *Report* (No. 8) *on Criminal Procedure.*

the evidence indicates probable guilt, the magistrate will hold the accused
for the action of a grand jury or prosecuting attorney. In the meantime
the accused may be released on bail, a right that the constitutions guarantee
except for capital offenses. Furthermore, if he feels that he is being held
in jail on insufficient grounds, or that he is forced to stay in jail because he
cannot raise what he regards as an excessive bail, he may apply to a court
for a writ of *habeas corpus*. He will then be brought into court, and a judge
will determine the legality of his restraint. The judge's decision may result,
of course, in his release, or in his being returned to jail to await further proceedings in his case.

3. INDICTMENT. On the basis of the magistrate's report of the preliminary hearing and from what other information the prosecuting attorney can
gather, that officer prepares an indictment and presents it to a grand jury.
This body, carried over from English practice, was formerly used in all states
for securing indictments, and it is still used in many of them. At common
law it was composed of from 12 to 24 members, though in some states a
smaller number is now provided. It considers the evidence presented by
the prosecuting attorney, collects evidence for itself if so minded (it seldom
is), and by majority vote decides what persons shall be held for trial. If
it votes to hold a particular individual for trial, the foreman endorses "true
bill" on the indictment. If a majority is convinced that there is no substantial charge against the individual, the indictment is marked *"ignoramus"* (we
ignore). The grand jury may not only pass upon cases presented to it by
the prosecuting officer, but it may also direct him to prepare other indictments
on the basis of evidence it uncovers.

Indictment by grand jury is often spoken of as a slow and cumbersome
method of bringing an accused to trial. Some states no longer require it,
and some others require it only for certain types of cases. In such states,
indictment is by an "information" prepared by the district attorney and filed
with the court having jurisdiction to try the case. Great care must always
be taken in preparing an indictment. The offender and his victim must be
named; the time, place, and character of the offense must be detailed; and
it must be shown that the offense was contrary to law.[29] A defective indictment often results in the discharge of an accused on a "motion to quash." [30]

4. ARRAIGNMENT. After the indictment, in due course the accused is
arraigned; that is, he is brought to the bar of the court to answer the accusation, a copy of which has been furnished him. An officer of the court asks
the accused to rise, states the charges, and then puts the question, "How
say you, guilty or not guilty?" If the accused pleads "guilty," there is then
no issue between him and the state, and the judge pronounces the sentence,
although before doing so he may hear testimony and argument that may
throw more light upon the case, thus aiding him in fixing a just sentence.

---

[29] See Callender, *op. cit.,* pp. 177–178, for a typical indictment.
[30] Occasionally, a purely technical defect will spoil an indictment, as in West Virginia
when "W. Virginia" was held insufficient to designate that state. 4 W. Va. 755 (1870).

The plea of "guilty" is often made when the defendant thinks he is quite likely to be convicted. Such a plea saves time and expense for the state, and usually results in a lighter sentence than the defendant would receive if found guilty by a jury. Not infrequently one reads of a defendant's changing his original plea of "not guilty" to "guilty." Occasionally, usually upon advice of counsel, a defendant changes his plea of "guilty" to "not guilty."

5. THE TRIAL. If the defendant pleads "not guilty" or refuses to plead at all (which is commonly treated as a plea of "not guilty"), he must then be tried by a jury.

The jury. In a few states he may waive jury trial, but in most states he has no option in this matter. The general rule is that the jury shall consist of twelve persons, although several states prescribe a smaller number for other than capital offenses. The jury is selected as in civil cases, the only differences being that a greater number of peremptory challenges are permitted and that great latitude is allowed in challenges for cause. The prejudices, the opinions, the knowledge, the associations, and what not, of each prospective juror are anxiously inquired into by counsel. It frequently happens that practically all intelligent persons in a community have knowledge of and an opinion concerning an important case that is brought to trial, the result being that they are disqualified as jurors and the box is filled with persons of a very low degree of intelligence. It is often suggested that alert citizens who would take an oath to return a verdict in accordance with the evidence presented at the trial would be much more likely to arrive at a correct decision than persons of low mentality who know nothing of a case previous to the trial, but there are many lawyers who are not impressed with the weight of this suggestion.

Court procedure. The prosecuting attorney opens the case for the state with a speech to the jury, outlining the charges against the defendant and the nature of the evidence he will offer to prove them. It is not the duty of this officer to secure a conviction of the accused unless he is guilty. It is his duty to see that justice is done. But, inasmuch as the prosecutor is often judged by the number of conviction scalps he wears on his belt, he sometimes becomes overzealous in his efforts. After his opening speech, he examines his witnesses. These may be, and usually are, examined by counsel for the defendant. When the state's case has been thus presented, the defendant's counsel then makes his speech to the jury, examines his witnesses, and turns them over to the prosecutor for cross examination. Each attorney, as in civil cases, objects to certain questions asked of witnesses by the other and takes exceptions to unfavorable judicial rulings. The testimony concluded, the prosecutor attempts to show the jury that the accused stands convicted; and the defendant's attorney follows him in what is usually a still greater effort to show that the state has failed to prove the guilt of his client.

The attorneys are supposed to confine their addresses to the evidence in the case; but this rule is very liberally interpreted and it would seem that it is practically ignored in some cases, despite the fact that the better element in the legal profession insists upon its observance. To save the accused from the penitentiary or from death, counsel may paint for the jury a picture of a broken-hearted wife and mother and of children much worse than orphaned; and he may speak at length upon many similar points that have no bearing upon the question to be decided, namely, the guilt or innocence of the accused. Although prosecutors are not quite so likely to go to such lengths, there are a few cases in which their emotional appeals rival those of the defense counsel. In a famous murder case in North Carolina, a prosecutor shouted at the jury that a certain labor union headquarters was "a whole section of hell! There was immorality there. Yes, *immorality!* Hugging and kissing in public. I'm old-fashioned. I'm a Sunday school man." He said that he was defending his community, where "the dove of peace hovers around the vine-clad door and the kindly light of an autumn sun kisses the curly hair of happy children." He spoke of union organizers as "fiends incarnate, stript of their hoofs and horns . . . from the wild plains of Soviet Russia." He knelt before the jury, holding the hand of the slain man's widow. In conclusion he recited a poem to Mother, and, to show the breadth of his charity, shook hands with a Communist.[31]

Following the closing speeches of the attorneys, the judge "charges" the jury. In this charge he informs them of the legal aspects of the case and tells them how to weigh the evidence that has been offered. The laws of most states prohibit the judge from commenting upon the evidence in such a way as to let the jury know his opinion concerning the guilt or innocence of the accused. The judge tells the jury that the accused is innocent unless the state has beyond a reasonable doubt proved him guilty. On the other hand, he cautions them that it is not necessary for the state to prove guilt beyond the possibility of a doubt. With these instructions, which in complicated cases may cover many pages, the jury retires to consider the verdict. Unanimity is almost invariably required for a decision in major offenses. Sometimes the verdict is quickly reached; but cases that make the newspaper headlines often hold the jury for hours, or even days. Sometimes it is impossible to reach any decision, in which case the jury is said to be "hung." For the less serious crimes, a number of states have modified the jury trial to the extent of requiring only a three-fourths or five-sixths majority for a verdict.

If a verdict of guilty is rendered and if the court overrules the frequently made motions in arrest of judgment and for a new trial, the judge pronounces the sentence. Before doing so, he may hear a plea for clemency from the attorney of the individual who stands convicted. If the unhappy man has a good record previous to the offense for which he is found guilty, the plea will probably not be in vain. The statutes commonly fix the maximum and minimum penalties, leaving the exact penalty for individual offenders to be determined by the judge, a discretion that a wise judge often applies on the side of clemency for persons who have fallen from grace but who are not past

[31] National Commission on Law Observance and Enforcement, *Report* (No. 11) *on Lawlessness in Law Enforcement,* pp. 319–320, and *Time,* Oct. 28, 1929, p. 13.

redemption.[32]   The sentence ends the work of the trial court, but on various grounds a subject of its adverse judgment may appeal to the higher state courts.[33]

Punishment for Crime

Formerly, capital punishment was administered for a great variety of crimes. As late as the reign of George III there were about two hundred offenses punishable by death; among these offenses were cutting down a tree and stealing goods in a shop to the amount of five shillings.   The same penalty was exacted for a number of crimes in the American colonies; but the number has steadily decreased, until now only five or six states have the death penalty for as many as four crimes, and in the majority of the states murder alone may carry that penalty.   A number of states have abolished the death penalty altogether.   Other punishments range from life imprisonment to short jail sentences and small fines, varying with the nature of the offense, the character of the offender, and, to some extent, the laws of the different states.

The criticism is often made that punishment as administered does not reform the criminal.   Nearly every prison is crowded.   The warden is by force of circumstances a custodian, who must operate the prison within his budget, rather than a reformer.   Considering these facts, it would be surprising if a majority of the prisoners were reformed, although some of them undoubtedly are.   Then, too, the trouble is not all within the prison walls. Prosecuting attorneys, who are sometimes bent only on securing the severest penalty; judges, who may lack understanding or who are held to a rigid formula by statute; juries, who are not infrequently swayed by prejudice and emotion; and respectable citizens, who sometimes show an unwillingness to give an ex-convict a new start in life, all must bear a share of the blame.[34]

AMELIORATION OF PUNISHMENT.   Punishments may be reduced in various ways.   The most sweeping method is by the executive pardon, which, if unconditional, wipes away all legal consequences of the crime.   In many jurisdictions a person convicted of a minor crime may be placed on probation and, if he maintains a proper standard of behavior, will not be required to serve a single day in prison.   Nearly all the states now have a parole sys-

---

[32] In a number of states the judge now imposes a maximum penitentiary sentence and an administrative board later fixes the exact time to be served.

[33] Appeal may be taken from the state supreme court to the Supreme Court of the United States only when a right under the federal Constitution has been claimed by a defendant and denied by the state court; for example, when it is claimed that "due process," a guaranty of the Fourteenth Amendment, is violated by state action.

Despite the safeguards surrounding an accused, it sometimes happens that an innocent person is convicted.   The most celebrated of recent cases is that of Bertram M. Campbell, who, as the result of mistaken identification, served more than three years in Sing Sing for a forgery he did not commit.   When his innocence was discovered, he was pardoned and awarded $115,000 for his wrongful imprisonment.

[34] See Warden Lewis E. Lawes, "Why Our Prisons Fail," *The New York Times Magazine*, Aug. 16, 1931.   For an encouraging report on improvements in prison administration, see A. H. MacCormick, "Progress in American State Prisons," *State Government*, Apr., 1949, pp. 112–115.

tem, a system under which an individual who has served a part of his sentence and who has been a good prisoner may be released from prison.   Such a person remains under the supervision of public authorities, however, and he may also receive assistance from them in obtaining employment and in "going straight."   The effective administration of the parole system is seriously impaired in a number of states because too few parole officers are employed. The success of a parole system depends largely upon the work of these officers, a fact that governors and legislatures are slow to realize.

VI. "JUSTICE AND THE POOR" [35]

It is impossible to deal in this work with the whole field of judicial administration, but there are two other problems that must be briefly considered. These are: (1) justice and the poor; and (2) defects of legal procedure.

The Theory and the Fact

Equality of justice is accepted as a fundamental principle in America, and in general the substantive law confers no favors upon particular classes; but the principle of equality often vanishes when individuals must fight for the rights accorded them by law.   Inability to pay court costs and fees and to buy the services of attorneys often separates the rich and the poor by a great gulf. Writing in 1919, R. H. Smith estimated that there were 35,000,000 persons in the United States unable to pay any appreciable amount for legal advice and assistance.[36]   The loss of homes, savings, and wages for lack of adequate counsel in civil cases is tragic enough, but the position of the unfortunates who are accused of violating a criminal law is still more pitiable.   Publicist Raymond Moley speaks of the great majority of the half million annually arraigned in the criminal courts of New York City as a helpless lot, constituting "not a problem of law enforcement as much as one of social welfare.   They are, in large part, merely careless, defective, or unfortunate beggars, vagrants, degenerates, crap shooters, peddlers without licenses . . . sneak thieves, 'dopes,' and small-time cheats. . . . All are bewildered, frightened, blindly seeking relief from their difficulties." [37]   Possibly the situation has been somewhat improved since those words were written, but certainly justice for the poor (and for the middle classes also, to a large degree) has not as yet been attained.

---

[35] G. E. Brand, "The Impact of the Increased Cost of Litigation," *Journal of the AJS,* XXXV (December, 1951), 102; E. A. Brownell, *Legal Aid in the United States* (1951); Justin Miller, "Lawyers and Judges and Legal Aid," *Journal of the AJS,* XXXVIII (June, 1954), 15; Raymond Moley, *Tribunes of the People* (1932); R. H. Smith, "Justice and the Poor," *Bulletin of the Carnegie Foundation for the Advancement of Teaching* (1919), No. XIII.

[36] *Ibid.,* p. 33.

[37] Quoted from "Justice for the Poor: A Task for New York," *The New York Times,* May 3, 1931, sec. 9, p. 1, by permission of the author and of the editors of *The New York Times.*   Acknowledgment is also made to the Yale University Press, since it has published Professor Moley's *Tribunes of the People* in which the statement above is reproduced practically unchanged.

And this is not the whole story. The poor man's justice may cost him more than the rich man pays for his. Competent investigators made a survey of the cost of civil litigation in New York for the year 1930. It was found that the inhabitants of the City of New York paid through public revenues an average of eight cents each (not including lawyers' fees) for justice in the Municipal Court, the civil court that settles finally the vast majority of the poor man's cases. On the other hand, the inhabitants paid an average of fifty cents each in public revenues for justice in the higher courts, the courts to which men of large affairs go for civil justice. As a result, litigants in the Municipal Court paid 71.1 per cent of the cost of administering justice in that court while those who used the higher courts in New York City paid only about 10 per cent of the cost. It is thus apparent that in New York City, at least, those who can least afford to pay for justice are required to pay about seven times as much as those who can most easily afford to pay.[38] Another major item in the cost of litigation is counsel fees, an item so large that people of small means are often prevented from going to court, and down-and-outs who are brought to court on criminal charges commonly have grossly inadequate counsel.

Steps Toward Reform

Efforts are being made, however, to assist the "forgotten man" in obtaining justice. Kansas (1923) authorized cities and counties to set up small claims courts with authority to decide cases in which the amount involved does not exceed twenty dollars. Massachusetts, New Hampshire, California, and three or four other states have similar systems, and so do several of the larger cities, including Chicago, Philadelphia, and Cleveland. These courts proceed with a minimum of formality, discourage the participation of lawyers, hold costs to a very low figure, and narrowly restrict the right of appeal.[39]

Legal aid societies, both private and public, now flourish in perhaps a hundred cities. A workman has a claim for a few dollars in wages; a hand laundress has not been paid because it is claimed that a shirt has not been returned; a divorced husband has ceased paying the ten dollars a week alimony ordered by the court, and his whereabouts is unknown; an injured laborer has encountered difficulties in collecting compensation due him; and a woman who rents one of her two plainly furnished rooms to a waitress has been arrested on her lodger's complaint that the landlady has stolen her clothes. Legal aid societies render assistance in such cases as these, and the best ones pride themselves upon serving their clients as efficiently as would a firm of private attorneys. The Legal Aid Society in New York City has about a hundred clients a day bringing such problems as unpaid wages, domestic controversies, personal injuries, and unsettled estates. The cases of those who come seeking help are usually trivial and petty; yes, as trivial and petty

[38] Summary in Graves, *op. cit.*, p. 662.
[39] Macdonald, *op. cit.*, pp. 240–241; Leonard Sawyer, *Municipal Courts of New Hampshire* (Bureau of Govt. Research, U. of N.H., 1949).

as an empty stomach or weeks in jail! The equal protection of the laws is without meaning if it does not give the laundress her wages as it awards damages to a millionaire who was injured in an accident through the fault of a billion-dollar corporation.

The Office of Friend of the Court is authorized by law for every county in the State of Michigan. The Office enforces alimony decrees for the benefit of minor children, gives service in matters relating to land contracts and mortgage foreclosures, and co-operates with the juvenile courts and other social agencies in their work of rehabilitation.[40]

What help is available for the indigent person who is facing criminal prosecution? For a long time the courts have customarily assigned counsel for such individuals, but in too many cases it has proved inadequate. In some areas the legal aid bureaus have furnished assistance, although it would appear that they are set up to give service primarily in petty (misdemeanor) cases. In order to give an individual charged with a felony counsel comparable to the prosecutor, voluntary defenders committees operate in a number of cities, New York City having one of the best. A few jurisdictions have established a public defender system, Los Angeles County leading the way (1913). It now functions in six or eight counties and cities in California and in perhaps a dozen large cities in other states. Only in Connecticut and Rhode Island, however, is it state-wide. The public defender is an officer, his duty being to defend the accused, and he enjoys essentially the same status in court as the prosecutor.[41] It is very doubtful whether any plans will or can be devised that will place the rich and the poor on the same footing in court; but the movements along the lines just indicated will place the poor in a more favorable position for gaining their rights.

Minorities and Justice

Another wrong or inequity in our treatment of accused persons is that minorities, unpopular minorities, even if they have some money for attorneys' fees, may have difficulty in getting "equal justice." It is not easy to maintain that a Negro who in intelligence and economic status compares favorably with a white man can with equal ease secure his legal rights in all the courts of the land. He is certain to be under the necessity of winning a favorable verdict from a white jury, and the juries before which his case is commonly tried are quite likely to be prejudiced against him because of his race. Does a labor agitator on trial for murder have only the task of defending himself from that charge; or is he also under the handicap of having to overcome a

[40] Graves, op. cit., pp. 734 ff., John S. Bradway, Legal Aid Bureaus (1935); F. E. Cooper and J. P. Dawson, "The Office of the Friend of the Court in Wayne County, Michigan," Annual Report of the Judicial Council of Michigan (1935); Edward Pokorny, "Friend of Court Aids Detroit Judges in Divorce Cases," Journal of the AJS, XXX (April, 1946), 166.

[41] Donald Freeman, "The Public Defender System," Journal of the AJS, XXXII (Oct., 1948), 74; David Mars, "The Public Defender System in Connecticut," State Government, Feb., 1954, p. 29; W. S. Stewart, "The Public Defender System is Unsound," ibid., (Dec., 1948), p. 115.

prejudice the prosecutor, or the judge, or the jury may have against him because he is an agitator? A "radical" is on trial for robbery, or embezzlement, or perjury. Will the fact that he is a "radical" make it more or less difficult to convict him? Here is a despised religious minority, receiving the sort of contempt and scorn that was heaped upon another religious minority, the early Christians. Will the members of this sect who violate local ordinances be caught and arrested by the police with more zeal than they employ in dealing with the general body of inhabitants; and will local magistrates deal as leniently with them as they do with the general body of citizens who violate ordinances? Democracy is an ideal, and equal justice for all is a part of that ideal. The complete attainment of the ideal is not possible, but a constant striving toward it is the standing obligation of a democratic society.

VII. SOME PROBLEMS OF LEGAL PROCEDURE [42]

The system of judicial administration is often criticized by laymen, lawyers, and judges. It is criticized, not only by idealists, who take as their standard of justice the statue of the beauteous and unseeing lady who holds in her hands the scales on which all the elements of any dispute are nicely weighed, but also by those who "judge justice" by a relative standard, having due regard for the limitations of the human beings who must administer it. It is pointed out that lawyers are primarily interested in winning a case, sometimes even to the extent of permitting an injustice to pass; that juries often fail to reach a just verdict; and that judges may lack the authority to control the proceedings and, at times, may even display ineptitude in operating the scales of justice. In fact, almost every phase of legal procedure is criticized.[43] It is said that from being a means of obtaining justice, procedure has become an end in itself; that attention has been concentrated on form to such an extent that justice is sometimes defeated.

The Law's Delay

A particular defect of procedure that is often singled out for special attack, and that includes many of the other defects, is delay. Delay is not only the cause of prolonged annoyance and expense, but it is perhaps the most frequent cause of miscarriage of justice. It is an old grievance. Hamlet numbered among the thousand natural shocks that flesh is heir to "the pangs of dispriz'd love and the law's delay"; and the "head chancery," a hold by which

[42] American Bar Association, Section on Judicial Administration, *A Handbook on the Improvement of the Administration of Justice* (1949); Jerome Frank, *Courts on Trial: Myth and Reality in American Justice* (1949); B. C. Keeney, *Judgment by Peers* (1949); Arthur T. Vanderbilt, *Men and Measures in the Law* (1949); *Journal of the AJS* relevant articles in practically every issue.

[43] To the layman, at least, legal terminology often appears archaic, a characterization humorously illustrated by an indictment, repeatedly read in court, much to the merriment of spectators and jury and to the annoyance of judge and prosecutor, charging a slender and dignified youth with "riotously and routously" assaulting a powerful policeman. A. Hamilton, M D., "What about the Lawyers?" *Harper's,* Oct., 1931, p. 546.

a boxer clinches the head of his helpless opponent under his arm, is so named because it symbolizes the all but hopeless state of many cases that entered the British chancery courts before the system was reformed (1873).

"Delay resembles the many-headed hydra of mythology," writes Professor Callender.[44] "It is an evil of many phases and very difficult of extirpation. It may appear at any stage of a lawsuit, be slain by a judicial Hercules, and appear again at a later stage. The many forms which it may assume make it difficult to attack. It is not an isolated problem. The delay may be the result of the procrastination of lawyers; it may be the result of an archaic system of pleading; it may be occasioned by the overcrowded condition of a court's calendar; it may be a consequence of faulty trial procedure; it may be the outcome of inadequate processes for enforcing a judgment; it may be the result of a complex judicial structure; it may be the consequence of a complicated system of appellate procedure, and so on."

Witnesses change their residence, their memories grow dim, and some die before they are called to court. The patience and funds of an honest litigant may be exhausted while his unscrupulous opponent may finally win the case by artful dodges around the sinuosities of legal procedure. Some states have set about to correct this condition by revising the rules of judicial procedure and by establishing a more or less unified system of judicial administration. Although the progress is slow, with both professional and lay opinion agreeing that procedure should be improved, it is reasonable to hope that the much needed overhauling is but fairly begun.

Defects in the Jury System

Common indeed is the complaint against the jury system. Judge Claude C. Coffin of Colorado draws up the following incisive indictment of juries.[45] "The jury poll, supposed to be a cross section of the county community, is at the outset by statutory exemptions purged of occupational types wherein we should find the highest degree of intelligence and integrity; then the panel is further purged of busy, first rate business and professional men by individual excuses. From the 'qualified' list of jurymen remaining are drawn the required number who in large majority have never before served as jurymen and who have little or no training or experience for the work at hand. But this is still not the end of the process of selecting 'qualified' jurors. Attorneys may then by the peremptory challenge remove from the list a certain number of those who seem more likely to give heed to the cause, which they are supposed to do, than to mind the parties and the pleaders, which they are supposed not to do." The judge has several other counts in his indictment. Judge John J. Parker of the Circuit Court of Appeals of the United States (Fourth District) finds the chief weakness of the jury system in the

[44] *American Courts* (1927 ed.), pp. 220–221. By permission of McGraw-Hill Book Co., publishers. See also, Edward S. Greenbaum, *The New York Times Magazine,* Feb. 24, 1955, p. 12.
[45] "Jury Trial Tragic but Not Entirely Hopeless," *Journal of the AJS,* XXV (June, 1941), 13.

fact, as noted above, that judges in many of the states are not permitted to give juries the assistance they need to understand and evaluate the evidence, an authority the federal judges possess and use to good advantage.[46]

Yet neither of these judges nor other intelligent critics of the jury system want to see it abolished. On the contrary, they are certain of its place in a democratic system of government. What they insist upon is the reform of the system. The essential features of this reform would be to improve the personnel of the jury by severely limiting classes, professions, and individuals who might be exempted or excused from service, and by giving the judge control of his court with the right and duty to assist jurors in weighing evidence. Other suggestions are that the number of jurors be reduced, that the unanimous verdict be abolished except perhaps in capital cases, that the jury be abolished for certain types of cases, and that jurors be made professional as are judges and lawyers. It has already been noted that a number of states have made some progress along one or more of these lines.

Defects Peculiar to Criminal Procedure

The same defects are generally apparent in both civil and criminal procedure, but certain procedural impediments are peculiar to the administration of criminal justice. A few of these demand serious attention. Sometimes, the magistrates who conduct the preliminary hearings are not properly qualified for their tasks, and there have been those who were corruptible. Failure to hold a hearing, or to conduct one properly, often means that the criminal goes free. It is proposed that the common practice of popular choice of magistrates give way to appointments, or that persons without legal training be declared ineligible for the office, or both. Some jurisdictions have acted upon these proposals. The grand jury is very generally conceded to have become a "venerable nuisance," a time-consuming method of determining what the committing magistrate and the prosecuting attorney have already decided; namely, that there is a *prima facie* case against an accused. Fortunately, many states have realized these facts, and some have abolished the grand jury completely; and a number of others have discontinued its use except for investigating general disorders and widespread conspiracies, a function that the grand jury may still usefully perform. Then there is the problem of selecting a jury in criminal cases, particularly the sensational ones.[47] The process may take days or weeks, a fact that is hardly less than astounding to those responsible for the administration of justice in other English-speaking countries. In those Commonwealths the challenge of prospective jurors is not permitted to run riot, and consequently the selection of a jury seldom takes more than an hour or two.

[46] "Improvements of Jury System Must Come," *Journal of the AJS*, XXVI (Oct., 1942), 71.
[47] Refer, for example, to the case of Dr. Samuel H. Sheppard, in Cleveland, Ohio, Oct., 1954.

Should the Right to Refuse to Testify Be Abolished?

The rights of persons accused of crime not infrequently operate to free the professional criminal who knows how to use them. No one questions the necessity of some of these rights, such as the right to public trial, to counsel, and to compel the attendance of witnesses on behalf of the accused. But the same cannot be said so readily of the right of an accused to refuse to testify.[48] In many civilized countries with superior systems of justice, this right does not exist. There is little doubt that it is an immunity which often prevents the uncovering of crime in this country. The criminal class jealously guards and frequently uses the right. On occasion the innocent man may find it advisable not to testify. It would appear that the repeal of the right to refuse to testify would make it more difficult for the guilty to escape, but that it might also deprive the innocent of adequate means of defense.

Since the accused may not be forced to testify in court, it has long been the practice of many police investigators to make him give evidence following arrest, using threats and violence toward the accused if he refuses to talk. This "third degree" administered in jails and at police stations is roundly criticized by many authorities, particularly by the National Commission on Law Observance and Enforcement.[49] It would seem that if a person charged with a crime could be compelled to testify in court, there would no longer be any good excuse for permitting the often-winked-at lawlessness incident to the "third degree." Despite the arguments that may be made against retaining the right of refusal to testify, most lawyers, including Dean Erwin N. Griswold of the Harvard Law School, want it retained, fearing that if the sieve is made too fine it may trap some of the innocent with the guilty.[50]

The Lawyers and Criminal Justice

Lawyers are officers of the court and they carry with the judge the responsibility for administering justice. The great majority of lawyers take this obligation seriously, but there are a few who lower the dignity of the courts, delay proceedings unnecessarily, and otherwise impede the turning of the wheels of justice. We read in the papers that "counsel roars at court—hits the ceiling" at an adverse ruling by a judge. For this type of conduct the legal profession must carry a part of the blame. Lawyers as a group should perhaps take another look at their code of conduct.

In defending a client in a criminal action, an attorney may be overly aggressive and domineering on his behalf; but, on the other hand, the canons of the American legal profession state: "No lawyer is obligated to act either

---

[48] It is generally held that comment by the prosecuting attorney upon the accused's failure to take the stand is a violation of his right to refuse to testify.

[49] *Report* (No. 11) *on Lawlessness in Law Enforcement.*

[50] For both sides of this question, see Claire B. Bird, "Our Constitutional Protection of Guilt," *Journal of the AJS,* XXV (June, 1941), 18, and Erwin N. Griswold, *The Fifth Amendment Today* (1955).

as adviser or advocate for every person who may wish to become his client."
Dean Robert G. Storey, when President of the American Bar Association,
called attention to the British tradition, to "the unwritten law that no barrister
may decline a brief—and that means refuse to try a case in court—except for
good reason." [51]   The Dean emphasizes the fact that the English tradition
results in bringing into court, even in some of the most shocking criminal
cases, counsel of the highest eminence. Of course all American lawyers
agree that an accused is entitled to counsel, but they deny the obligation of
any particular lawyer to defend any accused who might desire his services.
The result is that the radical or contemptible criminal defendant sometimes
has difficulty in finding a lawyer, and lawyers who have accepted such cases
have, on occasion, suffered a loss of standing.

Dean Storey suggests to his fellow-lawyers that they have too often followed
the more pleasant and more remunerative civil practice and neglected less
attractive but more significant criminal cases.   He wonders what thrill there
is "commensurate with gaining the acquittal of a fellow citizen unjustly charged
with felony."   It is a matter of common knowledge that many, if not most,
of the outstanding lawyers in America shun the criminal practice.   The result, stated in the words of one of America's most distinguished legal authorities, Dean Emeritus Roscoe Pound, is that "in the general run of criminal
cases, taking the country over, counsel fall far short of the standard which is
maintained for civil cases." [52]

Conclusion

Viewing broadly the administration of justice, both civil and criminal, it
may be said that there is still ample room for improvement.   Yet much
progress has been made during the past twenty-five or thirty years.   The
whole body of lawyers is rapidly becoming better organized for the purpose
of improving standards.   Formerly, membership in bar associations was
voluntary, but in the early 'twenties the integrated bar movement got under
way.   By statute or other directive slightly more than half the states now
have such a bar.   Under this system all the lawyers of a state are given the
organization necessary to enable them to function as a group in governing
admissions to the bar, improving discipline, and strengthening the bar generally.[53]

Modernized codes of procedure have been adopted by the federal government.   A few states preceded the national government in this endeavor and
others have followed suit, bringing the total up to eleven or twelve.   One of
the most encouraging factors is found in the interest and unremitting activity
of many outstanding legal scholars in improving the law and its administration.   In many jurisdictions the organized bar has been most helpful, play-

[51] Robert G. Storey, "The Legal Profession and Criminal Justice," *Journal of the AJS*,
XXXVI (April, 1953), 166.
[52] Quoted in *ibid.*, pp. 166–167.
[53] G. E. Brand, "Bar Organization and Judicial Administration—A New Horizon,"
Journal of the AJS, XXXIV (Aug., 1950), 38.

ing leading parts in the preparation of codes of procedure and in the promotion of other means for a speedier, simpler, and less expensive system of justice.

Reading List

Annual Report of the American Arbitration Association.

American Municipal Association, *Formal Professional Qualification Requirement of Judges* (1938).

Annals of the American Academy of Political and Social Science, Vol. 167, May, 1933, "The Administration of Justice"; Vol. 217, Sept., 1941, "Crime in the United States."

F. R. Aumann, *The Changing American Legal System* (1940).

S. E. Baldwin, *The American Judiciary* (1905), Chs. VII–XXV.

E. A. Brownell, *Legal Aid in the United States* (1951).

A. A. Bruce, *The American Judge* (1924).

C. N. Callender, *American Courts* (1927).

Benjamin N. Cardozo, *The Nature of the Judicial Process* (1925).

Z. Chafee, Jr., *Some Problems of Equity* (1950).

Council of State Governments, *State Court Systems* (1951 ed.).

W. F. Dodd, *State Government* (1928 ed.), Chs. X–XII.

Jerome Frank, *Courts on Trial: Myth and Reality in American Justice* (1949).

J. L. Frascona, *Business Law* (1954).

Abraham L. Furman, *Chief Council: The Ordeal of a Public Defender* (1933).

L. P. Goldberg and Eleanor Levinson, *Lawless Judges* (1935).

W. B. Graves, *American State Government* (1953 ed.), Chs. 16–19.

L. Hall and S. Glueck, *Cases and Materials on Criminal Law* (1940).

Erwin N. Griswold, *The Fifth Amendment Today* (1955).

Evan Haynes, Selection and Tenure of Judges (1944).

A. G. Hays, *Trial by Prejudice* (1933).

A. N. Holcombe, *State Government in the United States* (1931 ed.), Chs. XIII–XIV.

J. W. Hurst, *The Growth of American Law: The Law Makers* (1950).

Journal of the American Judicature Society (for current developments).

J. J. Kearney, *Clark and Marshall's Law of Crimes* (1940 ed.).

B. C. Keeney, *Judgement by Peers* (1949).

A. Lepawsky, *Judicial System of Metropolitan Chicago* (1932).

Henry T. Lummus, *The Trial Judge* (1938).

H. F. Lusk, *Business Law* (1951 ed.).

A. F. Macdonald, *American State Government and Administration* (1955 ed.), Chs. 11–12.

J. M. Maguire, "Poverty and Civil Litigation," *Harvard Law Rev.,* XXXVI (Feb., 1923), 361–404.

R. Moley, *Our Criminal Courts* (1930).

——, *Tribunes of the People* (1932).

National Commission on Law Observance and Enforcement, *Reports* Nos. 4, 8–10 (1931).

Association of the Bar of the City of New York, *Bad House-Keeping—The Administration of the New York Courts* (1955).

H. D. Nims, *Pre-Trial* (1951).

L. B. Orfield, *Criminal Procedure from Arrest to Appeal* (1947).

Albert S. Osborn, *The Mind of the Juror* (1937).

Richard O'Sullivan, *Inheritance of the Common Law* (1950).

Roscoe Pound, *Criminal Justice in America* (1945 ed.).

————, *Organization of Courts* (1940).

————, *Justice According to Law* (1951).

William A. Robson, *Civilization and the Growth of Law* (1934).

P. S. Sikes and J. E. Stoner, *Bates and Field's State Government* (1954 ed.), Chs. 18–19.

R. H. Smith, *Justice and the Poor* (1919).

———— and J. S. Bradway, "The Growth of Legal Aid Work in the United States," *Bull. U. S. Bureau of Labor Statistics,* No. 607 (1936 ed.).

J. N. Ulman, *A Judge Takes the Stand* (1933).

Arthur T. Vanderbilt, *Men and Measures in the Law* (1949).

Sam B. Warner and H. B. Cabot, *The Judges and Law Reform* (1936).

W. F. Willoughby, *Principles of Judicial Administration* (1929).

Questions and Problems

1. Draw a distinction between "advisory opinion" and "declaratory judgment."

2. Does your state have a unified court system? A judicial council? What improvements might be made in judicial organization in your state?

3. Discuss the various methods by which state judges are selected. What method of selection strikes the best balance between democratic and expert participation?

4. To what extent is the English law the law of the American states?

5. Make a list of the principal subjects with which our civil law deals.

6. Outline the main points of procedure in a civil case.

7. Explain the nature of an arbitration; a conciliation.

8. Define crime. Give the essential features of each of the principal felonies.

9. Indicate the steps in a typical criminal proceeding.

10. What are the principal shortcomings of the administration of criminal justice?

11. Discuss justice for the poor, the down-and-out, and minorities.

CHAPTER 7

STATE ADMINISTRATIVE

ORGANIZATION AND THE CIVIL SERVICE

In the preceding chapters our concern has been with the historic branches of state government—executive, legislative, and judicial. Here our purpose is to examine the administrative establishment. Administration, which belongs to the executive branch, may be roughly characterized as the executive, the enforcement arm of government, in action. It is through administrative organizations and their officers and employees that the laws, except those that require judicial enforcement, are brought to apply in the everyday life of the citizen.

I. ADMINISTRATIVE ORGANIZATION [1]

The Growth of the Tasks of Administration

A century and a half ago administrative activities were few and far between. There were no railroad or other public utility commissions because practically no public utilities existed. There was no board of agriculture because land was plentiful and everybody was supposed to know the art of farming, which consisted of clearing the land, sowing, reaping, and then moving on to new and very cheap land when a farm was worn out. Few states did more than endorse education, for each community provided for the teaching of the three R's in its own little school, if it wanted one, and any education beyond that was strictly a private matter and was paid for accordingly. There were no boards of health; for a few doctors scattered about over a commonwealth could "bleed and blister" the sick; and epidemics, since they were commonly regarded as manifestations of the wrath of God, could not

[1] A. E. Buck, *The Reorganization of State Government in the United States* (1938); J. C. Bollens, *Administrative Reorganization in the United States since 1939* (Bureau of Public Adm., U. of Calif., 1947); Council of State Governments, *Reorganizing State Government* (1950); W. B. Graves, *American State Government* (1953 ed.), Ch. 10; Leslie Lipson, "The Executive Branch in New State Constitutions," *Public Administration Review,* Winter, 1949, pp. 11–21.

be prevented. In those rugged days there were no factory inspectors, no mine rescue commissioners, and no body of any other description that looked after the interests of labor; for the majority of men worked for themselves or on farms, while the few who were employed in the more hazardous industries were deemed to have assumed all risks, and any attempt on the part of the state to protect them would have been considered an interference with their freedom.

Partly from lack of scientific knowledge, but chiefly because the need did not exist, state governments performed very few administrative functions before 1850. Industrialization, urbanization, science, and enlightenment along many lines have changed all this. The state now serves the public in scores of ways that were undreamed of by our agricultural civilization a hundred years ago, and it administers a few functions that were considered entirely outside the province of government thirty years ago. Administrative departments, boards, and commissions have been created by the dozens to take care of these services. The cost of performing the historic functions of the state is not one tenth as much as the cost of maintaining its modern public services. More than two thirds of all the state funds go to education, highways, and social security.

Creation of Administrative Agencies

The only state administrative officers one hundred and fifty years ago were the governor, lieutenant governor, secretary of state, attorney general, treasurer, and auditor (these are briefly discussed in Chapter 4). They were created by constitutional provision and remain constitutional officers. As the work of general administration grew, and, in particular, as the states seriously began to take on service functions, such as education, the construction and maintenance of highways, and the regulation of public utilities, new officers and agencies were created. About 1915 there were few states that could not boast of thirty or forty administrative organs, and some reached the hundred mark, and several multiplied this by two, producing a veritable administrative wilderness.

Two important differences are to be noted between the establishment of state and national administrative agencies. First, many officers, boards, and commissions are prescribed by the state constitutions, whereas the national administrative machinery is left entirely to congressional discretion. In the second place, although Congress has created a large number and several varieties of administrative agencies, it has made more successful efforts to keep them within the executive departments than have most of the states. Until quite recently state legislatures held a decided preference for boards and commissions. Each new need in the states was usually met by the creation of a new and practically independent administrative unit, even though the necessary machinery already existed. Consequently, there came to be much more duplication, overlapping, and general confusion in many state systems than there was in the national system.

The Need for Administrative Reorganization

Forty odd years ago the national government felt the necessity of studying its administrative system with a view to reorganizing it along more satisfactory lines. The states, for the most part, have felt this need with even greater urgency. About 1912, influenced perhaps by the investigations and recommendations made respecting national administration by President Taft's Efficiency and Economy Commission, several states started to look into their administrative households. In Illinois they found inefficiency and waste resulting from a lack of correlation and co-operation among the offices engaged in similar or related functions; separate boards for each state penal institution and normal school; some six boards dealing with agricultural matters, and about three times as many labor agencies; finance administration distributed among a number of elective and appointive officers, with no one carrying general responsibility; only a nominal power of supervision in the hands of the governor, which he could exercise only through his power of appointment and removal; and so many separate offices that the governor could hardly direct them even if he had adequate powers.[2] Conditions in New York, Massachusetts, Iowa, and some other states were found to be very similar to those in Illinois.

Principles of Reorganization

The various commissions of investigation and, in particular, experienced and careful observers of the administrative process, a number of whom served on the commissions, have made sweeping recommendations respecting administrative organization. Their principal points are summarized by the Council of State Governments in its *Reorganizing State Government*.[3] They are as follows:

1. Consolidate all administrative agencies into departments (from ten to twenty) organized by function.

2. Establish lines of authority from the governor down through the hierarchy by eliminating elective administrative officials and giving the governor the power to appoint and remove all department heads and such other authority as may be necessary to make him the supreme executive power.

3. Give the governor adequate staff agencies including personal advisers, administrative assistants, a budget officer, an accounting office, a personnel office, a purchasing office, and a planning agency.

4. Eliminate the work of boards and commissions except for quasi-legislative and quasi-judicial functions.

5. Retain or establish an auditor independent of the governor, the auditor's duties to be limited to post-audit of administrative transactions on which he should report to the legislature.

These recommendations have been rather severely criticized by many lay-

[2] J. M. Mathews, "Administrative Reorganization in Illinois," *Nat. Mun. Rev.* (1920), Vol. IX, No. 11 (Supplement), p. 742.
[3] Pages 3–5.

men and legislators as too extreme, tending toward executive "dictatorship." And among students of public administration there are those who hold that such recommendations are unrealisitic in that they assume a complete separation of executive and legislative power, which, in fact, has never existed nor could exist. Even administration, they suggest, requires co-operation between the two branches.[4] Without following the controversy further, we may say that administrative reorganization has, in general, been greatly influenced by the principles listed above, although few if any jurisdictions have made complete application of them.

The Progress of Reorganization

It would appear that at least half the states have undertaken rather ambitious programs of administrative reorganization. Among these we may mention Illinois, California, Idaho, Ohio, Pennsylvania, and Washington. Of the states that have undergone the most comprehensive reorganization we name New York, New Jersey, Georgia, and Missouri. Owing to the specific provisions of state constitutions, a complete reorganization usually requires a constitutional amendment, but nearly all of these states have used the statutory method. Georgia (1945), Missouri (1945), and New Jersey (1948) were fortunate, however, in that they were able to provide for reorganization in connection with constitutional revision.

In 1917 the Illinois legislature adopted an administrative code bringing some sixty administrative agencies into nine (later increased) departments, each headed by a single director appointed by the governor with the consent of the senate and removable by the governor "for cause." Individually, the directors are responsible to the governor for their departments; collectively, they may serve as his cabinet, although this practice has fallen into disuse. The different functions of each department are administered by superintendents, bureau chiefs, or similarly titled assistants, who are responsible to the director, although appointed, like him, by the governor and the senate. For those services that require the exercise of considerable quasi-legislative or quasi-judicial power, paid boards are attached to the appropriate departments. An important feature of the system is found in the finance department, through which the governor is enabled to exercise a substantial control of activities in the other departments. Among other things, this department prepares the annual budget, examines and approves or disapproves vouchers and bills of the several departments, and ascertains whether the prices paid for labor and materials are fair, just, and reasonable.

New York, under the leadership of Governor Alfred E. Smith, adopted a plan of reorganization that placed the governor in very definite control of administration. Under the provisions of a constitutional amendment, approved in 1925, the legislature, with due regard for functional relationships, placed nearly two hundred administrative agencies in eighteen (the

[4] See, for example, Charles S. Hyneman, "Executive-Administrative Power and Democracy," *Public Administration Review,* Autumn, 1942, p. 335; Marshall Dimock, "The Objectives of Governmental Reorganization," *ibid.,* Autumn, 1951, p. 233.

STATE GOVERNMENT OF MISSOURI UNDER THE OLD CONSTITUTION
(With Special Emphasis on the Administrative Structure)

VOTERS OF MISSOURI

GENERAL ASSEMBLY *
HOUSE OF REPRESENTATIVES
SENATE

STATE AUDITOR *

STATE TREASURER *

LIEUTENANT GOVERNOR *

GOVERNOR *

ATTORNEY GENERAL *

SUPERINTENDENT OF PUBLIC SCHOOLS *

SECRETARY OF STATE *

SUPREME COURT *

BOARD OF LAW EXAMINERS

LIBRARY

DRIVERS' LICENSES

PUBLICATIONS

MOTOR VEHICLE REGISTRATION

CORPORATION SUPERVISION

OFFICIAL RECORDS

DEPARTMENT OF EDUCATION

DEPARTMENT OF LAW

ACCOUNTING

AUDITING

INCOME TAX

COUNTY AUDITS & BUDGETS

SALES TAX

CUSTODY OF FUNDS

INHERITANCE TAX

PURCHASING DEPARTMENT

ADJUTANT GENERAL *

HIGHWAY PATROL

BUDGET DEPARTMENT

DEPARTMENT OF FINANCE (BANKING)

INSURANCE DEPARTMENT

BUREAU OF BUILDING AND LOAN SUPERVISION

DEPARTMENT OF OIL INSPECTION

GRAIN AND WAREHOUSE DEPARTMENT

DEPARTMENT OF LIQUOR CONTROL

DEPARTMENT OF LABOR & INDUSTRIAL INSPECTION

BUREAU OF MINES

DEPARTMENT OF AGRICULTURE

DEPARTMENT OF GEOLOGICAL SURVEY

SERVICE OFFICER

LEGEND

○ INDICATES POPULARLY ELECTED OFFICIAL

▭ INDICATES SINGLE-HEADED DEPARTMENT

▭ INDICATES BOARD OR COMMISSION

* INDICATES AGENCY HAS A CONSTITUTIONAL STATUS

174

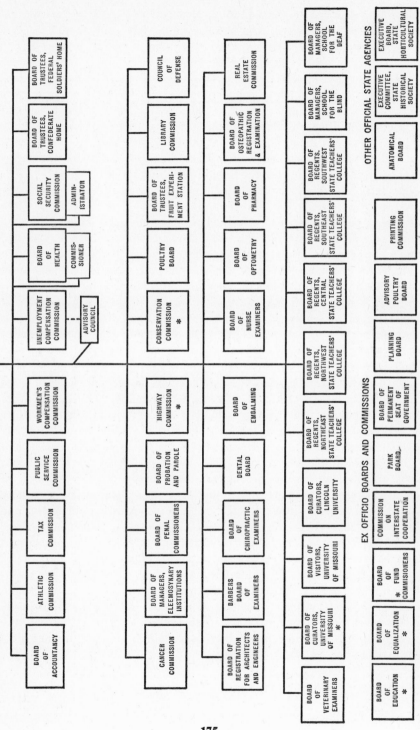

Prepared by Governmental Research Institute, St. Louis, Missouri, June, 1942

175

nineteenth was added by constitutional amendment in 1943) departments. Only the governor, lieutenant governor, comptroller, and attorney general remain elective officers. The governor, from his position as head of the "executive department" (the first of the nineteen departments), through his powers of appointment and removal, and through his cabinet conferences, has responsibility and authority sufficient to enable him to function as the chief administrator of the Empire State.[5] And still another state that has tied practically all the lines of administration in the executive chamber is Virginia (1927). Notwithstanding the fact that the movement was led in that State by a Jeffersonian Democrat, Governor Harry F. Byrd, the degree of integration achieved would scandalize the Sage of Monticello.

New Jersey is the state most recently to undergo substantial administrative reorganization. The Constitution (Article V, Section iv) of 1948 provides, in part, that all executive and administrative offices, including the historic ones of secretary of state and attorney general, shall be allocated within not more than twenty principal departments; that each department shall be under the supervision of the governor; that the department head shall be a single executive unless otherwise provided by law, appointed by the governor with the advice and consent of the senate and removable at the pleasure of the governor; and that where a board or commission heads a department the members thereof shall be appointed by the governor with the advice and consent of the senate, and may be removed in a manner provided by law. The legislature, in carrying out the mandate of the constitution, made extensive use of the reports of the Commission on State Reorganization, a body that had been functioning for four years. The legislative product might well be characterized as outstanding. Fourteen principal departments were established, the scores of administrative agencies and instrumentalities of the state being distributed among the departments in accordance with their functions. Thus, the Department of Law and Public Safety, operating under the direction of the attorney general, includes the subdepartments of law, state police, motor vehicles, weights and measures, and alcoholic beverage control; such professional boards as dentistry, embalmers and funeral directors, engineers and land surveyors, nursing, and veterinary medical examiners; and several other administrative agencies of the public safety variety. In like manner, all fiscal functions are administered through one department, that of the Treasurer. Under this system the governor is provided with a cabinet consisting of the fourteen department heads, persons appointed by him and directly responsible to him for the effective performance of the functions of their departments. This is administrative reorganization on a broad comprehensive scale, and it ought to produce satisfactory results.[6]

[5] F. D. Roosevelt, "Results in New York . . . ," *Nat. Mun. Rev.*, XIX (1930), 224; *Manual for the Use of the Legislature of New York*, 1953, pp. 485 ff.

[6] C. Wesley Armstrong, Jr., "Administrative Reorganization in New Jersey," *State Government*, Dec., 1948, pp. 244–247, 254–255; *New Jersey State Government: A Summary of*

Despite the valiant undertakings at reorganization reviewed above, the process throughout the nation has made only fair progress. As already noted, many elective public men and a few specialists in public administration fear the concentration of authority in the hands of the governor more than they deplore the probable waste and inefficiency of diffuse administration. Furthermore, an organized and integrated administration does not seem to stay that way. New functions are added to the tasks of administration and new machinery is established—and the not-so-long-ago reorganized system is again in need of reorganization.[7] Mention was just made of the Virginia administrative integration achieved under Governor Byrd. But twenty years later we read that the legislature of the Old Dominion State is "studying a plan to create a new administrative framework of 14 departments to handle the work now divided among 70 different governmental units," [8] and after two more years we have the report, "Virginia Reorganizes Again." [9] And so it goes.

THE LITTLE HOOVER COMMISSIONS. The first (Hoover) Commission on Organization of the Executive Branch of the Government of the United States (1947–1949) attracted wide attention. Since administrative organization is a continuing task, about three fourths of the states took advantage of the interest in the national Hoover Commission and set up little Hoover commissions to study and report on state problems of organization. The authority of these commissions varied considerably from state to state, from authorization to study all branches of the government to a limited assignment to consider such a subject as the revenue system. In general the commissions recommended about the same sort of administrative arrangements as were advocated by the earlier commissions. It should be noted, however, that the recommendations of the little Hoover commissions smell a little less of the lamp, are less insistent, for example, upon a specific limit to the number of departments or upon a particular division of functions among them.[10] As yet no sweeping changes appear to have come about as a result of the work of the latest commissions, but their activities in keeping the subject of administrative organization open for study is of itself a significant contribution to the solution of administrative problems.

Departmental Organization

The states vary considerably in the nature of the organizations they employ to perform the tasks of administration. The simplest type of organiza-

---

the *Organization and Functions of the Executive Branch* (Bureau of Government Research, Rutgers University, 1951).

[7] A number of authorities are skeptical of reorganization plans and of accomplishments under these plans. See, for example, F. W. Coker, "Dogmas of Administrative Reform," *Am. Pol. Sci. Rev.*, XVI (1922), 399; W. H. Edwards, "Has State Reorganization Succeeded?" *State Government*, Oct., 1938, pp. 183 ff.; and Harvey Walker, "Theory and Practice in State Administrative Reorganization," *Nat. Mun. Rev.*, April, 1930, pp. 249 ff.

[8] *News Bulletin*, Public Administration Clearing House, Feb. 16, 1948.

[9] R. B. Pinchbeck in the *Nat. Mun. Rev.*, July, 1950, p. 339.

[10] Ferrel Heady, "States Try Reorganization," *Nat. Mun. Rev.*, July, 1952, p. 334.

STATE GOVERNMENT OF MISSOURI UNDER THE NEW CONSTITUTION
(As Adopted by the People on February 27, 1945, Effective March 30, 1945)

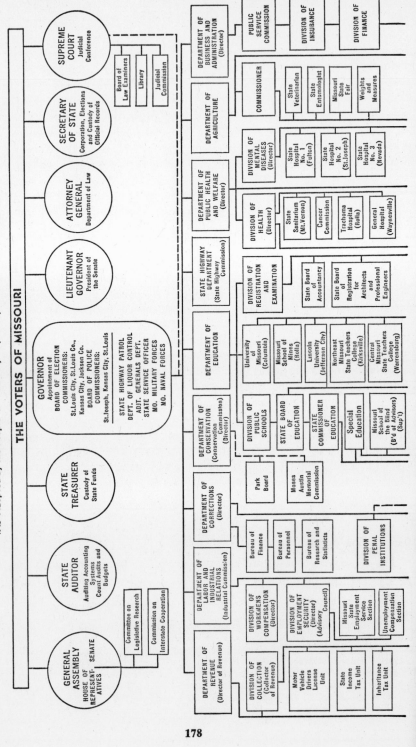

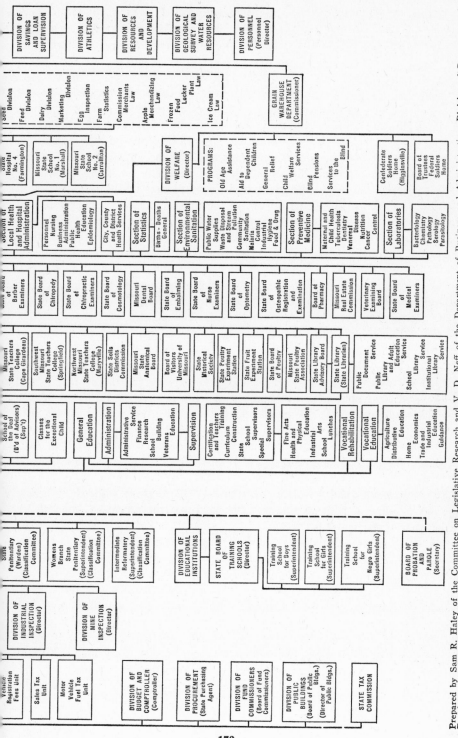

179

Prepared by Sam R. Haley of the Committee on Legislative Research, and V. D. Neff of the Department of Business and Administration, Division of Resources and Development. Reproduced by courtesy of the *Legislative Research Committee*, Jefferson City, Missouri.

tion, and the one that is commonly recommended, is found in those states that have an integrated administrative system. Missouri serves as a good example (see accompanying chart of its government under the constitution of 1945). That state has thirteen administrative departments. The heads of four of them, the secretary of state, the attorney general, the auditor, and the treasurer, are elected; the other department heads are appointed by the governor, with the exception of the director of conservation who is appointed by the conservation commission and the commissioner of education who is appointed by the Board of Education. It will be observed that the elective heads serve the old historic departments and that the appointive heads serve the modern departments, the ones that have the costly functions to perform. By looking at the units within any department we note that they all deal with subjects related to the general work of the department. It will appear also that such a scheme of organization does not necessarily abolish boards and commissions; that they may be left as appropriate agencies to perform those functions for which they are generally regarded as well fitted. Taking the plan as a whole, we have a very good demonstration of a large administrative organization that is yet arranged in such a manner as to make its work intelligible and enable a governor to supervise and direct it. Perhaps a score of other states have a departmental organization comparable to that of Missouri. New York and New Jersey have particularly good administrative set-ups.

The chart of Missouri's government under the old constitution (pages 174–175) serves as an example of organization, or disorganization, that is still prevalent in many states. A number of them have eight or more elective officials, officers practically independent of the governor. They have scores of boards and commissions, many appointed by the governor, some appointed by other officers, and some elective. A few services are headed by individual officials, but the broad system is all too prevalent, scant regard having been given to whether or not the service calls for this sort of direction. In 1950 Minnesota had 35 major departments, 13 of them with plural heads; Pennsylvania 42, with 18 plural heads; in Texas the score was 54 and 38; and in Oregon 78 and 66.[11]

Little Hoover commissions found 98 administrative agencies in Delaware, 115 in Arizona, and about 200 in Connecticut.[12] The head or heads of departments or other units in such states are usually made responsible to the governor, but how can a governor or anyone else maintain effective control over or be reasonably held responsible for a hundred or seventy-five or fifty separate agencies? The answer is that he cannot. Only through an administrative hierarchy with the number of departments held to a reasonable limit, with functions logically consolidated and apportioned among departments, is effective control of administration made possible.

[11] Council of State Governments, *Reorganizing State Government,* p. 17.
[12] Heady, *op. cit.,* p. 338.

II. PERSONNEL ADMINISTRATION [13]

We come now to the subject of state employees, of whom there are more than 600,000 (not including teachers), several states employing more than 25,000 each. These are the men and women who do the daily work of the state. They are the accountants, the engineers, the doctors, the nurses, the social securities specialists, the state policemen, the stenographers, the clerks, and others whom we see when we have business with the state. Are they under the merit system as are most of the federal employees? Are they adequately trained and scientifically selected? Are they properly classified and fairly and equitably compensated? These and other questions are appropriately raised in respect to administrative personnel programs.

The Extent of the Merit System

The spoils practice raged for years in the state and local civil service, as it did in the federal service from 1829 to 1883. Indeed, it may be said that the spoils poison spread into the federal administration from some of the states, notably from New York. Merit system acts were passed in New York and Massachusetts about the same time the first permanent merit system act was passed by the federal government (1883). Some twenty years later, Illinois and Wisconsin followed their example, and at the present time twenty-five states are listed as having comprehensive merit system programs. In all the other states a minimum merit program operates in conformity with the requirements of an amendment (1939) of the Federal Social Security Act. Those state departments that receive federal funds for public assistance and employment security must be operated under a merit system. The non-civil-service states commonly set up "merit system councils" to administer personnel policies of those state agencies that take part in the federal security program. A number of states that do not have "service-wide" coverage under a merit system, nevertheless provide for coverage in certain departments or services in addition to the social security agencies. Kentucky, Pennsylvania, and Washington, to mention just three states, have established such limited merit systems.

Formal adoption of the merit system does not necessarily mean that it is actually established. Politicians are forever finding short cuts to jobs for their friends, through securing the appointment of "reasonable" civil service commissioners, or by other means. Not infrequently the civil service laws are repealed, as in Arkansas (1939), and New Mexico (1941). Even those states that seek to protect the system by constitutional provision are not safe. The Michigan civil service law of 1937 rested upon a constitutional amendment, but that did not prevent the repeal of a number of its

[13] *The Book of the States, 1954–55,* pp. 177–197; Graves, *op. cit.,* Ch. 13; W. E. Mosher, J. D. Kingsley, and O. G. Stahl, *Public Personnel Administration* (1950 ed.); J. C. Phillips, *State and Local Government in America* (1954), Ch. 13; L. D. White, *Introduction to Public Administration* (1955 ed.), Chs. 21–30.

most excellent provisions (1939).   The basic reason for the slow progress
of the merit system is that the public is not decidedly averse to spoils.   Often
one hears heated denunciation of "politics" in the public service.   It usually
develops that a good Republican or an equally good Democrat is venting his
spleen at an administration of the other party.   Only when partisans criticize
their own party for corrupting the civil service is there evidence of sincere
devotion to the merit system.

EMPLOYMENT AND PAY ROLLS OF STATE AND LOCAL GOVERNMENTS, BY FUNCTION,
OCTOBER, 1952 *

Function	Number of Employees (in thousands)			October Pay Rolls (in millions)		
	State	Local	Total	State	Local	Total
Education, total	336	1,537	1,873	$75.6	$427.3	$502.9
Elementary and secondary schools	46	1,515	1,561	11.7	422.5	434.2
Institutions of higher education	259	22	281	56.5	4.8	61.3
Other	30	—	30	7.3	—	7.3
Highways	187	269	456	46.9	60.1	107.0
Public Welfare	37	56	93	9.1	12.5	21.5
Health	27	46	73	6.8	11.6	18.4
Hospitals	183	176	359	40.9	34.1	75.0
Police	21	217	238	6.1	61.0	67.1
Local fire protection	—	174	174	—	37.5	37.5
Natural resources	83	37	121	19.5	6.6	26.0
Sanitation	—	106	106	—	26.8	26.8
Local parks and recreation	—	61	61	—	14.0	14.0
Housing and community redevelopment	—	22	22	—	6.0	6.0
Employment security administration	44	—	44	12.8	—	12.8
State liquor stores	14	—	14	3.5	—	3.5
Local utilities	—	227	227	—	68.6	68.6
All other	172	489	661	49.6	86.9	136.6
TOTAL ALL FUNCTIONS	1,103	3,418	4,522	$270.8	$852.9	$1,123.7

* Adapted from *The Book of the States, 1954–55*, p. 185.
NOTE: As of January, 1954 the total number of civilian government employees in the
United States was 7,012,000.   Of the total 2,360,000 were federal, 1,133,000 state, and
3,519,000 local.   The figures include teachers and other educational personnel employed
by state and local governments.

Long ago the American public discarded its tolerance in the matter of
the political selection and removal of school teachers.   This relatively successful effort to remove politics from the schools would seem to indicate
that the people could have the merit principle in operation in all lines of
administrative activity if they really wanted it.   It may be said, however,
that the public is being slowly awakened to the necessity for improving
personnel standards in the public service, and that, despite a number of
instances of back-sliding on the part of states and local communities which
have adopted merit system laws, the general program for an improved civil

service has distinctly advanced, particularly since 1935. Since 1952 Alabama have given its merit system constitutional status; Georgia has extended coverage to eight departments; Louisiana has by constitutional amendment reestablished a state-wide merit system; Montana has provided for a department of state personnel; Nevada has established a state-wide civil service program; and five other states have made moves to strengthen their civil service.[14]

Operation of the Civil Service Laws

State civil service laws are administered by a civil service commission, a personnel board, a department of personnel, or by an agency with some such title, the members of which are commonly appointed by the governor. The commission, or whatever the personnel agency may be called, has general charge of the administration of the civil service laws, and the steady work for which it holds the legal responsibility is performed by an executive officer and staff.

The state civil service agencies have not, as a rule, attained the standard set by the federal commission. Furthermore, both state and federal commissions often have a common fault—that of giving too much attention to compliance with laws, rules, and regulations and not enough to the operational problems of department heads and other officers who must "get the work done." All too often state commissions have been under political domination, striving to do the will of the appointing officer, or even of a party leader holding no office. It seems that the state governments are unable to recruit for this service persons with as good qualifications as those who enter the federal service. This inability is due to various factors, among which may be mentioned the prestige of the federal service and its relative freedom from political interference.[15]

Salaries in the states are often inequitable. "Equal pay for equal work" is still a goal to be attained in many jurisdictions. Labor is usually better paid than the clerical and scientific forces, for powerful local labor organizations see to it that laborers in the public service receive the "going rate." Satisfactory salary adjustments depend upon scientific classification of positions. Although a number of studies of classification or standardization have been made, the results of such studies have not been put into effect as rapidly as the needs require; and where reclassifications have been made, considerable difficulty is always experienced in maintaining them against interested persons who present "special cases."

Promotion is based upon seniority, efficiency ratings, examinations, or the discretion of the administrative officer—usually upon a combination of these. In some states the opinion prevails that only a political "pull" will bring a promotion, and in many cases there is enough basis for this opinion to dis-

[14] *Book of the States, 1954–55,* pp. 177 ff.

[15] There is some complaint among state personnel officers to the effect that the federal service operates as a bit of a drain upon the state service; that the federal civil service steadily, if slowly, draws from the states some of the best state administrators and employees.

courage the civil service reformer as well as the capable employee who waits in vain for his promotion.

Discipline is imposed in a number of forms—deprivation of seniority, demerits, suspension, and others. The method of removal varies in form from removal at the discretion of a high administrative officer, as in the federal service, to removal upon the initiative of such officers, subject to the right of the employee to a judicial review. There is some dispute as to what form of removal best secures the interest of the employee and the public. The weight of authority seems to be on the side of the federal system, although it is conceded that more attention to recruitment might well lead to additional protection of the employee against removal.

As for retirement or pension systems, a number of our governments have in the last twenty years adopted some kind of plan. A few have liberal plans, but more commonly the annuity falls somewhat below this standard.

Problems and Trends in the Civil Service

A poser of long standing has been that of how to get capable, alert, dynamic personnel in the administrative services. It is an old story that in the contest for talent, government has often lost to business. But since the Great Depression government's position as a competitor with business has been greatly improved. Although the change has been more noticeable in the federal service, the states have shared somewhat in this development. Yet the fact remains that government must meet business as a rival for capable administrators, and government can do this rather effectively if it puts its best foot forward, emphasizing the many attractions of a public career.

Another problem of the civil service is that of reducing the number of amateurs and politicians in key administrative posts and turning the posts over to trained administrators. The tendency among legislators and elected administrative officials is to exempt the higher and better paid positions from the merit system. This tendency has been in part supported by the failure of our educational institutions to train adequately a sufficient number of general and expert administrators.[16] During the last twenty years, however, political officials have shown evidence of receding somewhat from their position that the best administrative posts should be reserved for faithful party workers, and the same score of years has witnessed a most encouraging growth of schools of public administration in nearly all of our best universities.

Of a number of other problems that might be mentioned, a major one concerns the civil service commission. As noted above, these agencies have in the past been concerned with the important (but nevertheless negative) functions of keeping spoils out of the civil service and with protecting employees against dismissal on political, racial, or religious grounds. These functions

---

[16] It is supported also by the failure (there are some exceptions) of American civil service systems to gear their examinations to any specific academic programs.

remain, but they are of less significance now than formerly because of a wider acceptance of the anti-spoils philosophy and because other factors have become of equal or greater importance for the merit system. Professor William Seal Carpenter, former president of the New Jersey civil service commission, observes that the current "problem is not so much that of 'keeping the rascals out' as it is that of getting intelligent and capable men and women to accept public employment." [17] The solution for this problem is not simple, but it certainly calls for the use of vision and imagination in the formulation of recruitment programs, qualities that commissions have seldom displayed in that connection. The formulation of a recruitment program is only an illustration of positive tasks that the modern personnel agency should undertake.

Modern administration requires that the personnel agency work closely with the chief executive, advising him in all phases of the personnel problem and supporting him in his efforts to utilize personnel to the best advantage. The bipartisan commission of amateurs, with its tradition of serving simply as a watch dog for the merit system, is unsuited for this rôle. Authorities commonly agree that the appropriate duties of a modern personnel agency can be best performed by a single individual, a professional director. Under such a plan the commission might be retained for the determination of policy and the adjudication of appeals, or the commission as we have known it might be abolished entirely, and a purely advisory commission or committee be substituted for it. Some states have moved in this direction, Maryland and Connecticut, among others. A single commissioner carries the full responsibility in Maryland, while in Connecticut a personnel director is associated with an advisory commission. In the latter state the director strengthens his position as head of the civil service through membership on the personnel board along with the governor and the commissioner of finance. This newer type of personnel officer is no less able to guard the merit system, to protect employees from unfair treatment, than the conventional commission, and as personnel adviser to the chief executive, he is in a position to work with the administration on recruitment, promotion, classification, salaries, and all the rest, to the end that the civil service be maintained at the highest efficiency and adequate for the needs of the state.

The foregoing should not be interpreted to mean that every civil service commission is grossly inadequate in dealing with the positive phases of a personnel program and that all the states should abolish them or transfer most of their duties to a director of personnel. A number of commissions are giving more attention to the positive side of their responsibilities. They are evolving comprehensive programs of personnel management, giving careful consideration to conditions of work, classification, salaries, improvement

---

[17] "Reformer's Task Never Done," *Nat. Mun. Rev.*, July, 1952, p. 342. This very penetrating article is composed of excerpts from Professor Carpenter's book, *The Unfinished Business of Civil Service Reform* (1952).

in the service, promotion, and various other factors that build morale and "esprit de corps," without which employees have a humdrum existence and the public their listless service.

Reading List

J. C. Bollens, *Administrative Reorganization in the States Since 1939* (Bureau of Pub. Adm., U. of Cal., 1947).

A. E. Buck, *The Reorganization of State Governments in the United States* (1938).

W. S. Carpenter, *The Unfinished Business of Civil Service Reform* (1952).

Civil Service Assembly . . . , *Employee-Training in the Public Service* (1941).

————, *Placement and Probation in the Public Service* (1946).

————, *Position-Classification in the Public Service* (1941).

————, *Recruiting Applicants for the Public Service* (1942).

————, National Civil Service League, and National Municipal League, *Model State Civil Service Law* (1946).

The Council of State Governments, *Reorganizing State Government* (1950).

C. R. Fish, *The Civil Service and the Patronage* (1904).

W. D. Foulke, *Fighting the Spoilsmen* (1919).

Good Government (bi-monthly).

W. B. Graves, *American State Government* (1953 ed.), Chs. X–XIII.

————, *Public Administration in a Democratic Society* (1950).

Leslie Lipson, *The American Governor: From Figurehead to Leader* (1939).

A. F. Macdonald, *American State Government and Administration* (1955 ed.), Chs. 16–17.

Michigan Commission on Reform and Modernization of Government, *Documents and Proceedings* (1938) and *Report of a Preliminary Survey* (1938).

W. E. Mosher, J. D. Kingsley, and O. G. Stahl, *Public Personnel Administration* (1950 ed.).

National Civil Service Reform League, *The Civil Service in Modern Government* (1936).

National Municipal Review (monthly).

New York State Constitutional Convention Committee, *Problems Relating to Executive Administration and Power* (1938).

J. M. Pfiffner and R. V. Presthus, *Public Administration* (1953 ed.).

J. C. Phillips, *State and Local Government in America* (1954), Ch. 13.

K. H. Porter, *State Administration* (1938).

Public Administration Review (quarterly).

Public Personnel Review (quarterly).

State Government (monthly).

L. D. White, *Introduction to the Study of Public Administration* (1955 ed.).

Questions and Problems

1. Why is the state administrative structure designed a century ago entirely inadequate for present needs?

2. Write a brief sketch on the development of state administrative agencies.

3. Devise a plan of state administrative organization that will at the same time preserve democratic principles and provide the framework for effective administration.

4. What administrative reorganization has been undertaken in your state? What more is needed?

5. Can it be said that administrative organization is a continuous process?

6. Outline the main features of departmental organization.

7. Discuss the progress of the merit system in state civil service.

8. Distinguish between the older (negative) functions and the newer (positive) functions of the personnel agency. Is there any necessary conflict between the two?

9. Assuming an adequate civil service law, what more is needed to assure the operation of the merit system?

CHAPTER 8

STATE AND LOCAL FINANCE

Fifty years ago there was complaint against the states and their local subdivisions for waste, extravagance, and the resulting high taxes. The criticism had justification, but even with all the mismanagement the cost by present-day standards was ridiculously low—not a tenth of the total we now accept with a wry smile or a shake of the head. Before 1914 most any tax structure would do, appropriations could be casual, and the supervision of expenditures practically nonexistent. We were getting along without bothering with such things. Today, the annual expenditures of New York City are larger than those of the national government in any year prior to the First World War, the aggregate of state and local expenditures (not far short of $25 billion) exceed the national debt in 1930, and the total annual cost of government in the United States is nearly $90 billion. To be sure, a large part of the dollar increase in cost is represented by inflation. Even since 1939 the purchasing power of the dollar has been cut in half. But the rise in cost is not explained solely by inflation. Expenditures of the national government for military purposes and state and local increases in expenditures for such old services as highways and schools and new expenditures such as those for social security add up to a very large total, even in terms of the 1939 dollars. Perhaps the clearest way to put the matter of cost is to say that one dollar out of every four now goes to government—national, state, and local. Finance at any level of government can no longer be incidental or casual. It is a major problem requiring the best efforts of the best minds.

Limitations Upon the Taxing Power

Before reviewing such matters of state finance as sources of revenue, budgeting, and borrowing money, certain limitations upon the taxing power should be noted.

There are three important federal limitations upon the power of state legislatures to tax. *First,* there is the limitation with respect to the taxing of commerce. The federal Constitution prohibits the states from levying import, export, or tonnage duties. Control of interstate commerce by the national government means that the states cannot tax interstate commerce. The states may, however, tax property as such, even though it is used in interstate or foreign commerce. Thus, the states may and do impose general property taxes upon railroad and steamship companies. What is prohibited is the taxing of an *act* of interstate or foreign commerce. *Second,* the state may not tax the national government or its instrumentalities.[1]

Third, state tax laws must satisfy a provision of the Fourteenth Amendment of the federal Constitution that reads: No state shall "deprive any person of life, liberty, or property, without due process of law; nor deny to any person within its jurisdiction the equal protection of the laws." As judicially interpreted, the due process clause means that a state may levy no taxes on property or rights not within its jurisdiction. This interpretation can get very technical, especially in relation to the taxing of intangible property. For example, it has been held that the State of Utah may impose a tax upon a transfer by death of shares of stock in the Union Pacific Railroad Company, a Utah corporation, even though the decedent resided in New York and kept his stock certificates there. Utah had the right to tax because the corporation owed its existence to that state.[2] The due process provision means also, among other things, that taxes may be levied only for public purposes (not for the special benefit of particular persons or corporations). It should be noted, however, that the Supreme Court of the United States now construes this tax limitation rather liberally in favor of the states, the Utah case just cited furnishing a good example of this generous attitude.

The equal protection provision might appear to mean that "everything and everybody" must be taxed alike, but it has no such meaning. As judicially construed, it prohibits only the harshest discriminations. For example, it prohibits a state from taxing stores in one locality at one rate and those in another at a different rate, but it permits the state to tax chain stores at one rate and "home-owned" stores at another. Equal protection means only that all persons and things in the same classification must be taxed in the same way.

In the greater number of state constitutions there are limitations identical with or very similar to the due process and equal protection provisions of the federal Constitution. Most state constitutions also require that all taxes be uniform upon the same class of property; for example, that an individual owning $100,000 worth of land and another owning $10,000 worth shall be taxed at the same rate per $100 value.

Cities, counties, and other local governments have no inherent power to tax. They may tax only under powers granted to them by charter, statute, or the state constitution. The limits that legislatures impose upon local areas commonly relate both to what may be taxed and to the maximum rates that may be levied. In exercising their taxing powers the local authorities are subject, like the state legislatures, to the limitations imposed by the federal Constitution and the constitution of the state.

---

[1] On limitations *one* and *two* see Chapter 1, section II, "Constitutional Limitations upon the States."

[2] State Tax Commission of Utah v. Aldrich, 316 U.S. 174 (1942).

I. SOURCES OF REVENUE [3]

Where is the money coming from?   At times it seems that taxing authorities simply seek to find somewhere, somehow, the needed revenue.   The problem is much bigger than that.   It is to hit upon a revenue system that will yield the necessary funds and impose the least possible strain upon the economy.   The best authorities yield uncertain answers to that question.   Here we shall limit ourselves to a brief consideration of the common sources of revenue and a comment of evaluation on each.

States draw their income from various sources.   Probably no two states have identical tax systems; but nearly all of them levy a general property tax, an inheritance tax, a corporation tax, unemployment compensation taxes, and certain others.

The General Property Tax

The general property tax is the oldest state tax, and the one from which practically all the revenue was formerly derived, but from which less than four per cent is derived at present.   It still carries nearly nine tenths of the revenue burden in most cities and counties.   The theory of the general property tax is simple.   Each person pays a tax determined by the value of his house, lands, horses, cattle, machinery, furniture, jewelry, stocks, bonds, mortgages, and so on.   This is an *ad valorem* tax—so much per hundred dollars of assessed valuation.   It falls alike upon all property owners, supposedly.   It was fairly satisfactory in the days when governments did not need much money, and when the earthly goods of most men consisted of real property and tangible personal property.   The farmer could not hide his buildings, fields, and live stock from the assessor; nor could he conceal easily the great hall clock or the "parlor" sofa.   Furthermore, the ordinary assessor had little difficulty in arriving at a fair valuation of these properties.   But the concentration of property in cities and the almost fabulous increase in the amount of intangible property (securities of various kinds) since the Civil War have changed all this.   City property is ordinarily much more difficult to evaluate than rural property; and the securities in the vaults of a trust company or brokerage house, whether held by rural or urban inhabitants, often escapes the assessor's rolls.   Indeed, the kindly assessor may rather encourage a timid individual to make no mention of his intangibles, since the general property tax rate in some states is almost confiscatory when applied to them.

ASSESSMENT.   The problem of assessing real and personal property for purposes of taxation calls for more than passing mention, for unscientific assessment constitutes a fundamental shortcoming in the administration of

[3] *The Book of the States, 1954–55*, pp. 201–234; W. Brooke Graves, *American State Government* (1953 ed.), Ch. 15; Harold M. Groves, *Financing Government* (1954 ed.); Lane W. Lanchester, *Government in Rural America* (1952 ed.), Chs. 6–7; *The Municipal Year Book* (1954), pp. 223 ff.; J. C. Phillips, *State and Local Government in America* (1954), Ch. 12; L. D. White, *Introduction to Public Administration* (1955 ed.), Chs. 16–19.

the general property tax. The assessors are local officers, usually elected, and seldom have any training for their important work. In most states the assessors are given written instructions, and in a few, some additional aids; but no amount of such help will reduce assessment to routine or give impartial valuations to property unless the assessors are honest and intelligent. The taxpayer often makes his own assessment, particularly his personal property assessment.[4]

The assessor walks into the home of a wealthy individual and makes dutiful inquiry about pianos, washing machines, electric refrigerators, and clocks; but he hardly notices the fine paintings on the wall or the oriental rug on the floor (unless he becomes conscious of not having properly cleaned his shoes before entering). Yet the rugs and the paintings are probably worth much more than the other articles enumerated. If the assessor places them on his list, he gives them the very low value that the owner mentions. The assessor moves on, feeling perhaps that justice has not been done, but not knowing just what he can do about it. He goes next to a home presided over by a proud but unsophisticated bride. Hardly realizing that she is talking to an assessor, she lists their modest properties at something approximating their full value. A more cheering version of this story has the husband, who is on friendly terms with the assessor, meeting that gentleman as he is leaving the house and setting him right as to the "real" value of the property. At any rate these fictitious cases illustrate the very common fact that assessments of personal property are made largely by the owners rather than by the assessor.

EQUALIZATION. Manifestly, assessments will vary greatly even among individuals visited by the same assessor, and they vary still more among the districts canvassed by different assessors. In order to reduce these inequalities, county or other district boards of review or equalization are authorized to hear complaints of individual taxpayers and to correct material injustices in assessments. These boards are also required to equalize assessments among the several districts or townships of a county, to the end that all may be equitably taxed. Ordinarily, however, only the grosser inequalities are corrected. When county authorities have passed upon assessments, the rolls are placed before a state tax commission or other state officers serving as a board of equalization. This board may order reassessments in particular counties or districts, or reassessments of particular kinds of property. It is also the duty of this board, or of some other state authority, to assess public utilities, such as railroad, telegraph, and telephone systems—properties that, because of their nature and extent, are not easily or equitably assessed by local authorities. A number of states have wisely entrusted the central tax commission with the power to supervise local assessments and to make investigations of the general conditions of taxation. Such commissions have greatly improved the taxation systems in several states.

CRITICISMS OF THE GENERAL PROPERTY TAX. It has already been shown

[4] On the problem of assessment and other phases of the general property tax in New Jersey, see John F. Sly, "A Century of Inequities," *Tax Review*, Feb., 1953.

that it is very difficult to get fair assessment of property. Ordinarily, real property and the general run of tangible personal property are not assessed in an equitable manner, and there are still wider disproportions in the assessment of other properties. The luxuries of the wealthy are usually assessed too low and intangibles are frequently not assessed at all. Taxes based upon unfair assessments are, of course, unfair. The burden falls with particular force upon the owners of real estate and tangible property, hitting the farmer as a class harder than any other.

But suppose all property is assessed alike—the tax is still subject to criticism, for the reason that some forms of property yield much greater income than others. A number of states have frankly recognized this, and they have provided for the classification of property for purposes of taxation. For example, intangibles have been placed in a special class and taxed at a lower rate than tangibles. What drove the intangibles into hiding originally was that the general property tax on their actual value was practically confiscatory. With the lower tax rate there is less urge to conceal them and less leniency for those who do conceal them. The result is that intangibles are now more commonly declared, the state gets more return for the lower rate than it did for the higher, and the owner of real estate and tangible personal property has some aid in supporting the government. But classification of property, although affording some relief, does not solve the tax problem, for ownership of property is neither a measure of ability to pay taxes nor of benefits the owner derives from government. Recognizing the unsatisfactory results of this general property tax, several states have abandoned it, leaving it for local government units. In desperation farmers and taxpayers' associations have compelled some states to place a limit on the rate of the general property tax. All the states have sought other sources of revenue.

Income and Inheritance Taxes

One of the other sources is the income tax. Thirty-one states levy a personal income tax and thirty-three levy such a tax on corporations. Delaware and New Hampshire impose the personal income tax only, and Connecticut, Pennsylvania, Rhode Island, and South Dakota impose the corporation income tax only. The personal income tax rates are graduated, but except in three or four states, the highest rate does not run beyond 8 per cent. The corporation income tax is commonly fixed at a flat rate, 2, 3, 4, or even a higher per cent. In a few states, notably Pennsylvania and Ohio, certain cities are permitted to levy income taxes. Washington, D.C., appears to have the highest rate—3 per cent for those with the largest incomes. The income tax is generally considered the most satisfactory, the soundest, of all taxes, being based on the ability to pay. There are, of course, limits to its possibilities, for the national government's large take from this source forces the states to keep their rates low. There is also the argument that when income taxes take so much from the larger incomes, persons with capital lose

STATE TAX COLLECTIONS, BY TYPE OF TAX, 1942–1953 *

| Tax Source | Amount in Millions(a) | | | | | | Change(b) Per Cent | | Per Cent Distribution | Per Capita(b,c) | |
	1953 (Prelim.)	1952	1950	1948	1946	1942	1952–1953	1942–1953	1953	1953	1942
Sales and gross receipts	6,199	5,730	4,670	4,042	2,803	2,218	8.2	179.5	58.8	40.01	16.76
General sales or gross receipts	2,433	2,229	1,670	1,478	899	632	9.2	284.8	23.1	15.70	4.78
Motor fuels	2,017	1,870	1,544	1,259	886	940	7.8	114.4	19.1	13.02	7.11
Alcoholic beverages	465	442	420	425	402	257	5.4	81.3	4.4	3.00	1.94
Tobacco products	467	449	414	337	198	130	4.0	259.4	4.4	3.01	.98
Insurance	316	284	241	193	145	113	11.2	178.8	3.0	2.04	.86
Public utilities	249	228	185	155	132	100	9.0	148.9	2.4	1.61	.76
Other	252	228	195	194	142	45	10.6	461.8	2.4	1.63	.34
License	1,630	1,476	1,228	1,000	783	708	10.4	130.2	15.5	10.52	5.35
Motor vehicles and operators	1,012	924	755	593	439	431	9.5	134.7	9.6	6.53	3.26
Corporations in general	266	226	176	149	121	93	17.5	185.6	2.5	1.72	.70
Alcoholic beverages	79	77	77	74	67	56	2.9	42.7	0.8	.51	.42
Hunting and fishing	76	70	60	48	33	24	9.2	215.6	0.7	.49	.18
Other	196	178	160	136	123	104	9.9	89.1	1.9	1.27	.78
Income	1,779	1,751	1,310	1,084	831	518	1.6	243.3	16.9	11.48	3.92
Individual income(d)	969	913	724	499	389	249	6.1	288.4	9.2	6.25	1.88
Corporation net income(d)	810	838	586	585	442	269	−3.3	201.4	7.7	5.23	2.03
Property	365	370	307	276	249	264	−1.3	38.0	3.5	2.36	2.00
Death and gift	222	211	168	179	141	110	5.2	102.1	2.1	1.43	.83
Severance	286	272	211	131	90	62	5.4	359.6	2.7	1.85	.47
Other	61	47	36	30	41	23	28.5	162.7	0.6	.39	.17
Total collections	$10,542	$9,857	$7,930	$6,743	$4,937	$3,903	7.0	170.1	100.0	$68.04	$29.50

* U.S. Bureau of the Census, *State Tax Collections in 1953*, as reproduced in *The Book of the States, 1954-55*, p. 225.

(a) Historical tax figures, by state, appear in Bureau of the Census, *Compendium of State Government Finances in 1952* and *Revised Summary of State Government Finances,*

1942-1950.
(b) Computed on the basis of amounts rounded to nearest thousand.
(c) Per capita figures for 1953 are based on 1952 population figures; those for

1942 are based on estimated total population of the forty-eight states on July 1, 1941 (132,300,000, excluding armed forces overseas).

(d) Individual income tax figures include corporation net income tax amounts for from one to three states in each fiscal year shown.

their incentive to put it to productive use, since the "government would get most of the profit anyhow."

The inheritance tax is employed in every state except Nevada. The rate of this excise on the privilege of a beneficiary to inherit property varies with the amount of the inheritance and with the beneficiary's degree of relationship to the deceased. The inheritance tax has a great deal to commend it. Often, but not always, an heir has done little to build up the fortune he inherits and thus has no very strong ground of complaint when the state takes a share of it. There are even strong individuals who have said that income and inheritance taxes help to bring about a more desirable distribution of wealth. It should be noted that income and inheritance taxes are not the state "gold mines" some people imagine them to be. Although in two or three states they may yield one third or more of the state revenue, taking the country as a whole, the income tax yields about 17 per cent of state revenue and the inheritance tax only about 2 per cent.

Franchises and Licenses

Some special type of tax is commonly levied upon corporate business and often upon other business. Taxes on corporations take varied and often complicated forms. One of the simpler forms is the corporation income tax, noted above. Corporations are usually required to pay a fee and organization tax at the time they start in business; then they pay an annual franchise tax (that is, a tax or fee for the privilege of doing business). The franchise tax is ordinarily a small percentage of the value of the capital stock of the corporation, or of its gross or net earnings, or of some of its other financial activities. A state may tax a foreign corporation (one chartered in another state) as it does its own, but the value it places on such a franchise must be determined only by the business the corporation does in the state.

Some state income is derived from licenses to sell alcoholic beverages, to hunt, and to fish. Income from these sources is but "chicken feed," however, compared with the funds that come from drivers' licenses and particularly from motor vehicle licenses. Between 9 and 10 per cent of the revenue the states receive from taxation is from licenses to possess and operate cars and trucks.

The Sales Tax

There are various forms of this tax, but the principal one is the retail sales tax. It was not in general use until 1933, when the depression brought it in as an emergency source of revenue. Although depression-born, it has shown no signs of departing with a partial restoration of normal times. It has been found to be a very productive source of revenue. Furthermore, it is very popular with tax-payers' associations, whose chief concern is to keep down taxes on real property. One often hears the statement that the sales tax broadens the base of taxation. Of course it does, but this means that many very poor people are brought within the ranks of taxpayers. There is little doubt that this tax bears much more heavily upon the poor than it does upon others, for the poor have to spend a very substantial part of their income for the bare necessities of life. It is true that this tax is no great burden in times of full employment and high wages; and it is, of course, possible to exempt, as some states do, such items as medicine and food from the tax. It now yields about one fifth of the revenue of the states.

THE GASOLINE TAX. There are special sales taxes on alcohol, tobacco, electricity, and other commodities and transactions, but the gasoline tax tops them all. The rate varies, but it averages around 5 or 6 cents a gallon, and it produces about 19 per cent of the revenue of the states. These funds are commonly ear-marked for highway purposes, but in periods of financial stringency, periods in which the gas tax still produced a handsome revenue, legislatures diverted some of the money to other uses. On the whole it is a rather satisfactory tax, one that is more or less painlessly extracted and for which the motorist usually feels that he is getting somewhere near his money's worth. A few cities and a number of small communities levy a gasoline tax, but most of the "gas money" that comes to local communities is collected by the states and passed on to the cities and counties for their streets and highways.

Insurance Trust Revenue *(omit)*

The foregoing discussion relates to the revenue raised by the state for the general purposes of government. A tax that was not included but of which notice should be taken is the payroll tax. It is imposed by the federal government and the laws of every state for unemployment compensation. The funds from this source, amounting to well over $1.5 billion annually, are deposited in a federal trust account.

Grants-in-Aid

Federal grants to the states for various programs (see Chapter 1, section V) now constitute a substantial part of the income of the states. In 1952 such grants totaled about $2,329 million, and they covered 17 per cent of state expenditures.[5] In turn the states follow a grant-in-aid policy for the benefit of local governments. The amount of state aid granted in 1952 was $5 billion, a sum representing more than a third of the state general expenditure. The grants are to counties, cities, towns, and school districts, and they are for education (almost exactly half the total), highways, public welfare, and other purposes (see table on page 196). State aid to local communities may find some justification in the more favorable position of the states for operating the taxing machinery, but it finds its special defense in the fact that taxable wealth is "spotty"; some areas have little and are thus unable to maintain adequate schools and other essential services without aid from the state.

[5] *The Book of the States, 1954–55,* p. 46.

II. FINANCIAL MANAGEMENT [6]

Before the First World War each spending agency of government, state or local, acted pretty much for itself in securing whatever appropriations it could get from council, commission, or legislature.   And it would then proceed to spend the money, subject only to a general check by an auditor as to the legality of expenditures.

STATE INTERGOVERNMENTAL EXPENDITURE, 1942–1952

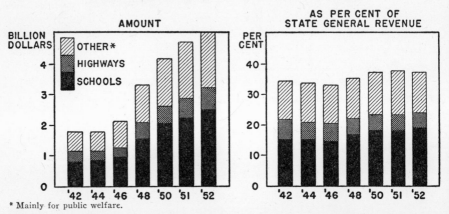

* Mainly for public welfare.

Reproduced by the courtesy of The Council of State Governments from *The Book of the States, 1954–55,* p. 55.

The table on National Totals of State Government Finance reproduced on pages 197–199 gives a picture of the development of services and the increase in costs that is representative also of local government.   With governments dealing in such large sums of money, a few taxpayers have called for reduction in service and a larger number have more loudly and more convincingly demanded greater efficiency in government operations.   There has been no appreciable response to the recommendations of the minority that services be curtailed, but the wider demand for efficiency and economy has produced a few results.   Since about 1915 many jurisdictions have instituted plans of fiscal management that include such processes as budgeting, the supervision of expenditures, post-auditing, and centralized purchasing.

The Budget

Before the First World War the idea was beginning to spread that order could be brought into government finance and some economies effected by the adoption of a budget system, and within a period of twenty years every state and most cities had formulated a budget plan.   Under such a plan the budget-making authorities (usually administrative officials) must decide what activities the government should undertake and how much each should cost, and they should also indicate where the money could come from, what sources

[6] See reference listed in note 1.

NATIONAL TOTALS OF STATE GOVERNMENT FINANCE, 1942–1952 *

Item	Amounts in Millions							Per Cent Change		Per Cent Distribution	Per Capita	
	1952	1951	1950	1948	1946	1944	1942	1951–1952	1942–1952	1952	1952	1942
Revenue and borrowing	$17,962	$16,831	$15,331	$12,736	$8,652	$7,721	$7,040	6.7	155.2	—	$117.73	$53.19
Borrowing	1,147	1,284	1,428	910	77	26	170	−10.7	576.4	—	7.25	1.28
Revenue, total	16,815	15,547	13,903	11,826	8,576	7,695	6,870	8.2	144.8	—	110.21	51.91
General revenue	13,429	12,402	11,262	9,257	6,283	5,465	5,132	8.3	161.7	100.0	88.02	38.77
Taxes, total(a)	9,857	8,933	7,930	6,743	4,937	4,071	3,903	10.3	152.5	73.4	64.61	29.49
Intergovernmental revenue	2,485	2,508	2,423	1,740	864	981	858	−0.9	189.8	18.5	16.29	6.48
From Federal Government	2,329	2,359	2,275	1,643	802	926	802	−1.3	190.5	17.3	15.26	6.06
Public welfare	1,149	1,185	1,107	731	432	415	369	−3.0	211.1	8.6	7.53	2.79
Education	293	329	345	320	99	215	137	−10.8	114.1	2.2	1.92	1.03
Highways	413	430	438	303	66	144	169	−4.0	143.6	3.1	2.70	1.28
Employment security administration	187	175	168	152	63	36	57	6.3	226.1	1.4	1.22	.43
Other	287	240	217	137	140	116	69	26.9	317.5	1.3	1.88	.52
From Local Governments	156	149	148	97	63	55	56	4.7	179.4	1.2	1.02	.42
Charges and miscellaneous general revenue	1,087	961	909	774	482	413	370	13.1	193.4	8.1	7.12	2.80
Liquor stores revenue	924	904	810	857	798	528	373	2.2	147.9	—	6.06	2.82
Insurance trust revenue	2,462	2,242	1,831	1,711	1,494	1,702	1,366	9.8	80.2	100.0	16.14	10.32
Employee retirement	579	500	425	296	193	142	115	15.6	402.6	23.5	3.79	.87
Unemployment compensation	1,597	1,483	1,176	1,203	1,162	1,405	1,134	7.6	40.8	64.8	10.46	8.57
Other	287	257	229	212	140	154	117	−5.9	146.2	2.5	1.88	.88
Debt outstanding at end of fiscal year, total	6,874	6,223	5,285	3,676	2,353	2,776	3,257	10.5	111.1	100.0	45.06	24.61
Long-term	6,640	5,974	5,168	3,568	2,328	2,768	3,096	11.1	114.5	96.6	43.52	23.39
Full faith and credit	4,926	4,688	4,209	3,070	1,970	2,281	2,641	5.1	86.5	71.7	32.29	19.95

NATIONAL TOTALS OF STATE GOVERNMENT FINANCE, 1942–1952 (continued)

Item	Amounts in Millions							Per Cent Change		Per Cent Distribution	Per Capita	
	1952	1951	1950	1948	1946	1944	1942	1951–1952	1942–1952	1952	1952	1942
Nonguaranteed	$1,714	$1,286	$958	$499	$358	$486	$455	33.3	276.7	24.9	$11.23	$3.44
Short-term	235	249	118	108	25	8	161	−5.9	45.8	3.4	1.54	1.22
Net long-term	5,620	4,944	4,246	2,911	1,727	2,112	2,563	13.7	119.2	81.8	36.84	19.37
Full faith and credit only	3,984	3,761	3,379	2,440	1,381	1,710	2,123	5.9	87.7	58.0	26.11	16.04
Expenditure and debt redemption	16,329	15,367	15,373	11,382	7,296	5,400	5,746	6.3	184.2	—	107.02	43.41
Debt redemption	495	346	291	202	231	240	403	42.8	22.8	—	3.24	3.04
Expenditure, total	15,834	15,020	15,082	11,181	7,066	5,161	5,343	5.4	196.4	—	103.78	40.37
General expenditure	13,697	12,972	12,250	9,469	5,245	4,508	4,549	5.6	201.1	100.0	89.78	34.37
Public safety	378	351	328	249	162	149	146	7.6	159.1	2.8	2.48	1.10
Public welfare	2,386	2,390	2,358	1,610	1,056	945	913	−0.2	161.4	17.4	15.64	6.90
Old age assistance	1,400	1,397	1,396	988	709	647	509	0.2	175.3	10.2	9.18	3.84
Aid to dependent children	506	520	480	306	153	121	134	−2.6	278.4	3.7	3.32	1.01
Other (including all public welfare administration)	479	473	481	315	195	177	270	6.9	77.4	1.3	3.14	2.04
Education	4,026	3,701	3,413	2,636	1,471	1,350	1,182	8.8	240.7	29.4	26.39	8.93
State institutions of higher education	1,180	1,166	1,107	895	397	380	296	1.2	298.3	8.6	7.74	2.24
Intergovernmental expenditure	2,525	2,248	2,054	1,554	953	861	790	12.3	219.6	18.4	16.55	5.97
Other	321	287	251	186	121	109	95	11.7	237.6	2.3	2.10	.72
Highways	3,290	2,955	2,668	2,016	952	838	1,134	11.3	190.2	24.0	21.56	8.56
Regular State highway facilities	2,266	2,105	1,953	1,476	606	534	771	7.7	193.8	16.5	14.85	5.83
State toll highway facilities	290	183	105	34	7	6	19	58.2	(b)	2.1	1.90	.14

Intergovernmental expenditure	$734	$667	$610	$507	$339	$298	$344	10.0	113.6	5.4	$4.81	$2.60
Health and hospitals	1,258	1,139	1,042	700	447	347	311	10.4	304.8	9.2	8.24	2.35
State hospitals and institutions for handicapped	968	864	788	533	308	253	235	12.1	311.2	7.1	6.34	1.78
Other	290	276	254	167	139	94	75	5.0	284.7	2.1	1.90	.57
Natural resources	548	518	477	346	209	165	160	5.9	241.6	4.0	3.59	1.21
Employment security administration	177	166	172	150	60	35	59	6.7	199.6	1.3	1.16	.45
General control	368	346	322	270	195	164	166	6.3	121.6	2.7	2.41	1.25
Miscellaneous and unallocable	1,202	1,333	1,407	1,493	692	515	479	−9.8	164.3	8.8	8.30	3.62
Veterans' services	143	335	462	633	54	1	1	−57.4	(b)	1.0	.94	—
State aid for unspecified purposes	510	513	482	428	357	274	224	−0.6	127.3	3.7	3.34	1.69
Interest	144	130	109	86	84	101	122	11.0	18.1	1.1	.95	.92
Other (includes intergovernmental aid for specified purposes n.e.c.)	470	426	417	345	196	138	132	7.1	255.3	2.0	3.08	1.00
Liquor stores expenditure	723	756	654	691	663	426	288	−4.3	150.9	—	4.74	2.18
Insurance trust expenditure	1,413	1,293	2,177	1,020	1,158	226	505	9.3	179.8	100.0	9.26	3.82
Employee retirement	247	200	163	123	92	71	65	23.4	277.8	17.5	1.62	.49
Unemployment compensation	971	916	1,845	756	965	65	369	6.0	163.2	68.7	6.37	2.79
Other	195	177	169	141	102	90	71	3.6	175.4	2.7	1.28	.54

* Reproduced by courtesy of the Council of State Governments from *The Book of the States, 1954–55*, pp. 204–205. (Material on "total expenditure by character and object" omitted.)

Note: Because of rounding, detail does not always add to total. Per capita and per cent figures are computed on the basis of amounts rounded to the nearest thousand.

(a) For detail, see Table 1 of section on "State Tax Collections in 1953," page 223 of *The Book of the States*.
(b) Not computed.

could be taxed and how much.   This operation calls for nothing less than the consideration and preparation of the whole government program, and that is its advantage.   After months of activity those responsible for preparing the financial program complete their task, and they submit the budget, a considerable document, to the final policy-determining body (council or legislature) for its action.   The significant point is that the legislative body has a carefully considered, specific, and concrete program upon which to act, a far cry from the odd assortment of proposals that came to it from a variety of sources in the good old days.

In many, if not most, of the rural units of government the budget idea has not taken effective hold.   State laws may require them to adopt a system, but the law may be vague and general and compliance with it "vague and general."   Arkansas and a number of local governments entrust the preparation of the budget to a committee of lawmakers.   Such a system may secure unified action with respect to revenue and appropriations in the legislature or council, but it fails to give administrative officers, who are in a better position to prepare and propose plans, a sufficient opportunity to render that valuable service.   Six or seven states and many local governments leave the preparation of the budget to a commission, which ordinarily consists of the chief executive (or his representative), several other administrative officers, and some members of the lawmaking body or bodies.   The theory behind this plan is that legislators should have a part in the original stages of budget preparation, and that having thus participated, they could defend it more intelligently before their colleagues.

THE EXECUTIVE BUDGET.   The plan that meets with the most general favor, one that is employed in about forty states and most cities, is known as the executive budget.   This plan varies somewhat among the governments, but broadly speaking, it follows the budget-making practice of the national government.   The governor or mayor, like the President, is responsible for its preparation.   A budget officer or one with some other title may do the work but the responsibility is that of the chief executive alone.   While departmental officials are preparing their estimates, the budget officer, speaking for his chief, is in frequent communication with them, often urging and sometimes forcing them to reduce their requests for funds.   Of course, this concentration of authority in the chief executive's hands greatly increases his power, but improvements in American government have generally been achieved by strengthening the executive hand.

THE LEGISLATIVE BODY AND THE BUDGET.   Regardless of how the budget is prepared, the legislature (or council) generally has the authority to deal with it as it sees fit.   If the budget has been carefully prepared, with due regard for the obligations of the government and a realistic conception of financial limitations, the legislative body may accept it as presented, although probably not until after lengthy and entirely appropriate consideration.   But the legislators may reduce particular items, strike out items, increase the amount for other items, or add new items.   But, in a sense, the budget as submitted puts the lawmakers on the spot. If they change it materially they must justify their actions to the public. It has turned out, therefore, that in spite of the legal authority of the legislative bodies to play havoc with the budget, they have usually displayed a degree of responsibility in relation to it.

In Maryland, New York, two or three other states, and a number of cities the legislative bodies have less freedom to deal with the estimates submitted than in other jurisdictions. In the Maryland group the representatives may strike out or reduce items in the executive budget, but they are prohibited from making any increases except for the legislative and judicial branches. This limitation appears to be a reasonable one since the executive authority surely ought to ask for sufficient appropriations.

Control of Expenditures

The spending agencies are not at liberty to "take their appropriations and run." Proper budgeting requires that expenditures be regulated. An appropriation is not an order to spend, but an authorization to spend under supervision.

ALLOTMENTS. The chief executive or a budget officer acting for him ordinarily requires each spending unit to make quarterly allotments of funds and to break these allotments down further under such headings as personal service, supplies, materials, and capital outlays. Most jurisdictions provide for flexibility in financial management by authorizing the transfer of funds from one heading to another, provided the permission of the chief executive is obtained.

ACCOUNTING. It goes without saying that an adequate system of accounting must be maintained. A few states and many local governments, particularly rural units, keep their accounts on a cash basis; they record no expenditures until bills are paid. This type of "house-keeping" may bring on difficulties. It does not give an accurate picture of outstanding obligations and committments. Books should be kept on an accrual method, a system under which encumbrances are recorded as soon as obligations are incurred. It is as important to know what is scheduled to be paid out as it is to know what has already been paid, and the accrual method provides that information. But an up-to-date accounting system does not stop at showing what disbursements have been made and what obligations are coming due; it should also reveal bad contracts and excessive costs, and thus lead to the stoppage of waste.

PURCHASING. Centralized purchasing is another means of bringing about order and economy in public expenditure. Fifty years ago each unit of administration purchased its own materials and supplies. That is still the practice in many governmental units, more especially the smaller ones; but most of the states and several hundred cities now follow a plan under which all or most purchases are made by a central agency. This agency may bring about economies by making large-scale purchases, standardizing and testing materials as to quality, and central storing. Obviously, the purchasing agency should be staffed with individuals who not only know how to get the best goods for the least money but also, how to work in harmony with other government personnel whose requisitions must pass through their hands. An inefficient purchasing agency is worse than none; it just produces more red tape and an otherwise satisfactory agency may find itself in difficulties if, in serving the more technical operating units, it fails to give full consideration to their very special needs.

THE AUDIT.   The methods of control outlined above are **executive** devices. They are the means by which the chief administrator may enforce economies and develop efficiency.   By what means may the legislature satisfy itself that the appropriations it makes are legally expended?   This service is the function of the auditor.   He is the servant of the legislature (or council) as the director of the budget, or the director of finance, is the agent of the chief executive.[7]   Rather commonly the auditor may pass upon the legality of a proposed expenditure and disallow it, if in his opinion it is contrary to law. Authorities take sides and give each other some stout blows on this question, some holding that the true function of an auditor is not to disallow proposed expenditures but to call to the attention of administrative officials any irregularities in their proposed expenditures and, if the warning is unheeded, report the situation to the legislature.   This is the executive view of the matter.   Those who view it from the legislative standpoint are convinced that nothing less than the power to disallow can make the auditor an effective agent of the legislative body.[8]

Borrowing Money

Any government must occasionally borrow money.   A number of the early state legislatures displayed considerable prodigality on this score, and, as a result, nearly all the states have placed limits upon the amounts the legislatures may borrow.   The federal Constitution imposes only one limitation—that the states may not borrow through the expedient of issuing bills of credit (paper money).   State constitutions contain such types of limitations as: a fixed sum; a sum that may not be exceeded except for certain specified purposes; a sum that may be exceeded only with the approval of the voters; and specifications with respect to the purposes for which money may be borrowed.[9]

Cities, counties, other local governments, and school districts are limited by state constitutions and laws as to the amounts they may borrow.   The limit is often expressed in terms of a certain percentage—5, 8, 10, etc.—of

[7] In West Virginia the legislative auditor is required to make "a continuous audit and analysis of the state budget" and report to the legislature "any misapplication of state funds or erroneous, extravagant or unlawful expenditures by any spending unit." *State Government*, May, 1953, p. 130.

[8] See White, *op. cit.*, Ch. 20.   See also J. W. Martin and Robt. Sawyer, "The Independent State Post-Audit," *State Government*, May, 1941, p. 107.

[9] But see "Circumventing Constitutional Debt Control," *Tax Review*, Aug., 1954.   The article is from *Constitutional Debt Control in the States*, a Tax Foundation study.

the assessed valuation of taxable property in the jurisdiction of the borrowing authority. It is frequently suggested that such limitations are too rigid, failing to take account of the capacity of different communities to carry debts, of the fluctuations of the economy, of over-lapping taxing authorities, each of which may incur the debt maximum, and of various other factors.

Students of the problem suggest that the legal limitations under which a local government may borrow might even be lowered, but that such limitations be made broadly flexible by the provision that borrowings beyond the limits named could be approved by a state administrative authority. Such state authority has been very helpful in North Carolina and some other states both in preventing unnecessary borrowing and in assisting the local authority with advice where borrowing is desirable.[10]

The question naturally arises: When should a government borrow, or, when is it permissible? Professor Jewell Cass Phillips summarizes the answer very neatly. He suggests that it is appropriate to borrow (1) for the construction of projects that are self-liquidating, such as power systems and turnpikes; (2) for the construction of highways and bridges and the erection of government buildings and school houses, all of which will be serviceable for a term of years; and (3) for meeting emergencies, such as floods, earthquakes, and similar disasters.[11] For the most part, borrowing has been in one of these categories, although an exception may be noted in state borrowing for the purpose of paying a soldiers' bonus.

A few states have practically no debt; in others it is of significant proportions, but in no state is the per capita debt more than a small fraction of that of the national government. Furthermore, although state debts increased from less than $3 billion in 1932 to about $7 billion in 1952, the debt of the latter year represented only 2.3 per cent of the annual national income while that of 1932 represented 6.9 per cent. The debt of all local governments in 1932 was about $16.6 billion, or 40 per cent of the national income; in 1952 it was about $20.5 billion or 7.4 per cent of the national income.

Governments borrow by issuing interest-bearing bonds, which are bought by investors. The period for which bonds are issued ordinarily varies with the duration of the benefit to be secured by the proposed expenditures— ten, twenty, or more years. An entire issue of bonds may be retired on a specified date of maturity. The government sets aside, or is supposed to set aside, a fund each year so that the entire principal will be on hand when the bonds mature. This is called the "sinking fund system." It is all right in theory, but in practice the authorities sometimes fail to build up the fund or lose part of it by bad investments. Hence, when the bonds mature, it becomes necessary to borrow again. A system that works better in practice and that many cities and some states now employ is the "serial bond system." By this system some bonds mature each year and are retired from current revenue.

---

[10] Phillips, *op. cit.*, pp. 269 ff.
[11] *Ibid.*, pp. 272–273.

Reading List

Roy G. and Gladys C. Blakey, *Sales Taxes and Other Excises* (1945).

A. E. Buck, *The Budget in Governments of Today* (1935).

Council of State Governments, *Federal Grants-in-Aid* (1949).

————, *The Book of the States, 1954–55.*

W. Brooke Graves, *American State Government* (1953 ed.), Chs. 14–15.

H. M. Groves, *Financing Government* (1954 ed.).

W. D. Durfee, Jr., *Intergovernmental Fiscal Relations* (1950).

A. H. Hansen and H. S. Perloff, *State and Local Finance in the National Economy* (1944).

The Commission on Intergovernmental Relations, *A Report to the President for Transmittal to the Congress* (1955).

International City Managers' Association, *Municipal Finance Administration* (1949 ed.).

————, *The Municipal Year Book* (1954).

Lane W. Lancaster, *Government in Rural America* (1952 ed.), Chs. 6–7.

H. L. Lutz, *Public Finance* (1947 ed.).

J. R. McKinley, *Local Revenue Problems and Trends* (1949).

National Municipal League, *Model Investment of State Funds Law* (1954).

————, *Model Real Property Tax Collection Law* (1954).

J. C. Phillips, *State and Local Government in America* (1954), Ch. 12.

B. U. Ratchford, *American State Debts* (1941).

Sidney Ratner, *American Taxation: Its History as a Social Force in Democracy* (1942).

Tax Foundation, *Recent Trends in State Expenditures, 1942–1947* (1948).

————, *Postwar Trends in State Debt: A State by State Analysis* (1950).

————, *Constitutional Debt Control in the States* (1954).

United States Bureau of the Census, *Compendium of State Government Finances* (annually).

L. D. White, *Introduction to Public Administration* (1955 ed.), Chs. 16–20.

Questions and Problems

1. What limitations does the federal Constitution impose upon the taxing powers of the states?   The state governments upon the local governments?

2. Outline the history of the general property tax as a source of revenue.   What use does your state now make of it?

3. What features of the income and inheritance taxes commonly commend them?

4. List the arguments for and against the sales tax.

5. Would you recommend that a single "best source of revenue" bear practically all of the state's tax burden?

6. Indicate the appropriate functions of executive officers and the members of the legislative body in budget-making.

7. What control should the chief executive have over funds after they have been appropriated by the legislature or council?   What control should the legislative body retain?

8. Under what conditions may a government appropriately borrow money? For what purposes has your state or city recently borrowed?

9. Give the "pros" and "cons" on the proposition that the national government only should levy an income tax. Would your reasoning be the same if the national government agreed to distribute a fixed percentage (say 10 per cent) of the amount collected to the states on the basis of wealth?

10. Evaluate the system under which states grant local communities funds in aid of education, road construction, and other services.

CHAPTER | 9

STATE ADMINISTRATIVE SERVICES

Having in chapters preceding examined briefly the administrative machinery through which state services are commonly performed and having given some attention to the methods by which they are financed, we are now to consider what these services are. A hundred years ago government functions were essentially negative, were primarily concerned with protecting the citizen against some of the more violent physical hazards, such as murder, burglary, and robbery, and against ancient economic gyps, such as false weights and measures. But even in the middle of the last century positive functions were not absolutely excluded. For example, nearly every state was to some extent encouraging public education and improving the means of transportation. Today, of necessity, the negative functions remain with us, and some new ones have been added, particularly those having to do with the regulation of business; but the chief emphasis is now on the positive functions: the construction and maintenance of highways, the protection of labor, the promotion of agriculture and conservation, health protection, social security, and education. These topics (excluding the development of highways, discussed elsewhere,[1] and including the regulation of business) constitute the subject-matter of this chapter.

I. THE REGULATION OF BUSINESS [2]

In the earlier days of our republic the national government was considerably interested in the promotion of business but gave very little attention to its regulation, the latter function being left primarily to the states. In recent years, although not neglecting the field of promotion, the national government has become so actively engaged in regulation that the casual observer might conclude that only the central government regulates business. This

[1] See Johnson's *American National Government* (1955 ed.), pages 490–496.
[2] Malvin Anshen and F. D. Wormuth, *Private Enterprise and Public Policy* (1954), pp. 121 ff., 137 ff., 176 ff., 325 ff., 413 ff.; A. F. Macdonald, *American State Government and Administration* (1955 ed.), Ch. 28; J. C. Phillips, *State and Local Government in America* (1954), Ch. 26; *The Book of the States 1954–55*, pp. 413–428. See also "Blue Books" of various states.

conclusion, however, would not be in accordance with the facts. The states
sions, and they have by no means been deprived of their powers to regulate
general business.
still carry full responsibility for regulating most trades, callings, and profes-

Occupational Licensing

From the very beginning the states controlled admission to certain professions by the license system, and as science, inventions, and our demands
have increased the number and variety of occupations and professions, the
license requirement has been extended to many of them. As of 1952 the
aggregate number of occupational licenses in the states was more than 1,200,
and the list started with abstracters and ended with yacht brokers. Every
state requires a license of accountants, architects, attorneys, chiropodists, den-
tists, dental hygienists, embalmers, engineers, nurses, optometrists, osteopaths,
pharmacists, physicians, teachers, and veterinarians; and in most states barbers, beauticians, chiropractors, funeral directors, insurance agents, practical
nurses, real estate salesmen, and surveyors are licensed. In some states
guide-dog trainers and horse-shoers must have a license. In a number of
states local communities are authorized to license persons to engage in such
trades as those of barber, beautician, electrician, and plumber. Occupational licenses and taxes yield the cities about 5 per cent of their revenue.

It is obvious that the purpose of the license is to make certain that an
individual has minimum qualifications for the profession or calling he seeks
to practice and that he will not be an undue hazard to the public health,
safety, or welfare. Each state fixes its own standard and there can be no
successful appeal from it unless it violates the "due process" or the "equal
protection" clause of the Fourteenth Amendment. Any requirements for
a particular license that have a reasonable relation to fitness for the performance of work for which license is sought is held to be reasonable and in
conformity with "due process" and "equal protection." Most states have
set up a separate board to examine candidates and grant licenses for each
profession or calling. It is well known that doctors examine doctors, accountants examine accountants, and so on; it could not be otherwise. Yet
there is complaint from time to time that the boards seem to show more interest in protecting the professions or callings than in guarding the public interest. In seeking to prevent abuses of that type and for reasons of economy,
about a third of the states have attempted to centralize licensing functions
by bringing the licensing boards, or a number of them, into a single department. But in a number of such states the boards continue with their old
independence, the department simply relieving them of routine administrative functions. Illinois is singled out as an example of a state that has
actually centralized the licensing function. The boards are retained for purposes of examining but the department is given powers of supervision and
inspection sufficient to enable it to prevent abuses.[3]

[3] *The Book of the States*, pp. 413–415.

The Regulations of Corporations—General

Considering that so much of modern business is conducted by corporations special (although brief) attention must be given to the part of the states in regulating them.

ISSUANCE OF CHARTERS. Certain types of business concerns may be chartered by the federal government, but the great majority of corporations have always had to look to the states for charters. The charter is the corporation's authorization to do business. It sets forth the manner in which the corporation shall be organized and the general methods by which it may conduct its business. A century ago legislatures commonly granted charters by special acts, but this practice has been generally abandoned. Under the present system, states have general corporation laws, and charters are issued in pursuance of these laws. A group applies to the secretary of state (or whatever authority is empowered to issue charters), who examines the application, makes sure that all terms of law are complied with, and then issues a charter upon receipt of a fee. A corporation is known as "domestic" in the state that issues the charter, and as "foreign" in other states. It is a very common practice for states to admit foreign corporations, a privilege for which they not infrequently exact a higher fee than they require of domestic corporations engaged in the same business. A state may not, however, prevent a corporate or natural person from engaging in interstate commerce, or burden such commerce by requiring a license for its conduct.

CONTINUOUS SUPERVISION. But the states do not issue charters of incorporation or grant foreign corporations the privilege of doing business and then let them pursue their merry course. Most of the states were satisfied with this procedure two generations ago; but in our time they exercise a continuous supervision over business organizations. Corporations are required to make various reports to the secretary of state or, better, to a corporation commission. Through an examination of these reports and by other checks the extent to which a corporation is observing the laws may be determined, and in the case of major violations the privilege of carrying on business may be revoked.

In order to protect the public from security frauds forty-seven states have enacted "blue-sky" laws. These statutes prohibit the issue of securities unless approved by state authority, which approval is given only when a company furnishes complete information concerning its financial condition and the nature of the securities it proposes to offer, and designates the property upon which the securities are to be based. In New York and several other eastern states the law has no application to dealers in advance of the sale of securities, but when fraud has been perpetrated the legal arm of the government then goes into action against the guilty party. "Blue-sky" laws do no more than protect the investor against fraud. He may still make very unwise purchases of securities. If the investor is a "sucker," the laws cannot remove him from that class.

Regulation of Corporations Affected with a Public Interest

Certain types of business are very close to the public, in that practically every citizen must depend upon them. In particular, banks, insurance companies, and public utilities come within this group. Such business is said to be "affected with a public interest." It would be absurd to expect each person to determine the soundness of a bank or an insurance company. Government must do what it can to make these concerns safe.

1. BANKS. Inasmuch as the federal government has assumed ever-increasing (but not exclusive) responsibility for the regulation of banks, that subject is commonly treated in books on the national government.[4]

2. INSURANCE. The public must put its trust and savings in insurance companies as in the banks; and, for the same reason, the states must regulate the business of insurance. Although, in 1944, the Supreme Court held that the national government might through its power over interstate commerce reach certain transactions of insurance companies, the states are still, and with the approval of Congress, essentially in control of the business.[5] Most of the states have exercised this power with considerable energy since New York (1905) investigated the practices of insurance companies. A state administrative authority, often the superintendent of insurance, is required to keep an eye on the assets of the companies, to see that their funds are invested in sound securities, and otherwise to enforce the state laws designed for the protection of policy-holders. Some states have themselves gone into the insurance business. For example, North Dakota insures against hail, fire, and tornadoes; and a larger number insure against industrial accidents. Whether insurance is undertaken by states or by companies chartered by them, it is a business that calls not only for honesty but for technical talent of a high order.

3. PUBLIC UTILITIES. Certain other businesses, monopolistic in character, call for special regulation by the states. To this class belong the railroads, bus lines, and telegraph and telephone systems, electric power, and gas. Concerning these utilities, it may be said that, although the states continue to regulate them in their intrastate business, the federal government, through its power over interstate commerce and navigation, has rather effectively entered the field. State laws govern such subjects as the granting of franchises, the issuing of stocks and bonds, the quality of the service rendered, the rates to be charged, and, in addition, require reports from the companies.

These matters cannot possibly be regulated in detail by law. For specific application of the laws the states have created state and local public utility commissions, endowing them with powers similar to those held by the national Interstate Commerce Commission. These commissions hold exten-

---

[4] See Johnson, *op. cit.*, pages 463–467.

[5] Under Public Law 15 of 1945 Congress agreed, in effect, to leave the regulation of insurance to the states for three years, subject to the exception that the federal anti-trust laws are applicable to it.

sive hearings in respect to rates and other matters brought before them by utility companies or the public. Their decisions are always subject to judicial review on points of law, and in many jurisdictions on facts as well. Manifestly the commissions' duties require a high degree of talent and integrity. There has been some difficulty in finding men with sufficient qualifications to fill these positions. Complaint is made that they are much more likely to side with the companies than with the public. This condition may exist because men holding the view of the companies are often appointed commissioners, or possibly because the companies are usually represented by better legal talent than is the public. There is complaint also that the courts are sometimes unfriendly to the decisions of commissions that favor the public. Granted that the commissions do not and cannot always satisfy the public and that the courts may occasionally block their best efforts, it is generally agreed that commission regulation is superior to the old system, which was essentially that of nonregulation.

A number of cities own their utilities, particularly gas and electric plants. Since small electric plants cannot be conducted economically, a few states have authorized communities to combine in "utility regions." This authorization offers a sort of standing threat to power companies to give better rates and services. It does not mean that these communities will immediately enter the power business. Perhaps the majority of Americans, until 1933 at least, looked with disfavor upon public ownership and operation of utilities, preferring to solve the problem by official regulation and informal adjustments with private companies. In any event the issue is one that should be determined on the basis of local conditions and needs—not by politics and blood pressures.[6]

II. LABOR AND INDUSTRIAL RELATIONS [7]

Labor is now the subject of no little concern to the national [8] government, but, in order to be subject to its laws, labor must be employed by the national government, or be engaged in foreign or interstate commerce, or be occupied with activities that feed commerce, or with some other activity within the scope of national authority. All other labor remains under state jurisdiction. Before the national government interested itself in labor's welfare, the more progressive industrial states were providing a minimum of protection for labor. At the present time most of the states have comprehensive labor laws. Naturally these vary a great deal from state to state; but they commonly apply to such subjects as collective bargaining, hours and conditions of work, wages, labor disputes, and workmen's compensation.

[6] On the national government's power projects, see Johnson, *op. cit.*, pp. 569 ff.

[7] Anshen and Wormuth, *op. cit.*, Ch. 17; J. H. Leek, *Government and Labor in the United States* (1952); Macdonald, *op. cit.*, Ch. 29; *The Book of the States, 1954–55*, pp. 385–412.

[8] See Johnson, *op. cit.*, Ch. 19.

The Status of Trade Unions

The right of labor to organize and bargain collectively with employers is now generally recognized. The right of a particular craft to strike for such purposes as an increase in wages or to prevent a reduction is also recognized, but striking simply to assist another union is generally held to be illegal.

The methods that the strikers may employ are limited. The "sit-down" strike was declared illegal by the Supreme Court of the United States.[9] Picketing is usually permissible if it consists only of attempts to persuade others not to take the strikers' jobs. Intimidation by threats or violence is illegal. The difficulty of drawing a line between persuasion and intimidation is at once apparent. Formerly, employers often sought injunctive relief against strikers and they frequently obtained it. Long ago the injunction proved to be such an effective weapon in breaking strikes that it became one of labor's principal grievances. In response to labor's demands practically every state now has statutory provisions limiting the use of the injunction in labor relations cases. The primary boycott (the agreement of a union group not to patronize an "unfair" employer) is now generally recognized as a lawful labor weapon. On the other hand, the secondary boycott (an attempt of a union to prevent third parties from patronizing an employer) is illegal under the laws of a number of states.

In the last twenty years or so we have heard considerable discussion of such union devices as "union shop," "closed shop," "check-off," and "maintenance of membership." The closed shop is one in which only union men may be employed, and a union shop is one in which a nonunion man may be employed, but must become a member within a specified period. About a fourth of the state prohibit both types of shops. The check-off, forbidden by law in some states and authorized in others if assented to by the employer, is the system under which employers deduct union dues from wages and pay them to the union. Maintenance of membership is an agreement between an employer and a union providing that employees may be union members or not but that all who are members shall continue as such during the life of the contract or lose their jobs. Some states permit it; others do not. It is obvious that such devices greatly strengthen the unions and that state laws respecting them will vary among the states in accordance with their industrial development, the strength of the unions, and the attitude of citizens generally.

Hours of Labor

1. MEN. A few decades ago, the hours of work, like all other problems of labor, were left entirely to the employer and the employee to determine. But the great advantage of the employer over the employee has led many states to come to the assistance of the latter. Men are still expected to be

[9] National Labor Relations Board v. Fansteel Metallurgical Corporation, 306 U.S. 240 (1939).

able to take care of themselves, but there are certain exceptions to be noted. Quite a few states have fixed the eight-hour day for those employed by them or by local governments. It seems also that states may require contractors on public works to observe the eight-hour day. Such laws exert an appreciable influence over private employment.

There is no question of a state's authority to fix the hours of labor for its own employees. How far can it go in fixing a limit for private employees? Such laws interfere with the freedom of contract and may be judicially stricken down as being in violation of constitutional provisions that no person shall be deprived of life, *liberty* (of contract in such cases), or property without due process of law. But where the courts are convinced that labor is in actual need of protection, they hold that the freedom of contract must give way to the police power of the state. Thus, as long ago as 1898 the Supreme Court sustained a Utah statute limiting labor in mines to eight hours a day.[10] A few years later it held invalid a New York statute limiting labor in bakeries to ten hours,[11] although in 1917 this decision was practically overruled when the Oregon ten-hour factory law was sustained.[12] There is now no doubt that the states may limit the hours of labor of men in dangerous or unhealthful employment; and it is generally believed that, in keeping with the policy of the national government to limit hours, they may limit the hours of employment in industry generally.

2. WOMEN AND CHILDREN. Recognizing the difference between the physical capacity of men and women, the courts have generally upheld statutes for the protection of women that would have been declared invalid if applied to men. "Due process" has been made to yield to the obligation of the states to safeguard their women. Child labor legislation easily passes judicial scrutiny. Children are wards of the state, and the state owes them special protection. All states prohibit the employment of children under fourteen, fifteen, or sixteen in mines and factories, and children within a specified age group above this limit may not be employed beyond a stipulated number of hours and unless they hold an employment certificate. The hours of labor for children often are limited in other types of employment. Not infrequently night work is prohibited altogether. Compulsory school attendance laws also have the effect of limiting child labor. It should be added that child labor laws, like any others, are sometimes indifferently enforced.

Conditions for Work

GENERAL. Some years ago a miner, humorously fatalistic, told the writer that he always examined his lunch before going into the mines and that if he found articles of diet for which he had a particular weakness, he ate them at once, not risking the chance of being deprived of them by being

---

[10] Holden v. Hardy, 169 U.S. 366.

[11] Lochner v. New York, 198 U.S. 45 (1905).

[12] Bunting v. Oregon, 243 U.S. 246 (1917). On the application of "due process" to this and the cases mentioned in notes 10 and 11, see Johnson, *op. cit.*, Chapter 5, section IV, pages 107–108 and Chapter 19, section III, pages 530–531.

killed before twelve o'clock! The hazards of mining are not so great now as they were, for the states have made serious attempts to lessen them. The requirements for ventilation, safety lamps, and various other safety appliances, enforced by inspection officers, have added somewhat to the miner's allotment of years. Factories are similarly required to provide for the safety of their employees. Whizzing saws and other dangerous machinery must be covered as far as possible. Suction pipes must be installed to take up the dust that would otherwise go into workmen's lungs. The manufacturing of articles in the home of workers, commonly called "sweating," is prohibited or restricted in many states. Laundries and bakeries must conform to standards of sanitation fixed in the interest of the health of employees and the public. These are but a few typical health, safety, and comfort measures that the states have enacted for employees. Usually they are upheld as being proper exercises of the states' police power, due process of law being reserved to strike down those measures that, in the opinion of the courts, are unreasonable or arbitrary uses of that power.

CONDITIONS FOR THE EMPLOYMENT OF WOMEN. Most of the states now take a number of precautions relative to the employment of women. About half the states require that women be given one day of rest out of seven, a requirement that is also applicable to men in six or seven states. More than half the states specify a certain period for meals, and a half dozen or more states call for rest periods. Some twenty states place limitations on night work for adult women, and half the states prohibit their employment at any time in certain enterprises, mines and barrooms being most commonly specified. Most of the states have "seating" laws for women, and ten or so have prohibitions respecting their lifting or carrying heavy weights in connection with employment. Thirteen or more states prohibit discrimination in pay on the grounds of sex. Connecticut, Missouri, Washington, and three other states prohibit the employment of women in certain industries for specified periods before and after childbirth.[13]

Wages

The freedom of contract gives way in certain particulars to the urgent necessity of protecting labor in the collection of wages. Long ago the Supreme Court of the United States held valid a Tennessee statute which required that store orders issued in payment of wages must be redeemed in cash.[14] The same Court upheld an Arkansas statute providing that, where miners were being paid by the ton for their output, coal should be weighed before being screened.[15] Of course it was argued that such statutes deprived employers and employees of their freedom to make the kind of labor contracts they desired, and that the statutes were therefore contrary to "due process"; but the Court said in the latter case: "laws . . . enacted for the

[13] *The Book of the States,* pp. 398–401.
[14] Knoxville Iron Co. v. Harbison, 183 U.S. 13 (1901).
[15] McLean v. Arkansas, 211 U.S. 539 (1909).

protection of the public health, safety, or welfare . . . may be valid notwithstanding they have the effect to curtail or limit the freedom of contract."

Formerly, when states attempted to fix minimum wages, they soon ran against the constitutional snag of "due process." Of course the states may fix wages for those employed on public works, but fixing wages for private employment is another matter entirely. At first they attempted to do so only for women and children. Before 1920 Congress, the legislatures in a third of the states, and the legislative bodies in nearly all of the European countries had enacted such laws. The supreme courts in several of the states sustained them, and the Supreme Court of the United States, by an equal division (Mr. Justice Brandeis not sitting), affirmed the favorable decision of the Supreme Court of Oregon.[16] A few years later, however, the Supreme Court held invalid the act of Congress that provided for the minimum wage for women and children in the District of Columbia.[17]

In 1933 the New York legislature passed a carefully drafted minimum wage law designed to overcome the objections the Supreme Court had made to the law enacted by Congress for the District of Columbia. But the Court and employers, and therefore in violation of the due process provision of the found, five to four, the New York Act to be an oppressive exercise of the police power, an infringement upon the "freedom of contract" of workers Fourteenth Amendment.[18] "It is difficult to imagine any grounds," said Justice Stone, in dissent, "other than our own personal economic predilections, for saying that the contract of employment is any the less an appropriate subject of legislation than are scores of others in dealing with which this Court has held that legislatures may curtail individual freedom in the public interest." Ten months later, the five-four majority against minimum wages changed to five-four for minimum wages, Justice Roberts shifting his position. Speaking for the new majority, Chief Justice Hughes declared: "The Constitution does not speak of freedom of contract. It speaks of liberty and prohibits the deprivation of liberty without due process of law. . . . But the liberty safeguarded is liberty in a social organization which requires the protection of law against the evils which menace the health, safety, morals, and welfare of the people." [19] More than half the states now have minimum wage laws for women and children. Furthermore, since the authority of Congress to fix minimum wages for *men* engaged in or making goods to be shipped in interstate commerce (Fair Labor Standards Act of 1938) has been sustained as being within the commerce power and not in violation of due process of law,[20] it is assumed that state minimum wage laws for men in like manner meet the test of due process. Massachusetts, New York, and several other states have enacted minimum wage laws for men.

16 243 U.S. 629 (1917).
17 Adkins v. Children's Hospital, 261 U.S. 525 (1923).
18 Morehead v. New York, 298 U.S. 587 (1936).
19 West Coast Hotel Company v. Parrish, 300 U.S. 379 (1937).
20 United States v. Darby Lumber Co., 312 U.S. 100 (1941).

Employment Service

In former times when the laborer needed assistance in securing employ
ment he commonly resorted to private employment agencies operating on
a fee basis. These agencies sometimes engaged in rather sharp practices,
particularly in periods when jobs were scarce, and as a result the states found
it necessary to regulate their charges and procedures. Such organizations
still operate, but most of the states also furnish employment service. Every
year tens of millions of workers go to these services for employment counsel-
ing interviews and placement. In 1952 public employment offices placed
15.5 millions and in 1953 about the same number, a majority of them on farm
jobs.[21] The service is particularly valuable for seasonal employment and
an aid to the employer hardly less than to the employee.

Fair Employment Practices

Most of us give lip service at least to the principal that there should be
no discrimination in employment on account of race, color, nationality, or
religion. Until a decade or so ago that is where the issue stood, with employers, employees, and labor unions exercising discrimination or not as they
saw fit. A segment of the population, probably a fairly large one, still holds
that discrimination can be removed only by education and good conscience;
others take the position that a little law can do much to remove employment
discrimination. During the last war the national government attempted, with
some success, to prevent such discrimination, and since the war a dozen or
more states have enacted fair employment practices legislation. New York,
New Jersey, Oregon, Washington, and four or five other states have mandatory laws that carry penalties for their violation. In such states a board
or commission is commonly empowered to receive complaints, conduct investigations, and issue orders against discriminating practices, such orders
being subject to judicial review. Indiana, Kansas, and several other states
attempt to meet the problem more by the educational and conciliatory approach. It may well be that some states are ready for antidiscrimination
laws with "teeth in them," others for the advisory type, and still others retain
such a sentiment for discrimination that any remedial legislation would be
a dead letter.

Workmen's Compensation for Accidents

Tens of thousands of workmen are killed and injured in line of duty every
year. Formerly, the only method by which they or their relatives could
obtain compensation was to institute suit against the employers. Occasionally, handsome damages would be collected by a lawyer who impressed
a jury with his pleas for a wife, or widow, and six dependent children of the
victim of an industrial accident. But more often the employers were saved
by the old common-law defenses of "contributory negligence," "fellow serv-

[21] *The Book of the States,* pp. 403–404.

ant," and "assumption of risk." [22]   All the states have abolished these defenses in industrial accident cases, thus placing employees in a much more favorable legal position.   Furthermore, they have provided for systems of industrial insurance.

This is the way a typical system works: Employers are required to establish funds from which compensation shall be paid to injured workmen.   Such workmen no longer go to court for compensation, but an industrial commission hears their cases and fixes the amount of compensation for each in proportion to the extent of the injury.   The procedure is relatively speedy and free from technicalities, the employer being no longer allowed to set up the old common-law defenses noted above.   These laws in the interest of the disabled veterans of industry who had been engaged in developing the wealth of the state may be sustained upon the same theory as pensions for soldiers wounded in defending it.   "A machine as well as a bullet may produce a wound and the disabling effect may be the same," said the Supreme Court of the United States in upholding a statute of the State of Washington. [23]   Sickness, as well as accidents, may arise from causes directly traceable to employment.   Accepting this fact, a number of states have extended the provisions of their compensation acts to cover diseases attributable to occupations. [24]

The Settlement of Industrial Disputes

National labor relations legislation (Taft-Hartley and others) is, of course, restricted in its application to activities in interstate commerce.   Industrial disputes arising in enterprises not engaged in or feeding such commerce are within the jurisdiction of the states.   Practically every state now offers some means of seeking a solution to disputes arising between employees and employers.   It may happen that a high official of a state, possibly the governor, acting not under a law but simply using the prestige of his office and his qualities of persuasion, may bring about a settlement, but that method is unreliable as a means of settling the general run of labor-management controversies. Many states have established a service of conciliation and mediation.   Ordinarily this service enters a dispute only at the request of the parties involved. The parties may ask for a conciliator, whose chief function is to keep them in a talking and bargaining mood until they reach a settlement.   Or, they may ask for a mediator whose function it is to enter the discussion and offer suggestions, compromises, and solutions for their difficulties.   The request for and acceptance of the services of a conciliator or mediator does not bind the parties to the dispute to reach a solution.

With arbitration we have a system under which a third party actually makes a binding settlement.   The parties to a dispute resort voluntarily to arbitra-

---

[22] For explanation of these defenses see Johnson, *op. cit.,* p. 520.
[23] Mountain Timber Co. v. Washington, 242 U.S. 219 (1917).
[24] On unemployment compensation and vocational rehabilitation, see Johnson, *op. cit.,* pp. 588 and 591.

tion, but the agreement to arbitrate carries with it the obligation to accept the award of the arbitrator.   Back in 1920 Kansas sought to make resort to arbitration compulsory in essential industries, including public utilities, mining, fuel, food, and clothing.   The Supreme Court of the United States declared the act void, saying in particular that the food, clothing, and fuel industries were not "affected with a public interest" and were not therefore subject to regulation of the type attempted.[25]   But in this mid-century period it is extremely unlikely that the Court would construe so narrowly the police power of the states.[26]   In recent years six or seven states have made arbitration compulsory in those labor-management disputes arising in public utilities and other essential services, and it seems that such legislation stands judicial scrutiny.   Arbitration is by no means the final answer to industrial disputes.   For one thing, the opposing parties usually dislike it, and, for another, Americans generally seem to prefer the give and take of negotiation to the decision of a final authority.

III. AGRICULTURE AND CONSERVATION [27]

Although the national government has moved forward on a wide front to promote agriculture and to conserve natural resources, such federal activity has not caused the states to withdraw from those functions.   It has rather encouraged them to do more.

State Services to Agriculture

Every state has an executive department, or other administrative establishment, fully occupied with carrying out numerous statutes enacted for the dual purpose of benefiting the farmer and the consumer.   It is common knowledge that there is much state co-operation with the federal agricultural agencies.   Other phases of the state agricultural program are in response to particular regional needs or relate to matters on which the national government has not as yet devised a co-operative program.   In gaining some idea of the part of the states in promoting agriculture we cannot do better than review the program of a progressive state with diversified agriculture.

The New York State Department of Agriculture and Markets, organized into a dozen bureaus and certain other agencies, is charged with the duty of enforcing and administering scores of statutes appropriate to its title.[28]   The bureau of animal industry licenses cattle dealers and baby chick auctions; issues certificates of enrollment for stallions; tests dairy cattle for tuberculosis; conducts programs of calfhood vaccination and for pullorum testing of poultry; enforces the serum and vaccine law and the baby veal law; and

---

[25] Wolff Packing Co., v Ct. on Ind. Rel., 262 U.S. 522 (1923) and 267 U.S. 552 (1925).
[26] See, for example, Nebbia v. People of New York, 291 U.S. 502 (1934).
[27] *The Book of the States, 1954–55,* pp. 350–384; Blue Books or Manuals of the several states; Richard T. Ely and George S. Wehrwein, *Land Economics* (1940); Guy H. Smith, *Conservation of Natural Resources* (1950).
[28] *Manual for the use of the Legislature of the State of New York,* 1953, pp. 563 ff.

enforces animal quarantines. The bureau of food control licenses manufacturers of frozen desserts, processing plants, commercial feeding stuffs, refrigerated warehouses and locker plants, and slaughterhouses (outside metropolitan area); registers fertilizers; and enforces the state pure food law, egg grading law, turpentine and linseed oil law, caustic products law, and the kosher foods and bread enrichment law. The bureau of markets engages in such activities as inspecting farm produce for grade certification; issuing market information; registering merchant truckmen; licensing and bonding commission merchants; assisting co-operative marketing associations; and enforcing specific laws respecting the grading and sale of apples, grapes, and maple products. The bureau of milk control licenses and bonds milk dealers; licenses milk plant managers and testers; enforces the milk control law and dairy products law; and co-operates with federal agencies in administering the New York Metropolitan Milk Marketing Order and administers orders for Niagara Frontier and Rochester Milk Marketing areas. The bureau of plant industry inspects and certifies nurseries; administers controls for dangerous insect pests and plant diseases; inspects apiaries and issues permits for moving bees; and enforces seed and insect poisons laws.

Officials of the state department of agriculture issue weigh-master licenses and enforce the weights and measures law and the coal, coke, and charcoal law in co-operation with local officials. The bureau of dog licenses administers the dog law; issues supplies to local officials charged with the responsibility of licensing dogs; and investigates certain cases of claims for domestic animals killed by dogs. Another bureau co-operates with the other state agencies that have direct responsibility for administering the state's 47 institution farms, advising such agencies on the care and development of land, crop rotation, and so on. This does not complete the list of functions of the New York department but it is sufficient for a sample. It will have been observed that the concern of the State of New York is quite as much with the interest of the consumer and the general public as it is with the welfare of the farmer, the stock raiser, the dairyman, and other producers, factors that may not be so well balanced in a few other states.

State Conservation

The federal conservation program is wide in scope and far-reaching in its ramifications, but that program does not exclude the state or local governments from the field. Supplementing the work of the national government and co-operating with it in a number of its functions, state conservation services assume importance. In a number of states these services are not integrated—are scattered about among various boards and commissions—but nearly half of the states gather them into a single department headed by a director. Whatever the organization may be, the administrators are charged with numerous duties and powers respecting soil conservation, water resources, mineral resources, forests, fish and game, and parks.

Soil conservation, essential to continued productivity, is a good example of federal-state co-operation.   Similarly, the conservation of water resources is essentially a joint enterprise, the national government giving attention primarily to the great rivers and watersheds and the states to the innumerable local problems of water supply and use.   The protection of water sources from pollution and depletion is an elementary obligation of the state and local governments.   No less urgent in many states is the matter of flood control. The larger the population becomes, the more highly urbanized and industrialized we get, the more attention we must give to water supply.   Quite aside from our concern with water as such, with water for domestic and industrial use, we have the problem of hydroelectric power.   Most states have an agency that keeps watch on power developments, gives special attention to future hydroelectric needs, and co-operates with the Federal Power Commission and other federal power agencies.

Much more closely connected with water resources than many of us realize are the forests.   Without the forest watersheds we would have very little steady water supply, and alternate periods of flood and drought.   Furthermore, the resulting land erosion would stagger the imagination.   In any case, we need the forest for itself; for its timber, its protection to wildlife, and the pleasure it brings.   Every state has some unit of its government responsible for the protection and development of its forests.   Such agencies devise means of preventing, detecting, and fighting fires, maintain nurseries and distribute young trees and shrubs, advise owners on forest management, and, under certain conditions, reclaim wornout forest land for the state.   Most of the forest land under state jurisdiction is in private hands, but that fact does not lessen the interest of the state in doing what it can to preserve the forests in order to lessen the danger of floods and the menace of erosion and to make it yield its full potential in forest products.

A fish and game service has long since become indispensable as a conservation agency.   Such an agency conducts studies and researches on wildlife and applies its findings to its development and preservation in correlation with other, and major, uses of the land.   Thus, during a twenty year period, the Missouri game management section was able so to rehabilitate the deer herd that the annual legal harvest was triple the size of the herd at the beginning of the period.   It did almost equally well with raccoons, quail, rabbits, and squirrels.   These results were accomplished by increasing game cover with plants and shrubs (which were at the same time useful to the farm) and by devising more scientific methods of trapping predatory animals.   In the same state a fisheries section annually stocks thousands of farm ponds and hundreds of lakes with fish, and pushes a program of stream management that in one year included the planting of over a million channel catfish and hundreds of thousands of small mouth bass and trout.[29]

Many of the states have vast mineral resources and nearly all of the states have made movements toward their development and conservation.   Geological surveys to determine the location, quality, and quantity of minerals have

[29] *Official Manual, State of Missouri, 1954–55*, pp. 307 ff.

been in progress for more than a century and much has been accomplished. Viewed from the strict conservationist angle, however, the results have been far from noteworthy.   For the most part, the minerals located were in, or fell into, private hands and were usually mined for the quickest profits.   An exception may be noted in the case of oil.   Even back in the "coal oil" days, New York and Pennsylvania, in the appropriate exercise of their police powers, enacted statutes designed to prevent wastage at the wells.   Such legislation is now common in oil producing states, although most of it falls short of a medium standard of conservation.   Practically all of the gas and oil producing states have signed an Interstate Oil Compact under which they agree to foster study and research on conservation methods and to establish production quotas.   Congress has supported this program, and specifically prohibits the transportation in interstate commerce of oil produced in any state in excess of the quota.

Planning

Although Americans have had some experience with planning, especially in cities, we have been very slow to come to the realization that the best use of our national resources can be brought about only after careful studies of those resources have been made and plans for their development have been formulated and adopted.   With this idea in mind the President, in 1934, established the National Resources Board.   This agency, later designated the National Resources Planning Board, had only advisory functions, but they were comprehensive.   It did excellent work for ten years, but it was never popular with Congress, which, in a huff at its recommendations for the postwar period, abolished it.

In the 'thirties planning boards or councils were established by nearly all the states, and some of these states united in forming regional planning commissions.   The idea of planning was even adopted in some counties. State planning boards, largely through their full-time research staffs, made studies and recommendations on such subjects as population and population trends, land-use, housing, water resources, fiscal policies, and governmental organization.   State planning is now a little less inclusive than it was before 1949.   The present emphasis is upon industrial development.   Some states have progressed along this line to the point where they are providing financial aid for new industries.   In 1953 Illinois, Pennsylvania, and several other states were permitting municipalities to finance the construction of industrial buildings for lease to private enterprise.   The present-day planning and development agencies commonly have a program of advertising state products, climate, and scenery.   Only a few of the older agencies follow the pattern of the original (1930's) state planners and give major emphasis to planning for the fullest development and use of natural resources.[30]   One is tempted to believe there is more to be gained by the long-

[30] *The Book of the States, 1954–55,* pp. 350–351.

range, more inclusive, planning than by concentrating simply upon bringing new industries and tourists to a state.

IV. PUBLIC HEALTH AND WELFARE [31]

In the days when our population was predominantly rural, safeguarding the public health was only one of the minor functions of government. It is quite true that there was much more need for health services than was generally recognized, but neither the scientific knowledge nor the sense of government obligation existed in those times. During the last hundred years, and particularly since 1930, the situation has been greatly changed. Increased population, industrialization, and urbanization have brought the need, science has supplied many of the answers, and public pressure has furnished the stimulus for government action. Health protection was formerly largely the province of local governments; later the states assumed a large part of the obligation; and now the national government also plays a most significant part. The entrance of the national government into the field has not caused state and local governments to withdraw from it. On the contrary, federal participation has stimulated state and local activity. The story of the development of public welfare is about the same as that of public health. Prior to the Civil War the feeble-minded, the crippled, the blind, to say nothing of the unemployed and the aged, were left to find what succor they might from private sources. Local governments assumed a grudging obligation for only a few of the most tragic cases. Private charity still flourishes and should continue to do so, but governments now assume the major role of caring for the unfortunate. In this program the national government takes a leading part, but here we shall limit our discussion to the states.

Organization of State Health Agencies

The states have established state boards of health, often giving them the power to issue important orders and regulations for the purpose of carrying into effect general statutes relative to the public health, and always giving them the authority to investigate health conditions and to supervise the work of subordinate health officers. Not infrequently a state board of health is given a considerable degree of control over local agencies. Of course, a board cannot carry on the routine work of health protection. This is carried on by administrative officials and employees, subject to the general supervision of the board. The executive head of the administrative forces has some such title as "state health officer" or "director of public health."

[31] *The Book of the States, 1954–55,* pp. 289–329; Council of State Governments, *The Mental Health Programs of the Forty-Eight States* (1950); I. V. Hiscock, *Community Health Organization* (1950); A. F. Macdonald, *American State Government and Administration* (1955 ed.), Chs. 23, 25; A. P. Miles, *An Introduction to Public Welfare* (1949); J. C. Phillips, *State and Local Government in the United States* (1954), Chs. 23–24; W. G. Smillie, *Public Health Administration in the United States* (1947 ed.); R. C. White, *Administration of Social Welfare* (1950 ed.).

The administrative services of the typical department of health are divided into appropriate bureaus, with doctors, chemists, engineers, and other scientists and technicians assigned to each according to the need. It should be stated here that not all the public health functions are monopolized by the department of that name. Departments of agriculture, education, social security, or other administrative agencies usually have a good share.

Functions of State Health Agencies

Space permits only a partial enumeration of the functions of the health agencies.[32]

(1) The collection of vital statistics and the assembling of other information contributing to a knowledge of health conditions and trends.

(2) The imposition and maintenance of the very old service of quarantine, the compulsory isolation of persons with contagious diseases.

(3) The maintenance of hygienic laboratories for the purpose of making bacteriological examinations of various kinds.

(4) The establishment of hospitals for the care of persons unable to pay for private treatment. A number of states make special efforts to provide treatment for the tuberculous.

(5) The administration of the vaccination laws and the distribution of vaccines.

(6) The medical examination of school children—now a general and splendid service, often leading to correction of defects that if undiscovered until later life might not yield to treatment.

(7) The operation of a bureau of child hygiene, which reaches the preschool child, giving physical and mental examination, advising parents, and so on.

(8) The enforcement of laws relative to sewage disposal and water supplies.

(9) Inspections of factories, canneries, packing plants, and similar establishments.

(10) The enforcement of state food and drug acts.

(11) Joining with the national government in scientific efforts to reduce the number of cases of venereal disease and to cure existing cases. Their aim is accomplished chiefly by the dissemination of information, consultation services for health officers and private physicians, and free distribution of drugs.

(12) The treatment of the mentally ill—a responsibility that states have long assumed but one they have often negligently discharged. As ignorance has grudgingly given way to science, the states have improved their services; but in many states the application of science still lags woefully behind knowledge, and legislatures are all-too-reluctant to make appropriations for the proper care of the mentally ill.

(13) Educating the public in elementary health precautions, a program

[32] For a fuller discussion see P. S. Sikes and J. E. Stoner, *Bates and Field's State Government* (1954 ed.), pp. 423–428.

many states have carried forward in a very satisfactory manner, the schools serving as the principal media.[33]

RECENT DEVELOPMENTS. The bare listing above of the principal functions of the health agencies tells a very incomplete story. It may be given more emphasis by reference to some of the newer developments. Fifty years ago tuberculosis (then commonly called "consumption" or the "white plague") was one of the principal killers. Improved methods of treatment have greatly reduced the death rate from this disease, and consequently, most of its terrors. New drugs and treatment centers, strongly supported by public education, have somewhat reduced the incidence and tragic effects of venereal disease. Diabetes and other chronic diseases, frequently found among older people, present a special problem in a country in which the life span is steadily being lengthened. About a third of the states now operate diabetes control programs. Occupational health is a matter of concern in a number of states. Recent investigations include studies of workers exposed to radiation in uranium mines and to hazards associated with X-ray installations. The states are grappling with the problem of atmospheric pollution and even with excessive noise in industry.

Millions of Americans are in poor mental health. For some time now we have had a limited knowledge of how to deal with the insane, but until relatively recent times we understood practically nothing of the problems and sufferings of those who were not insane but mentally maladjusted. There was, of course, some state recognition of this broad phase of the mental health problem before Congress acted (1946), but it was this national legislation that led to remedial action in all the states. The National Mental Health Act provides for professional assistance to the states and makes grants of money, provided the states "match the federal dollar." A number of states have established a special agency for the administration of mental health, a procedure which carries the recognition that the problem is quite different from that involved in general health administration. The states have been relatively generous in financing the new program, increasing their appropriations for it from $2.5 million in 1948 to $10 million in 1953. The heart of the program lies in the community clinics, hundreds of which have been established. The mental health program is just getting under way, but the beginning is significant.

State Institutions for Dependents

In the rugged days of a century ago dependents of almost every description and condition were often sent to county poorhouses. A more enlightened society has gradually segregated the various classes and established separate state institutions for them. About the first class to be thus segregated was the insane. The harmless insane were brought from the poorhouses and the violent insane from the jails, and were given appropriate care, sometimes

---

[33] The licensing of doctors, nurses, and many other professional people (see page 207) represents another means of protecting the public health.

in private asylums subsidized by the state and sometimes in state hospitals. The latter method of care is at present almost universal. Mental defectives now constitute the largest class of public dependents. Somewhat in keeping with the advance of knowledge concerning the feeble-minded, the epileptic, and other classes of unfortunates, nearly all of the states have established separate institutions for them. Educational institutions are maintained at state expense for the deaf, the dumb, and the blind. These individuals are not charity cases. They receive their training under the sound theory that they are entitled to public education, just as are the other youths in the state. Furthermore, if the state did not educate them, many of them would become its dependents.

THE PROBLEM OF ADMINISTRATION. The management of these institutions, including the difficult tasks of selecting properly qualified personnel, purchasing large quantities of supplies, and keeping "politics" out of both duties, is full of perplexities. Formerly, the practice was to create a board for each institution, but the newer tendency is to put all similar establishments under the same board. In some states this movement has gone so far that all correctional institutions, including prisons, as well as the charitable establishments, are placed under a single, general agency. It is generally thought that a centralized plan is the better; that it makes for uniform practices, secures a higher quality of service, and effects economy in management and in the purchase of supplies. But it is usually found difficult to keep the spoils system out of the management of institutions, whatever the plan of supervision may be. In any case of mismanagement the inmates of charitable institutions are the chief sufferers. Every little while we hear of brutal treatment, impure food, or some other indefensible condition (always promptly denied by those in authority) at a charitable institution. Although the condition complained of sometimes exists only in the imagination of some soft-hearted or excitable person, all too often there is much truth in the charge.

Modern Social Welfare

The poor have always been with us and they may be with us to the end of time, but the manner of caring for them can change. One used to give alms to the poor, the alms being, sometimes, quite as much for the good of the donor's soul as for the stomach of the poor. In any event, such gifts were indiscriminate and usually inadequate. Within the memory of men of middle age the poorhouse is a well-known institution. Both almsgiving and the poorhouse are passing (have just about passed) out of the picture. Society has decided that those in need should be maintained in decency, in such a way that they can maintain their self-respect and, should be given such assistance as will enable them, if possible, to take their place as productive members of society. Before 1935 a number of states and local communities were beginning to move in response to the sentiment described, but the passage in that year of the National Social Security Act fixed the more enlightened plan in American practice. Inasmuch as the author discusses the Social Security Act in his *American National Government* (Chapter 21), at this point he notes only that the states have taken full advantage of it; that they have established appropriate departments for its administration; and that in co-operation with the national government on the one hand and with local governments on the other, they now have welfare or social security programs designed to give nearly all necessary assistance to those in need and without depriving them of their dignity or of their status as first class citizens.

V. PUBLIC EDUCATION [34]

Education is perhaps America's biggest enterprise; its greatest social activity. For it we spend approximately $6 billion a year, employ a million teachers, and attempt to educate or train some 25 million students. Despite the fact that professional authorities and assorted critics have written numerous books and innumerable articles on it, the author of any book on American government must be bold enough to give it a little more than passing mention.

Federal Support of Education

Although education has been, and still is, primarily a state and local obligation, the national government has not neglected the field. Long ago, as noted in Chapter 1, under "Federal Aid to the States," Congress set aside lands for public schools and later provided for land-grant colleges in the several states, eventually supplementing the land grants with money grants. More recently Congress has made larger appropriations for agricultural education, agricultural extension, scholarships, and so on. Much of this aid is administered by the United States Office of Education, which is also very helpful to state and local authorities in its research and advice on matters of general educational policy. In developing its defense program during the Second World War and later, the national government has awarded numerous contracts to various institutions of higher learning for experiment and research. Not an inconsiderable part of the income of a few of the best universities in the land comes from this source. It goes without saying that any national appropriation for education is accompanied by the national authority to see that certain procedures and standards are maintained in the expenditure thereof.

State Educational Policy

With a few exceptions the colonies left education to private individuals and institutions. But following the Revolution the idea of elementary educa-

[34] The Council of State Governments, *The Forty-Eight State School Systems* (1949); Newton Edwards and H. G. Richey, *The School and the American Social Order* (1947); New York State Regents' Inquiry, *Education for American Life* (1938); B. F. Pittenger, *Local Public School Administration* (1951); The Tax Foundation, *Public School Financing, 1930–1954.*

tion at public expense gained rapidly, and in the course of time this became the practice in every nook and corner of the country.[35]   Secondary schools and state universities were added to the state program; but not always in logical sequence, the university sometimes being established first.   In our own time we find that the constitution and laws of a state usually call for elementary, secondary, and vocational schools, teachers' colleges, an A. and M. college, a university, and certain other institutions of learning.   State laws also prescribe in considerable detail the methods by which education shall be financed, stipulating, for example, the manner in which funds shall be raised for the higher institutions, what part of the total cost, if any, of secondary and elementary education shall be chargeable to the state, and how the local units shall raise their quotas of the cost.   The laws also commonly provide for a state school board and a superintendent of schools, charging them jointly or separately with the duties of making rules and regulations respecting the state public school system, conducting inspections, licensing teachers, collecting statistics, and similar responsibilities.   Ordinarily, the board determines questions of policy, and the administrative work is done by the superintendent.   The state colleges and universities are very commonly left free of the state school board and the superintendent of schools. A separate board, often a separate board for each institution, administers them.

HIGHER EDUCATION.   Although a few of the Eastern states with very old privately endowed universities have no state institution by that name, all the other states have.   Attendance in the universities and state colleges, as well as in the private institutions of higher learning, has increased most remarkably in the past generation.   In the old days the favored few went to college to acquire the learning and culture a "gentleman" was supposed to have; the masses now go for the purpose of receiving training that will enable them to make a living.   The colleges have responded to this new demand, particularly the state institutions, by offering vocational courses in an array of subjects never dreamed of by the pedagogues of a hundred years ago and which amaze the European and bring forth some adverse criticism in our own country.   Liberal education is not omitted from the curricula, but critics say that undue emphasis is given the vocational subjects.   Still, there is a great deal to be said both for the democracy that provides it and for the system itself, the system that prepares students for callings other than the learned professions.   Another feature of our higher educational system is the opportunity it "gives a poor boy to work his way through college."   This opportunity, which does not exist in many other countries, is often referred to as one of the glories of the American system. The "poor boy" does not always eventually triumph, as in the story, but he is given his chance.   Those who cannot attend college have their chance also.

---

[35] Long after their establishment, however, the "free schools" in some sections of the country, particularly the South, were looked upon as schools for the poor and were sometimes openly referred to as such.

The college goes to them through its extension professors sent to give courses at local centers and through the correspondence courses that can be taken wherever mail is delivered.

PUBLIC SCHOOLS. The state usually fixes minimum standards for the public schools, exercises some general supervision to make certain that those standards are maintained, grants a subsidy for the support of the schools of each district, and leaves the rest to local initiative and enterprise. Each county, city, township, or whatever the unit may be has its school board of laymen, and the larger units have their professional superintendents also. The board has general authority in school matters and quite often has the power, within certain limits, to fix the school levy. Communities almost invariably take great pride in and often make considerable sacrifice for their public schools. We take it as a matter of course that the school building shall be the best and most conspicuous structure in a small town. A number of distinguished foreigners who have found many features of American culture about which to make caustic comment are favorably impressed with the dominance of our public schools. In the town and to some extent in the cities the school is not just the school, but it furnishes a public forum and is a center for recreation and social life as well.

As for courses of instruction, preparation for college is not forgotten; but the "practical" courses are emphasized more and more—courses that will fit the students to become breadwinners. Nearly all the larger cities have special vocational schools for training students in electrical installation, plumbing, printing, stenography, cooking, sewing, and a host of other trades and callings. Night schools are now commonly provided for youths who must earn a living during the day and for adults who did not have advantages earlier. A number of cities provide junior colleges and a few have established municipal universities. Schools for such classes of unfortunates as the tuberculous have been founded in some areas.

The Problem of Finance

Approximately one fourth of the state and local revenue goes for education. It is generally thought that the schools are worth the money and that less waste and extravagance occur with school expenditures than with most other public expenditures. However, in times of economic recession, the schools have sometimes been the special target of attack. The small salary of the thrifty teacher now appears very large to the struggling business man. The whole school system is attacked as extravagant. It is right that the schools should be asked to reduce costs; but straight percentage reductions, easy to calculate and often employed, often result in the curtailment of a particular school service that we should be most anxious to preserve.

A special financial problem is that of the rural school. The cost is high and many rural communities are poor, even in relatively prosperous times. Since the funds must be raised primarily from taxable property in the district, it follows that taxpayers in a poor area will have to pay much higher school taxes for the same type of school than are paid by their more favored brethren in a wealthy district. A partial solution lies in the consolidation of schools. But, while consolidation gives better schools, it does not improve the financial situation a great deal for the impoverished areas forming the larger district. A better solution is for the state to assume more financial responsibility for the schools and give aid to local communities in proportion to their needs and deserts. During the past twenty-five years the trend has been strongly in this direction (see table). Every state now pays a part of the cost of operating the public schools. The amount of such grants-in-aid varies from 85 per cent in Delaware to 7 per cent in New Hampshire and Nebraska, but the average is approximately 40 per cent.

PUBLIC SCHOOL REVENUE RECEIPTS BY GOVERNMENTAL SOURCE *
(In millions of dollars and by percentage distribution, selected school years 1930–1951)

School Year Ending	Total Revenue Receipts	Source			Percentage Distribution		
		Local	State	Federal	Local	State	Federal
1930	2,088.6	1,727.6	353.7	7.3	82.7	16.9	.4
1932	2,068.0	1,649.2	410.6	8.3	79.7	19.9	.4
1934	1,810.7	1,365.9	423.2	21.5	75.4	23.4	1.2
1936	1,971.4	1,383.2	578.4	9.8	70.2	29.3	.5
1938	2,222.9	1,540.4	656.0	26.5	69.3	29.5	1.2
1940	2,260.5	1,536.4	684.4	39.8	68.0	30.3	1.7
1942	2,416.6	1,622.3	760.0	34.3	67.1	31.4	1.4
1944	2,604.3	1,709.3	859.2	35.9	65.6	33.0	1.4
1946	3,059.8	1,956.4	1,062.1	41.4	63.9	34.7	1.4
1948	4,311.5	2,514.9	1,676.4	120.3	58.3	38.9	2.8
1950	5,437.0	3,115.5	2,165.7	155.8	57.3	39.8	2.9
1951	5,946.8	3,401.6	2,360.6	184.6	57.2	39.7	3.1

* Reproduced from The Tax Foundation, *Public School Financing, 1930–1954* (Project Note No. 36, 1954), p. 21.

NOTE: Detail will not necessarily add to totals because of rounding. Data include minor amounts for summer and adult schools.

Source: U.S. Office of Education.

It has been very seriously argued that federal subsidies are necessary if the children in the poor states are to have educational advantages equal to those of children in the wealthy states. Bills introduced in Congress providing for such subsidies have met with strong opposition from those who would avoid any addition to the federal budget unless it is absolutely necessary; or who object to aid to public schools when no such aid is provided for parochial and other private schools; or who favor a vigorous and local autonomy in school matters and therefore, oppose any further federal activity in the field of public education. Whatever the merits of the proposal may be, at this writing; opinion both in Congress and out appears to be predominantly against national grants-in-aid to the public schools.

The Freedom to Teach and to Learn

Finance may not be the principal problem facing the schools. Many authorities genuinely interested in education would say that a problem of equal or greater magnitude is that of the freedom of teachers and students to pursue knowledge, truth.[36] In recent years our understandable and entirely proper concern for internal security has caused anxiety in certain quarters respecting the loyalty of teachers in universities, colleges, and the public schools. Why teachers as a class have fallen under the suspicion of disloyalty is not easy to answer. It may be because teachers have so many ideas and raise so many questions. And neither new ideas nor questioning of old ideas, if only as an exercise, are popular in times of stress. It is true that a few, a very, very small fraction of 1 per cent, of the teachers have been found to be Communists. A much higher percentage has liberal views, views that many persons, some of whom are ignorant or vicious, equate with disloyalty. Even conservative teachers, particularly in the social sciences, must deal with material that is unconventional, leftist, and radical. In the climate of opinion that has prevailed in these "cold war" years teachers thus unfortunately become suspect.

Legislatures, school boards, and private groups devise means of insuring loyalty in the schools. Few intelligent citizens object to the purpose of legislative bodies and school boards to exclude from the teaching profession persons who advocate or teach the overthrow of the government of the United States by force and violence. But a larger number of public-spirited citizens raise questions as to the propriety and effectiveness of some of the methods adopted to accomplish that end, and suggest that they might well result in interfering with the freedom to teach and, of course, with the freedom to learn. Furthermore, not infrequently, private organizations go beyond school authorities with their lists of subversive activities, associations, books, and magazines, and bring tremendous pressure to bear upon teachers to observe their "black lists." It has developed in many communities that a teacher must be more than ordinarily cautious about what organizations he joins, what social causes he supports, what books and magazines he reads, or advises his students to read, what meetings he attends, and what persons he selects for friends and associates. Such conditions probably do not make what is already the hard life of the Communist much harder, but they make it much more difficult for the liberal, the unconventional, and the unorthodox. It is questionable whether a school system in which only conservative teachers feel free, while all others are supercautious and fearful, is one that is representative of the best traditions of American education.

Surely a teacher must be loyal to his country. He must also be loyal to his profession. He has a deep professional obligation to acquaint students with

---

[36] There is much current literature on this subject, and a great deal of it is found in general works on civil liberties. See, for example, "Internal Security and Civil Rights," *The Annals of the American Academy of Political and Social Science,* Vol. 300 (July, 1955).

facts and opinions of many shades and varieties. Who is to tell the teacher what facts he is to present and what opinions (labeled as such) he is to ventilate? If the decision is not the teacher's, then he is not a teacher. He must claim the right that he must have to function as a teacher—the right to present facts, the disconcerting as well as the satisfying, to explore, to experiment, to reflect, and above all, to share his mental processes and his findings with his students. If the public denies him the right to make full use of his mental faculties, it limits at the same time the educational opportunities of American youth. Indeed, the freedom to teach is not designed to license instructors as a privileged class, but to endow students with their American birthright, the freedom to learn.

Reading List

Grace Abbott, *From Relief to Social Security* (1942).

Melvin Anshen and W. D. Wormuth, *Private Enterprise and Public Policy* (1954).

John Bauer, *The Public Utility Franchise: Its Functions and Terms under State Regulation* (1946).

J. R. Commons and J. B. Andrews, *Principles of Labor Legislation* (1936 ed.).

The Council of State Governments, *The Book of the States, 1954–55,* Section VI.

————, *The Forty-Eight State School Systems* (1949).

————, *Higher Education in the Forty-Eight States* (1952).

————, *The Mental Health Programs of the Forty-Eight States* (1950).

M. E. Dimock, *Regional Factors in National Planning* (1935).

P. H. Douglas, *Social Security in the United States* (1939 ed.).

Newton Edwards and H. G. Richey, *School in the American Social Order* (1947).

R. T. Ely and G. S. Wehrwein, *Land Economics* (1940).

H. G. Epsy, *Public Secondary School* (1939).

W. Gee, *The Social Economics of Agriculture* (1934).

H. D. Gideonse, *Higher Learning in a Democracy* (1937).

C. S. Golden and Harry Reullenburg, *The Dynamics of Industrial Democracy* (1942).

T. S. Harding, *Two Blades of Grass* (1947).

I. V. Hiscock, *Community Health Organization* (1950).

R. M. Hutchins, *Higher Learning in America* (1936).

The Commission on Intergovernmental Relations, *A Report to the President for Transmittal to the Congress* (1955).

C. H. Judd, *Problems of Education in the United States* (1934).

C. C. Killingsworth, *State Labor Relations Acts* (1948).

A. Levenstein, *Labor Today and Tomorrow* (1945).

A. F. Macdonald, *American State Government and Administration* (1955 ed.), Chs. 23–30.

A. P. Miles, *Introduction to Public Welfare* (1949).

H. C. Morrison, *School and Commonwealth* (1937).

H. S. Mustard, *Government in Public Health* (1945).

New York State Regents' Inquiry, *Education for American Life* (1938).

T. L. Norton, *Public Education and Economic Trends* (1939).

J. C. Phillips, *State and Local Government in America* (1954), Chs. 20–26.

B. F. Pittenger, *Local Public School Administration* (1951).

Public Welfare Directory (1949).

P. L. Reason and Others, *Common Core of State Educational Information* (U. S. Office of Educ., 1953).

J. D. Russell and C. H. Judd, *American Educational System* (1940).

W. F. Russell, *How to Judge a School* (1954).

P. S. Sikes and J. E. Stoner, *Bates and Field's State Government* (1954 ed.), Chs. 15–17.

S. H. Slichter, *The Challenge of Industrial Relations* (1947).

W. G. Smillie, *Public Health Administration in the United States* (1947 ed.).

G. H. Smith, *Conservation of Natural Resources* (1950).

H. M. Somers and Anne R. Somers, *Workmen's Compensation* (1954).

The Tax Foundation, "Public School Financing, 1930–1954" (Project Note No. 36, 1954).

A. G. Taylor, *Labor Problems and Labor Law* (1938).

Harold Taylor, *On Education and Freedom* (1954).

P. A. Waring and W. M. Teller, *Roots in the Earth* (1943).

R. C. White, *Administration of Social Welfare* (1950 ed.).

S. T. Williamson and Herbert Harris, *Trends in Collective Bargaining* (1945).

Questions and Problems

1. Discuss the power of the states to regulate business.

2. Trace the efforts of the states to protect women and children in industry. How does it happen that "due process of law" no longer operates as a primary obstacle to such legislation?

3. How have the states attempted to protect workmen from accidents and disease and to compensate incapacitated workmen?

4. Indicate the trends in labor legislation in your state during the last 20 years.

5. Have the states done as much for the farmer as they have for the industrial worker?

6. List the services to agriculture that are provided by your state.

7. Does your state have a planning board or commission? If so, what has it achieved?

8. How do the states protect the public health?

9. Comment upon the economic and social implications of this statement: *Each family should take care of its own dependents.* And this: *Each community should take care of its own indigent.*

10. What are the pros and cons of federal aid for the public schools?

11. To what extent is the freedom to teach and learn limited in your community? Are such limitations appropriate?

CHAPTER | 10

RURAL GOVERNMENT

Everyone knows that state government is not the only government in a state; that within any state and under its control there are commonly hundreds of other government units—cities, counties, districts, and special units. Indeed our earliest and always most numerous associations with government are with these local units, and the degree of happiness and contentment we find under government largely depends therefore upon the efficiency, the vitality, and the responsiveness of the governing authorities in these units. In the present chapter our attention is directed to the county, essentially an area of rural government, and to other rural jurisdictions.

Dependency of the States upon County Administrative Agencies

The states have administrative organization and personnel sufficient to perform only a minor fraction of the services they now offer. To a considerable extent they must rely upon local administrative agencies, particularly upon the counties, for the performance of routine state services. State law requires your birth certificate, but it is issued by a local official, probably by a county official. State law likewise requires a hunting license, a car license, a marriage license, but you go to the county courthouse to get them. State law regulates land transfers, wills, and divorces, but the counties take care of the administrative details. State law fixes certain standards for milk and other products on the market, but the county and city officers have the burden of enforcing these standards. The state establishes a minimum requirement for public education, but the county and city authorities are charged with the responsibility of enforcing them. Commit a crime (against the state), and you are arrested by a county or city officer, prosecuted by a county officer, tried by a judge elected by the county, and hear the verdict from a county jury. If found guilty, you may be sent to the *state* penitentiary. This process of illustration could be continued to monotony. To be sure, counties and cities, particularly the latter, have a number of local functions to perform, but a very significant phase of local government is that of serving the state in an administrative capacity.

232

Legal Status of Counties

"While the county is an agency of the state, it is likewise a creature of the state." [1]   It is created by the state, at all times subject to its control, and may be abolished by it.   This complete power over counties was in earlier times held almost exclusively by the legislature; but it was not long until some of the states started the practice of protecting counties from legislatures through constitutional provisions prohibiting the changing of boundaries, the moving of the county seat, and the like, without the assent of the people affected.

I. RURAL GOVERNMENTAL ORGANIZATION

County Officers

The county has no clear separation of powers along the traditional executive, legislative, and judicial lines.   It has no chief executive; and a number of its officers, subject to no unified control, perform functions that are both judicial and administrative.

1. THE BOARD.   The most important governing body in the county is the elective county board (known also by various other names), which functions in every state except Rhode Island, although neither the board nor the county as a unit of government is of any particular importance in the other New England states. The typical board has three or five members, but in a few states the number may run to fifty or more.   They meet as actual needs and laws require, both of which vary among the states and counties within the same states.   In some jurisdictions, the boards, during the time they are not in session, make a considerable use of committees.   Board members are ordinarily paid on a per diem basis, although in a few large counties of some states fairly substantial salaries are provided.

These bodies have no powers other than those allowed by the constitution and legislature of the state.   In general, they are empowered to control county finances, subject to restrictions as to the amount of taxes that may be levied and the purposes for which such taxes may be used and to like restrictions as to borrowing money; to construct county roads and bridges; to erect and maintain courthouses, jails, and other county buildings; to license and regulate dance halls, bathing beaches, and other places of recreation and amusement; to legislate on local matters (in a few states); to organize townships; to appoint a few officers, such as the county physician; to exercise a measure of supervision over the elective officers; to establish polling places and administer certain other features of the election laws; and to establish and maintain institutions for the care of the needy and, subject to national and state law, to make certain decisions on questions of social security administration.

2. OFFICERS ASSOCIATED WITH THE ADMINISTRATION OF JUSTICE.   In all counties there are a number of officers who are associated with the administra-

[1] Cook County v. Chicago, 142 N.E. (Ill.) 512 (1924).

tion of justice.   Among these we mention the prosecuting attorney, the sheriff, and the coroner.   Although in a legal sense these officers are regarded as state officials, they are locally elected and the citizens regard them as "their" local officers.[2]

Prosecuting attorney. The prosecuting attorney (known also by various other titles, such as "state's attorney," "county attorney," and "prosecutor"), a county officer commonly elected, is a familiar figure about the trial courts. He serves as counsel for the grand jury, aiding it in preparing indictments; and in many states he may bring an accused person to trial without going through the formality of securing an indictment from a grand jury.   He must conduct the prosecution of all offenders in the name of the state.   Clearly the activity of this officer determines very largely the degree of law enforcement a county will attain.   Some prosecutors have winked at lawlessness or at certain types of offenses; others, frequently young lawyers, have made records as prosecutors, and steadily climbed the political ladder from that first round. The prosecuting attorney also represents the state and the county in civil suits to which they happen to be parties, and he acts as a legal adviser to other county officers.

Sheriff. The sheriff is another important county officer usually elected by the people.   A powerful and somewhat romantic figure in the English counties centuries ago, he now has only a few administrative duties to perform in that country.   In the American county he must, as far as possible, prevent breaches of the peace, and arrest offenders; serve the writs issued by the courts; summon juries; execute the court's judgments; administer the county jail; and discharge other duties imposed by law. Since the historic sheriff has so many civil functions, his time for the police duties that are appropriate to his office is limited.   Furthermore, he is usually untrained for such work and his politically appointed deputies are equally deficient.   Although local law-enforcement officers formerly regarded state police with some jealousy and resentment, they now accept them, even welcome them, as allies in their police work.   The truth is that the office of sheriff as a law-enforcement agency has fallen behind the times; it is with few exceptions quite incapable of coping with the modern criminal.   Such officers will probably remain ineffective as long as they are on an elective and political basis.

Coroner. Another officer who held a post of honor and trust in the England of long ago is the coroner.   This office has declined much further than that of sheriff.   The coroner now has only the duty of inquiring into the cause of death produced by accident, or where the deceased had not been attended by a physician, or where foul play is suspected.   It is the duty of the coroner to summon a jury, examine witnesses, seize evidence, and aid in apprehending suspects.   Everyone knows that only pathologists or others trained in science can determine the cause of death.   Yet the elected office of coroner is often filled by a political hack who knows nothing.   Not in-

[2] See Lane W. Lancaster, *Government in Rural America* (1952 ed.), pp. 49–51.   This is an excellent book on a subject about which little is written.

GOVERNMENT OF WHITMAN COUNTY, WASHINGTON

STATE DEPARTMENT OF PUBLIC WELFARE

EXTENSION SERVICE WASHINGTON STATE COLLEGE

STATE DEPARTMENT OF AGRICULTURE

ELECTION BOARD *

FINANCE COMMITTEE **

COUNTY ELECTORATE

COMMISSIONERS *** (3)

JUSTICES OF THE PEACE (11)

1 2 3 4 5 6 7 8

9 10

11 12 13 14 15 16 17 18

SCHOOL DISTRICTS (25)

ROAD DISTRICT

FIRE PROTECTION DISTRICTS (3)

LIBRARY DISTRICT

1. AUDITOR
2. TREASURER
3. ASSESSOR
4. CLERK
5. PROSECUTING ATTORNEY
6. SHERIFF
7. SUPERINTENDENT OF SCHOOLS
8. SUPERIOR COURT JUDGE
9. PROBATION OFFICERS
10. BOARD OF EDUCATION
11. HORTICULTURAL INSPECTOR
12. WELFARE ADMINISTRATOR
13. HEALTH OFFICER
14. ROAD ENGINEER
15. WEED CONTROL SUPERVISOR
16. AGRICULTURAL AGENT
17. 4-H CLUB AGENT
18. HOME DEMONSTRATION AGENT

○ Appointive offices

▢ Elected by local residents but components of state judicial system.

* Auditor, prosecuting attorney and chairman of board of commissioners.

** Treasurer, auditor and chairman of board of commissioners.

*** Commissioners are ex officio board of equalization, board of health, welfare board and road commissioners,

Prepared by Professor Paul Beckett, The State College of Washington

frequently it is filled by an undertaker who may thus pick up a little extra business.   A number of jurisdictions have "done something about" the office of coroner.   Massachusetts, Virginia, and other states have transferred the duties of coroner to the prosecutor, giving him the authority to call in medical experts as needed.   In Connecticut the coroner is appointed by a court, must be a lawyer, and is required to leave the medical duties of the office to an appointed examiner, who shall "without delay repair to and take charge of the body" of any person who comes to "a violent, sudden, or untimely death."   The appointed medical examiner is, of course, the logical successor to the coroner, and that is the trend.[3]

(FINANCE OFFICERS.   Several county officers are responsible for various phases of finance. (The *assessor* is a county official in about half the states; in the others he is chosen by towns or districts.   He is almost invariably an elected official.   In the chapter on state and local finance it was observed that assessment is a rather technical matter and that it is often very poorly performed.   One of the reasons for inefficient performance is that the elected assessor, particularly in the small districts, is likely to be subject to pressure, subtle or otherwise.   If he wants to be re-elected, he must be "careful," must be "reasonable," about the values he places on properties.   Another reason for assessment inadequacies is that assessors, quite aside from their political status, are usually poorly equipped for their duties.   The appointment of assessors would not necessarily take them out of politics, but it might help. Appointment by units as large as counties, or larger, and under civil service requirements, would most certainly result in improving the qualifications of assessors and in making them less amenable to "influence."   The public is slow to accept the merit system for the assessor, however, because of its devotion to democracy in local government and perhaps more particularly because it likes the idea of the assessor being subject to a little influence.   Yet in a number of cities progress has been made in the direction of securing qualified assessors and in devising scientific methods of assessment.

The county *treasurer,* like the assessor, is commonly elected.   It is his duty to receive, deposit in banks, and disburse the county funds in accordance with the laws, which are usually so explicit that the treasurer has little discretion.   Not so long ago it was quite common for the treasurer to receive for his own pocket the interest—sometimes a large amount—on county funds deposited in banks.   This practice is now generally prohibited by law.   Treasurers very commonly receive substantial salaries or even more substantial compensation in fees.   Many scandals and shady transactions have been revealed in connection with the depositing of county funds.   Banks have taken care of the treasurer's bond in return for the deposits; banks of political friends have been favored, even to the extent of being given deposits when known to be unsound.   A number of states have sought to remedy these con-

---

[3] There seems to be unanimity among authorities on local government that the coroner's duties can be performed only by a professional.   See Lancaster, *op. cit.*, pp. 170–173, and references there cited.

ditions by giving the county board the authority to select the depositaries, although a board as well as a treasurer might sometimes get off the straight and narrow path.

In addition to his work for the county the treasurer ordinarily acts as an agent for the collection of state funds, and in some states he receives and passes on to local units of the county the funds designated for them. In a number of states, however, money is collected by towns and townships at considerable more expense than the county system of collection entails.

The *auditor* is a county finance officer found in about a third of the states. His duties consist primarily of examining and approving bills and claims against the county. Following his favorable action, the county board ordinarily orders payment. Where there is no auditor, the county clerk, whose chief duties are described below, serves in somewhat the same capacity. Indeed, except perhaps in the very populous counties, there is no need for both auditor and clerk.

4. OTHER OFFICERS. Some twenty-five states have the office of county *clerk,* usually elective. The clerk keeps the records of the proceedings of the county board; prepares and distributes ballots for elections; issues certain licenses; makes reports as required by law; and performs numerous other ministerial and clerical tasks that vary considerably from state to state. Where there is no county clerk, these duties are discharged by the clerk of a court or other officer or officers.

A *register of deeds* is about as common in the counties as the county clerk. His chief duty is to keep the public records of the sale and transfer of real estate. This is an important function in a country where real property changes hands so frequently; and in those states that have no register of deeds, some other county officer, usually the clerk, keeps these records. There are many other county officers—school, road, welfare, etc.,—varying in number, titles, and duties among the states and even among the counties of a particular state. The elective officers mentioned above are able to carry out the administrative work of the ordinary county; but in the more populous areas, hundreds or even thousands of assistants, deputies, and clerks are employed. In a few counties such assistants are engaged under the merit system.

Subdivisions of the County

THE TOWN. For purposes of community government, counties are subdivided in one way or another in every state. In the New England states this subdivision is the town, a unit that dates from early colonial times. In these states it is an older and much more vital unit of government than the county. The term "town" has various meaning in different parts of the country and often several meanings in the same locality. The farmer says, "I am going to town," meaning to the little cluster of houses and stores, the village. The boy in the village says, "I am going up (or down) town," meaning that he is going a quarter of a mile to the point where the village trading is done. It is difficult for many Americans to understand that the New England town is a rural area averaging about twenty-five square miles, which usually includes a village. In theory, the town is governed by the whole body of citizens, who assemble at the town meetings, make the local laws, and elect a clerk and other town officials to carry out these laws and the many duties imposed by state authorities. This theory borders on the fact in those communities that are still chiefly agricultural and consequently not overburdened with population. But in industrial areas with more than 10,000 or 15,000 inhabitants, many of whom are non-native or floaters, the system breaks down and most likely falls into the hands of a machine.

Ordinarily, city government is more competent for administering the affairs of the more populous communities, and that form is usually adopted when the town system becomes too unwieldy. The town or township system was adopted by a number of states outside of New England; but only in the Central states is there much resemblance to the New England system. Even in the Central states the town is of much less importance than in New England. This reduced significance came about because in the Middle West the town is subordinate to the county; because roads, schools, and some other local functions are usually administered by separate authorities; and because the town includes the rural population only.

2. COUNTY DISTRICTS. In the Southern and Western states, counties are divided into administrative units known variously as magisterial districts, civil districts, and precincts. Ordinarily villages, and sometimes the smaller cities located within the district, are parts of the district organization. Such districts are convenient areas for the conduct of elections and the administration of petty justice, schools, and rural roads. An important characteristic of these districts is their almost complete subordination to the county. They were created for administrative purposes and their authority is exceedingly limited. Neither in the South, because of its earlier development along county lines, nor in the West, because of its wide, sparsely settled areas, has there been developed anything approximating the vigorous local government of the rural New England town.

3. SPECIAL DISTRICTS. The regular county districts, particularly in the South and West, have not been found equal to the performance of a number of administrative functions. Consequently, special districts have been created for schools, highways, drainage, irrigation, and the like. More than twenty-five years ago Professor F. H. Guild found forty-seven varieties of such districts under eighty-nine different titles.[4] Special districts may or may not have boundaries conforming to those of a county, regular district, or township.

[4] "Special Municipal Corporations," Nat. Mun. Rev., XVIII (1929), 319–323. See also J. A. Fairlie and C. M. Kneier, County Government and Administration (1930), pp. 476–508; William Anderson, The Units of Government in the United States (1942 ed.); Bureau of the Census, Governments in the United States in 1952 (1953). The number of special districts increased by about 50 per cent from 1942 to 1952, the figure for the latter date, according to the Bureau of the Census, stood at 12,319. Of these, fire districts constituted 2,272; drainage, 2,174; soil conservation, 1,981; cemeteries, 911; housing, 863; highways, 774; water supply, 665; irrigation, 641; and sanitation, 429.

Their boundaries are determined by the area of need, not by the arbitrary lines of some pre-existing political unit. They have another advantage over the regular districts in that they are created to administer special functions— health, mosquito abatement, and so on. Still another advantage is in finance. Counties and the regular districts are commonly limited by law in the amount of taxes they may levy and the money they may borrow; but, by creating a special district, it is ordinarily possible to get funds sufficient for a given purpose. We might add that this circumvention is not always appreciated by the taxpayers. Officers of the special districts are appointed by county or state authorities in a number of instances, although popular election is the usual method of selection. Effort is made in a few states to guarantee that the appointed officials shall be qualified for the positions they hold; but there are few cases in which the requirement goes beyond the "suitable and competent person" generality.

Quite naturally several local government districts, sometimes coextensive and sometimes overlapping, with their special functions, and frequently with independent taxing powers, cause considerable confusion and waste. The problem here, as with the state administrative system, is one of coordination and consolidation, a problem that in rural areas has hardly been touched.

State Control of Local Officers

1. JUDICIAL CONTROL. Since counties and their subdivisions are concerned so largely with the administration of state laws, it is highly desirable that state officials be authorized to exercise some control over local officers. A degree of control is exercised by the courts, which, for example, by writ of *mandamus* may compel a county board to levy a tax to pay the amounts due on county bonds and by writ of injunction may restrain county officers from illegally changing the county seat or creating a debt in excess of that authorized by law. Courts are frequently empowered to remove local officers for corruption, incompetence, and similar causes; and in a few states judges have the duty of appointing certain county officers. But court control over officers corrects only the worst abuses and mistakes, and it is highly technical and cumbersome in any case.

2. ADMINISTRATIVE CONTROL. Any effective control or supervision over local officers must come from the central administrative authorities, as France and other countries of Continental Europe learned long ago. Control of our local officials, as far as such control was exercised at all, has been very largely in the hands of legislatures during the greater part of our history. This was the old English system, now considerably modified in favor of administrative control in that country and to a somewhat lesser extent in the American states. Administrative control in America takes several general forms. (1) Appointment of a few local officers is by state authorities. For example, in Massachusetts and Rhode Island the governor may appoint medical examiners. (2) State authorities may fix the standard of attainment for certain employees who are selected by local officials as is illustrated by the state standards set

for teachers who are appointed by local boards and superintendents.   (3) The power to remove certain local officers is vested in state authorities in several states.   Thus, the governor of New York may remove sheriffs and district attorneys and the governor of Wisconsin may remove district attorneys and coroners.   (4) Local authorities may be required to make reports to state authorities.   State officers may also have the power to inspect and advise, and, on occasion, command, local officers.   (5) Payment of subsidies by the state to local communities for roads, schools, welfare, and other services, under the conditions that the local units meet state standards, operates as a very effective means of central control.[5]   Such subsidies, and the control that goes along with them, have increased by leaps and bounds since 1933.   (6) State supervision of local finances is partially accomplished by state boards of equalization that have authority to adjust assessments of property for purposes of taxation, by the requirement that local communities shall follow specific budget practices, and by a degree of supervision over local indebtedness.   Although these state administrative powers may seem comprehensive, it must be noted that not all of them are exercised in every state and that in some other states the supervisory powers are exercised with extreme leniency.

Only four or five states have an administrative setup adequate to exercise effective control over local government and the agencies of control in those states are designed to deal almost exclusively with matters of finance.   In New Jersey, for example, there is a director of local government and a local government board.   The board is authorized to take control of a local unit if it defaults on its debts, carries a budget deficit for two years in excess of 5 per cent of the tax levy, or has certain other financial difficulties.   The director of the division of local government keeps a sharp eye on the debt situation and has the power to require local levies sufficient to reduce deficits. He has, also, the power to prescribe uniform accounting systems for local governments, to supervise their audits, and to enforce the laws relating generally to local finance.[6]

Criticisms and Proposals for Improvements

For over one hundred and fifty years the American county has stood practically as it stands today.   It was organized in colonial times to suit the needs of rural America and the states later admitted to the Union came with their counties organized to serve the needs of their rural civilization.   The county still functions with some degree of success in rural areas, but it seldom achieves any noteworthy triumphs in urban communities.   In small or sparsely populated rural counties the per capita cost of administration is usually high and in the metropolitan areas the county administrative system is often corrupt and almost always ineffective in dealing with the many technical activities it

---

[5] Fairlie and Kneier, *op. cit.,* pp. 92 ff.

[6] Lancaster, *op. cit.,* pp. 314 ff. and W. B. Graves, *American State Government* (1953 ed.), pp. 796 ff.

is supposed to assume. The stronghold of the spoilsman, with an organization that in truth belongs to the "ox cart" days, the county does not hold a place as a promising unit of government. Furthermore, the counties have fallen into financial difficulties and they have called loudly to the states for financial aid, bewailing at the same time their gradual loss of the power of self-government. In addition to these and many other criticisms of county government, we have the problem of special areas mentioned above.[7]

What solutions are offered? Abolish the counties and set up six or eight or a dozen administrative units to do their work? This proposal may have some merit, but essentially the same result could be achieved by county consolidation. That solution appears to be a sound one, and it is very easy to pick up a map, erase a few boundary lines, and mark out a few county seats. But the task is not easy beyond that point. For one thing, the least populous counties, the ones that for economic reasons ought to be consolidated, are usually very large in area, so that consolidation would raise the problem of convenience to the citizens. On the other hand, many counties covering extremely small areas are very populous, so that the economic reason for consolidation loses much of its force. Furthermore, the people in the counties, particularly in the rural counties, want them to remain as they are. They have grown up with them; that is the way they know them; and they have an almost superstitious aversion to any tampering with the county boundary. Perhaps a fourth of the counties could be consolidated to advantage, but for reasons of sentiment and politics, consolidation is most difficult to accomplish. The inhabitants of the county seat will vote against it to a man and so will all the other citizens of the county who feel that they might suffer some slight inconvenience. But the chief factor that will defeat such a proposal is the vague fear that this movement is but the beginning of a scheme to rob the counties of all power, a fear fed by all of the county politicians, who for obvious reasons are opposed to consolidation. So great is the opposition to consolidation that it has been found difficult or impossible to place an amendment in a state constitution that would *permit,* much less require, the people of counties to vote on the question.

Another type of consolidation that has been proposed and that has met with a little favor is the city-county combination. This is discussed in the next chapter.

There is another type of consolidation, the consolidation of functions. For example, small and poor counties might combine for the purpose of maintaining a county hospital or a health unit or some other service. This is hardly as satisfactory as a complete consolidation, but it has some merit (and some disadvantages) and it has been achieved in a few cases.

Considerable attention has been devoted to the problem of improving county administration by the introduction of some sort of executive management.

[7] The obstacles to efficient county government as well as the plans for improving it are well set forth by Lancaster, *op. cit.,* particularly in Chs. 2, 5, and 15.

There are those who believe that the county should adopt a manager system similar to the city-manager plan.[8] Although this plan has been advocated for some years and a few states have authorized its adoption, the number of counties that have installed it is relatively small, not over twenty-five. Whatever merits the plan may have for cities, there is no convincing evidence that it fits the needs of the counties. For one thing, the smaller counties cannot afford it. Furthermore, there are some authorities who believe that the manager system would disturb the relationship now existing between county and state in respect to the joint administration of such services as health and welfare.[9]

Perhaps Professor William Anderson was right in fixing his aim on the more than 150,000 units of government in existence in 1941.[10] Fully realizing that his plan to abolish nine out of ten of these units would in all probability never be accepted, he nevertheless presented it as a desirable goal. He would abolish the 118,308 school districts he found in 1941, leaving the schools to be administered by city or county authority, but under state control. Since 1941 a number of states have made considerable progress in reducing the number of such districts (in 1952 the Bureau of the Census reported 67,346). In like manner Anderson would abolish practically all the special districts. His blueprints call for the disappearance of the townships except in New England, where rural towns would be consolidated. The small villages he would deprive of their corporate existence. He would create city-counties in every area having a city of at least 50,000 population, giving such units of government the functions of the city, the county, and the school district. For rural areas he would leave the counties to administer state-wide services, such as schools, health, and welfare, and he would leave with these counties any purely rural functions. Of course, he advocates extensive consolidation for rural counties.

There are, then, many suggestions and plans for the improvement of county government, but very few of them have met with any enthusiasm from county and state officers or from the people. Counties continue for the most part to manage their affairs badly. They make increasing demands on the states for financial aid, while they proclaim, "never before has it been so necessary for counties to stand together in the preservation of local autonomy." Obviously it is not possible to receive funds from the state without at the same time giving the state a larger share in the administration of the services for which funds are advanced. In the last twenty years the trend toward state control of highways, education, public welfare, and health administration has been observed even by those who give these matters little attention. This result is

[8] See *National Municipal Review*, Dec., 1948, p. 612, May, 1949, p. 243, July, 1953, p. 331, Sept., 1953, p. 393, May, 1954, p. 250, and many other issues. See also E. W. Weidner, "A Review of the Controversy over County Executives," *Public Administration Review*, VIII (Winter, 1948), 18.

[9] Lancaster, *op. cit.*, pp. 344–348.

[10] *Op. cit.*, pp. 45–47.

inevitable because the states have the broader taxing powers, they have the technical staffs necessary for administration, and they are therefore better able to administer large functions. The counties should retain their purely local functions, but science and technology have made many local functions state-wide functions. Yet this development toward centralization does not mean that the county is passing completely out of the picture. It does and should remain a vital administrative unit, subject of course to state supervision. In particular, the county should continue to play a large part in administering those services, such as education and social security, that so intimately touch the life of the individual. But even if such services should be transferred completely to the state (an unlikely event), the county may still record wills, mortgages, and deeds, issue various types of licenses, and perform numerous other routine functions for the state. Furthermore, as the people, young and old, find more leisure the county may well busy itself with maintaining parks, playgrounds, theaters, libraries, and similar facilities that develop mental and physical health and combat delinquency.

II. TWO RURAL ADMINISTRATIVE SERVICES

The functions of counties and smaller units of government include large shares in the administration of justice, education, highways, health, and welfare. Inasmuch as the writer has considered the first, second, and third of these elsewhere,[11] only health and welfare administration will be briefly examined here, and our attention will be directed primarily to the predominantly rural areas.

Health Administration

Much poetry has been written about the country, mostly by people who no longer live in it; some fiction has a rural setting, but hosts of people believe more fiction about farm and country than reputable writers would be guilty of endorsing. One of these fictions has it that the country, being such a healthful place in which to live, has little or no public health problem. The truth is, however, that rural communities have their full share of measles, whooping cough, diphtheria, influenza, lobar pneumonia, and diarrhea, and almost a monopoly on diseases traceable to polluted water, food, or soil—such diseases as hookworm, malaria, dysentery, and typhoid. Furthermore, although the death rate in the country is slightly lower than in the city, physical defects of a debilitating kind are more common in the country. This evidence is abundantly sufficient to show that rural areas have their health problem, a problem made difficult of solution in part because of the widespread ignorance of the nature of disease among rural populations.[12]

Health organization in rural communities was established in the day when

[11] See Chapter 6 on the administration of justice; pages 225–230 on education; and the writer's *American National Government* (1955 ed.), pages 490–496 on highways.
[12] Lancaster, *op. cit.*, pp. 285 ff.

diseases were believed to be transmitted largely, if not exclusively, from personal contact and smells. Consequently, the unit of administration (such as it was) was small—the town, a county district, and, less often, the county. Even when knowledge of disease transmission became more general, the smaller units of administration were commonly retained. Small communities are usually unable to provide health services worthy of the name because the cost is beyond their means. The county is now regarded as the smallest area populous enough and wealthy enough to provide those preventive and educational services that constitute the modern public health program. Such a program calls for full-time, permanent organization for health services; for at least one medical health officer, a nurse, a sanitary inspector, and a clerk. The minimum services to be rendered include the recording of vital statistics, the assembling of data on and the control of communicable diseases; the inspection of water and food supplies and the enforcement of hygenic regulations applicable thereto; the maintenance of nursing service for mothers and infants.[13]

Very few rural counties have established these services. Country people generally do not see any great need for them; moreover, even the minimum standard outlined above would be a heavy financial drain on a number of the rural counties. What progress has been made in rural health protection has come largely from the educational activities and financial support offered by private organizations like the Rockefeller Foundation and the Commonwealth Fund and by the state and national governments. Indeed, adequate health protection can hardly be expected to reach the majority of rural communities without education, supervision, and financial subsidies from the state or national government. And in recent years these state and national aids have become substantial.

Welfare Administration

One of the oldest responsibilites of local government is the care of the indigent—"poor relief." Until recently the needy were commonly regarded as unworthy, shiftless nuisances, and treated accordingly. Local officials granted the minimum of food, clothing, and fuel to certain applicants and often denied it to others who were equally in want. The indigent sick, the aged, the feebleminded, deserted wives and children, and other unfortunates were given indoor relief; that is, they were sent to an institution known as the poorhouse, almshouse, county farm, or county home. Whatever its name, the place was about the same, a poorhouse, and a Virginia Board of Public Welfare characterized it as "a perfect testimonial of man's inhumanity to man, as well as a conspicuous example of inefficient and reactionary government." [14] The same characterization would have applied to a few of these "homes" in a number of other states. The authorities suggested that substantial improvements could be made, both in economy of administration and in the treatment accorded the inmates, by co-operation among the counties in materially reduc-

13 Lancaster, *op. cit.,* p. 295.
14 Fairlie and Kneier, *op. cit.,* p. 283.

ing the number of institutions. Virginia has made significant progress in this direction, and some other states have followed the same procedure.

But neither outdoor aid, doled out in groceries and clothing, nor even well-administered homes for the aged and broken quiet the modern social conscience, which is quickened to the conviction that the poor may be worthy and deserve assistance that will enable them to maintain their self-respect. The ill who are without funds should receive proper medical care, the aged should be pensioned and thus be enabled to remain in their own homes, and dependent mothers and children should be given financial assistance. That is the practice of our time; and it has just about closed the almshouses and abolished the old "grocery order" type of relief.

This newer and humane philosophy was not born of the Great Depression, but it gained general acceptance during that period. Not only did the 'thirties witness a wide change in attitude toward the unfortunate on the part of the general population but they also saw the abandonment of the idea that relief was a local problem. Indeed, we practically stopped thinking about "relief," preferring instead *social welfare* or *social security,* and on a national basis. The national government through its Social Security Act (1935) pretty well fixes the minimum standards of assistance and the states, even the reluctant ones, conform in order to get a share of the federal social security grant. But the state-federal welfare program does not remove the counties from the picture. The operation of the program where it really counts—the granting of financial assistance to the blind, to dependent children, to the aged—is in the hands of the county. The nation and the state wisely hold the county to merit system personnel in welfare administration, and inspectors and supervisors keep a check on what the county is doing, but the fact remains that the county is the basic unit in the administration of several features of the social security program. It could not well be otherwise; units of administration there must be, and if the counties were not in existence to provide them, somewhat similar areas of local administration would have to be provided.

Reading List

William Anderson and E. W. Weidner, *State and Local Government in the United States* (1951).

A. W. Bromage, *American County Government* (1933).

Laverne Burchfield, *Our Rural Communities* (1947). A bibliography.

Council of State Governments, *State-Local Relations* (1946).

H. Emerson and M. Luginbuhl, *Local Health Units for the Nation* (1945).

J. A. Fairlie and C. M. Kneier, *County Government and Administration* (1930).

W. Kilpatrick, *Problems in Contemporary County Government* (1930, and *State Supervision of Local Finance* (1940).

J. H. Kolb and E. de S. Brunner, *A Study of Rural Society* (1946 ed.).

L. W. Lancaster, *Government in Rural America* (1952 ed.).

T. B. Manny, *Rural Municipalities* (1930).

National Municipal League, *The County Manager Plan* (1950), pamphlet.

National Municipal Review (monthly).

Lowry Nelson, *Rural Sociology* (1948).

fession (1934); C. P. Taft, *City Management: The Cincinnati Experiment* (1933).

New York Bureau of Municipal Research, *Report on County Government in Virginia* (1928).

J. E. Pate, *Local Government and Administration* (1954).

J. C. Phillips, *State and Local Government in America* (1954).

The President's Research Committee on Social Trends, *Recent Social Trends* (1933), Chs. I, X.

H. Quick, *A New Kind of County Government* (1925).

J. F. Sly, *Town Government in Massachusetts* (1930).

C. F. Snider and N. F. Garvey, "County and Township Government in 1947," *Am. Pol. Sci. Rev.,* XLIII (Feb., 1949), 53.

Tennessee Valley Authority, *County Government and Administration in the Tennessee Valley States* (1940).

C. R. Tharp, *Social Security and Related Services in Michigan, Their Administration and Financing* (1946).

P. W. Wager, *County Government Across the Nation* (1950).

R. H. Wells, *American Local Government* (1939).

G. A. Works and S. O. Lesser, *Rural America Today* (1942).

Questions and Problems

1. What functions does your home county perform for the state?

2. How much discretion have your county officers over such matters as education, road construction, and public health?

3. Diagram the structure of your county government. Who is at the head of it?

4. Comment upon this statement: *If the people in every town, or township, or similar unit of local government displayed lively interest in that unit a happy future for the nation would be assured.*

5. What changes have been made in local rural government in your state since 1900? What trends are observable?

6. To what extent does your state employ financial subsidies in order to induce the counties to provide more adequate services in such fields as education and road construction? Are there other reasons why the states provide such subsidies?

7. How does the problem of public health show the logic of the trend toward centralization in government?

8. Comment upon this statement: *If those in need were allowed only the barest minimum of aid we could easily carry the cost and social security would be no threat to free enterprise.*

CITY GOVERNMENT AND ADMINISTRATION

It is not the purpose to trace here the growth of the American city, our change from an agricultural civilization to one predominantly industrial and urban.   Nor is it feasible to review the interesting if not always inspiring story of the development of the American city as an agency of government.   Many other writers have dealt with these subjects, and to them the student is referred. All that is attempted here is a brief discussion of the city's governmental structure and an outline of some of its administrative services.

I. CITY GOVERNMENTAL ORGANIZATION [1]

The City and the State

The city to a lesser extent than the county discharges certain functions for the state and to a much greater extent than the county administers to local needs.   Like the county, the city is a creature of the state.   It was formerly the creature of the state legislature; but because the legislature often used its exclusive powers unwisely, constitutional restrictions were placed upon its authority over cities.   These restrictions are now numerous and vary a great deal among the several states; but, in general, they are limitations on the authority of the legislature to do such things as grant charters to cities by special act, amend charters without the consent of the inhabitants of cities affected, and authorize cities to tax and borrow money beyond a stipulated percentage of the valuation of taxable property.   It may be said that, although in theory the city is in essentially the same position of dependence upon the state as is the county, in actual fact the city is more independent than the county because of the constitutional limitations upon the legislature respecting its control of city affairs.

THE CITY CHARTER.   Each city has a charter, a sort of constitution.   It is acquired in various ways.   In some states the legislature may still grant each

---

[1] A. W. Bromage, *Introduction to Municipal Government and Administration* (1950); E. S. Griffith, *Current Municipal Problems* (1933); C. M. Kneier, *City Government in the United States* (1947 ed.); A. F. Macdonald, *American City Government and Administration* (1951 ed.); W. B. Munro, *Municipal Administration* (1934); J. M. Pfiffner, *Municipal Administration* (1940); C. E. Ridley and O. F. Nolting, *The City-Manager Profession* (1934); C. P. Taft, *City Management: The Cincinnati Experiment* (1933).

city a charter by a special act, and each charter may be different.   This power
to grant charters by special act gives the legislature and the cities too much
opportunity to play politics.   There are states that have tried the expedient
of requiring the legislatures to classify cities and give all in the same class the
same charter.   The trouble here is that cities may be so classified, as they were
at one time in Ohio, that practically every city will be in a class to itself, and the
special charter system will again prevail.   A few states have a set of charters,
allowing a city to adopt the one best suited to its needs.   This is known as the
"optional charter" system.   Although it appears satisfactory, cities have often
failed to find charters to meet their specifications.

Some years ago students of municipal problems pinned their faith on the
home rule charter as the solution of many of the city's ills.   It is now authorized in sixteen or more states that include many of the largest cities.   A small
group of citizens, chosen by the voters or otherwise, drafts the charter for a
city.   It is then referred to the voters, whose approval puts it into effect, although in some states it must go through the formality of receiving legislative approval.   The home rule charter must not, of course, contain provisions
contrary to the Constitution and laws of the state.   Home rule does not, then,
confer upon the people of a municipality the authority to control their government completely.   "It simply means," explains Professor Austin F. Macdonald, "that state supremacy will be exercised only with regard to matters
of state-wide concern, and that in local affairs authority will rest with each
community." [2]   But what are purely local affairs?   And is a matter once
conceded to be one of purely local significance to remain forever in that classification?   It is not easy to draw the line between subjects appropriate for
local control and those best suited for state action, and the picture does
change.   Legislatures and courts have tended to guard state powers jealously,
to give restrictive interpretations of what the home rule cities may do.   The
home rule principle is, therefore, from the standpoint of the cities, often withheld or unduly limited in practice.[3]

Its content.   By whatever method the charter may be acquired, it provides for the government of the city and the conduct of its business, usually
in great detail.   It creates the municipal corporation (the city as a legal
entity); provides for the framework of government; names the officials,
the manner in which they shall be chosen, the length of their terms, and
similar details; outlines the powers of the corporation and of its various
officers; prescribes the method for letting contracts; lays down the rules
to be observed in city finance; elaborates a municipal employment system;
and makes detailed stipulations on scores of other subjects.   The charter
of any one of several of the larger cities fills a sizable volume.   An important point to be noted is that the city has no powers except those delegated

[2] *Op. cit.,* p. 86.   See also Rodney L. Mott, *Home Rule for American Cities* (1949).
[3] For restrictions imposed by the West Virginia legislature, see H. J. Shamberger, "Home
Rule Still a Farce," *Nat. Mun. Rev.* Nov. 1954, p. 523.

by state authority and found chiefly in the charter. Unlike the powers delegated to the national government in the federal Constitution, which are construed liberally by the federal courts, powers enumerated in the city charter are construed strictly by state judicial authority.

TYPES OF STATE CONTROL. Cities are controlled by the state, although the amount of state "interference and obstruction" in city affairs varies in accordance with constitutional provisions affecting local government, the nature of the city charters, the composition of legislatures, and the attitude of the courts. This state control was formerly exercised almost exclusively by the legislatures, and it is still very largely in the hands of those bodies. Not only must the city look to the legislature for its authority but also, in a number of states, it must go to a legislature in which the rural communities have a majority of the representatives, although they have less than a majority of the population. This unequal representation exists because, as was explained in Chapter 5, the rural areas once had a large majority of the population and because their representatives, using their initial advantages, have refused to grant the cities their fair quota of representatives. This struggle of the city against the legislature is nowhere better illustrated than in Illinois.[4] The City of Chicago bitterly protests against this discrimination, and it frequently raises the complaint that the legislature will not grant it the authority necessary to conduct its local affairs. In 1925 the Chicago Council unanimously passed a resolution of secession from the state! This bizarre gesture is indicative of the city reaction against rural-state domination.

Legislative control of cities may not always mean unfriendly control, but it commonly means inflexible control. Laws are made applicable to all cities, or to cities in certain classes, without allowance for the special requirements of particular cities. Yet, if we are to have legislative control, it seems best to exercise it in this manner, for legislative acts for individual cities would produce a train of abuses, as they did before special legislation was prohibited.

Another type of control, administrative control, is used extensively in European countries and is growing in our own. The French and, to a lesser extent, the English grant through their central legislative bodies the very widest powers to local government units. But they provide also that these local units in exercising such powers shall be under very close administrative supervision imposed by the central administrative authority. The administrative officers in approving or vetoing a city budget or some proposed municipal undertaking are not limited to the consideration of legality, but they may consider the financial standing of the city, the usefulness of the proposed project, the effect on the surrounding community, and any number of other factors. Clearly the great advantage of administrative control is in its flexibility. It should be equally clear that unless the administrators who exercise this control are well trained, capable, thoroughly honest, and disinterested, the cities will suffer from discriminations and arbitrary acts

4 Kneier, *op. cit.,* pp. 116 ff.

to a number and degree beyond the capacity of an ordinary state legislature to impose. The European countries have been fairly successful in developing administrators who possess the necessary qualities.

There is not a great deal of state administrative control over cities in the United States, but there is a decided trend in that direction, particularly in the fields of education, health, public welfare, and finance. Since 1919 an Indiana law has authorized ten taxpayers to petition the State Board of Tax Commissioners to review either a local tax levy or a local bond issue proposal. The taxpayers have not failed to exercise the privileges conferred, nor has the State Board hesitated to order local authorities to make substantial reductions. North Carolina has taken what is commonly regarded as an extreme step. In 1931 it established a Local Government Commission composed of three state officers *ex officio* and six citizens appointed by the governor. The Commission is authorized to consider local bond issues from such angles as necessity, adequacy, their effect on the tax situation, and the condition of sinking funds. An issue of bonds not approved by the Commission may, however, be made with the approval of the voters. The state authority exercises a close supervision over the investment of sinking funds, and acts as virtual receiver over any unit of government that defaults on its bonds.[5] State grants-in-aid are very common now, and wherever there are such grants there are accompanying arrangements for state supervision.

Federal-city Relations

Prior to 1933 the cities had only a very few associations with the federal government. Such relationships were utterly informal and consisted largely of information the federal government made available through its Office of Education, the Public Health Service, the Bureau of the Census, and other agencies. A more direct association that runs back to the 'twenties is that of the FBI and the municipal police. It was the Great Depression, however, that brought the federal and city governments into direct and significant contact. The public works program called for federal grants to states, *cities,* and other public bodies. Formerly, the federal government prohibited any use of its highway grants to the states for the purpose of constructing city streets, but during the depression it made the requirement that a fourth of the emergency highway grant must be used for streets. In 1935 WPA advanced large sums to the cities for the purpose of putting the unemployed to work on athletic fields, parks, streets, and other construction jobs. During the same distressing period, Congress came to the relief of the financially embarassed cities with the Municipal Bankruptcy Act.[6]

During the Second World War cities co-operated with the federal Office of Civilian Defense, accepting loans of equipment and federal civilian defense rules along with it. In the same years cities swollen in population by war industries were given federal aid for housing and essential municipal services.

[5] W. B. Graves, *American State Government* (1953 ed.), p. 798.
[6] See page 22 and Johnson, *American National Government* (1955 ed.), p. 510.

Since the war cities have continued to receive federal assistance for the clearance of slum areas. Of the current large federal appropriations for highways, substantial shares go for construction in the cities, and hundreds of municipal airports have been and are being constructed under a federal-aid-to-the-cities plan. Now that the national authorities and the cities have found each other there is no likelihood that they will ever be completely separated.[7] Co-operation is an advantage to both. The process does not remove the cities from the legal control of the states, but it is almost certain to weaken the influence of the states with the cities. It would appear, however, that if such functions as slum clearance, airport construction, and civilian defense can better be performed by direct federal-city arrangements, there would be no valid objection to them because they might in some measure change the state-city relationships.

The Conventional Form of City Government

The form of city government that brought us through the nineteenth century is the mayor-council plan. It is modeled largely after the structure of the national and state governments, emphasizing the separation of legislative and executive powers. Indeed, the cities followed these models even to the extent of establishing bicameral councils, although these have now been abandoned in every city in favor of the single chamber. Following the states again, the cities at first gave their chief executive officers few powers, but the trend for many years has been in the direction of strengthening the position of mayor. Since 1900 the mayor-council plan of city government has been challenged, first by the commission plan and later by the council-manager plan. Yet the mayor-council system, the only system our grandfathers knew, remains the leading type of municipal government. Nearly half the cities of over 30,000 population still employ it in varying forms.

Authorities on municipal government commonly differentiate between "weak mayor" and "strong mayor" types of mayor-council government. In the former type the department heads as well as the mayor are commonly elective and there are various administrative boards elected or appointed for overlapping terms. Such a system lacks the unity that is necessary for successful administration. Consequently it is generally considered entirely inadequate for modern needs. Many cities have gone over to the strong mayor type of government. This system ordinarily gives the mayor the authority to veto acts of the council, appoint and remove department heads, prepare the budget for presentation to the council, and administer the budget after it has been approved. Students of city government prefer this type above any other except the council-manager plan. We should add that there is no clear line of distinction between strong and weak mayor city governments, for there are variations from strong "strong mayor" to weak "weak mayor" among the several thousand mayor-council cities.[8] There is no diffi-

[7] See *Municipal Year Book* for recent developments.
[8] National Municipal League, *Forms of Municipal Government* (pamphlet, 1951).

culty, however, in identifying the cities that stand at either end of the scale, there being very general agreement, for example, that Cleveland, Detroit, and, since 1954, New Orleans (see chart on pages 260–261) are among the cities in which the mayor is definitely the responsible head of the city administration. In the paragraphs that follow we shall give a composite picture of the mayor-council system, placing the emphasis upon the strong mayor type of organization.

THE COUNCIL. The council formerly exercised practically all the powers of city government. It still has the commanding place in the weak mayor cities, but it has rather steadily lost power to the mayor in the others. It is always elected by the people, commonly for a period of two years. Usually councilmen are chosen by wards, sometimes at large, and in a few instances by a combination method. Councils vary a great deal in size (not necessarily in accordance with the size of cities); but the tendency is to make them small, fifteen or twenty councilmen being considered sufficient in most cities. A few of the large cities pay councilmen fair salaries; usually they receive very little. Councils meet as often as necessary—weekly or fortnightly meetings being most common. They organize and proceed very much as do state legislatures, relying upon standing committees for the greater part of the routine work.

The powers of the councils vary with charters and state laws, but every council has some legislative and administrative authority. Councils in general may pass ordinances (laws) on such subjects as the following: the structure of city government, as far as the charter and general state law leave it unprescribed; street traffic, sanitation, health, fire prevention, and numerous other matters that fall under the broad "police" power of the city; revenue, appropriations, and other problems of city finance, always subject, of course, to limitations imposed by the state; the granting of franchises to streetcar and bus companies and other public utilities, again under strict limitations prescribed by state law; and the management of city property. On the administrative side the council has few powers, except in the weak mayor cities. Councils still make appointments to some offices, but appointments are usually made by the mayor subject to the approval of the council. In the strong mayor cities offices are filled by the mayor alone. However small the council's legal part in appointments may be, there are many individual members who by devious means and indefatigable efforts secure places for their friends and supporters in the city's vineyard.

THE MAYOR. A century ago the mayor was chiefly a figurehead and the council had the power, but the success of mayors in handling affairs as compared with the councils' mediocre achievements and the rapid growth of administrative functions, particularly in the past fifty years, have placed the mayor in the ascendancy in most cities. He is elected by the people; usually serves a two-year term, although the four-year term is growing in favor; receives a substantial salary in the larger cities—not infrequently more than the governor of his state. Although some mayors have been conspicuous playboys, jokes, crooks, or frauds, the greater number of them are of higher caliber than councilmen. A few mayors have gone on to high national office; but for one reason or another, mayors commonly do not seek, or at least fail to find, the favor of the voters outside the cities.

His powers. The mayor is the official head of the city. He handles communications between the city and outside governing authorities, issues proclamations, receives delegations, entertains distinguished visitors, and represents the city in other formal matters. He is the city's chief administrator, being charged with the very broad duty (usually without adequate powers in the weak mayor cities) of directing the various administrative units that perform the numerous services for the urban population. As already stated, he usually has a wide appointing power, commonly and sometimes unfortunately shared with the council.

The preparation of a budget was formerly considered a legislative matter, but the strong mayor cities now pass this responsibility to the mayor and other executive officers. The financial program for revenues and expenditures prepared by the mayor and his staff is submitted to the council, which may both strike out and reduce items; but in a growing number of cities the council is not permitted to vote increases over the mayor's recommendations. This restriction as to increases in the budget is singularly effective in preventing wasteful, "pork barrel" appropriations.

Just as the President and the governor, the mayor may recommend legislation to the co-ordinate governing body, the council, and often bring about its passage through his political influence and through a judicious use of the patronage. Following the national and state practice, the mayor is usually given the power to veto ordinances of the city council, a power that he uses frequently for good or ill, depending upon his qualifications and temperament. His veto is seldom overridden by the council, a two-thirds majority being commonly required for that purpose.

GROWTH OF CITY FUNCTIONS. The council, the mayor, a few constables, some volunteer firemen, and perhaps a few other public-spirited individuals, were able to carry on the affairs of a city a hundred years ago; for in those days the city authorities were expected to do little besides pass an occasional ordinance, preserve the peace, keep the streets (often just dirt roads) passable, and make some crude efforts in the direction of sanitation. Now this is all changed. Large cities provide a hundred, or even two hundred services —libraries, schools, museums, playgrounds, bathing beaches, swimming pools, dispensaries, tuberculosis camps, and so on. Services have grown because the cities have grown, because science has made new services possible, and because the people demand them. The annual cost of these functions in any one of our largest cities runs into several hundred million dollars.

ADMINISTRATIVE STRUCTURE. Manifestly the work of the city can no longer be performed by the mayor and the council. The council serves as a board of directors, and the mayor is the general manager, or should be. The work is done through an elaborate administrative organization employing, in large cities, thousands of individuals. Functions are distributed among departments—five, ten, twenty, or more—as in the national and state systems. Departments are headed by single officials or boards, the former being preferred for most departments, the latter being used almost invariably for such services as schools, libraries, and recreation. The department heads are appointed by the mayor in the strong mayor cities: in others they may be elected or appointed, the practice varying among the cities and departments of the same city. Sometimes the mayor can control them and sometimes his authority is only nominal, his power depending upon the nature of the administrative structure and upon the mayor himself. Within each department there are as many bureaus, divisions, and sections as the several services of a department demand. These subdivisions are headed by officials who are commonly responsible to their immediate superiors. In a strong mayor system the lines of responsibility run from subordinate to superior until they all finally reach the mayor, who is in a general way responsible to the people.

Newer Forms of City Government

Undisturbed for a century and a half was the American's devotion to the check and balance theory of government. The division of authority between executive and legislative branches, with all the attendant bickerings, recriminations, deadlocks, and stalemates, the average citizen regarded as the Palladium of his liberties. Even the "practical, hard-headed" business man pinned his political salvation to it, and many of them who scorn the systems of advertising in vogue a generation ago still glow with satisfaction at the mention of this check and balance device of the Fathers. Possibly the mayor-council division in the cities would have continued unchallenged to this day but for two catastrophes. One befell the city of Galveston and brought forth the Commission plan of city government, and the other befell the city of Dayton and in turn brought forth the Manager plan. To be sure, both plans had been used earlier in other cities, but the dramatic introduction to these new devices in these cities gave them popularity.

THE COMMISSION PLAN: *Launched at Galveston.* In the late summer of 1900 a huge tidal wave, driven by a wind of terrific velocity, drowned some seven thousand citizens of Galveston and destroyed property to the value of millions. For years the government of that city had stood as a match in corruption and inefficiency for any municipal government in America. The tidal wave did not wash it away, but it did result in its displacement. Continuing their old course and grossly negligent in dealing with the emergency, the city government found a number of its functions taken over by the Deepwater Commission, previously formed to promote harbor interests. This Commission asked a few of the city's leading lawyers to draft a new charter. Their charter, approved by the legislature, provided for a government by a commission of five, to whom was delegated all municipal authority. The best citizens were willing to present themselves to the electorate for the office of commissioner and they were elected. The old political organization went into hiding. Soon the city was a model in public improvements and in financial management. Special reporters were sent to Galveston; magazine articles were written about it; and the Galveston Plan became the talk of reformers and serious students of public affairs the country over.

What was the Galveston Plan? It was a plan very similar to those used in the boroughs of colonial America and in Sacramento, New Orleans, and a few other cities shortly after the Civil War. It provided that all legislative, executive, and administrative power should be vested in a single commission of five men. One of the commissioners was designated Mayor-President, but "Mr. Mayor-President" was simply the chairman of the Commission, the titleholder, neither enjoying the honors nor carrying the duties commonly associated with either side of his rather pretentious title. As a group, the commissioners passed ordinances and performed all other duties related to general policy. As individuals, each supervised the work of a city department, the actual administration of the departments being left to an officer with the proper technical qualifications. Here was in operation a plan of city government, enthusiastically acclaimed, that boldly set aside the traditional separation of powers.

The Des Moines refinements. Although the Galveston experiment was admittedly a success, the rank and file of Americans hesitated to advocate it for general use. They were concerned about a five-man government with no "checks and balances," fearful of a government that might proceed quickly to an objective. The plan therefore spread slowly until Des Moines (1907) erected safeguards against the commission. The Des Moines Plan simply superimposed upon the earlier plan certain democratic institutions already in use—the recall, the initiative, and the referendum. Here were the checks against possible arbitrary authority.

The Des Moines Plan spread rapidly, receiving modifications as it spread. During the ten years following the action at Des Moines nearly every state authorized the use of the new system in some form or other, and about five hundred cities adopted it. Since 1917 very few cities have installed the commission system. Some cities have gone back to the mayor-council system; a larger number have abandoned the commission plan for the newer manager type of city government. In 1949 even Des Moines voted to shift to the manager plan, and in 1954 New Orleans abandoned commission government for the strong mayor type. Today the commission system is fast losing ground, although it is still in use in many small cities and a few larger ones, including Newark and Portland, Oregon.

Defects of the commission plan. There are good reasons for the decline in the use of the commission form of city government. The fusion of administrative functions and policy-making functions is contrary to American traditions and does not work well. Administrative work requires one type of man and policy-making another. Seldom are the two qualities found in the same individual. The absence of a responsible chief executive is particularly to be deplored. The multiple executive system provides for no brake on the activities of the departments, no co-ordination. It makes no one responsible for the over-all view and general supervision. It establishes no one authority to whom the voters can go with their troubles and complaints. In a sense, there is not just one city administration, but five, or as many as there are commissioners.

The commissioners vote *and* spend the appropriations. No administrative officer has the responsibility of keeping the budget within reasonable limits. Each department prepares its own estimates and, wanting them to be approved, goes along with the other departments on their budget requests. Each department may thus build up its own "empire." This is not to say that every commission city is poorly governed, but only that the system itself has serious defects, easily lends itself to waste and inefficiency. Good government is possible under almost any system if those responsible for its operation are capable and devoted to the public interest.

In 1949 a body of distinguished citizens and experts in New Jersey made a study of that state's municipal government, including the government of 59 commission cities. After noting the weaknesses of the commission system substantially as indicated above, the report of this body stated that "the commission form has proved to be a transition device. It was an immediate, more or less accidental, answer to the overcomplicated check and balance system of the nineteenth century with bicameral municipal legislatures, weak mayors, and numerous separately elected officials and boards. Subsequent experience has demonstrated that it was, however, by no means a completely satisfactory or final answer." [9] During the last thirty years, cities seeking to improve their system of government have commonly turned, not to the commission, but to the council-manager plan.

THE COUNCIL-MANAGER PLAN: *Its origin.* In 1908 Staunton, a city in the Shenandoah Valley of Virginia, installed the first city manager plan, as it was called. Three years later, Lockport (N.Y.) presented to the legislature a draft of a charter embracing the manager system and asked that cities below 50,000 population be authorized to adopt it. The legislature did not act upon the suggestion, but the Lockport Plan was widely advertised. The next year (1912) several small cities in North Carolina and South Carolina adopted the city manager plan. While the Lockport Plan was receiving wide publicity, a committee in Dayton, Ohio, was busy studying charters. It recommended the city manager type of charter. Under the new home rule amendment to the state constitution a city could have a charter of its own selection. Consequently, a large committee was appointed to push the campaign for a popular vote on the manager plan. While the campaign was in progress, a devastating flood hit the city. A few months later the people voted for the manager plan. No doubt the flood had something to do with the popular vote on the question, but, coming as it did with the move-

[9] National Municipal League, *op. cit.*, pp. 8–9.

ment for the new charter, it probably had more to do with advertising the new city manager plan than with the favorable vote the plan received in Dayton.

Its growth. The new plan spread rapidly from the time (1913) Dayton adopted it. It has maintained a steady growth to date, having, in 1954, about 1,200 cities operating under it. In about six cases out of seven the cities adopted a manager charter; in the others they simply installed it by ordinance. The latter procedure is commonly frowned upon because momentary dissatisfaction might lead to the repeal of the ordinance before the plan has had an opportunity to justify itself. Not only have adoptions grown steadily, but the friends of the system have found great encouragement in two other facts. It has been adopted by a number of the larger cities, by about one fifth of those with a population of over 100,000. The second encouraging fact is that it has been abandoned by few cities—about 30. Most of the backsliders were small cities, and half of them dropped the plan during the depression when whatever government that happened to be functioning was subject to attacks. Cleveland abandoned it in 1931, but the reasons were primarily political, having little relation to the merits of the manager system. It can be said, then, that the council-manager plan is still spreading and that it has demonstrated its suitability for medium-sized cities, such as Cincinnati, Dayton, Oakland, and Rochester. It remains to be tried in the very largest cities.

Its principal features. The council-manager form of government is a logical development from the commission form. Indeed considerable evidence indicates that the earliest designers of the manager system thought they were simply improving the existing commission plan. That improvement was in the concentration of executive authority in the hands of one man. The manager plan, as it was soon developed and as it stands today, passing over certain variations, provides for a small council of three, five, or seven members, who are elected at large on a nonpartisan ticket. This council has all the ordinance-making power, and it elects and removes the manager. The manager need not be, and usually is not, a resident of the city at the time of his appointment. This is a very fine feature of the plan, for it enables the council to pick the best man available and it makes possible a managership profession.

The manager is the chief administrator in every sense of the word. He appoints all administrative officers and employees; he directs their work; and he promotes the industrious and capable and removes the inefficient. This ideal is not always attained, for in some cities a few elective officers remain and in others the council has a share, official or unofficial, in naming administrative officers. The manager is charged with the duty of keeping the council informed of the "state of the city" and of recommending to its consideration such measures as he shall deem necessary and expedient. It should be observed that nearly all of the cities with the manager plan continue the office of mayor, leaving that official the duty of presiding over the council and the pleasant ceremonial functions that commonly go with the office of mayor. The manager is thus left free for the real work of administration.

Manager and council. The council formulates and adopts policies, often upon the recommendation of the manager; the manager's duty is to see that the policies are executed, even if he does not approve of some of them. In some cases the council has paid little attention to the recommendations of the manager, and the manager usually interprets this situation to mean that he lacks the council's confidence and resigns. On occasion the council has interfered with the details of administration. This interference violates a basic principle of the plan, that the manager be unhampered in directing administration. It may indicate only a lack of confidence in a particular manager; but if it is chronic with the council, the manager plan will eventually fail.

When the plan is operating on a normal basis, the council commonly takes the advice of the manager on administrative matters and frequently follows his lead on questions of policy. This procedure is proper, for the manager is a trained professional giving all his time to his work and the councilmen are properly amateurs. Yet the council should never become a rubber stamp for the manager, certainly not on questions of policy. On what parks the city should lay out, what zoning ordinances it should enact, what hospitals should be erected, what streets should be opened up, and on other matters relating to plans and projects the council should hear the manager, but the decisions should be based upon the independent judgment of the council, the elected representatives of the people.

Under the mayor-council government the people are represented by both arms of the government. Under the manager-council type they are represented only by the council. It is important, therefore, that under the latter type of government, the council take its responsibilities seriously. If, as sometimes happens, the people look to the manager rather than to the council as the responsible authority on matters of city policy, that situation usually presages the beginning of the end of the manager system of government and almost certainly foreshadows the end of the career of a particular manager in a given city. The manager is on safe ground in urging the council to adopt a policy, but definitely overstepping the bounds if he should publicly advocate a policy before the council has approved it. But once the council has adopted a policy, the manager may support it publicly, unless, perchance, it should become an issue in the election of councilmen. In short, a manager may not only be a guide to the council but he may also be a discreet community leader.[10]

Managership as a profession. Despite the fact that some managers have become involved in politics, sometimes because the local situation made it

---

[10] This is the view of the managers' function as expressed by Charles E. Ridley, Director of the City Managers' Association (letter to the author, Oct. 31, 1949). A similar view is held by C. A. Harrell, manager of Norfolk, Va. See his "The City Manager as a Community Leader," *Public Management,* Oct., 1948, p. 290.

HARTFORD'S CITY GOVERNMENT

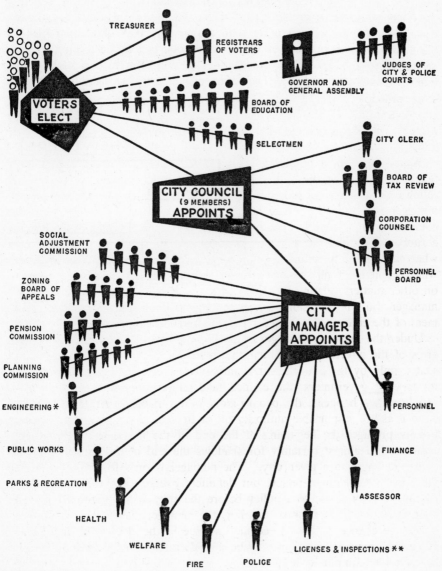

* City Engineer is also a member of Planning Commission.
** Being created by combining offices of Building Inspection and Weights & Measures.

From the *Annual Report of the City of Hartford, 1948–1949*, p. 6.

inevitable and sometimes because the managers made the mistake of assuming a political rôle, managership is a profession.[11]   This status it must maintain if the council-manager plan is to be a continued success. Some of the evidences of the professional status of managership may be briefly indicated: (1) The salaries paid are such as to make the position of manager attractive. Managers are paid much more than mayors in cities of comparable size. Managers of cities between 50,000 and 100,000 population receive a median salary of over $13,000; mayors of cities in that class receive slightly more than half that amount. (2) The tenure of managers has steadily lengthened.

ORGANIZATION OF NEW ORLEANS' NEW (STRONG-MAYOR) FORM OF GOVERNMENT

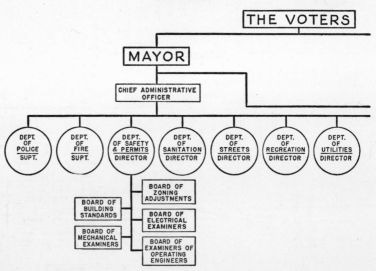

Adapted from the *Annual Report of the Mayor of New Orleans, 1953–1954*, pp. 2–3.

In 1921 it was two years; at present it is four years. (3) Successful managers are often promoted—offered positions in cities that pay higher salaries. This form of recognition was infrequent during the early years of the plan; now it is not at all uncommon. (4) The managers have developed a professional spirit. A City Managers' Association was formed in 1914, an association that has steadily grown in importance and that has, among other things, produced a code of ethics for managers. (5) In keeping with these developments, an interest in training managers has become very pronounced. The Managers' Association has given attention to this problem, and several educational institutions have outlined courses of training for those who hope to enter the profession. It may be said that the preparation generally considered desirable emphasizes engineering, public finance, accounting, munici-

11 For significant facts and figures on the manager, see "An Analysis of City Managers," *Public Management*, Jan., 1954, pp. 5–9 and *Municipal Year Book*, 1954, pp. 163–165, 529 ff.

pal administration, and city-planning. Of course, a manager must be an executive, but there is some question as to what courses, if any, train one to be an executive. An essential feature of any such training should be a period of "internship" in a managers' office. Efforts have been made to provide for this, but not many managers will or can make room for an "apprentice," or "intern."

The council-manager plan has not taken hold in cities with populations above half a million. Some of these cities, however, are following a promising development that associates with the mayor a chief administrative officer who is responsible for the bulk of the managerial work, thus leaving the mayor free to devote himself to his duties as high policy planner and strategist (see accompanying chart of the government of New Orleans).[12]

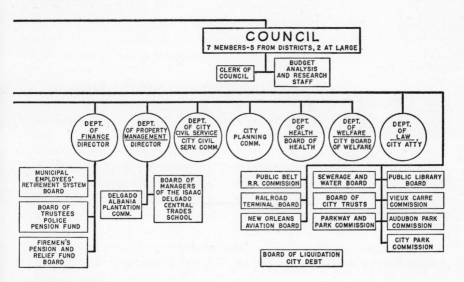

The Problem of Metropolitan Areas

Simultaneously with the growth of our great cities, the small cities and villages that were formerly some miles removed from them have extended their own boundaries until they are contiguous with those of the hub cities. New York, Chicago, and several other municipal leviathans are partially surrounded by satellite cities. A great metropolitan area thus formed is physically, and to a large extent, economically and socially, a single urban unit; but governmentally the area is composed of a number of separate corporations.

Some years ago legal consolidation of surrounding cities with the greater city was quite common and the results were reasonably satisfactory; but

[12] On the council-manager plan, see E. S. Griffith, *Current Municipal Problems* (1933); C. E. Ridley and O. F. Nolting, *The City-Manager Profession* (1934); C. P. Taft, *City Management: The Cincinnati Experiment* (1933); *Public Management*, published monthly by the International City Managers' Association; and Wallace S. Sayre, "The General Manager Idea for Large Cities," *Pub. Adm. Rev.*, XIV (1954), 253.

the newer communities, because of the likelihood of a higher tax rate, a feeling of social superiority, or for other reasons, seem less inclined to be annexed now than a generation ago. Yet it seems fair to assume that fire and police protection, water supply, sanitation—in fact, that practically every important municipal function—could be more economically and more efficiently administered by one government than by half a dozen. Unity of action in certain functions is sometimes secured by the creation of special districts. Thus, thirteen cities of Southern California are included in a single district for water supply; and a sanitary district takes care of sewage disposal for the Chicago metropolitan area.[13] But the consolidation of a particular function of several contiguous cities is only a piece-meal method of attaining the desired administrative entity for metropolitan areas. It is a step in the right direction, but leaves too many functions to be independently administered by the authorities of the separate cities.

CITY-COUNTY CONSOLIDATION. The city area is ordinarily a part of the territory of the county. County officers have authority in its urban as well as in its rural sections. Since county and city governments have some identical functions, their jurisdictions in respect to these functions overlap. For example, the sheriff and the other law enforcement officers of the county may legally act in the city, despite the fact that the city has its own police officers. In actual practice the county enforcement officers usually confine their activities to the rural districts. Moreover, legal provision is sometimes made to give city authorities practically exclusive control within the city. This exclusive authority often appears in the domains of education and welfare administration. Nevertheless, there is still too much duplication and confusion resulting from the overlapping authority of city and county officers.

A few states have attempted to correct these conditions by city-county consolidation. The city and county of Philadelphia were practically consolidated in 1854, although the county officers still have certain functions. San Francisco, Baltimore, St. Louis, and Denver are detached from counties and have governments independent of them. In Virginia all cities are closed to county authorities, the cities administering both municipal and county functions. Some other examples might be given, but the progress of such consolidations is slow. Rural communities frequently oppose a city-county consolidation because it means to them an increase in taxes, and they oppose the detachment of the cities from the counties because it means a heavy loss in taxable property. The opposition is logical enough in both cases.

THE POSSIBILITY OF "REGIONS." Even if counties and cities have the constitutional authority to consolidate or separate, and vote to do one or the other, the problem of the metropolitan area is left unsettled in many regions. This disorganized condition exists because an urban area may extend into several counties or into several states. The problem then be-

[13] Kneier, *op. cit.*, pp. 361–362.

comes very complex. To meet this situation, a number of students of the metropolitan area are now recommending a new political unit to be called the "region." [14] This unit would be given the authority to deal with such matters as sanitation, health, transportation, and planning for all areas of government within a designated metropolitan community. There is much to be said for the proposal, but before such a plan can be put into operation the electorate, the state legislatures, and Congress (to approve interstate compacts) must be converted to it. To be sure, as indicated above, government units in certain regions have united upon specific functions—water in the southern California area and sewage disposal in the Chicago area. The Boston region has a number of authorities whose jurisdiction extends over that metropolitan district. The Port of New York Authority, a shining example of regional co-operation, was established by compact between New York and New Jersey with the approval of Congress. Yet the big job remains to be done—the job of organizing the metropolitan region to exercise authority in all matters of common interest in the area.

II. CITY ADMINISTRATIVE SERVICES [15]

City administrative functions include zoning, police protection, fire fighting and fire prevention, traffic regulation, health services, and several others. We shall limit ourselves to consideration of police, fire, and health services.

The Police System

DEVELOPMENT OF THE POLICE SYSTEM. The great cities of the ancient world had fairly adequate police protection, but its almost complete absence in the medieval cities was one of the principal reasons why life in them was precarious. Indeed, the same lack of protection made the day unsafe and the night hideous in English cities until well into modern times. The only guardians of the law were the residents, who took turns walking the unlighted streets, perhaps whistling in futile attempts to hide their fear. Substantial citizens busy with their private affairs hired loafers and disabled men to take their turn as watchmen. In London, bellmen were chosen to supplement the watchmen, but they proved no more efficient. Both were the common subjects of jests, and rowdies often made them the victims of rough

---

[14] On the general subject of the metropolitan area, see Victor Jones, *Metropolitan Government* (1942); Macdonald, *op. cit.,* Ch. 7; C. E. Merriam, S. D. Parratt, and Albert Lepawsky, *The Government of the Metropolitan Region of Chicago* (1933); Mary F. Parton, *Metropolis: A Study of New York* (1939); Coleman Woodbury (ed.), *The Future of Cities and Urban Development* (1953).

[15] American Public Health Association, *Standards of Healthful Housing: Planning the Neighborhood* (1948); A. W. Bromage, *Introduction to Municipal Government and Administration* (1950), Chs. 24–31; I. V. Hiscock (ed.), *Community Health Organization* (1950 ed.); International City Managers' Association, *Municipal Police Administration* (1943) and *Municipal Fire Administration* (1946); V. A. Leonard, *Police Organization and Management* (1951); J. J. McCarthy, *The Science of Fighting Fire* (1943); Macdonald, *op. cit.,* Chs. 21–29; Bruce Smith, *Police Systems in the United States* (1949 ed.); W. G. Smillie, *Public Health Administration in the United States* (1947 ed.).

practical jokes. Crime flourished to such a degree that the London gentleman who had to be abroad at night took a guard with him. All this went on until 1839, when Robert Peel, the Home Secretary in the British Cabinet, persuaded Parliament to create a professional police system. Hooted and jeered, occasionally violently assaulted, early policemen did not have a pleasant life, but it was not long until the high character of their work earned them the respect, even the affection, of the public.

Until after the middle of the nineteenth century American cities attempted to preserve order in the old English way, and with as little success. A group of students, having taken their examinations and "out to make an evening of it," might conclude the celebrations by beating up "the watch." A legislative investigation of conditions in New York City led to the adoption, in 1844, of a police system patterned after the new British model. As the New York force soon displayed greater energy in suppressing crime than the unorganized and undisciplined peace officers had shown, in the course of a few years practically all the larger cities followed the new model.

MODERN POLICE ORGANIZATION. The police in a few of the large cities are under state control. This arrangement is not unreasonable, since the policemen are engaged chiefly in enforcing state laws. But the cities bear the cost, and they usually resent state "interference" in their affairs. Consequently, municipal authorities are allowed to direct the police in nearly all cities. In many large cities a board or a single commissioner has general charge of the city's police. The commissioner method, because it offers less opportunity for political manipulations and provides full-time service and unity of command, is commonly employed. Commissioners are rarely appointed from the force, men of broader experience and more general qualifications being preferred. Often, however, they are just politicians. Lawyers, doctors, real estate men, barbers, bankers, undertakers, and others are appointed to the post in rapid succession, two years being about the average tenure. The board or commissioner is charged with the broad duties of determining policy and organizing and managing the police force. In some cities the chief administrators must be guided by civil service rules in such matters as making appointments and promotions.

In immediate command of the police force is a chief of police, commonly selected from the force. Smaller cities usually do not feel the need of both commissioner and chief, and, in consequence, they frequently combine the functions of both officers in that of the chief of police. Attached to the headquarters of the chief are various inspectors, sergeants, and patrolmen. Stationed in precincts or districts are captains, with their lieutenants, sergeants, and patrolmen, each captain being a sort of chief in his district but very definitely responsible to the big chief at the central station. Large cities usually have intermediate units, divisions, one for every four or five precincts. The chief officer of a division is usually known as "inspector."

Police training. Formerly it was thought the policemen needed no special training. It was believed that physical strength and common sense, backed up by a club, a gun, and a pocket manual, made a patrolman. One commissioner explained how he fitted a man for the task: "I say to him that now he is a policeman, and I hope he will be a credit to the force. I tell him that he doesn't need anybody to tell him how to enforce the law; that all he needs to do is to go out on the street and keep his eyes open. I say 'You know the Ten Commandments, don't you? Well, if you know the Ten Commandments and you go out on your beat and you see somebody violating one of those Commandments, you can be sure that he is also violating some law.' " [16] Such grossly inadequate "training" gives us policemen as unprepared for ordinary patrol duty as the commissioner who gave it.

Years ago the Europeans learned that policemen should be trained, and they provided facilities for such training; but only in the past thirty years have American cities responded to this crying need. Many cities still leave their officers to follow their common sense and the Ten Commandments, although some of these easy-going municipalities select their men under civil service rules. Other cities not discounting the importance of common sense or a knowledge of the Commandments, select their recruits by competitive examinations, and then give them instruction in police powers and duties, elementary law, rules of evidence, legal procedure, first aid, the handling of prisoners, criminal identification, report writing, and other subjects. The comprehensive three-year curriculum for police officers at Berkeley, California, has attracted wide attention, and it is commonly rated as among the best in the country, certainly as one of the few in-service curricula that represents a broad conception of desirable qualities in a police officer and an ambitious program to develop them.

But the best in-service training may fail to provide the best possible police officers. Modern police problems are so varied, so complicated, and the knowledge that can be brought to their solution so woven into the total fabric of our society that education in the arts and sciences no less than training in specific skills is now often recommended for future police officers. At least eight colleges and universities [17] now recognize this need to the extent that they offer degree programs in police science and administration.

Police duties. As the private soldier does the fighting for an army, so the patrolman is the principal law enforcer for the police department. He is on active duty eight hours a day, on reserve for another eight hours, and free the remaining time. On duty he may walk or use a motorcycle or an automobile, his means of transportation depending upon the character and length of his beat. He must cover his patrol within a certain designated time, keep his eyes open for violations of law, give particular attention to suspicious characters and disreputable places, and make arrests when necessary. Often a law is violated in such a trivial manner that an official

[16] Quoted in Macdonald, *op. cit.,* p. 503 from *Report of the Sub-Committee on Police to the Crime Commission of New York State,* p. 27.

[17] Including the University of California, the University of Southern California, Indiana University, and the State College of Washington. See Leonard, *op. cit.,* pp. 151–158.

warning accompanied by a smile is sufficient; another infraction may be of such a nature as to call for a stern reprimand; a third may be properly dealt with only by a prompt arrest. The patrolman is therefore a walking judge, handing out decisions in very minor cases and determining what cases are sufficiently grave to warrant regular legal prosecution. The patrolman must also serve as a sort of information bureau, report accidents, and carry out any special orders of his superiors. In recent years traffic regulation has become a special police problem. Bells, lights, "one-way streets," and "no U turns" all help; but personal supervision is necessary. Patrolmen are detailed from the regular force for this work, often after special training for it. To the average citizen the traffic officer is now a more familiar figure than the patrolman.

Major crimes are commonly committed by experts, organized experts. The trails they leave can be followed only by officers of the law whose skill at detection is equal to the professional criminals' art of concealment. Patrolmen who seem to have an aptitude for this highly scientific work of investigation and detection are sometimes detailed for it, but the selection of the detective force by special civil service tests should give a better qualified personnel. The latter method is now used in a number of cities. Whatever the method of selection may be, the necessity for special training for this service is now generally recognized. Despite improvement in recent years, we are still behind the great European cities in the type of personnel attracted to the service and, following somewhat logically from this, in the application of science to detection.

CRITICISM OF THE POLICE SYSTEM. The police force of a typical American city is grossly inefficient. Crime flourishes, and few arrests are made. "The American professional criminal," says Professor A. F. Macdonald, "soon learns that his occupation is safe as well as lucrative, provided he takes care to avoid violence." [18] What is the reason for this? In 1931 the National Commission on Law Observance and Enforcement investigated police organization and activities and made an unflattering report, to put it mildly.[19] Many other investigations and studies have been made, among the more significant of the recent ones being those of the Special Senate (Kefauver) Committee to Investigate Organized Crime in Interstate Commerce [20] and the study by a Commission of the American Bar Association on Organized Crime and Law Enforcement.[21] The three investigations or studies mentioned were concerned with a much wider area than the municipal police, but each of their reports contained significant material on policemen and police administration.

The Commission of the Bar Association criticizes the local police systems on the point of organization. For example, the Chicago police department

---

[18] *Op. cit.*, p. 499.
[19] *Report* No. 14, pp. 1–9.
[20] *Senate Reports* 141, 307, 725, 82nd Cong., 1st sess. (1951).
[21] *Report* in two vols. (1952).

has, or has had, nineteen separate units reporting to the police commissioner and the Boston department, twenty-seven. Experts generally agree that effective administrative control is not possible if an official is responsible for more than six or eight units. Related functions should be combined under subordinate officials who alone should report to the chief.[22]

The Commission on Law Observance found that the average tenure of the chief in the great cities was 2.41 years. In cities the country over, the average now seems to be four or five years. Tenure is still short and insecure, and it is largely the result of political appointment and control. There is not much hope for improvement at the top until the more sordid politics, at least, is taken out of this position. The Committee on Law Observance called attention to "the well-known and oft proved alliance between criminals and corrupt politicians which controls, in part, at least, where it does not wholly do so, the police force of our large cities." Twenty years later, the Kefauver Committee came to about the same conclusion. Any such alliance, arrangement, or understanding between the police and the criminals is obviously fatal for law enforcement.

The dismal failure of some enforcement officers to live up to their oath of obligation as public servants is a tragedy for the whole police force and the public. This failure results in part from inadequate character investigation at the time the appointment is made. Such investigations should uncover evidences of dishonesty, unreliability, laziness, failure to discharge financial obligations, addiction to alcohol, bad associations, and so on.[23]

But character, indispensable as it is, is not enough. Training is essential, and training is what the policemen do not get in 90 per cent of the enforcement units in the country. It frequently consists of nothing more than a talk by the chief and assignment with an experienced officer for up to one month. New York City gives a ninety-day recruit course, something that appears to be reasonably adequate. In-service training, training to keep policemen up-to-date, is not common, and where it is given, the "teachers" are often incapable and their "students," naturally enough, bored.[24]

Among the proposals that the Commission of the American Bar Association makes for improving police systems is one relating to the functions of the state. The Commission says the state should provide police training schools, centralized information, and statistical and crime detection services; set standards for police efficiency; inspect local police departments; and perhaps offer grants-in-aid to those departments that meet the state standards. But this Commission and all other authorities are united on the point that the first requirements for improving the police are intelligence and integrity.[25] Laws, regulation, training, and organization all fail in one respect—as substitutes for character.

[22] Commission of the American Bar Association, *Report on Organized Crime and Law Enforcement*, I, 180–181.
[23] *Ibid.*, pp. 185–186.
[24] *Ibid.*, pp. 187–189.
[25] *Ibid.*, pp. 31–33, 203 ff.

Fire Protection

THE IMPORTANCE OF FIRE PREVENTION.   Fire losses in the United States amount to more than a million dollars a day.   Our per capita losses are much higher than those of any European country.   Yet we have the best fire-fighting forces and equipment in the world.   In 1917–1919 our soldiers in France often remarked that medium-sized French cities seemed to have no force or apparatus for fighting fires, whereas in American cities of the same size there was the daily drama of shrieking sirens, roaring motors loaded with equipment and firemen, motorists pulling over, and pedestrians scurrying to places of safety.   Asked to state how much property he had seen destroyed by fire in France, the doughboy often admitted he had seen no fires.   Now the French do have an occasional fire and they do have an organized system of fire fighting; but this is not their major line.   Their efforts are concentrated upon *preventing* the occurrence of fires, rather than in fighting them.   So well does this policy succeed in European countries generally that they have not felt the necessity of developing the fire-fighting art to the point of American efficiency.   They are willing to concede that we are the champion fire fighters of the world.   How do the Europeans prevent fires?   In the first place, lumber is so expensive that few persons want to erect frame buildings.   In the second place, their laws prohibit frame structures in any area where they will constitute a fire menace.   And, in the third place, the use of fire in dwellings and places of business is thoroughly regulated by law.   In recent decades American cities have seen the wisdom of fire prevention.   Although they may still lay disproportionate emphasis upon fire fighting, the matter of prevention has been seriously undertaken.

AMERICAN METHODS OF PREVENTION.   All our large cities have rather elaborate regulations respecting fire prevention, and nearly all other cities have rules more or less suited to their needs.   The rules commonly fix fire limits; that is, areas in which only buildings of a certain fire-resisting type may be constructed.   There is a lot of talk about fireproof buildings, but there is no such building.   There are buildings that will not burn, but no buildings that will not crumble when subjected to high temperatures, temperatures that may be developed by neighboring buildings in conflagration.   Hence, even the so-called fireproof (actually only fire-resisting) buildings are not safe unless all buildings in the same area are constructed of noncombustible materials.   Of course, some flexibility is provided for in the fire-prevention rules.   Buildings such as theaters, in which a fire would likely cause loss of human life, may have no wood materials except for trimmings.   Stores and shops are ordinarily allowed wood floors and partitions, but no other use of timber is permitted.   Still more wood may be allowed in the structure of other buildings.   It should be noted that these ordinances prescribing the type of building materials that may be used are not retroactive—they apply only for buildings to be erected; they do not require the demolition of structures standing at the time such ordinances are passed.

Equal in importance to the rules themselves is their enforcement. A staff of trained inspectors must be provided. Cities have commonly failed to engage a sufficiently large and competent staff. They have not always found honest men. It costs a little more to conform to the building material requirements, and it has been found that inspectors are sometimes lenient in this matter. Contractors who have good standing at the city hall know that the inspectors are not going to bother them overmuch. Then, too, the people who risk their lives in unsafe buildings are not particularly concerned about the enforcement of the fire-prevention ordinances. They are not sufficiently educated on the subject of fire prevention either to demand that fire ordinances be enforced or to refrain from acts of individual carelessness that often cause fires. Perhaps, after all, we Americans enjoy our fires! [26]

THE FIRE DEPARTMENT. Fire fighting will always be necessary; prevention will only lessen the need for it. Until around 1850, American cities relied upon volunteer fire brigades for this function. Boys about town who wanted some excitement or who saw fire fighting as an avenue of approach to politics were quite willing to "run," and they did it very well, although rival companies, arriving at a conflagration about the same time, occasionally fought each other and almost forgot the fire. All cities of any considerable size now have full-time, professional firemen. The chief of the fire department is commonly appointed by the mayor, and the other officers of the department are selected in about the same manner as police officers. The ordinary firemen are usually selected under civil service rules requiring competitive examinations. When appointed, they are given a little training, very little in some cities, and assigned to places as engineers and hosemen. The fire-fighting force, like the police force, is distributed over the city at conveniently located stations, a captain being in charge of each station. It may be of some interest to note here that, although an American city has fewer policemen than a European city of the same size, it has about twice as many firemen, and pays three times as much for fire protection.

Fire-fighting equipment. Cities usually keep their fire-fighting equipment up to date. Horses and steam engines have given way to motors, and ladder trucks now have ladders of the quick-lifting aërial type. Chemical extinguishers are in use everywhere. Heavy streams of water are forced through turret pipes and deluge sets. High pressure systems are installed for the business districts, the pressure sometimes being as much as 300 pounds per square inch and delivering as much as 1,000 or even 1,500 gallons a minute. Smoke helmets and gas masks enable firemen to go where they never went before and come out alive. Pulmotors enable them to resuscitate persons who have been overcome by smoke. Within three minutes after an alarm has sounded, a company is usually at the scene of the fire, a stream is turned

26 Macdonald, *op. cit.,* pp. 513–516.

on, and, says one chief, "in a few minutes the furniture goes floating out of the window." [27]   This remark indicates that in extinguishing a fire more damage may be done than is caused by the fire itself.   Many fire-fighting units do not seem to be concerned about this, but the more progressive ones carry waterproof covers, brooms, mops, and so on, and do systematic salvage work.

PRIVATE FIRE PROTECTION.   Factories, department stores, and other large commercial establishments do not rely solely upon the city for fire protection.   They have their watchmen, who make the rounds and punch clocks to give proof that periodic inspection was actually made.   Mechanical watchmen and fire extinguishers in the form of automatic sprinklers are usually installed, frequently under legal requirement.   These are sealed with a substance that melts when a fire breaks out, thereby releasing the water to deluge the affected area and to sound an alarm attached to the sprinkler-head.   Some years ago it was estimated that private persons and establishments pay about one third as much for fire protection as the cities spend on their fire departments. [28]

Health Services

The cities are now very much alive to their responsibilities respecting the health of their inhabitants.   The states fix the health standards that municipalities must attain, and they ordinarily exercise sufficient control to make sure that the standards are maintained; but many cities go far beyond the standards required by state law and, in addition, include functions not mentioned in the law.

ADMINISTRATIVE ORGANIZATION.   Many cities still have boards of health for general supervisory purposes; but a number of authorities feel that the board of health is unnecessary and sometimes in the way—that, in any case, regular administrative officers, who are quite competent to take over the duties of the board, must be employed.   Whether a city makes use of a board or not, a health officer is in direct charge of the administrative activities.   In large cities the department of health is divided into several divisions or bureaus, each charged with particular functions and having assigned to it the necessary physicians, laboratory experts, inspectors, and other specialists.

FUNCTIONS.   With certain exceptions the work of the city's health forces is similar to that performed by state agencies.   Of course, city authorities have no subordinate agencies to supervise, and they must intensify some activities that do not engage the major attention of state authorities and add a few that concern those authorities only incidentally.   Working in congested areas, city authorities must be most vigilant for communicable diseases, quick to impose quarantines when such diseases are found or reported, and careful to disinfect the premises when an illness has terminated.   Eternal vigilance is one of the prices of a city's pure milk supply.   Used by practically everyone

[27] Quoted in Munro, *Municipal Government and Administration* (1923), Vol. II, p. 254.
[28] *Ibid.*, pp. 255–256.   See also Bromage, *op. cit.*, pp. 544 ff.

and an especially fine food for children, milk and its products are unfortunately very easily subject to contamination and therefore often bring disease and death. Many cities have the most stringent regulations respecting the testing and quality of milk sold to their inhabitants. Samples of milk are constantly being taken from wagons on the streets and tested in laboratories. Inspection of the dairies that ship milk to the city is also a regular proceeding.

The "smoke nuisance" is entirely a city problem. It is not, as a student once told the writer, the problem of preventing individuals from smoking tobacco, but the problem of forcing manufacturers and others maintaining smokestacks belching forth clouds of ugly, dirty smoke, often laden with poisonous gases, to abate the smoke nuisance. Many cities have successfully met the situation by requiring all large users of soft coal to install smoke consumers. Other regulations and activities of city health authorities, being of a character similar to those mentioned under state and county health functions, are omitted from this discussion.[29]

The Health Phases of Other Services

Several services vitally connected with health are administered by other than health departments, or by health and other authorities combined. Among these may be mentioned housing, sanitation, water supply, and recreation. The health phases of these services are fundamental, and they are here treated to the practical exclusion of the others.

HOUSING. Housing conditions in nearly all of our large cities and in some of the small industrial cities and towns have for years amounted almost to a national scandal. Lacking sufficient light, air, living space, and toilet facilities, living in crowded rooms, or a room, often with a lodger or two to help piece out an existence, the unskilled worker's family has a hard and not infrequently losing fight against disease and moral deterioration. Some would lay all the blame on the shiftlessness of the laborer and dismiss the subject. No doubt some of the fault lies there; but city governments have generally recognized that not all the circumstances are under his control, and consequently have come to his aid with housing regulations, some cities with elaborate ones. These codes contain a number of provisions respecting such matters as building materials, fire escapes, and stairs—provisions designed to lessen the fire hazard. But requirements respecting light, air and sanitation— predominantly health regulations—are treated even more extensively. Such regulations limit the amount of lot space a building may occupy; state the minimum requirements for floor space and windows; and prescribe the minimum standards for water, toilet facilities, drainage, and so on. Often the regulations are meager enough, as instanced by the requirement that there shall be running water on every floor, accessible to every family; but they do afford some protection to tenants. The laws are also designed to bring

---

[29] For fuller discussion, see Bromage, *op. cit.,* Ch. 29, Macdonald, *op. cit.,* Ch. 28, and other standard works on municipal government.

the tenants up to certain standards. For example, the keeping of poultry and swine in tenements is prohibited. "They kept the pig in the parlor" was found to be very near a reality, not just the words of a song.[30]

Promotion of housing. The difficulties involved in devising just the right sort of legal regulations and enforcing them have caused many authorities to approach the housing problem from another angle, the angle of promotion. This phase of housing was by no means lost sight of in the President's Conference on Home Building and Home Ownership (1931). This Conference published eleven volumes of reports, which constitute the most comprehensive publication yet made in housing science. To date not a great deal has been done to promote housing. Certain private corporations in New York, Newark, Chicago, and a few other cities have erected tenements that are let to workers at reasonable rates; but relatively few families are accommodated and the rent is still above what the unskilled wage-earners are able to pay. Many European cities have adopted the scheme of municipal housing; but, with the present state of political control in practically all branches of American city government, authorities generally issue warning against the undertaking on this side of the Atlantic. As an encouragement for the erection of model apartments, New York grants tax exemption on those that do not rent for more than a stipulated maximum per month. A few housing organizations have constructed tenements under this law. Another means of aiding housing is through cheap government credit. This method is common in European countries, but until recently its acceptance made but little headway in our own.

Federal housing projects. Since 1932 the federal government has taken a very active interest in housing development, this being one of several problems that that government, almost ignoring the states, has approached through direct relationship with the cities. In 1932 Congress authorized the RFC "to make loans to corporations formed wholly for the purpose of providing housing for families of low income, or for reconstruction of slum areas, which are regulated by state or municipal law as to rents, charges, capital structure, rate of return, and areas and methods of operation," provided such undertakings were self-liquidating in character. This idea was something new. But for various reasons the federal public housing program did not really get under way until the passage of the National Housing Act of 1937. This legislation left the state and municipal authorities the initiative, but it provided for federal loans and subsidies for low-rent housing and slum clearance programs. The local authority submitted plans for construction to the national authority; and if such plans met the federal requirement that costs should not exceed a stipulated sum ($4,000 per family unit in all except the large cities), the federal government would make loans, at low rates of interest, covering 90 per cent of the cost. The federal government also made outright grants for the construction of low-rent units to be occupied by families who would be otherwise obliged to live in the slums.

[30] Macdonald, *op. cit.,* pp. 612 ff.

The federal housing program is tied up with slum clearance, the standard plan (to which exceptions are permitted) being that for each modern unit constructed a slum unit must be demolished. Such projects cost a great deal of money in large cities, where slum dwellings may stand on land valued at four or five dollars per square foot. Not a few housing authorities suggested that new construction be undertaken in areas where land is less costly, and that slum clearance be retarded for the time being. The program was pushed forward, however, as originally planned. The states with large urban communities were almost unanimous in permitting such areas to engage in public housing under the federal plan. Before 1942 many cities had taken advantage of this privilege, and the Federal Public Housing Authority had approved housing projects costing hundreds of millions. Of course this development was suspended or given new direction by the war.

Postwar housing problems. Between 1942 and 1946 there was practically no construction of dwellings except in the defense areas. Many of those were of no value for peacetime; some were too flimsy, and others were in the wrong place. Furthermore, there were many more families in 1946 than there were in 1942. Following the war it was estimated that about three million low and moderate cost houses were urgently needed for veterans and others, and that some twelve million dwelling units would be needed in the next ten years. The National Housing Agency made comprehensive recommendations as to ways and means, and Congress made some effort to relieve the situation, particularly by an appropriation of $400,000,000 to be used as premium payments to makers of new materials required in unconventional types of construction. The program lagged, however, because of a shortage of building materials (nonresidential construction perhaps getting more than its share), plumbing equipment, and other essentials, and because of rising costs.[31] In the meantime war veterans lived in trailers or doubled-up with relatives and friends or total strangers, and concocted fantastic schemes for getting a place of their own or even a little privacy. Such glaring housing inadequacies mean not only inconvenient, unsanitary, and unhealthful living, but they may also cause divorce and broken homes. In Congress and out discussion and debate on the housing situation continued for several years, and the Housing Act of 1949 was the result.

The act of 1949 authorizes federal loans and grants to municipal agencies for the purpose of clearing slums and blighted areas. Grants may be made to help local communities absorb up to two thirds of the loss sustained in acquiring and preparing slum areas for development. Areas thus reclaimed by the local authorities are sold or leased to private builders who agree to construct apartments and houses for low-income families. The plan was to provide for the construction of some 800,000 housing units, but progress has been slow. Both before and after the enactment of the law it was fought as socialistic, extravagant, wasteful, and not in line with the "American way of life." Consequently, Congress has withheld appropriations, making available not

[31] *United States News,* Sept. 6, 1946, p. 54, and Oct. 25, p. 26.

much more than token funds.   In 1954 the President asked for appropriations for 140,000 units over a four-year period—a modest request and much less than was necessary to meet the objectives of the act of 1949—but Congress provided for only 35,000 units and for one year.   It is true that there has been considerable private housing construction in recent years, but little of this benefits the 10 million or more families without adequate housing who are in the lower than $5,000 income class.[32]

SANITATION.   A few generations ago the pedestrian, picking his way down a slimy street, was much less on the lookout for traffic than for dishwater and other refuse that might be thrown at any time from a window or door of a city dwelling.   Rubbish and garbage also took their place in gutters, and swine and dogs came and helped themselves.   Occasionally a good rain would sweep some of the noisome mess out of the city.   Sewage disposal was almost as primitive.   One of the chief reasons for the good health record of modern cities is found in their progress in sanitation, in the collection and removal of wastes under the direction of sanitary engineers.   It must be said, however, that sanitation is more than a branch of public health; a great deal of it, the removal of ashes and rubbish, for example, simply contributes to public convenience.

Garbage would probably be a menace to public health, and unquestionably a nuisance, if not properly disposed of.   It is ordinarily collected by city employees, but sometimes by private contractors.   It is disposed of in various ways, a number of which are quite satisfactory.   These are: towing it to sea, if far enough out; feeding it to hogs; burning it or reducing it, that is, cooking the grease out to be used for such purposes as the manufacture of soap.   The residue makes a good fertilizer base.

Quick and effective collection and disposal of sewage is absolutely essential to the public health.   A soldier in the front line is in less danger than his civilian brother would be in a city without a sewage system.   Every city must have this type of subway service, and the spent water supply, carrying human, household, and industrial wastes, must be kept moving to avoid trouble.   In large cities the trunk mains are six or eight feet in diameter.   Not the least of the marvelous things in Paris is its sewage system, its great horseshoe-shaped main tunnels being from fifteen to twenty feet in diameter.   The sewage flows in a trough beneath a projecting footpath, and above this path there are galleries that carry the city water mains, electric lighting, telegraph, and telephone wires, pneumatic postal tubes, and pipes containing compressed air to be used as power.

Cities dispose of their sewage in various ways.   Those near the sea run the sewage into it—at a point several miles from land, to avoid polluting the beach.   A number of cities on the Great Lakes empty sewage into them; cities on rivers usually make use of them, the Mississippi getting at least two billion gallons a day.   Sufficient water renders the sewage harmless, but in those

---

[32] For a rather critical article on the failure of Congress to maintain the housing program, see the *New Republic*, Oct. 11, 1954, Part 2, pp. 10–12.

areas of rapid growth the amount of sewage deposited has sometimes polluted the water. Cities not having this natural means for disposal must take care of their sewage by filtering or other processes.

WATER SUPPLY. Every city must have an abundant supply of water. It is essential to safety, convenience, and health. Ancient Rome was well supplied through her great aqueducts. The inhabitants of medieval cities used but little, and that was often impure, coming chiefly from rivers and wells. The modern city gets its water from various sources—springs, lakes, rivers, and mountains. Water unfit for use in the condition the city finds it, is carried through water-treatment plants, where it is filtered, chlorinized, or given other treatment necessary to make it harmless. A few may still prefer the "cold, pure, wholesome water" from the farmhouse well (which may be located in a little valley with the pigpen on one side and the stable on the other), but people of moderate intelligence know that the health risk as between it and city water is easily ten to one.

RECREATION. Realizing that recreation facilities are essential to the physical and mental health of both young and old, every city has made some provision for them. Young people must play in order to use up surplus energy; and if the opportunity for play is not given, they often get into mischief and land in the juvenile court. Occasionally they make mischief even of their play, if it is unsupervised. Progressive cities, therefore, not only provide large playgrounds in every section where there are a few hundred children, but they engage playground supervisors as well. Many cities, however, furnish inadequate playgrounds and maintain no supervision over them. The value of economy is not underestimated, but there is some doubt as to the wisdom of this particular economy. Parks are places of recreation and play for all classes and ages. A few decades ago one might see in a park a sign, "five dollars fine for walking on the grass." Fortunately, we have learned that parks are made for the people, not the people for the parks. Although all the cities have parks, only a small proportion of them have park systems— parks of different types, in the different sections of the city, or even outside, connected with tree-lined boulevards. Although we might wish that more cities would turn their attention to the need for additional playground facilities and more enlightened planning for parks, there is no great reason for discouragement, considering what has been accomplished in these directions in recent decades. During the depression years, however, shortsighted economy cut very heavily into the recreational program in some cities.

Reading List

American Bar Association Commission on Organized Crime, *Organized Crime and Law Enforcement* (1952).
American Public Health Association, *Standards of Healthful Housing* (1948).
A. W. Bromage, *Introduction to Municipal Government and Administration* (1950).
Reports of Special (Kefauver) *Committee to Investigate Organized Crime in In-*

terstate Commerce, Senate Reports, 141, 307, 725, 82nd Cong., 1st sess. (1951).

M. L. Colean, *American Housing* (1944).

Federal Bureau of Investigation, *Standards in Police Training* (1939).

E. S. Griffith, *Current Municipal Problems* (1933).

I. V. Hiscock (ed.), Community Health Organization (1950 ed.).

H. G. Hodges, *City Management, Theory and Practice of Municipal Administration* (1939).

International City Managers' Association, *Municipal Police Administration* (1943).

——, *Municipal Fire Administration* (1946).

Victor Jones, *Metropolitan Government* (1942).

C. M. Kneier, *City Government in the United States* (1947 ed.).

V. A. Leonard, *Police Organization and Management* (1951).

A. F. Macdonald, *American City Government and Administration* (1951 ed.).

R. D. McKenzie, *The Metropolitan Community* (1933).

Public Management (monthly), Journal of the International City Managers' Association.

R. L. Mott, *Home Rule for American Cities* (1949).

The Municipal Year Book.

National Municipal Review (monthly).

National Resources Committee, *Our Cities, Their Role in the National Economy* (1937).

New York Bureau of Municipal Research, *City and County of Denver* (1914); *City and County of San Francisco* (1916); *City and County of Philadelphia* (1923).

Mary F. Parton, *Metropolis: A Study of New York* (1939).

J. M. Pfiffner, *Municipal Administration* (1940).

T. H. Reed, *Municipal Government in the United States* (1934 ed.).

C. E. Ridley and O. F. Nolting, *The City-Manager Profession* (1934).

W. G. Smillie, *Public Health Administration in the United States* (1947 ed.).

Bruce Smith, *Police Systems in the United States* (1949 ed.).

Social Science Research Council, *City Manager Government in the United States* (1940).

——, *City Manager Government in Nine Cities* (1940).

——, *City Manager Government in Seven Cities* (1940).

C. P. Taft, *City Management: The Cincinnati Experiment* (1933).

L. D. White, *The City Manager* (1927).

S. Winston, *Social Aspects of Public Housing: An Evaluation of North Carolina's Experience* (1947).

Coleman Woodbury (ed.), *The Future of Cities and Urban Development* (1953).

——, *Urban Development: Problems and Practices* (1953).

H. B. Woolston, *Metropolis: A Study of Urban Communities* (1938).

Harold Zink, *Government of Cities in the United States* (1939).

Questions and Problems

1. What types of city charters are permissible in your state?

2. Indicate the extent to which the cities are controlled by the state; the national government.

3. Explain the structure of the conventional type of city government. Do you

find in it any features which a state might use with profit in its own government?

4. Draw up a list of the best features of the commission plan of city government. What are its reputed weaknesses?

5. Diagram the structure of the council-manager type of government. What elements of this system stand out as particularly American?

6. Comment upon this statement: *The best type of city government in respect to structure and organization produces the best possible city government.*

7. What problems of local government might be solved if we could bring political organization into conformity with geography?

8. Write a 200-word essay on city police problems, with particular reference to your own city (if you live in one).

9. Can you show that American methods of protection from fire indicate both the strength and weakness of our skills and methods?

10. How do you explain the fact that public health protection in the cities has made more rapid progress than rural health protection?

MODEL STATE CONSTITUTION *

FIFTH EDITION, 1948

Article I

BILL OF RIGHTS

SECTION 100. *Political Power.*[1] All political power of this state is inherent in the people, and all government herein is founded on their authority.

SECTION 101. *Inherent Rights.* All persons are by nature equally free and independent and have certain inherent rights; namely, the enjoyment of life and liberty, with the means of acquiring and possessing property, and pursuing and obtaining happiness and safety.[2] These rights carry with them certain corresponding duties to the state.

SECTION 102. *Legal Rights.* No citizen shall be disfranchised, or deprived of any of the rights or privileges secured to any other citizen, unless by the law of the land; nor shall any person be deprived of due process of law, or be denied the equal protection of the laws. There shall be no imprisonment for debt and a reasonable amount of the property of individuals may be exempted from seizure or sale for payment of any debt or liabilities.

SECTION 103. *Right to Organize.* Citizens shall have the right to organize, except in military or semi-military organizations not under the supervision of the state, and except for purposes of resisting the duly constituted authority of this state or of the United States. Public employees shall have the right, through representatives of their own choosing, to present to and make known to the state, or any of its political subdivisions or agencies, their grievances and proposals.[3] Persons in private employment shall have the right to bargain collectively through representatives of their own choosing.

SECTION 104. *Searches and Seizures.* The right of the people to be secure in their persons, houses, papers and effects, against unreasonable searches and seizures, shall not be violated; and no warrants shall issue but upon probable cause supported by oath or

* Drafted by the Committee on State Government of the National Municipal League and reproduced by the courtesy of the League. The explanatory articles that accompany the Model and published by the League are most helpful.

[1] The Committee has adopted the policy of inserting short headings at the beginning of each paragraph; these are intended as aids to reference and have nothing to do with the legal operation or judicial interpretation of the sections.

[2] Virginia constitution, article I, section 1.

[3] New Jersey constitution, article I, section 19.

278

affirmation, and particularly describing the place to be searched, and the persons or things to be seized. Evidence obtained in violation of this section shall not be admissible in any court against any person.

SECTION 105. *Writ of Habeas Corpus.* The privilege of the writ of habeas corpus shall not be suspended, unless, in case of rebellion or invasion, the public safety requires it, and then only in such manner as shall be prescribed by law.

SECTION 106. *Rights of Accused Persons.* In all criminal prosecutions, the accused shall have the right to demand a specific statement of the charges against him, and to appear and defend himself in person and by counsel; to meet the witnesses against him face to face; to have process to compel the attendance of witnesses in his behalf; and to have a speedy public trial in the county or district in which the offense is alleged to have been committed, unless he shall waive this right in order to secure a change of venue.

SECTION 107. *Double Jeopardy; Excessive Bail.* No person shall, after acquittal, be tried for the same offense. All persons shall, before conviction, be bailable by suffi-cient sureties, except for capital offenses when the proof is evident or the presumption great.[4]

SECTION 108. *Right of Assembly.* The right of the people peaceably to assemble, and to petition the government, or any department thereof, shall never be abridged.

SECTION 109. *Freedom of Speech.* There shall be no law passed nor executive action taken abridging the freedom of speech or of the press.

SECTION 110. *Freedom of Religion.* No law shall be passed respecting the establish-ment of religion, or prohibiting the free exercise thereof.

SECTION 111. *Freedom from Legislative Abuses.* The power of the state to act in tht general welfare shall never be impaired by the making of any irrevocable grant of special privileges or immunities.

SECTION 112. *Eminent Domain.* Private property shall not be taken or damaged for public use without just compensation.

SECTION 113. *Sanction.* Any citizen or taxpayer may restrain the violation of any provision of this constitution by a suit with leave of the general court of justice, upon notice to the chief law officer of the state.

Article II

SUFFRAGE AND ELECTIONS

SECTION 200. *Qualifications for Voting.* Every duly registered citizen of the age of eighteen years who shall have been a citizen for ninety days, and an inhabitant of this state for one year next preceding an election, and for the last ninety days a resident of the county and for the last thirty days a resident of the election district in which he [5] may offer his vote, shall have equal voting rights at all elections in he election disrict of which he shall at the time be a resident, and not elsewhere, except as hereinafter provided, but no person shall become entitled to vote unless he is also able, except for physical disability, to read and write English; and suitable laws shall be passed by the legislature to enforce this provision.

[4] Based on provisions in the Iowa and New Jersey bills of rights.
[5] The masculine pronoun is here used generically; see section 1201.

SECTION 201. *Absent Voting.* The legislature may, by general law, provide a manner in which qualified voters who may be absent from the state or county of their residence may register and vote, and for the return and canvass of their votes in the election district in which they reside.

SECTION 202. *Disqualifications from Voting.* No person who shall receive, accept, or offer to receive, or pay, offer or promise to pay, or withdraw or withhold or threaten to withdraw or withhold any money or other valuable consideration as a compensation or reward for the giving or withholding of a vote at an election shall vote at such election. No person under conviction of bribery or of any infamous crime shall exercise the privilege of the suffrage.

SECTION 203. *Residence.* For the purpose of voting, no person shall be deemed to have gained or lost a residence simply by reason of his presence or absence while employed in the service of the United States; or while engaged in the navigation of the waters of this state, or of the United States, or of the high seas; nor while a student at any institution of learning; nor while kept at any almshouse, or other asylum, or institution wholly or partly supported at public expense or by charity; nor while confined in any public prison.

SECTION 204. *Registration of Voters.* Laws shall be made for ascertaining, by proper proofs, the citizens who shall be entitled to the privilege of the suffrage and for the registration of all qualified voters. Registration shall be upon personal application in the case of the first registration of any voter and shall be completed at least ten days before each election. Such registration shall be effective so long as the voter shall remain qualified to vote from the same address or for such other period as the legislature may prescribe.

SECTION 205. *Methods of Voting.* Voting at all elections or on referenda shall be by such method as may be prescribed by law, provided that secrecy of voting be preserved. The legislature shall have power to provide for the use of mechanical devices for voting or counting the votes.

SECTION 206. *Election Officers.* All officers and employees charged with the direction or administration of the election system of the state and of its civil divisions shall be appointed in such manner as the legislature may by law direct, provided that appointment shall be made according to merit and fitness, to be determined, so far as practicable, by competitive examination.

SECTION 207. Regular elections shall be held annually on the first Tuesday after the first Monday in November; but the time of holding such elections may be altered by law.

Article III

THE LEGISLATURE

SECTION 300. *Legislative Power.* The legislative power shall be vested in a legislature, which may delegate to other public officers the power to supplement statutes by ordinances, general orders, rules, and regulations, provided a general standard or principle has been enacted to which such delegated legislation shall conform. All such delegated legislation, promulgated by state officers, departments, offices, or agencies, shall be reported to the legislative council, and shall be adopted and published in accordance with a fair procedure prescribed by law. The legislature may delegate to the legislative council authority to approve or disapprove ordinances, general orders, rules, and regulations supplementing existing legislation.

SECTION 301. *Composition of the Legislature.* The legislature shall be composed of a single chamber of such number of members as may be prescribed by law, but not to exceed........members. Except as otherwise provided in this constitution, any qualified voter shall be eligible to membership in the legislature.[6]

SECTION 302. *Election of Members.* The members of the legislature shall be chosen by the qualified voters of the state for a term of two years by proportional representation, under a method to be prescribed by law. For the purpose of electing members of the legislature, the state shall be divided into districts, composed of contiguous and compact territory, from each of which there shall be elected from three to seven members, in accordance with the population of the respective districts. The term of members of the legislature shall begin on the first day of December next following their election.

SECTION 303. *Apportionment.* After each decennial census, the secretary of the legislature shall reallot the number of members assigned to each district, in accordance with the changes in the population of the several districts. The boundaries of the districts and the total number of members may be altered only by law and not more frequently than once in each census period.

SECTION 304. *Time of Election.* The members of the legislature shall be elected at the regular election in each odd numbered year, beginning in 19.....

SECTION 305. *Vacancies.* Whenever a vacancy shall occur in the legislature, it shall be filled by a majority vote of the remaining members from the district in which said vacancy occurs, or in such other manner as may be provided by law. If, after thirty days following the occurrence of a vacancy, it remains unfilled, the governor shall appoint some eligible person for the unexpired term.[7]

SECTION 306. *Compensation of Members.* The members of the legislature shall receive an annual salary, as may be prescribed by law, but the amount thereof shall neither be increased nor diminished during the term for which they are elected.

SECTION 307. *Sessions.* The legislature shall be deemed a continuous body during the biennium for which its members are elected. It shall meet in regular sessions quarterly or at such times as may be prescribed by law. Special sessions may be called by the governor or by a majority of the members of the legislative council.

SECTION 308. *Organization and Procedure.* The legislature shall be judge of the election, returns and qualifications of its members, and may by law vest in the courts the trial and determination of contested elections of members. It shall choose its presiding officer, and a secretary who shall serve for an indefinite term. It shall determine its rules of procedure; it may compel the attendance of absent members, punish its members for disorderly conduct and, with the concurrence of two-thirds of all the members, expel a member; and it shall have power to compel the attendance and testi-

---

[6] The committee recommends a unicameral legislature but believes that most of the provisions of this *Model State Constitution* are applicable to the bicameral system, with slight modification, in any state which may wish to retain it.

[7] Some authorities prefer a recount of the ballots cast at the original election which have been left unrepresented as a result of the vacancy. This prevents a district majority from appropriating to itself a vacated seat of a district minority.

mony of witnesses and the production of books and papers either before the legislature as a whole or before any committee thereof.

SECTION 309. *Legislative Immunity.* For any speech or debate in the legislature, the members shall not be questioned in any other place.

SECTION 310. *Local and Special Legislation.* The legislature shall pass no special act in any case where a general act can be made applicable, and whether a general act can be made applicable shall be matter for judicial determination. No local act shall take effect until approved by a majority of the qualified voters voting thereon in the district to be affected, except acts repealing local or special acts in effect before the adoption of this constitution and receiving a two-thirds vote of all the members of the legislature on the question of their repeal.

SECTION 311. *Transaction of Business.* A majority of all the members of the legislature shall constitute a quorum to do business but a smaller number may adjourn from day to day and compel the attendance of absent members. The legislature shall keep a journal of its proceedings which shall be published from day to day. The legislature shall prescribe the methods of voting on legislative matters, but a record vote, with the yeas and nays entered in the journal, shall be taken on any question on the demand of one-fifth of the members present. Mechanical devices may be employed to record the votes of members.

SECTION 312. *Committees.* The legislature may establish such committees as may be necessary for the efficient conduct of its business. Each committee shall keep a journal of its proceedings as a public record. One-third of all the members of the legislature shall have power to relieve a committee of further consideration of a bill when the committee to which it was assigned has not reported on it. Notice of all committee hearings and a clear statement of all subjects to be considered at each hearing shall be published one week in advance in the journal.

SECTION 313. *Bills and Titles of Bills.* No law shall be passed except by bill. Every bill, except bills for appropriations and bills for the codification, revision or rearrangement of existing laws, shall be confined to one subject, which shall be expressed in the title. Bills for appropriations shall be confined to appropriations.

SECTION 314. *Passage of Bills.* No bill shall become a law unless it has been read on three different days, has been printed and upon the desks of the members in final form at least three legislative days prior to final passage, and has received the assent of a majority of all the members. No act shall become effective until published, as provided by law.

SECTION 315. *Action by the Governor.* Every bill which shall have passed the legislature shall be presented to the governor; if he approves he shall sign it, but if not he shall return it with his objections to the legislature. Any bill so returned by the governor shall be reconsidered by the legislature and if, upon reconsideration, two-thirds of all the members shall agree to pass the bill it shall become a law. In all such cases the vote shall be by roll call, and entered on the journal.

If any bill shall not be signed or returned by the governor within fifteen days after it shall have been presented to him it shall be a law in like manner as if he had signed it, except that, if the legislature shall be in recess at the end of such fifteen-day period, the governor may sign the bill at any time during the recess or return it with his objections upon the reconvening of the legislature, and if the legislature shall adjourn finally before the governor has acted on a bill that has been presented to him less than fifteen days before, it shall not become law unless the governor sign it within thirty days after such adjournment.

SECTION 316. *Referendum on Legislation.* Any bill failing of passage by the legislature may be submitted to referendum by order of the governor, either in its original form or with such amendments which were considered by the legislature as he may designate. Any bill which, having passed the legislature, is returned thereto by the governor with objections and, upon reconsideration, is not approved by a two-thirds vote of all the members but is approved by at least a majority thereof, may be submitted to referendum by a majority of all the members. Bills thus submitted to referendum shall be voted on at the next succeeding regular election occurring at least sixty days after action is taken to submit them, unless the legislature shall provide for their submission at an earlier date.

SECTION 317. *Legislative Council.* There shall be a legislative council consisting of not less than seven nor more than fifteen members, chosen by and from the legislature. Members of the legislative council shall be chosen by the legislature at its first session after the adoption of this constitution and at each subsequent session following a regular election. Members of the legislative council shall be elected in such a manner as the legislature shall direct, and when elected shall continue in office until their successors are chosen and have qualified. The legislature, by a majority vote of all the members, may dissolve the legislative council at any time and proceed to the election of a successor thereto.

SECTION 318. *Organization of Legislative Council.* The legislative council shall meet as often as may be necessary to perform its duties. It shall choose one of its members as chairman, and shall appoint a director or research; it shall adopt its own rules of procedure, except as such rules may be established by law. The secretary of the legislature shall serve ex officio as secretary of the council.

SECTION 319. *Duties of the Legislative Council.* It shall be the duty of the legislative council to collect information concerning the government and general welfare of the state and to report thereon to the legislature. Measures for proposed legislation may be submitted to it at any time, and shall be considered and reported to the legislature with its recommendations thereon. The legislative council may also recommend such legislation, in the form of bills or otherwise, as in its opinion the welfare of the state may require. Other powers and duties may be assigned to the legislative council by law.

SECTION 320. *Compensation of Members of the Legislative Council.* Members of the legislative council shall receive such compensation, additional to their compensation as members of the legislature, as may be provided by law.

Article IV

INITIATIVE AND REFERENDUM

SECTION 400. *The Initiative.* The people reserve to themselves power by petition to propose laws and amendments to this constitution, and directly to enact or reject such laws and amendments at the polls. This reserved power shall be known as the initiative.

SECTION 401. *Initiative Procedure.* An initiative petition shall contain either the full text of the measure proposed, or an adequate summary thereof, and, to be valid, shall be signed by qualified voters equal in number to at least......per cent of the total vote cast for governor in the last preceding regular election at which a governor was chosen. An initiative petition proposing a constitutional amendment shall be signed by........[a greater] per cent of the qualified voters of the state. Not more than one-fourth of the signatures counted on any completed petition shall be those of the voters of any one county. Initiative petitions shall be filed with the secretary of the legislature for report by the legislative council. If the proposed measure is not enacted into law at the next ensuing session of the legislature or, in the case of a constitutional amendment, if it is not passed at such session and repassed at the first session meeting at least six months thereafter, the question of the adoption of the measure shall be submitted by the secretary of the legislature to the qualified voters at the first regular election held not less than sixty days after the end of the session which fails to take the indicated action, except that a constitutional amendment shall be submitted at the second regular election after each session. The legislature may provide by law for a procedure by which the sponsors may withdraw an initiative petition at any time prior to its submission to the people.

SECTION 402. *The Referendum.* The people also reserve to themselves power to require, by petition, that measures enacted by the legislature be submitted to the qualified voters for their approval or rejection. This reserved power shall be known as the referendum.

SECTION 403. *Referendum Procedure.* A referendum petition against any measure passed by the legislature shall be filed with the secretary of the legislature within ninety days after the adjournment of the session at which such measure was enacted and, to be valid, shall be signed by qualified voters equal in number to not less than........ per cent of the total vote cast for governor at the last preceding regular election at which a governor was chosen. Not more than one-fourth of the signatures counted on any completed petition shall be those of the voters of any one county. The question of approving any measure against which a valid referendum petition is filed shall be submitted to the voters at the first regular or special election held not less than thirty days after such filing.

SECTION 404. *Effect of Referendum.* A referendum may be ordered upon any act or part of an act, except acts continuing existing taxes and acts making appropriations in amounts not in excess of those for the preceding fiscal year. When the referendum is ordered upon an act, or any part of an act, it shall suspend the operation thereof until such act, or part, is approved by the voters.

The filing of a referendum petition against one or more items, sections, or parts of an act shall not delay the remainder of the measure from becoming operative. No act shall take effect earlier than ninety days after the adjournment of the legislative session at which it was enacted, except acts declared to be emergency measures. If it be necessary for the immediate preservation of the public peace, health, or safety that a measure become effective without delay, the facts constituting such necessity shall be stated in a separate section, and if, upon a record vote entered in the journal, two-thirds of all the members of the legislature shall declare the measure to be an emergency measure, it shall become effective at the time specified therein; but no act granting or amending a franchise or special privilege, or creating any vested right or interest, other than in the state, shall be declared an emergency measure. If a referendum petition be filed against an emergency measure, such measure shall be operative until voted upon, and if not approved by a majority of the qualified voters voting thereon, it shall be deemed repealed.

SECTION 405. *Special Elections.* Any referendum measure shall be submitted to the qualified voters at a special election if so ordered by the governor or if a separate petition requesting a special election be signed by.........per cent of the qualified voters. Any such special election shall be held not less than one hundred and twenty nor more than one hundred and fifty days after the adjournment of the legislative session at which the act was passed.

SECTION 406. *Passage of Constitutional Amendments and Laws by the Initiative and Referendum.* Each measure shall be submitted by a ballot title, which shall be descriptive but not argumentative or prejudicial. The ballot title of any initiated or referred measure shall be prpeared by the legal department of the state, subject to review by the courts. The veto power of the governor shall not extend to measures initiated by, or referred to, the qualified voters. Any measure submitted to a vote of the qualified voters shall become law or a part of the constitution only when approved by a majority of the votes cast thereon, provided that, in addition, no initiative measure shall become effective unless the affirmative votes cast therefor shall equal 30 per cent of the total vote cast for governor at the last preceding regular election at which a governor was chosen. Each measure so approved shall take effect thirty days after the date of the vote thereon, unless otherwise provided in the measure. If conflicting measures referred to the people at the same election shall be approved by a majority of the votes cast thereon, the one receiving the highest number of affirmative votes shall prevail to the extent of such conflict.

SECTION 407. *Restrictions on Direct Legislation Procedure.* The initiative shall not be used as a means of making appropriations of public funds, nor for the enactment of local or special legislation. No measure submitted by the initiative shall contain therein the name of any person to be designated as administrator of any department, office or agency to be established by the proposed law or constitutional amendment.

No law shall be enacted to hamper, restrict or impair the exercise of the powers herein reserved to the people. No measure adopted by vote of the qualified voters under the initiative and referendum provisions of this constitution shall be repealed or amended by the legislature within a period of three years except by a two-thirds vote of all the members.

Article V

THE EXECUTIVE

SECTION 500. *Establishment of the Executive.* The executive power of the state shall be vested in a governor, who shall be chosen by the direct vote of the people for a term of four years beginning on the first day of December next following his election.

SECTION 501. *Election of the Governor.* The governor shall be elected at the regular election in each alternate odd numbered year, beginning in 19....... Any qualified voter of the state shall be eligible to the office of governor.

SECTION 502. *Legislative Powers.* The governor shall, at the beginning of each session, and may at other times, give to the legislature information as to the affairs of the state, and recommend such measures as he shall deem expedient. He shall have the power of veto over bills approved by the legislature, as prescribed in section 315 of this constitution.

The governor, the administrative manager, and heads of administrative departments shall be entitled to seats in the legislature, may introduce bills therein, and take part in the discussion of measures, but shall have no vote.

SECTION 503. *Executive and Administrative Powers.* The governor shall take care that the laws are faithfully executed, and to this end shall have power, by appropriate action or proceeding brought in the name of the state in any of the judicial or administrative tribunals or agencies of the state or any of its civil divisions, to enforce compliance with any constitutional or legal mandate, or restrain violation of any constitutional or legal duty or right by any department, office, or agency of the state or any of its civil divisions; but this power shall not be construed to authorize any action or proceeding against the legislature.[8]

He shall commission all officers of the state. He may at any time require information, in writing or otherwise, from the officers of any administrative department, office or agency upon any subject relating to their respective offices. He shall be commander-in-chief of the armed forces of the state (except when they shall be called into the service of the United States), and may call them out to execute the laws, to suppress insurrection or to repel invasion.

SECTION 504. *Executive Clemency.* The governor shall have power to grant reprieves, commutations and pardons, after conviction, for all offenses, subject to such regulations as may be prescribed by law relative to the manner of applying therefor.

SECTION 505. *Administrative Manager.* The governor shall appoint an administrative manager of state affairs, whose term shall be indefinite at the pleasure of the governor. The governor may delegate any or all of his administrative powers to the administrative manager. The administrative manager shall be assisted by such aides as may be provided by law.

SECTION 506. *Administrative Departments.* There shall be such administrative departments, not to exceed twenty in number, as may be established by law, with such powers and duties as may be prescribed by law. Subject to the limitations contained in this constitution, the legislature may from time to time assign by law new powers and functions to departments, offices and agencies, and it may increase, modify, or diminish the powers and functions of such departments, offices, or agencies, but the governor shall have power to make from time to time such changes in the administrative structure or in the assignment of functions as may, in his judgment, be necessary for efficient administration. Such changes shall be set forth in executive orders which shall become effective at the close of the next quarterly session of the legislature, unless specifically modified or disapproved by a resolution concurred in by a majority of all the members.[9]

All new powers or functions shall be assigned to departments, offices or agencies in such manner as will tend to maintain an orderly arrangement in the administrative pattern of the state government. The legislature may create temporary commissions for special purposes or reduce the number of departments by consolidation or otherwise.[10]

---

[8] Follows *Report* of the 1947 New Jersey Committee for Constitutional Revision.

[9] This follows a procedure that has become fairly well standardized in the federal government.

[10] Follows New York State constitution, article V, section 3.

The heads of all administrative departments shall be appointed by and may be removed by the governor. All other officers in the administrative service of the state shall be appointed by the governor or by the heads of administrative departments, as provided by article IX of this constitution and by supporting legislation. No executive order governing the work of the state or the administration of one or more departments, offices and agencies, shall become effective until published as provided by law.

SECTION 507. *Impeachment.* The legislature shall have the power of impeachment by a two-thirds vote of all the members, and it shall provide by law a procedure for the trial and removal from office of officers of this state. No officer shall be convicted on impeachment by a vote of less than two-thirds of the members of the court hearing the charges.

SECTION 508. *Succession to Governorship.* In case of the failure of the governor to qualify, or of his impeachment, removal from office, death, resignation, inability to discharge the powers and duties of his office, or absence from the state, the powers and duties of the office shall devolve upon the presiding officer of the legislature for the remainder of the term, or until the disability be removed.

Article VI

THE JUDICIARY

SECTION 600. *Establishment of the Judiciary.* The judicial power of the state shall be vested in a general court of justice which shall include a supreme court department and such other departments and subdivisions and as many judges as may be provided by law.

SECTION 601. *Jurisdiction.* The general court of justice shall have original general jurisdiction throughout the state in all causes, including claims against the state. The jurisdiction of each department and subdivision of the general court of justice shall be determined by statute or by general rules of the judicial council not inconsistent with law, provided that the legislature shall determine the jurisdiction of the supreme court department by law.

SECTION 602. *Selection of Justices and Judges.* The chief justice shall be elected by the qualified voters of the state at a regular election in an odd numbered year in which a governor is not elected. He shall hold office for a term of eight years, beginning on the first day of December next following his election.

Whenever vacancies occur the chief justice shall appoint the other judges of the general court of justice from eligible lists containing three names for each vacancy, which shall be presented to him by the judicial council. The term of office of each judge so appointed shall be twelve years, subject to recall, removal, or retirement as hereafter provided. After any appointed judge shall have served for four years, the qualified voters of the state or of a judicial district shall decide at the next regular election whether he shall be retained or recalled from office. The judicial council, subject to any general rules that the legislature may prescribe by law, shall determine on the basis of the record of the judge's service in what, if any, particular district the question of his retention or recall shall be submitted. A separate ballot shall be used (unless voting machines are employed) on which there shall appear no other question than that of the retention or recall of the judge. If a majority of the votes on the question are against retaining the judge, his term shall end upon the thirtieth day next following the election.

The judicial council shall designate a judge to act in place of the chief justice in case of a vacancy in the office or in case of the absence of the chief justice from the state or of his inability to discharge the powers and duties of his office. In case of a vacancy, a new chief justice shall be elected for a full term at the next regular election held in an odd numbered year in which a governor is not elected, unless the legislature provides by law for an earlier election to fill an unexpired term.

SECTION 603. *Establishment of Judicial Council.* There shall be a judicial council, to consist of the chief justice, who shall preside at its meetings, one other member of the supreme court department, and two judges of other departments of the general court of justice to be designated for four years by the chief justice; three practicing lawyers, to be appointed by the governor for overlapping terms of three years, from an eligible list containing three times as many names as there are appointments to be made and presented to him by the governing board of the state bar association; three laymen citizens of the state, to be appointed by the governor for overlapping terms of three years; and the chairman of the judiciary committee of the legislature. The judicial council shall meet at least once in each quarter, at a time and place designated by the chief justice.

SECTION 604. *Powers of the Judicial Council.* The judicial council, in addition to the other powers conferred upon it by this constitution or by law, shall have power to make or alter the rules relating to pleading, practice, or procedure in the general court of justice. It shall also have power to make rules respecting the administration of the general court of justice, including rules prescribing the duties of the administrative director and his subordinates and all other ministerial agents of the court, determining the location of offices and places of sittings of the various departments and subdivisions of the general court of justice, and establishing or altering judicial districts for the handling of specified types of judicial business.

Rules of pleading, practice, and procedure shall be effective only when published as provided by law and the legislature may repeal, alter, or supplement any of them by a law limited to that specific purpose. All other rules made by the judicial council shall be subject to any statutes theretofore or thereafter enacted.

SECTION 605. *Judicial Administration.* The chief justice shall be the presiding justice of the supreme court department and shall be the executive head of the general court of justice, exercising the powers conferred by this constitution, by law, and by rules of the judicial council.

The chief justice, subject to rules of the judicial council, shall assign judges to service in the several departments, subdivisions, and judicial districts and shall designate such presiding judges therein as may be required by law or by rule of the judicial council. Presiding judges shall serve on such conditions and with such administrative responsibilities and such powers of appointment, assignment, and control over calendars as may be determined by law or by rule of the judicial council.

The chief justice shall appoint an administrative director of the general court of justice to serve at his pleasure, the clerk of the supreme court department, and all other ministerial agents of the general court of justice whose appointment is not by law or by rule of the judicial council vested in the administrative director of the general court of justice, the clerk of the supreme court, or the presiding judges.

The chief justice shall supervise the work of the general court of justice and of all its agents. He shall publish an annual report covering the business done by every department, subdivision, district or agency of the general court of justice and stating the condition of the dockets at the close of the year. He may require periodic or special reports from any judicial officer or agent.

SECTION 606. *Retirement and Removal.* The legislature shall provide by law for retirement of judges. The chief justice may assign a retired judge to temporary active service as need appears at any time prior to the end of the term for which he had been appointed.

The legislature may, upon due notice of reasons given and opportunity for defense, remove from office any judge upon the concurrence of two-thirds of all the members. Judges and ministerial agents of the general court of justice may be removed for cause, after due notice and opportunity for defense, by the judicial council.

SECTION 607. *Compensation.* All remuneration for the services of judges and court officials shall be paid from an appropriation by the legislature. The annual compensation paid to any judge shall be neither increased nor diminished during the term of office to which he shall be elected or appointed.

SECTION 608. *Fees, Costs, and Fines.* All fees collected in any department of the general court of justice or by any officer thereof shall be collected and received by the administrative director and shall be accounted for by him monthly and paid to the state treasury. The judicial council shall have power to establish or alter fees to be collected in the several court departments, within such limits as the legislature may by law establish.

SECTION 609. *Ineligibility to Other Offices.* No judge shall hold any office or public employment, other than a judicial office, during the term for which he shall have been elected or appointed, nor shall he engage in the practice of law or other gainful occupation during his continuance in office. No judge shall be eligible for election to any non-judicial office until two years after the expiration of the full term for which he was appointed or elected.

SECTION 610. *Disqualifications in Certain Cases.* No judge shall sit in any case wherein he may be interested, or where either of the parties may be connected with him by affinity or consanguinity within such degrees as may be prescribed by law, or where he shall have been of counsel in the case, or on appeal from a trial in which he presided.

SECTION 611. *Writ of Habeas Corpus.* Each judge of the general court of justice shall have power to issue writs of habeas corpus.

Article VII

FINANCE

SECTION 700. *Powers of Taxation.* The power of taxation shall never be surrendered, suspended, or contracted away.

SECTION 701. *Borrowing Power.* The credit of the state or any civil division thereof shall not in any manner, directly or indirectly, be given or lent to or used in aid of any individual, association, or private corporation.

SECTION 702. *Debt Limitations.* No debt shall be contracted by or in behalf of this state unless such debt shall be authorized by law for a single project or object distinctly specified therein; and no such law shall, except for the purpose of repelling invasion, suppressing insurrection, defending the state in war, meeting natural catastrophes, or redeeming the indebtedness of the state outstanding at the time this constitution is approved, take effect until it shall have been submitted to the qualified voters at a regular election and have received a favorable majority of all votes cast upon such question at such election; except that the state may by law borrow money to meet appropriations for any fiscal year in anticipation of the collection of the revenues of such year, but all debts so contracted in anticipation of revenues shall be paid within one year.

SECTION 703. *The Budget.* Three months before the opening of the fiscal year, the governor shall submit to the legislature a budget setting forth a complete plan of proposed expenditures and anticipated income of all departments, offices and agencies of the state for the next ensuing fiscal year. For the preparation of the budget the various departments, offices and agencies shall furnish the governor such information, in such form, as he may require. At the time of submitting the budget to the legislature, the governor shall introduce therein a general appropriation bill to authorize all the proposed expenditures set forth in the budget. At the same time he shall introduce in the legislature a bill or bills covering all recommendations in the budget for new or additional revenues or for borrowing by which the proposed expenditures are to be met.

SECTION 704. *Legislative Budget Procedure.* No special appropriation bill shall be passed until the general appropriation bill, as introduced by the governor and amended by the legislature, shall have been enacted, unless the governor shall recommend the passage of an emergency appropriation or appropriations, which shall continue in force only until the general appropriation bill shall become effective. The legislature shall provide for one or more public hearings on the budget, either before a committee or before the legislature in committee of the whole. When requested by not less than one-fifth of all the members of the legislature it shall be the duty of the governor to appear in person or by designated representative before the legislature, or before a committee thereof, to answer any inquiries with respect to the budget.

The legislature shall make no appropriation for any fiscal period in excess of the income provided for that period. The governor may strike out or reduce items in appropriation bills passed by the legislature, and the procedure in such cases shall be the same as in the case of the disapproval of an entire bill by the governor.

SECTION 705. *Appropriations for Private Purposes Prohibited.* No tax shall be levied or appropriation of public money or property be made, either directly or indirectly, except for a public purpose, and no public money or property shall ever be appropriated, applied, donated, or used directly or indirectly, for any sect, church, denomination, or sectarian institution. No public money or property shall be appropriated for a charitable, industrial, educational or benevolent purpose except to a department, office, agency or civil division of the state.

SECTION 706. *Expenditure of Money.* No money shall be withdrawn from the treasury except in accordance with appropriations made by law, nor shall any obligation for the payment of money be incurred except as authorized by law. The appropriation for each department, office, or agency of the state, for which appropriation is made, shall be for a specific sum of money, and no appropriation shall allocate to any object the proceeds of any particular tax or fund or a part or percentage thereof.[11]

No appropriation shall confer authority to incur an obligation after the termination of the fiscal period to which it relates. The governor shall have authority to reduce expenditures of state departments, offices and agencies under appropriations whenever actual revenues fall below the revenue estimates upon which the appropriations were based, or when other changed circumstances warrant economies, and, through allotments or otherwise, to control the rate at which such appropriations are expended during the fiscal year, provided that the legislature, by resolution concurred in by a majority of all the

[11] Follows Georgia constitution, article IX, paragraph 1.

members, may exempt specific appropriations for the legislative department from the exercise of this power by the governor.

SECTION 707. *Purchasing Methods.* All public purchases made by the government of this state, or by any of its cities, counties, or other civil divisions, shall, so far as practicable, be made under a system of competitive bidding. Centralized purchasing shall be practiced wherever practicable.

SECTION 708. *Post-auditing.* The legislature shall, by a majority vote of all the members, appoint an auditor who shall serve during its pleasure.[12] It shall be the duty of the auditor to conduct post-audits of all transactions and of all accounts kept by or for all departments, offices and agencies of the state government, to certify to the accuracy of all financial statements issued by accounting officers of the state, and to report his findings and criticisms to the governor and to a special committee of the legislature quarterly, and to the legislature at the end of each fiscal year. He shall also make such additional reports to the legislature and the proper legislative committee, and conduct such investigation of the financial affairs of the state, or of any department, office or agency thereof, as either of such bodies may require.

SECTION 709. *Excess Condemnation.* The state, or any civil division thereof, appropriating or otherwise acquiring property for public use, may, in furtherance of such public use, appropriate or acquire an excess over that actually to be occupied by the improvement, and may sell such excess with such restrictions as shall be appropriate to preserve the improvement made. Bonds may be issued to supply the funds in whole or in part to pay for the excess property so appropriated or acquired; and such bonds, when made a lien only against the property so appropriated or acquired, shall not be subject to the restrictions or limitations on the amount of indebtedness of any civil divisions prescribed by law.[13]

Article VIII

LOCAL GOVERNMENT

SECTION 800. *Organization of Local Government.* Provision shall be made by general law for the incorporation of counties, cities, and other civil divisions; and for the alteration of boundaries, the consolidation of neighboring civil divisions, and the dissolution of any such civil divisions.

Provisions shall also be made by general law (which may provide optional plans of organization and government) for the organization and government of counties, cities, and other civil divisions which do not secure locally framed and adopted charters in accordance with the provisions of section 801, but no such law hereafter enacted shall become operative in any county, city, or other civil division until submitted to the qualified voters thereof and approved by a majority of those voting thereon.

SECTION 801. *Home Rule for Local Units.* Any county or city may adopt or amend a charter for its own government, subject to such regulations as are provided in this constitution and may be provided by general law. The legislature shall provide one or more optional procedures for nonpartisan election of five, seven or nine charter commissioners and for framing, publishing, and adopting a charter or charter amendments.

[12] Or it may be provided that the legislature shall contract with qualified public accountants to conduct all post-audits for the state. The auditor or auditors should, in any case, be certified public accountants.

[13] Follows Ohio constitution, article XVIII, section 10.

Upon resolution approved by a majority of the members of the legislative authority of the county or city or upon petition of 10% of the qualified voters, the officer or agency responsibile for certifying public questions shall submit to the people at the next regular election not less than sixty days thereafter, or at a special election if authorized by law, the question "Shall a commission be chosen to frame a charter or charter amendments for the county (or city) of . . . . ?" An affirmative vote of a majority of the qualified voters voting on the question shall authorize the creation of the commission.

A petition to have a charter commission may include the names of five, seven or nine commissioners, to be listed at the end of the question when it is voted on, so that an affirmative vote on the question is a vote to elect the persons named in the petition. Otherwise, the petition or resolution shall designate an optional election procedure provided by law.

Any proposed charter or charter amendments shall be published by the commission, distributed to the qualified voters and submitted to them at the next regular or special election not less than thirty days after publication. The procedure for publication and submission shall be as provided by law or by resolution of the charter commission not inconsistent with law. The legislative authority of the county or city shall, on request of the charter commission, appropriate money to provide for the reasonable expenses of the commission and for the publication, distribution and submission of its proposals.

A charter or charter amendments shall become effective if approved by a majority of the qualified voters voting thereon. A charter may provide for direct submission of future charter revisions or amendments by petition or by resolution of the local legislative authority.

SECTION 802. *Powers of Local Units.* Counties shall have such powers as shall be provided by general or optional law. Any city or other civil division may, by agreement, subject to a local referendum and the approval of a majority of the qualified voters voting on any such question, transfer to the county in which it is located any of its functions or powers, and may revoke the transfer of any such function or power, under regulations provided by general law; and any county may, in like manner, transfer to another county or to a city within its boundaries or adjacent thereto any of its functions or powers, and may revoke the transfer of any such function or power.

SECTION 803. *County Government.* Any county charter shall provide the form of government of the county and shall determine which of its officers shall be elected and the manner of their election. It shall provide for the exercise of all powers vested in, and the performance of all duties imposed upon, counties and county officers by law. Such charter may provide for the concurrent or exclusive exercise by the county, in all or in part of its area, of all or of any designated powers vested by the constitution or laws of this state in cities and other civil divisions; it may provide for the succession by the county to the rights, properties, and obligations of cities and other civil divisions therein incident to the powers so vested in the county, and for the division of the county into districts for purposes of administration or of taxation or of both. No provision of any charter or amendment vesting in the county any powers of a city or other civil division shall become effective unless it shall have been approved by a majority of those voting thereon (1) in the county, (2) in any city containing more than 25 per cent of the total population of the county, and (3) in the county outside of such city or cities.

SECTION 804. *City Government.* Except as provided in sections 802 and 803, each city is hereby granted full power and authority to pass laws and ordinances relating to its local affairs, property and government; and no enumeration of powers in this constitution shall be deemed to limit or restrict the general grant of authority hereby conferred; but this grant of authority shall not be deemed to limit or restrict the power of the legislature to enact laws of statewide concern uniformly applicable to every city.[14]

The following shall be deemed to be a part of the powers conferred upon cities by this section when not inconsistent with general law:

(a) To adopt and enforce within their limits local police, sanitary and other similar regulations.

(b) To levy, assess and collect taxes, and to borrow money and issue bonds, and to levy and collect special assessments for benefits conferred.

(c) To furnish all local public services; and to acquire and maintain, either within or without its corporate limits, cemeteries, hospitals, infirmaries, parks and boulevards, water supplies, and all works which involve the public health and safety.[15]

(d) To maintain art institutes, museums, theatres, operas, or orchestras, and to make any other provision for the cultural needs of the residents.

(e) To establish and alter the location of streets, to make local public improvements, and to acquire, by condemnation or otherwise, property within its corporate limits necessary for such improvements, and also to acquire additional property in order to preserve and protect such improvements, and to lease or sell such additional property, with restrictions to preserve and protect the improvements.

(f) To acquire, construct, hire, maintain and operate or lease local public utilities; to acquire, by condemnation or otherwise, within or without the corporate limits, property necesary for any such purposes, subject to restrictions imposed by general law for the protection of other communities; and to grant local public utility franchises and regulate the exercise thereof.

(g) To issue and sell bonds, outside of any general debt limit imposed by law, on the security in whole or in part of any public utility or property owned by the city, or of the revenues thereof, or of both, including in the case of a public utility, if deemed desirable by the city, a franchise stating the terms upon which, in case of foreclosure, the purchaser may operate such utility.

(h) To organize and administer public schools and libraries.

(i) To provide for slum clearance, the rehabilitation of blighted areas, and safe and sanitary housing for families of low income, and for recreational and other facilities incidental or appurtenant thereto; and gifts of money or property, or loans of money or credit for such purposes, shall be deemed to be for a city purpose.[16]

SECTION 805. *Public Reporting.* Counties, cities and other civil divisions shall adopt an annual budget in such form as the legislature shall prescribe, and the legislature shall by general law provide for the examination by qualified auditors of the accounts of all such civil divisions and of public utilities owned or operated by such civil divisions, and provide for reports from such civil divisions as to their transactions and financial conditions.

[14] General grant follows New York constitution. Last clause follows Wisconsin constitution.

[15] Michigan constitution, article VIII, section 22.

[16] Paragraph (b) gives general bonding power, subject to general limitation by general law and paragraph (g) gives additional bonding power for public utilities, etc. Paragraph (i) is an addition agreed to by the Committee on Revision of the Model City Charter. In relation to this section, see sections 709 and 1004.

SECTION 806. *Conduct of Elections.* All elections and submissions of questions provided for in this article or in any charter or law adopted in accordance herewith shall be conducted by the election authorities provided by general law.

Article IX

THE CIVIL SERVICE [17]

SECTION 900. *General Provisions.* In the civil service of the state and all of its civil divisions, all offices and positions shall be classified according to duties and responsibilities, salary ranges shall be established for the various classes, and all appointments and promotions shall be made according to merit and fitness to be ascertained, so far as practicable, by examinations, which, so far as practicable, shall be competitive.[18]

SECTION 901. *Administration and Enforcement.* There shall be a department of civil service which shall, in accordance with the provisions of this article and the laws enacted pursuant thereto, administer the personnel functions of the state and of such of its civil divisions as elect to come under the jurisdiction of the department. For the administration of the personnel functions of civil divisions that do not elect to come under the jurisdiction of the department, and which do not make provisions for the administration of their personnel functions in a home rule charter adopted pursuant to section 801 of this constitution, provision shall be made by law. No payment for any employment hereunder shall be made without the affirmative certification by the department, or of a designated local authority in the case of a civil division over which the department does not have jurisdiction, as to the legality of such employment. The legislature shall enact laws necessary to carry out the provisions of this article and the department shall make such rules as may be necessary to carry out the provisions and intent of such laws.

SECTION 902. *Legislative and Judicial Employees.* Employees of the legislature shall be selected in conformity with the provisions of this article and shall be appointed and supervised by the secretary of the legislature. Employees of the courts likewise shall be selected in conformity with the provisions of this article, and shall be appointed and supervised as provided in this constitution or as may be prescribed by law.

Article X

PUBLIC WELFARE

SECTION 1000. *Public Education.* The legislature shall provide for the maintenance and support of a system of free common schools, wherein all the children of this state may be educated,[19] and of such other educational institutions, including institutions of higher learning, as may be deemed desirable.

SECTION 1001. *Public Health.* The protection and promotion of the health of the inhabitants of the state are matters of public concern and provision therefor shall be made by the state and by such of its civil divisions and in such manner and by such means as the legislature shall from time to time determine.[20]

SECTION 1002. *Public Relief.* The maintenance and distribution, at reasonable rates, or free of charge, of a sufficient supply of food, fuel, clothing, and other common neces-

[17] Draft prepared through the cooperation of committees representing the National Municipal League, the Civil Service Assembly of the United States and Canada, and the National Civil Service League.

[18] In part from New York State constitution, article V, section 6.

[19] New York State constitution, article IX, section 1.

[20] New York State constitution, article XVII, section 3.

sities of life, and the providing of shelter, are public functions, and the state and its civil divisions may provide the same for their inhabitants in such manner and by such means as may be prescribed by law.[21]

SECTION 1003. *Public Inspection of Private Charitable, Correctional, or Health Institutions and Agencies.* The state shall have the power to provide for the inspection by such state departments, offices or agencies, and in such manner as the legislature may determine, of all private institutions and agencies in the state, whether incorporated or not incorporated, which are engaged in charitable, correctional, or health activities.[22]

SECTION 1004. *Public Housing.* The state may provide for low rent housing for persons of low income as defined by law, or for the clearance, replanning, reconstruction and rehabilitation of substandard and insanitary areas, or for both such purposes, and for recreational and other facilities incidental or appurtenant thereto, in such manner, by such means, and upon such terms and conditions as are prescribed elsewhere in this constitution or as may be prescribed by law.[23]

SECTION 1005. *Conservation.* The conservation, development and utilization of the agricultural, mineral, forest, water and other natural resources of the state are public uses, and the legislature shall have power to provide for the same and to enact legislation necessary or expedient therefor.[24]

SECTION 1006. *Sightliness, Order and Historic Asociations.* The natural beauty, historic associations, sightliness and physical good order of the state and its parts contribute to the general welfare and shall be conserved and developed as a part of the patrimony of the people, and to that end private property shall be subject to reasonable regulation and control.

SECTION 1007. *Powers of the State.* The enumeration in this article of specified functions shall not be construed as a limitation upon the powers of the state government. The state government shall have full power to act for the government and good order of the state and for the health, safety, and welfare of its citizens, by all necessary and convenient means, subject only to the limitations prescribed in this constitution and in the constitution of the United States.

Article XI

INTERGOVERNMENTAL RELATIONS

SECTION 1100. *Federal-State Relations.* Nothing in this constitution shall be construed in such manner as to impair the constitutionality of any act passed by the legislature for the purpose of making effective the cooperation of the state with the federal government under any legislation which Congress has the power to enact.

SECTION 1101. *Interstate Relations.* The legislature shall provide by law for the establishment of such agencies as may be necessary and desirable to promote cooperation on the part of this state with the other states of the Union. The legislature may appropriate such sums as may be necessary to finance its fair share of the cost of any interstate activities.

[21] Combines New York State constitution, article XVII, section 1, and the Massachusetts constitution, Amendments, article XLVII.
[22] Adapted from New York State constitution, article XVII, section 2.
[23] Adapted from New York State constitution, article XVIII, section 1; see also sections 709 and 804 (i).
[24] Adapted from Massachusetts constitution, Amendments, article XLIX.

SECTION 1102. *Cooperation of Governmental Units.* Agreements may be made by any county, city, or other civil division with any other such civil division, or with the state, or with the United States, for a cooperative or joint administration of any of its functions or powers, and the legislature shall have power to facilitate such arrangements.

SECTION 1103. *Consolidation and Cooperation of Local Units.* The legislature may, by appropriate legislation, facilitate and encourage the consolidation of existing civil divisions, or the establishment of cooperative enterprises on the part of such civil divisions.

Article XII

GENERAL PROVISIONS

SECTION 1200. *Self-Executing Clause.* The provisions of this constitution shall be self-executing to the fullest extent that their respective natures permit. The legislature, the governor, and the judicial department shall each have power to take any action consistent with its nature in furtherance of the purposes of this constitution and to facilitate its operation.

Whenever legislation shall be needed to carry out a mandate of the constitution, the governor shall call the matter to the attention of the legislature, and he may issue an executive order to carry out the mandate. Every such executive order shall be transmitted to the legislature while it is in session and shall become effective as law sixty days after its transmittal unless it shall have been modified or replaced by a resolution concurred in by a majority of all the members of the legislature.

SECTION 1201. *Equal Rights.* Whenever in this constitution the term "person," "persons," "people," or any personal pronoun is used, the same shall be interpreted to include persons of both sexes.[25]

SECTION 1202. *Oath of Office.* All officers of the state—legislative, executive and judicial—and of all the civil divisions thereof, shall, before entering upon the duties of their respective offices, take and subscribe to the following oath or affirmation: "I do solemnly swear (or affirm) that I will support and defend the constitution of the United States, and the constitution of the state of............, and that I will faithfully discharge the duties of the office of............to the best of my ability."

Article XIII

CONSTITUTIONAL REVISION

SECTION 1300. *Amending Procedure.* Amendments to this constitution may be proposed by the legislature or by the initiative. When the initiative is used, the procedure set forth in sections 401 and 406 of this constitution shall be followed.

Amendments proposed by the legislature shall be twice agreed to by record vote of a majority of all the members and each time entered on the journal, a period of not less than six months having intervened between such approvals. Amendments thus approved shall be submitted to a vote of the qualified voters at the first regular or special statewide election held not less than two months after the second action by the legislature.

SECTION 1301. *Constitutional Conventions.* The legislature, by an affirmative record vote of a majority of all the members, may at any time submit the question "Shall there be a convention to amend or revise the constitution?" to the qualified voters of the

---

[25] Follows New Jersey constitution, article X, paragraph 4.

state. If the question of holding a convention is not otherwise submitted to the people at some time during any period of fifteen years the secretary of the legislature shall submit it at the general election in the fifteenth year following the last submission.

The legislature, prior to a vote on the holding of a convention, shall provide for a preparatory commission to assemble information on constitutional questions to assist the voters, and if a convention is authorized the commission shall be continued for the assistance of the delegates. If a majority of the qualified voters voting on the question of holding a convention approves it, delegates shall be chosen at the next regular election not less than three months thereafter unless the legislature shall by law have provided for election of the delegates at the same time that the question is voted on or at a special election.

Any qualified voter of the state shall be eligible to membership in the convention, to which as many delegates shall be elected from each existing legislative district as there are representatives in the legislature from that district. Election shall be by proportional representation, in the same manner as for members of the legislature. The convention shall convene not later than one month after the date of the election of delegates and may recess from time to time.

No proposal shall be submitted by the convention to the voters unless it has been read on three different days in the convention, has been printed and upon the desks of the delegates in final form at least three days on which the convention was in session prior to final passage therein, and has received the assent of a majority of all the delegates. The yeas and nays on any question shall, upon request of one-tenth of the delegates present, be entered in the journal. Proposals of the convention shall be submitted to the qualified voters at the first regular or special statewide election not less than two months after final action thereon by the convention, either as a whole or in such parts and with such alternatives as the convention may determine.

SECTION 1302. *Adoption of Revision or Amendments.* Any constitutional revision or amendment submitted to the voters in accordance with this article shall become effective by approval of a majority of the qualified voters voting thereon. The provisions of section 406 concerning ballot titles, effective dates of approved measures and the resolution of conflicts among such measures shall apply to all measures for amendment or revision of the constitution.

Article XIV

SCHEDULE

SECTION 1400. *Effective Date.* This constitution shall be in force from and including the first day of . . . . 19 . . . ., except as herein otherwise provided.

SECTION 1401. *Existing Laws.* All laws not inconsistent with this constitution shall continue in force until specifically amended or repealed, and all rights, claims, actions, orders, prosecutions, and contracts shall continue except as modified in accordance with the provisions of this constitution.

SECTION 1402. *Officers.* All officers filling any office by election or appointment shall continue to exercise the duties thereof, according to their respective commissions or appointments, until their offices shall have been abolished or their successors selected and qualified in accordance with this constitution or the laws enacted pursuant thereto.

SECTION 1403. *Choice of Officers.* The first election of governor under this constitution shall be in 19 . . . . . The first election of chief justice under this constitution

shall be in 19 . . . . .   The first election of members of the legislature under this constitution
shall be in 19 . . . . .

SECTION 1404. *Establishment of the Legislature.* Until otherwise provided by law,
members of the legislature shall be elected from the following districts: The first district
shall consist of the counties of . . . . and . . . . , and said district shall be entitled to . . . . . . members in the legislature, etc. [The description of all the districts from
which the first legislature will be elected should be inserted in similar language.]

If by . . . . [date] the legislature has not prescribed by law a system of proportional representation for the election of members of the first legislature under this constitution, such members shall be selected by the Hare system of proportional representation, each voter having a single transferable vote, under regulations promulgated by the
governor.

SECTION 1405. *Administrative Reorganization.* The governor shall submit to the
legislature orders embodying a plan for reorganization of administrative departments in
accordance with section 506 of this constitution prior to . . . . [date]. These orders shall become effective as originally issued or as they may be modified by law on [a
date three months later] unless any of them are made effective at earlier dates by law.

SECTION 1406. *Establishment of the Judiciary.* The general court of justice shall be
inaugurated on September 15, 19 . . . .   Prior to that date the justices, judges, and
principal ministerial agents of the general court of justice shall be designated or selected
and any other act needed to prepare for the operation of the general court of justice shall be
done in accordance with this constitution.

The judicial power vested in any court in the state shall be transferred to the general
court of justice and the justices and judges of the [here name all the courts of the state
except justice of the peace courts] holding office on September 15, 19 . . . . , shall become
justices and judges of the general court of justice and shall continue to serve as such for
the remainder of their respective terms and until their successors shall have qualified.
The justices of the [here name the highest court of the state] shall become justices of the
supreme court department, and the judges of the other courts shall be assigned by the
chief justice to appropriate service in the other departments of the general court of
justice, due regard being had to their positions in the existing judicial structure and to
the districts in which they had been serving.

The judicial council shall be organized as soon as practicable after the adoption of this
constitution. The first members of the judicial council shall include the chief justice
[the chief justice elect, when one has been chosen under the new constitution], together
with a justice who will become a member of the supreme court department and two
judges who will become members of other departments of the general court of justice.
Prior to . . . . [date], the legislature and the judicial council shall adopt all needed
legislation and rules for the satisfactory operation of the general court of justice and
the chief justice [or chief justice elect] shall organize the court.

INDEX

DATE DUE
